Strategic Management

DOI: https://doi.org/10.21061/strategicmanagement

Strategic Management

adapted by

Reed Kennedy

with

Eli Jamison, Joe Simpson,
Pankaj Kumar, Ayenda Kemp, Kiran Awate,
and Kathleen Manning

PAMPLIN COLLEGE OF BUSINESS

IN ASSOCIATION WITH

VIRGINIA TECH. PUBLISHING

BLACKSBURG, VIRGINIA

Contents

Copyright and License Information

Pamplin College of Business
Pamplin Hall, RM 1030
880 West Campus Drive
Blacksburg, VA 24061, USA

Virginia Tech Publishing
Virginia Tech University Libraries
560 Drillfield Drive
Blacksburg, VA 24061, USA

Peer Review: This work benefited from peer review and contributions of five subject matter experts; one recent business graduate also reviewed and contributed to this work.

Accessibility Statement: Virginia Tech Publishing is committed to making its publications accessible in accordance with the Americans with Disabilities Act of 1990. The HTML and screen reader–friendly PDF versions of this book utilize header structures and include alternative text which allow for machine-readability.

Publication Cataloging Information

Kennedy, Reed, author
   Strategic Management / Reed Kennedy
   Pages cm
   ISBN 978-1-949373-94-3 (print-color)
   ISBN 978-1-949373-89-9 (print-black & white)
   ISBN 978-1-949373-96-7 (ebook-PDF)
   ISBN 978-1-949373-95-0 (ebook-Pressbooks)
   DOI: https://doi.org/10.21061/strategicmanagement
   1. Management. 2. Strategy
   I. Title
   HD30.28.K45

Cover Design: Kindred Grey

Acknowledgments

Publication of this work was made possible in part by the University Libraries at Virginia Tech through its Open Education Initiative (https://guides.lib.vt.edu/oer/grants), which provides development assistance and financial support to Virginia Tech faculty who wish to use, create, or adapt openly licensed teaching materials to support student learning. The University Libraries also contributed faculty and staff labor. Reed Kennedy's contributions were supported by the Pamplin College of Business at Virginia Tech.

Introduction

Goals for this Book

This textbook is intended for seniors in undergraduate business programs taking a capstone course in strategic management. Most business school students begin with a broad introductory business course before concentrating on courses in their major. This textbook and corresponding course, MGT 4394 "Strategic Management," are designed for the other end of the business curriculum. More specifically, the goal is to refocus business students from their major at the end of their time in school and help them understand how businesses become successful by leveraging their competitive advantages. While it is true that strategic management functions are typically the purview of senior leadership in a company, newly minted business graduates and their employers directly benefit when new employees understand their role in helping their organization to strategically achieve its goals.

About this Book

The book begins with a general introduction to the key themes and topics of strategic management. In the chapters that follow students first learn how to conduct a case analysis, measure organizational performance, and conduct external and internal analyses. Next they learn the various strategies used by firms: business/competitive level, corporate level, international, and innovation strategies. The final two chapters focus on implementing strategy and corporate ethics. Ethical considerations are integrated throughout the textbook.

Target Audience

This textbook is intended for a wide range of business students including those majoring in marketing, management, business administration, accounting, finance, real estate, business information technology, and hospitality and tourism. Ideally, students in each of these majors will take a strategic management course during their final semester before graduation. This book will guide them through this course as they prepare to transition from the classroom to a competitive business marketplace.

Features of this Book

- Example-rich narrative
- Graphic elements which illustrate and reinforce concepts

- Linked online glossary (glossary appears at the end for PDF and print)
- Numerous case examples and 'Strategy at the Movies'
- Section-level videos, key takeaways, and exercises
- Linked end of section references for additional reading
- Embedded navigation and image alt-text for screen readers
- Free online and in PDF, and in print at vendor cost of production
- Open license, Creative Commons BY NC-SA 3.0 (https://creativecommons.org/licenses/by-nc-sa/3.0) permits customization and sharing
- Instructor community portal enables sharing of ancillary resources
- Register your Use form allows instructors to opt in to receive book updates
- Errata and report-an-error/share-a-suggestion forms promote currency

If course modules are used, the textbook easily separates into six modules.

- MODULE 1 Introduction to Strategic Management: Chapters 1 and 2
- MODULE 2: External Analysis: Chapter 3
- MODULE 3: Internal Firm Analysis: Chapters 4 and 5
- MODULE 4: Innovation, Corporate and International Strategies: Chapters 6, 7, 8, and 9
- MODULE 5: Executing Strategy: Chapter 10
- MODULE 6: Leading an Ethical Organization: Chapter 11

For students who prefer to learn by listening, external video links are provided at the end of each section addressing the topic of that section. Other students may find these videos helpful as an alternative source of information and as an aid for review.

The short introductions at the start of each chapter are intended to assist students in understanding the flow of the course, and how the chapter builds upon previous chapters. It also helps students to have a brief overview of the chapter and its content.

The vignettes, illustrations, and examples use companies and personalities that today's student would be familiar with. The pictures in the book should add interest to the student.

Major terms that students need to know are hyperlinked with definitions. These terms and definitions are also provided in a glossary at the end of the book.

Textbook Development

Strategic Management is an adaptation of a previously published textbook (more on this below). A group of six strategic management instructors in the Pamplin College of Business at Virginia Tech were involved in deeply adapting, revising, supplementing, and developing that work into the textbook you are now reading. Kennedy, who had taught the course multiple times and served as the course coordinator, took the role of primary contributor and chief textbook reviser. The other five, all Ph.Ds in strategy or a related field, served as editors.

In addition, the Research and Editorial Assistant, a recent Pamplin graduate provided a student perspective on the text, and the Design Specialist, a graduating senior, re-worked illustrations and created new figures to make them more presentable to students. The team of six editors revised the outline of the original textbook, deciding which topics to add and which ones to delete. After solidifying the outline, the lead author deleted extraneous content, composed new content, and updated content as needed. The five editors then made suggestions on content, format, illustrations, grammar, etc. Finally, the Assistant Director of Open Education in the University Libraries at Virginia Tech guided the book through the development and production processes leading up to its publication by Virginia Tech Publishing. Multiple staff formatted the text in Pressbooks, offered feedback to the editorial team, and provided copy editing and proofreading. The resulting book has been published in both online versions (Pressbooks, ePub, and PDF) and printable on-demand versions.

Attribution and Scope of Revision

This textbook is adapted from the openly licensed textbook *Mastering Strategic Management* (https://dx.doi.org/10.24926/8668.1401) published in 2011 under a Creative Commons Attribution NonCommercial ShareAlike 3.0 (https://creativecommons.org/licenses/by-nc-sa/3.0) licence, revised and hosted by the University of Minnesota Libraries Publishing Service in 2015. The 2011 version of the book was written by two authors who held administrative and leadership roles at major U.S. universities. It was published in 2011 by a publisher who requested that neither the authors nor publisher receive attribution. This new version uses much of the same content and structure of the 2011 and 2015 versions, with the following significant changes:

- Alignment of book to learning outcomes
- Updated examples and illustrations
- Addition of linked section-level videos
- Re-ordering of some chapters
- Addition of Chapter 5: Synthesis of Strategic Issues and Analysis" on the SWOT framework and strategic issues.
- Additional mini-case studies on The Bottom of the Pyramid and COVID-19

A more detailed list of changes is available in the book's Version Notes at the end of the book.

The revision process involved adding content in certain areas while removing dated or less relevant content to better align with learning objectives. We also gave the book a general refresh by adding illustrations, examples, and applications from companies and brands more relatable to today's students.

Strategy instructors collaborated to determine which content to supplement or delete. This coordinated effort from diverse perspectives provides more consistency among instructors in teaching the content of the course.

An additional goal of the editorial team was to provide an affordable alternative to existing expensive strategic management textbooks. The ever-increasing costs of a college education convinced us that a strong, no-cost textbook would benefit not only Virginia Tech students but students at other colleges and universities as well.

Impact

Our hope for this textbook is that it will enlighten and prepare students for entering the business world. After reading it they should come away with a much better grasp of the ways that organizations operate at the strategic level to be successful. Not only will they be better accountants, or whatever their particular major is, they will be better prepared as employees, especially as they rise in responsibility and take on more strategic roles in their organizations. Ultimately, we hope they will become better critical thinkers and have the ability to analyze the full range of situations they will face in their professional lives.

Also, it is hoped that instructors in other colleges and universities will appreciate the content and structure of this textbook and adopt it for their students, providing a textbook solution for them at no cost.

Instructor Resources

How to Adopt This Book

This is an open textbook. That means that this book is freely available and you are welcome to use, adapt, and share this book with attribution according to the Creative Commons NonCommercial ShareAlike 3.0 (CC BY NC-SA 3.0) license https://creativecommons.org/licenses/by-nc-sa/3.0. (This license does not apply to third-party works (images, illustrations, etc.)

Instructors reviewing, adopting, or adapting this textbook are encouraged to register at http://bit.ly/strategy-interest. This assists Virginia Tech's Open Education Initiative in assessing the impact of the book and allows us to more easily alert instructors of additional resources, features and opportunities.

Finding Additional Resources for your Course

The main landing page for the book is http://hdl.handle.net/10919/99282.

This page includes:

- Links to multiple electronic versions of the textbook (PDF, ePub, HTML)
- Ordering information for softcover print-on-demand copies
- Links to supplementary resources
- Links to the instructor resource-sharing portal
- Link to errata document

Sharing Resources You've Created

Have you created any supplementary materials for use with *Strategic Management* such as presentation slides, activities, test items, or a question bank? If so, please consider sharing your materials related to this open textbook. Please tell us about resources you wish to share by using this form: http://bit.ly/strategy-interest or by directly sharing non-assessment resources under an open license to the public-facing instructor sharing portal https://www.oercommons.org/groups/strategic-management-instructor-group/5209.

Customizing this Book

The Creative Commons Attribution NonCommercial-ShareAlike 3.0 license https://creativecommons.org/licenses/by-nc-sa/3.0/legalcode on this book allows customization and redistribution which is NonCommercial, that is "not primarily intended for or directed towards commercial advantage or monetary compensation."

Best practices for attribution are provided at https://wiki.creativecommons.org/wiki/Best_practices_for_attribution.

This book was created in Pressbooks and is most easily customized using the Pressbooks platform or by editing on the PDF on a page-by-page basis. For additional considerations and methods of customization, see: *Modifying an Open Textbook: What You Need to Know*, https://press.rebus.community/otnmodify.

Feedback

To report an error or omission, please use https://bit.ly/strategic-feedback.

We welcome additional feedback at publishing@vt.edu.

Chapter 1: Mastering Strategy: Art and Science

Learning Objectives

After reading this chapter, you should be able to understand and articulate answers to the following questions:

1. What is the difference between strategic management and strategy?
2. Why does strategic management matter?
3. What are intended, emergent, and realized strategies?
4. What is the history of strategic management?
5. What is the basic strategic management process?

1.1 Introduction

Successful organizations have found that a strategic management process helps them achieve their goals within a dynamic and competitive environment. Strategic management is a comprehensive process designed for firms to best use their resources and capabilities to provide superior firm performance. Analysis of the external, competitive, and internal environments help shape the strategies that a firm pursues to be successful. Strategies are broad goals that, as accomplished, help the organization move forward toward its vision.

Strategy formation goes back to ancient times, particularly used in warfare. Although not perfect, the strategic management process creates a framework for an organization to look outside of itself and set a course for success. The remaining chapters in this textbook walk students through this framework, providing tools for diagnosing the external, competitive, and internal environments to the development and implementation of strategies. The process should always be performed with a framework of corporate ethics and values to limit the temptation to cross the line where an organization should not go.

Figure 1.1: Elon Musk, CEO of Tesla

Will Tesla Make It?

On January 7, 2020, Tesla Inc. became the most valuable US automaker in history. Valued at $81.39 billion, Tesla passed Ford Motor Company as most valuable. Approximately two weeks later, Tesla passed Volkswagen to become the second most valuable car company worldwide. Still well behind Toyota, which has a $233 billion market capitalization, Tesla's growth is unprecedented in the automotive industry. Can Tesla become number one worldwide?

Despite tremendous growth, Tesla has its share of problems as well. Its founder, Elon Musk, tweeted that the company's stock price was too high; sending the stock tumbling, the Model 3 lost Consumer Reports recommendations, and COVID-19 shutdowns of factories slowed production. These problems raise serious questions. Will Elon's Twitter use continue to cause problems? Are the quality problems going to tank Tesla's growth? Can Tesla emerge from the COVID-19 shutdown successfully?

The company faces stiff competition from automakers attempting to regain their footholds in a highly aggressive market. Competitors are attempting to compete in the same areas as Tesla. Porsche's Taycan, a Tesla competitor, got a huge win with a purchase from Bill Gates. As competitors continue to develop autonomous capabilities and better electric batteries, will Tesla continue to dominate US auto markets?

References

Langley, K. (2020, January 7). Tesla is now the most valuable US car maker of all time. *Wall Street Journal*. https://www.wsj.com/articles/tesla-is-now-the-most-valuable-u-s-car-maker-of-all-time-11578427858.

Johnson, M. (2020 January 24). Tesla becomes world's second most valuable carmaker. *The Hill*. https://thehill.com/policy/transportation/automobiles/479712-tesla-becomes-worlds-second-most-valuable-carmaker.

Olsen, P. (2019, November 14). Tesla Model 3 loses CR recommendation over reliability issues. *Consumer Reports*. https://www.consumerreports.org/car-reliability-owner-satisfaction/tesla-model-3-loses-cr-recommendation-over-reliability-issues.

Siddiqui, F. (2020, May 1). Tesla stock plummets more than 10 percent after Elon Musk tweets valuation is 'too high.' *Washington Post*. https://www.washingtonpost.com/technology/2020/05/01/musk-tesla-stock.

Matousek, M. (2020, February 18). Elon Musk took a shot at Bill Gates after the Microsoft founder said he bought Porsche's electric sports car instead of a Tesla – here are the details on Gates' new car. *Business Insider*. https://www.businessinsider.com/porsche-reveals-taycan-turbo-and-taycan-turbo-s-production-model-2019-9.

Image Credits

Figure 1.1: Maurizio Pesce. Elon Musk at Tesla Factory Fremont CA. CC BY 2.0. Retrieved from https://flic.kr/p/emx5tu.

1.2 What is Strategic Management?

Defining Strategic Management

Issues such as those currently faced by Tesla are the focus of **strategic management** because they help answer the key question examined by strategic management—"Why do some firms outperform other firms?" More specifically, strategic management examines how actions and events involving top executives (such as Elon Musk), firms (Tesla), and industries (the electric car market) influence a firm's success or failure. Strategic management involves the utilization or planned allocation of resources to implement major initiatives taken by executives on behalf of stakeholders to improve performance of firms in an environment. Formal tools exist for understanding these relationships, and many of these tools are explained and applied in this book. But formal tools are not enough; creativity is just as important to strategic management. Mastering strategy is therefore part art and part science.

This introductory chapter is intended to enable students to understand what strategic management is and why it is important. Because strategy is a complex concept, we begin by explaining what strategy is. Types of strategies and the history and critique of strategic management are introduced. Lastly, students are presented with the process of strategic management that firms use.

Figure 1.2: Strategic management within a firm is accomplished by a team of senior people.

Defining **strategy** is not simple. Strategy is a complex concept that involves many different processes and activities within an organization. It involves goals and objectives that an organization needs to achieve to be successful in the marketplace. The development of these goals, however, requires a strategic management process to be done correctly and thoroughly.

A strategy is typically a higher level, broad goal, without a lot of specifics. It is long-term in nature. It provides the direction that an organization wants to move toward to be more successful. New or revised strategies may be developed as a result of changes in the business environment, such as what happened during the COVID-19 pandemic. Firms also routinely revise or create new strategies, often annually, by assessing and reacting to external and competitive forces and to maximize organizational performance. By identifying their resources and capabilities, firms attempt to deploy these through strategies that will give them a competitive advantage, so consumers will buy their product or service instead of a competitor's.

Section Video

What is Strategic Management? What does Strategic Management mean? [03:48]

The video for this section further explains strategic management and strategies.

You can view this video here: https://youtu.be/g-wf6A0ailA.

Key Takeaway

- Strategic management focuses on firms and the different strategies that they use to become and remain successful. Firms develop strategies, or longer range goals, to achieve success in the competitive marketplace. In the dynamic environment in which firms exist, firms may alter their strategies as conditions change.

Exercises

1. Have you developed a strategy to manage your career? Should you make it more detailed? Why or why not?
2. What business that you visit regularly seems to have the most successful business model? What makes the business model work?

References

Markoff, J. (1996, May 14). Apple unveils strategic plan of small steps. *New York Times.* http://www.nytimes.com/1996/05/14/business/apple-unveils-strategic -plan-of-small-steps.html.

Porter, M. E. (1996, November–December). What is strategy? *Harvard Business Review,* 61–79.

Reuters. (2011, March 1). Philadelphia area pizza owner used mice vs. competition–police. *Reuters*. https://www.reuters.com/article/us-crime-pizza-idUSTRE7207MU20110301.

Image Credits

Figure 1.2: fauxels (2019). "Photo of people looking on laptop." CC BY-SA 4.0. Retrieved from https://www.pexels.com/photo/photo-of-people-looking-on-laptop-3182812/.

Video Credits

Audiopedia. (2017, April 4). *What is strategic management? What does strategic management mean?* [Video]. YouTube. https://youtu.be/g-wf6A0ailA.

1.3 Intended, Emergent, and Realized Strategies

A few years ago, a consultant posed a question to thousands of executives: "Is your industry facing overcapacity and fierce price competition?" All but one said "yes." The only "no" came from the manager of a unique operation–the Panama Canal! This manager was fortunate to be in charge of a venture whose services are desperately needed by shipping companies and that offers the only simple route linking the Atlantic and Pacific Oceans. The canal's success could be threatened if transoceanic shipping were to cease or if a new canal were built. Both of these possibilities are extremely remote, however, so the Panama Canal appears to be guaranteed to have many customers for as long as anyone can see into the future.

When an organization's environment is stable and predictable, strategic planning can provide enough of a strategy for the organization to gain and maintain success. The executives leading the organization can simply create a plan and execute it, and they can be confident that their plan will not be undermined by changes over time. But as the consultant's experience shows, only a few executives–such as the manager of the Panama Canal–enjoy a stable and predictable situation. Because change affects the strategies of almost all organizations, understanding the concepts of intended, emergent, and realized strategies is important (Table 1.1). Also relevant are deliberate and unrealized strategies. The relationships among these five concepts are presented in Figure 1.3, "A Model of Intended, Deliberate, and Realized Strategy" (Mintzberg & Waters, 1985).

Table 1.1 Strategic Planning and Learning: Intended, Emergent, and Realized Strategies

Intended Strategy	Emergent Strategy	Realized Strategy
David McConnell aspired to be a writer. When his books weren't selling he decided to give out perfume as a gimmick.	The perfumes McConnell gave out with his books were popular, inspiring the foundation of the California Perfume Company.	The company changed its name to Avon in 1939, and its direct marketing system remained popular for decades. Avon is now available online and in retail outlets worldwide.
When father and son team Scott and Don Rasmussen were fired from the New England Whalers, they envisioned a cable television network that focused on sports events in the state of Connecticut.	As the network became successful, ESPN has branched out beyond the local softball games and demolition derbies that were first broadcasted.	ESPN is now billed as the worldwide leader in sports, owning several ESPN affiliates as well as production of ESPN magazine, ESPN radio, and broadcasting for ABC.
In 1977, a cash-strapped advertiser gave a radio station managed by Lowell Paxson 112 electric can openers to pay off an overdue bill. The can openers were offered over the air for $9.95 and quickly sold out.	An idea emerged. Soon the radio station featured a regular show called "Suncoast Bargaineers." In 1982, Paxson and a partner launched the Home Shopping Club on local cable television in Florida.	The Home Shopping Network evolved into a retail powerhouse selling on their own channel on television. With the increased popularity of online shopping and competitors like Amazon, their success has faltered.

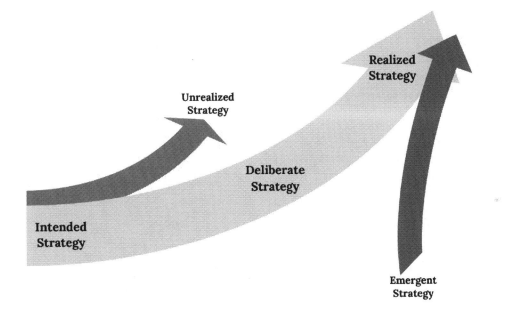

Figure 1.3: A Model of Intended, Deliberate, and Realized Strategy

Intended Strategy

An **intended strategy** is the strategy that an organization hopes to execute. Intended strategies are usually described in detail within an organization's strategic plan. When a strategic plan is created for a new venture, it is called a business plan. As an undergraduate student at Yale in 1965, Frederick Smith had to complete a business plan for a proposed company as a class project. His plan described a delivery system that would gain efficiency by routing packages through a central hub and then pass them to their destinations. A few years later, Smith started Federal Express (Funding Universe, n.d.), a company whose strategy closely followed the plan laid out in his class project. FedEx has achieved a ranking among the World's Most Admired Companies according to Fortune magazine. Certainly, Smith's intended strategy has worked out far better than even he could have dreamed (Donahoe, 2011; Memphis Business Journal, 2011).

Emergent Strategy

Emergent strategy has also played a role at Federal Express. An emergent strategy is an unplanned strategy that arises in response to unexpected opportunities and/or challenges. Sometimes emergent strategies result in disasters. In the mid-1980s, FedEx deviated from its intended strategy's focus on package delivery to capitalize on an emerging technology: facsimile (fax) machines. The firm developed a service called ZapMail that involved documents being sent electronically via fax machines between FedEx offices and then being delivered to customers' offices. FedEx executives hoped that ZapMail would be a success because it reduced the delivery time of a document from overnight to just a couple of hours. Unfortunately, the ZapMail system had many technical problems that frustrated customers. Even worse, FedEx failed to anticipate that many businesses would simply purchase their own fax machines. ZapMail was shut down, and FedEx lost hundreds of millions of dollars following its failed emergent strategy. In retrospect, FedEx made a costly mistake by venturing outside of the domain that was central to its intended strategy: package delivery (Funding Universe, n.d.).

Emergent strategies can also lead to tremendous success. Southern Bloomer Manufacturing Company was founded to make underwear for use in prisons and mental hospitals. Many managers of such institutions believe that the underwear made for retail markets by companies such as Calvin Klein and Hanes is simply not suitable for the people under their care. Instead, underwear issued to prisoners needs to be sturdy and durable to withstand the rigors of prison activities and laundering. To meet these needs, Southern Bloomers began selling underwear made of heavy cotton fabric.

An unexpected opportunity led Southern Bloomer to go beyond its intended strategy of serving institutional needs for durable underwear. Just a few years after opening, Southern Bloomer's performance was excellent. It was servicing the needs of about 125 facilities, but unfortunately, this was creating a vast amount of scrap fabric. An attempt to use the scrap as stuffing for pillows had failed, so the scrap was being sent to landfills. This was not only wasteful but also costly.

One day, co-founder Don Sonner visited a gun shop with his son. Sonner had no interest in guns, but he quickly spotted a potential use for his scrap fabric during this visit. The patches that the gun shop sold to clean the inside of gun barrels were of poor quality. According to Sonner, when he "saw one of those flimsy woven patches they sold that unraveled when you touched them, I said, "Man, that's what I can do" with the scrap fabric. Unlike other gun-cleaning patches, the patches that Southern Bloomer sold did not give off threads or lint, two by-products that hurt guns' accuracy and reliability. The patches quickly became popular with the military, police departments, and individual gun enthusiasts. Before long, Southern Bloomer was selling thousands of pounds of patches per month. A casual trip to a gun store unexpectedly gave rise to a lucrative emergent strategy (Wells, 2002).

Realized Strategy

A **realized strategy** is the strategy that an organization actually follows. Realized strategies are a product of a firm's intended strategy (i.e., what the firm planned to do), the firm's deliberate strategy (i.e., the parts of the intended strategy that the firm continues to pursue over time), and its emergent strategy (i.e., what the firm did in reaction to unexpected opportunities and challenges). In the case of FedEx, the intended strategy devised by its founder many years ago—fast package delivery via a centralized hub—remains a primary driver of the firm's realized strategy. For Southern Bloomers Manufacturing Company, realized strategy has been shaped greatly by both its intended and emergent strategies, which center on underwear and gun-cleaning patches.

In other cases, firms' original intended strategies are long forgotten. An **unrealized strategy** refers to the abandoned parts of the intended strategy. When aspiring author David McConnell was struggling to sell his books, he decided to offer complimentary perfume as a sales gimmick. McConnell's books never did escape the stench of failure, but his perfumes soon took on the sweet smell of success. The California Perfume Company was formed to market the perfumes; this firm evolved into the personal care products juggernaut known today as Avon. For McConnell, his dream to be a successful writer was an unrealized strategy, but through Avon, a successful realized strategy was driven almost entirely by opportunistically capitalizing on change through emergent strategy.

Strategy at the Movies

The Social Network

Did Harvard University student Mark Zuckerberg set out to build a billion-dollar company with more than 2.6 billion active users? Not hardly. As shown in 2010's The Social Network, Zuckerberg's original concept in 2003 had a dark nature. After being dumped by his girlfriend, a bitter Zuckerberg created a website called "FaceMash" where the attractiveness of young women could be voted on. This evolved first into an online social network called TheFacebook that was for Harvard students only. When the network became surprisingly popular, it then morphed into Facebook, a website open to everyone. Facebook is so pervasive today that it has changed the

Figure 1.4: The Social Network demonstrates how founder Mark Zuckerberg's intended strategy gave way to an emergent strategy via the creation of Facebook.

way we speak, such as the word friend being used as a verb. Ironically, Facebook's emphasis on connecting with existing and new friends is about as different as it could be from Zuckerberg's original mean-spirited concept. Certainly, Zuckerberg's emergent and realized strategies turned out to be far nobler than the intended strategy that began his adventure in entrepreneurship.

Key Takeaway

- Most organizations create intended strategies that they hope to follow to be successful. Over time, however, changes in an organization's situation give rise to new opportunities and challenges. Organizations respond to these changes using emergent strategies. Realized strategies are a product of both intended and realized strategies.

Exercises

1. What is the difference between an intended and an emergent strategy?
2. Can you think of a company that seems to have abandoned its intended strategy? Why do you suspect it was abandoned?
3. Would you describe your career strategy in college to be more deliberate or emergent? Why?

References

Donahoe, J. A. (2011). Forbes: Fred Smith's fortune grows to $.21B. *Memphis Business Journal*. http://www.bizjournals.com/memphis/news/2011/03/10/forbes-fred-smiths-fortune-grows-to.html.

Funding Universe. (n.d.). *Fedex Corporation History*. http://www.fundinguniverse.com/company -histories/FedEx-Corporation-Company-History.html.

Fortune: FedEx 8th 'most admired' company in the world. *Memphis Business Journal*. (2011). http://www.bizjournals .com/memphis/news/2011/03/03/fortune-fedex-8th-most- admired.html.

Mintzberg, H., & Waters, J. A. (1985). Of strategies, deliberate and emergent. *Strategic Management Journal*, 6, 257–272.

Wells, K. (2002). *Floating off the page: The best stories from the Wall Street Journal's middle column*. Simon & Schuster. pg 97.

Image Credits

1.4 The History of Strategic Management

Those who cannot remember the past are condemned to repeat it.

– George Santayana, *The Life of Reason*

Santayana's quote has strong implications for strategic management. The history of strategic management can be traced back several thousand years. Great wisdom about strategy can be acquired by understanding the past, but ignoring the lessons of history can lead to costly strategic mistakes that could have been avoided. Certainly, the present offers very important lessons; businesses can gain knowledge about what strategies do and do not work by studying the current actions of other businesses. But this section discusses two less obvious sources of wisdom: (1) strategy in ancient times and (2) military strategy. This section also briefly traces the development of strategic management as a field of study.

Strategy in Ancient Times

Perhaps the earliest-known discussion of strategy is offered in the Old Testament of the Bible (Bracker, 1980). Approximately 3,500 years ago, Moses faced quite a challenge after leading his fellow Hebrews out of enslavement in Egypt. Moses was overwhelmed as the lone strategist at the helm of a nation that may have exceeded one million people. Based on advice from his father-in-law, Moses began delegating authority to other leaders, each of whom oversaw a group of people. This hierarchical delegation of authority created a command structure that freed Moses to concentrate on the biggest decisions and helped him implement his strategies (Table 1.2 "Strategy in Ancient Times"). Similarly, the demands of strategic management today are simply too much for a chief executive officer (the top leader of a company) to handle alone. Many important tasks are thus entrusted to vice presidents and other executives.

In ancient China, strategist and philosopher Sun Tzu offered thoughts on strategy that continue to be studied carefully by business and military leaders today. Sun Tzu's best-known work is *The Art of War*. As this title implies, Sun Tzu emphasized the creative and deceptive aspects of strategy.

Strategic management borrows many ideas from ancient uses of strategy over time. The following anecdotes provide a few notable examples of historical actions that remain relevant for the study of modern strategy. Indeed, the Greek verb strategos means "army leader" and the idea of stratego (from which we get the word strategy) refers to the idea of destroying one's enemies through the effective use of resources.

Table 1.2 Strategy in Ancient Times

1491 BC:
Moses uses hierarchical delegation of authority during the exodus from Egypt. Dividing a large set of people into smaller groups creates a command structure that enables strategies to be implemented.
500 BC:
Sun Tzu's The Art of War provides a classic handbook on military strategy with numerous business applications, such as the idea "to win without fighting is the best." This type of approach was used by businesses, such as Gap Inc. when they decided to create their own stores rather than competing for shelf space for their clothing within traditional department stores.
70 BC:
Roman poet Virgil tells the story of the Trojan horse, a classic strategic ploy where the Greek forces hid a select number of soldiers in a large wooden horse that the Trojan army took into their heavily guarded city gates. Once inside the city, Greek soldiers were able to open the gates and allow in reinforcements which eventually led to the end of the war.
c. 530:
King Arthur rules Britain. Legend says he made his famed round table so that no one, including him, would be seen as above the others. His mission to find the Holy Grail serves as an exemplar for the importance of the central mission to guide organizational actions.

One of Sun Tzu's ideas that has numerous business applications is that winning a battle without fighting is the best way to win. Apple's behavior in the personal computer business offers a good example of this idea in action. Many computer makers such as Toshiba, Acer, and Lenovo compete with one another based primarily on price. This leads to price wars that undermine the computer makers' profits. In contrast, Apple prefers to develop unique features for its computers, features that have created a fiercely loyal set of customers. Apple boldly charges far more for its computers than its rivals charge for theirs. Apple does not even worry much about whether its computers' software is compatible with the software used by most other computers. Rather than fighting a battle with other firms, Apple wins within the computer business by creating its own unique market and by attracting a set of loyal customers. Sun Tzu would probably admire Apple's approach.

Perhaps the most famous example of strategy in ancient times revolves around the Trojan horse. According to legend, Greek soldiers wanted to find a way to enter the gates of Troy and attack the city from the inside. They devised a ploy that involved creating a giant wooden horse, hiding soldiers inside the horse, and offering the horse to the Trojans as a gift. The Trojans were fooled and brought the horse inside their city. When night arrived, the hidden Greek soldiers opened the gates for their army, leading to a Greek victory. In modern times, the term Trojan horse refers to gestures that appear on the surface to be beneficial to the recipient but that mask a sinister intent. Computer viruses also are sometimes referred to as Trojan horses.

A far more noble approach to strategy than the Greeks' is attributed to King Arthur of Britain. Unlike the hierarchical approach to organizing Moses used, Arthur allegedly considered himself and each of his knights to have an equal say in plotting the group's strategy. Indeed, the group is thought to have held its meetings at a round table so that no voice, including Arthur's, would be seen as more important than the others. The choice of furniture in modern executive suites is perhaps revealing. Most feature rectangular meeting tables, perhaps signaling that one person—the chief executive officer—is in charge.

Another implication for strategic management offered by King Arthur and his Knights of the Round Table involves the concept of mission. Their vigorous search to find the Holy Grail (the legendary cup used by Jesus and his disciples at the Last Supper) serves as an exemplar for the importance of a central mission to guide organizational strategy and actions.

Lessons Offered by Military Strategy

Key military conflicts and events have shaped the understanding of strategic management (Table 1.3). Indeed, the word strategy has its roots in warfare. The Greek verb strategos means "army leader" and the idea of stratego (from which we get the word strategy) refers to defeating an enemy by effectively using resources (Bracker, 1980).

A book written nearly five hundred years ago is still regarded by many as an insightful guide for conquering and ruling territories. Niccolò Machiavelli's 1532 book *The Prince* offers clever recipes for success to government leaders. Some of the book's suggestions are quite devious, and the word Machiavellian is used today to refer to acts of deceit and manipulation.

Two wars fought on American soil provide important lessons about strategic management. In the late 1700s, the American Revolution pitted the American colonies against mighty Great Britain. The Americans relied on nontraditional tactics, such as guerilla warfare and the strategic targeting of British officers. Although these tactics were considered by Great Britain to be barbaric, they later became widely used approaches to warfare. The Americans owed their success in part to help from the French navy, illustrating the potential value of strategic alliances.

Nearly a century later, Americans turned on one another during the Civil War. After four years of hostilities, the Confederate states were forced to surrender. Historians consider the Confederacy to have had better generals, but the Union possessed greater resources, such as factories and railroad lines. As many modern companies have discovered, sometimes good strategies simply cannot overcome a stronger adversary.

Two wars fought on Russian soil also offer insights. In the 1800s, a powerful French invasion force was defeated in part by the brutal nature of Russian winters. In the 1940s, a similar fate befell German forces during World War II. Against the advice of some of his leading generals, Adolf Hitler ordered his army to conquer Russia. Like the French before them, the Germans were able to penetrate deep into Russian territory. As George Santayana had warned, however, the forgotten past was about to repeat itself. Horrific cold stopped the German advance. Russian forces eventually took control of the combat, and Hitler committed suicide as the Russians approached the German capital, Berlin.

Five years earlier, Germany ironically had benefited from an opponent ignoring the strategic management lessons of the past. In ancient times, the Romans had assumed that no army could cross a mountain range known as the Alps. An enemy general named Hannibal put his men on elephants, crossed the mountains, and caught Roman forces unprepared. French commanders made a similar bad assumption in 1940. When Germany invaded Belgium (and then France) in 1940, its strategy caught French forces by surprise.

Figure 1.5: General Hannibal from Carthage, who led his troops on elephants to cross the Alps to attack the Romans.

The top French commanders assumed that German tanks simply could not make it through a thickly wooded region known as the Ardennes Forest. As a result, French forces did not bother preparing a strong defense in that area. Most of the French army and their British allies instead protected against a small, diversionary force that the Germans had sent as a deception to the north of the forest. German forces made it through the forest, encircled the allied forces, and started driving them toward the ocean. Many thousands of French and British soldiers were killed or captured. In retrospect, the French generals had ignored an important lesson of history: do not make assumptions about what your adversary can and cannot do. Executives who make similar assumptions about their competitors put their organizations' performance in jeopardy.

Strategic management often borrows lessons as well as metaphors from classic military strategy. For example, major business decisions are often categorized as "strategic" while more minor decisions (such as small changes in price or the opening of a new location) are referred to as "tactical" decisions. Here are a few select examples of classic military strategies that hold insights for strategic decisions today.

Table 1.3 Classic Military Strategy

1532:
Machiavelli's book *The Prince* offers clever recipes for success to government leaders. Some of the book's suggestions are quite devious, and the word Machiavellian comes to refer to acts of deceit and manipulation.

1775:
The American Revolutionary War between the United States and Great Britain begins. Weaker American forces win the war in part by relying on nontraditional tactics such as guerrilla warfare and the strategic targeting of British officers. They also depend on help from the French navy, illustrating the potential value of strategic alliances.

1815:
Napoleon's defeat at Waterloo demonstrates how spreading resources too thin can result in defeat of even one of the most famed militaries of all time.

1865:
The American Civil War ends. Historians consider the Confederacy to have had better generals, but the Union possessed greater resources. Sometimes good strategies simply cannot overcome a stronger adversary.

1944:
Following a series of deceptions designed to confuse and fool German forces, the Allies launch the D-Day invasion in an effort to liberate Europe from Nazi control.

Strategic Management as a Field of Study

Universities contain many different fields of study, including physics, literature, chemistry, computer science, and engineering. Some fields of study date back many centuries (e.g., literature), while others (such as computer science) have emerged only in recent years. Strategic management has been important throughout history, but the evolution of strategic management into a field of study has mostly taken place over the past century. A few of the key business and academic events that have helped the field develop are discussed next.

The ancient Chinese strategist Sun Tzu made it clear that strategic management is partially art. But it is also part science. Major steps toward developing the scientific aspect of strategic management were taken in the early twentieth century by Frederick W. Taylor. In 1911, Taylor published *The Principles of Scientific Management*. The book was a response to Taylor's observation that most tasks within organizations were organized haphazardly. Taylor believed that businesses would be much more efficient if management principles were derived through scientific investigation. In *The Principles of Scientific Management*, Taylor stressed how organizations could become more efficient through identifying the "one best way" of performing important tasks. Implementing Taylor's principles was thought to have saved railroad companies hundreds of millions of dollars. Although many later works disputed the merits of trying to find the "one best way," Taylor's emphasis on maximizing organizational performance became the core concern of strategic management as the field developed.

Also in the early twentieth century, automobile maker Henry Ford emerged as one of the pioneers of strategic management among industrial leaders. At the time, cars seemed to be a luxury item for wealthy people. Ford adopted a unique strategic perspective, however, and boldly offered the vision that he would make cars the average family could afford. Building on ideas about efficiency from Taylor and others, Ford organized assembly lines for creating automobiles that lowered costs dramatically. Despite his wisdom, Ford also made mistakes. Regarding his company's flagship product, the Model T, Ford famously stated, "Any customer can have a car painted any color that he wants so long as it is black." When rival automakers provided customers with a variety of color choices, Ford had no choice but to do the same.

The acceptance of strategic management as a necessary element of business school programs took a major step forward in 1959. A widely circulated report created by the Ford Foundation recommended that all business schools offer a capstone course. The goal of this course would be to integrate knowledge across different business fields such as marketing, finance, and accounting to help students devise better ideas for addressing complex business problems. Rather than seeking a "one best way" solution, as advocated by Taylor and Harvard's business policy course, this capstone course would emphasize students' critical thinking skills in general and the notion that multiple ways of addressing a problem could be equally

Figure 1.6: The Model T Ford, the first production car produced on an assembly line.

successful in particular. The Ford Foundation report was a key motivator that led US universities to create strategic management courses in their undergraduate and master of business administration programs.

Although strategy has been important throughout history, strategic management as a field of study has largely developed over the past century. Below are a few key business and academic events that have helped the field evolve.

Table 1.4 The Modern History of Strategic Management

Year	Notable event
1909	Ford first produces its classic Model T.
1911	Frederick W. Taylor publishes *The Principles of Scientific Management.*
1912	The precursor to the modern strategic management course was created at Harvard Business School under the title of "Business Policy."
1925	A&W Root Beer becomes America's first franchised restaurant chain.
1959	The Ford Foundation recommends that business school curricula include a capstone course that integrates knowledge across business fields in order to help solve complex business problems.
1962	Alfred Chandler publishes *Strategy and Structure: Chapters in the History of the Industrial Enterprise.*
1962	Sam Walton opens the first Wal-Mart in Arkansas, relying on a strategy that emphasized low prices and high levels of customer service.
1980	The *Strategic Management Journal* is created.
1995	The launch of Amazon.com by founder Jeff Bezos is perhaps the pivotal event in creating internet-based commerce.
2001	Enron Corporation declares bankruptcy after a series of disclosures reveal that the firm's stellar performance had been a product of fraud and corruption.
2005	Thomas Friedman's book *The World is Flat: A Brief History of the Twenty-First Century* suggests that many advantages that firms in developed countries like the United States take for granted are disappearing.
2010	Walmart becomes the largest company in the world.
2018	Apple becomes the first company to be worth $1 trillion.
2020	Walmart is still the highest revenue producing company in the world.

In 1962, business and academic events occurred that seemed minor at the time but that would later give rise to huge changes. Building on the business savvy that he had gained as a franchisee, Sam Walton opened the first Walmart in Rogers, Arkansas. Relying on a strategy that emphasized low prices and high levels of customer service, Walmart grew to 882 stores with a combined $8.4 billion dollars in annual sales by 1985. A decade later, sales reached $93.6 billion across nearly 3,000 stores. In 2010, Walmart was the largest company in the world. In recent years, Walmart has arguably downplayed customer service in favor of cutting costs. Time will tell whether deviating from Sam Walton's original strategic positioning will hurt the company.

Two pivotal events that firmly established strategic management as a field of study took place in 1980. One was the creation of the *Strategic Management Journal*. The introduction of the journal offered a forum for researchers interested in building knowledge about strategic management. Much like important new medical findings that appear in the *Journal of the American Medical Association* and *The New England Journal of Medicine*, the *Strategic Management Journal* publishes path breaking insights about strategic management.

The second pivotal event in 1980 was the publication of *Competitive Strategy: Techniques for Analyzing Industries and Competitors* by Harvard professor Michael Porter. This book offers concepts such as five forces analysis and generic strategies that continue to strongly influence how executives choose strategies more than thirty years after the book's publication. Given the importance of these concepts, both five forces analysis and generic strategies are discussed in detail in Chapter 3 "Evaluating the External Environment" and Chapter 6 "Selecting Business-Level Strategies", respectively.

Many consumers today take web-based shopping for granted, but this channel for commerce was created recently. The 1995 launch of Amazon by founder Jeff Bezos was perhaps the pivotal event in creating internet-based commerce. In pursuit of its vision "to be earth's most customer-centric company," Amazon has diversified far beyond its original focus on selling books and has evolved into a dominant retailer. Powerful giants have stumbled badly in Amazon's wake. Sears had sold great varieties of goods (even including entire houses) through catalogs for many decades, as had JCPenney. Neither firm created a strong online sales presence to keep pace with Amazon, and both eventually dropped their catalog businesses. As often happens with old and large firms, Sears and JCPenney were outmaneuvered by a creative and versatile upstart.

Ethics have long been an important issue within the strategic management field. Attention to the need for executives to act ethically when creating strategies increased dramatically in the early 2000s when a series of companies such as Enron Corporation, WorldCom, Tyco, Qwest, and Global Crossing were found to have grossly exaggerated the strength of their performance. After a series of revelations about fraud and corruption, investors in these firms and others lost billions of dollars, tens of thousands of jobs were lost, and some executives were sent to prison.

Like ethics, the implications of international competition are of central interest to strategic management. Provocative new thoughts on the nature of the international arena were offered in 2005 by Thomas L. Friedman. In his book *The World Is Flat: A Brief History of the Twenty-First Century*, Friedman argues that many of the advantages that firms in developed countries such as the United States, Japan, and Great Britain take for granted are disappearing. One implication is that these firms will need to improve their strategies if they are to remain successful.

Looking to the future, it appears likely that strategic management will prove to be more important than ever. In response, researchers who are interested in strategic management will work to build additional knowledge about how organizations can maximize their performance. Executives will need to keep track of the latest scientific findings. Meanwhile, they also must leverage the insights that history offers on how to be successful while trying to avoid past mistakes.

Key Takeaway

- Although strategic management as a field of study has developed mostly over the last century, the concept of strategy is much older. Understanding strategic management can benefit greatly by learning the lessons that ancient history and military strategy provide.

Exercises

1. What do you think was the most important event related to strategy in ancient times?
2. In what ways are the strategic management of business and military strategy alike? In what ways are they different?
3. Do you think executives are more ethical today as a result of the scandals in the early 2000s? Why or why not?

References

Bracker, J. (1980). The historical development of the strategic management concept. *Academy of Management Review*, 5(2), 219–224.

Image Credits

Figure 1.5: Verlag, Phaidon. "A marble bust, reputedly of Hannibal, originally found at the ancient city-state of Capua in Italy." Public Domain. Retrieved from https://commons.wikimedia.org/wiki/File:Mommsen_p265.jpg.

Figure 1.6: ModelTMitch. "1925 Ford Model T touring, built at Henry Ford's Highland Park Plant in Dearborn, Michigan." CC BY-SA 4.0. Cropped. Retrieved from https://commons.wikimedia.org/wiki/File:1925_Ford_Model_T_touring.jpg.

1.5 Contemporary Critique of Strategic Management

This book focuses attention on the widely accepted approaches that frame the contemporary practice and understanding of strategic management. The field of strategic management has always had its critics, and, as with any academic discipline, this criticism has challenged the field to adapt and improve over time. Over time, both practitioners and scholars have voiced concerns about various areas of the strategic management process, and this section summarizes the general critiques to deepen your own ability to critically consider the processes of strategic management in your own organizations and career.

The kinds of concerns about strategic management differ depending upon who is voicing them. From the perspective of firm managers or executives, commonly expressed concerns target the high levels of investment required in order to get more benefit than cost from an effective strategic management process. For strategic management to be done well, it is typically a complex process that is high in cost, time, and difficulty (Cameron, 2019; Katsanos, 2019). Further, some decision makers are skeptical of the ability of strategic management to achieve its goal: to accurately anticipate an unknown future (Cameron, 2019; Llopis, 2019). Some critics go so far as to suggest that committing to a strategy may limit a firm's ability to respond to a changing environment when companies "make future decisions on obsolete data" (Cameron, 2019). In the opening paragraph of Michael Raynor's bestselling book *The Strategy Paradox*, he says:

"Most strategies are built on specific beliefs about the future. Unfortunately, the future is deeply unpredictable. Worse, the requirements of breakthrough success demand implementing strategy in ways that make it impossible to adapt should the future not turn out as expected. The result is the Strategy Paradox: strategies with the greatest possibility of success also have the greatest possibility of failure" (2007, p. 1).

In his book, Mr. Raynor goes on to discuss that survivorship bias is an issue because the strategies of firms that survive are evaluated more than those that fail. The issue of survivorship bias also is a research area within the field of strategic management. Additionally, other strategy scholars raise concerns about how the dominant approaches to strategic management reinforce existing assumptions about power and inequalities within organizations (e.g., affecting gender, race, etc.) and in the global market (i.e., reproducing the same "winners" and "losers") (Knights & Morgan, 1991; Levy et al., 2011; Montgomery et al., 1989).

Some critiques focus on the inadequacies of specific strategic tools or theories. For example, some scholars challenge existing firm-level, resource-based approaches for its inability to adequately assess and capture changing contexts and capabilities (resource-based approaches are introduced in Chapter 5) (Bromiley & Fleming, 2002; Teece, 2019). Finally, the field of strategic management has been critiqued for being too concerned with achieving immediate, business "results" (Montgomery et al., 1989), and at other times, for not being attuned enough to the real-time, practical needs of business (Pricop, 2012).

It is evident that there are plenty of reasons to think critically about how a firm's decision makers choose to engage in their strategic management processes. Ultimately, responsibility for determining a firm's strategic approach is left to the discretion of the firm's executive team. While the theories, tools, and resources introduced throughout this text are well-researched, time-tested, and best practices in the field of strategic management, no approach is perfect, nor is it intended to be.

References

Bromiley, P., & Fleming, L. (2002). 15. The resource-based view of strategy: a behaviorist critique. *The Economics of Choice, Change and Organization: Essays in Memory of Richard M. Cyert* (319). Edward Elgar Publishing.

Cameron, S. (2019). What are some disadvantages of strategic management? *bizfluent*. https://bizfluent.com/info-7933037-disadvantages-strategic-management.html

Katsanos, K. (2019). What are some disadvantages of strategic management. *Chron.* https://smallbusiness.chron.com/disadvantages-strategic-management-80740.html

Knights, D., & Morgan, G. (1991). Corporate strategy, organizations, and subjectivity: A critique. *Organization Studies, 12*(2), 251-273.

Levy, D. L., Alvesson, M., & Willmott, H. (2011). Critical approaches to strategic management. In M. Alvesson & H. Willmott (Eds.), *Critical Management Studies, 14,* 92-110. Los Angeles: Sage.

Llopis, G. (2019). Corporate strategies were not designed for today's age of personalization. *Forbes.* https://www.forbes.com/sites/glennllopis/2019/11/04/corporate-strategies-were-not-designed-for-todays-age-of-personalization/#5da602a51d06

Montgomery, C. A., Wernerfelt, B., & Balakrishnan, S. (1989). Strategy content and the research process: A critique and commentary. *Strategic Management Journal, 10*(2), 189-197.

Pricop, O. C. (2012). Critical aspects in the strategic management theory. *Procedia – Social and Behavioral Sciences, 58,* 98-107. doi:https://doi.org/10.1016/j.sbspro.2012.09.983

Raynor, M. E. (2007). The strategy paradox: Why committing to success leads to failure (and what to do about it). *Currency.*

Teece, D. J. (2019). A capability theory of the firm: an economics and (strategic) management perspective. *New Zealand Economic Papers, 53*(1), 1-43.

1.6 Understanding the Strategic Management Process

Strategic management is a process that involves building a careful understanding of how the world is changing, as well as a knowledge of how those changes might affect a particular firm. CEOs, such as late Apple founder Steve Jobs, must be able to carefully manage the possible actions that their firms might take to deal with changes that occur in their environment. We present a model of the strategic management process in Figure 1.7, "Overall Model of the Strategic Management Process". This model also guides our presentation of the chapters contained in this book.

MODULE 1: Introduction to Strategic Management

Chapter 1: Mastering Strategy – Art and Science

Chapter 2: Assessing Organizational Performance

MODULE 2: External Analysis

Chapter 3: Evaluating the External Environment

MODULE 3: Internal Firm Analysis

Chapter 4: Evaluating the Internal Environment

Chapter 5: Synthesis of Strategic Issues and Analysis

MODULE 4: Business-Level, Innovation, Corporate and International Strategies

Chapter 6: Selecting Business-Level Strategies

Chapter 7: Innovation Strategies

Chapter 8: Selecting Corporate-Level Strategies

Chapter 9: Competing in International Markets

MODULE 5: Executing Strategy

Chapter 10: Executing Strategy through Organizational Design

MODULE 6: Leading an Ethical Organization

Chapter 11: Leading an Ethical Organization: Corporate Governance, Corporate Ethics, and Social Responsibility

Figure 1.7: Overall Model of the Strategic Management Process

The strategic management process begins with an understanding of strategy and performance. As we have noted in this introductory chapter, strategic management is both an art and a science, and it involves multiple conceptualizations of the notion of strategy drawn from recent and ancient history. In Chapter 2 "Assessing Organizational Performance", we focus on how the organization's mission and vision shape the development of the firm's strategy. Consequently, how managers understand and interpret the performance of their firms is often central to understanding strategy.

Environmental and internal scanning is the next stage in the process. Managers must constantly scan the external environment for trends and events that affect the overall economy, and they must monitor changes in the particular industry in which the firm operates. For example, Apple's decision to create the iPhone demonstrates its ability to interpret that traditional industry boundaries that distinguished the cellular phone industry and the computer industry were beginning to blur. At the same time, firms must evaluate their own resources to understand how they might react to changes in the environment. For example, intellectual property is a vital resource for Apple. Between 2008 and 2010, Apple filed more than 350 cases with the US Patent and Trademark Office to protect its use of such terms as apple, pod, and safari (Apple Inc.).

A classic management tool that incorporates the idea of scanning elements both external and internal to the firm is SWOT (strengths, weaknesses, opportunities, and threats) analysis. Strengths and weaknesses are assessed by examining the firm's internal resources, while opportunities and threats refer to external events and trends. The value of SWOT analysis parallels ideas from classic military strategists such as Sun Tzu, who noted the value of knowing yourself as well as your opponent. Chapter 3 "Evaluating the External Environment" examines the topic of evaluating the external environment in detail, and Chapter 4 "Evaluating the Internal Environment" presents concepts and tools for managing firm resources. Synthesizing the information gained in the external and internal analysis into a SWOT framework is addressed in Chapter 5. The SWOT is then used to formulate the strategic issue(s) that the firm must deal with as it formulates strategies.

Strategy formulation is the next step in the strategic management process. This involves developing specific strategies and actions. Certainly, part of Apple's success is due to the unique products it offers the market, as well as how these products complement one another. A customer can buy an iPod that plays music from iTunes—all of which can be stored in Apple's Mac computer (Inside CRM Editors, n.d.). In Chapter 6 "Selecting Business-Level Strategies", we discuss how selecting business-level strategies helps to provide firms with a recipe that can be followed that will increase the likelihood that their strategies will be successful. In Chapter 7, "Innovation Strategies", we present insights on the role innovation plays in strategy development and implementation. Chapter 8

Figure 1.8: *The importance of knowing yourself and your opponent is applicable to the knowledge of strategic management for business, military strategy, and classic strategy games such as chess.*

"Selecting Corporate-Level Strategies" focuses on selecting corporate-level strategies, and Chapter 9 "Competing in International Markets" presents possibilities for firms competing in international markets. Strategy implementation is the final stage of the process. One important element of strategy implementation entails crafting an effective organizational structure and corporate culture. For example, part of Apple's success is due to its consistent focus on innovation and creativity that Steve Jobs described as similar to that of a start-up. Chapter 10 "Executing Strategy through Organizational Design" offers ideas on how to manage these elements of implementation. The final chapter explores how to lead an ethical organization through corporate governance, social responsibility, and sustainability.

Section Video

Strategic Management Process [04:35]

The video for this lesson explains the strategic management process.

You can view this video here: https://youtu.be/o0U0gwvnhek.

Key Takeaway

- Strategic management is a process that requires the ability to manage change. Consequently, executives must be careful to monitor and to interpret the events in their environment, to take appropriate actions when change is needed, and to monitor their performance to ensure that their firms are able to survive and, it is hoped, thrive over time.

Exercises

1. Who makes the strategic decisions for most organizations?
2. Why is it important to view strategic management as a process?
3. What are the four steps of the strategic management process?
4. How is chess relevant to the study of strategic management? What other games might help teach strategic thinking?

References

Apple Inc. Litigation. In *Wikipedia*. en.wikipedia.org/wiki/Apple_Inc._ litigation.

Inside CRM Editors. (n.d.). *Effective strategies Apple uses to create loyal customers*. Retrieved from https://it.toolbox.com/blogs/inside-crm/11-effective-strategies-apple-uses-to-create-loyal-customers-100109.

Image Credits

Figure 1.7: Kindred Grey (2020). "Chapter Layout for Strategic Management." CC BY-SA 4.0. Retrieved from https://commons.wikimedia.org/wiki/File:Chapter_Layout_for_Strategic_Management.png.

Figure 1.8: Shirinsokhan, Mahmoudreza. "Chess" CC BY-NC 2.0. Retrieved from https://flic.kr/p/bPNmxi.

Video Credits

Afra Alnaimi. (2014, November 29). *Strategic Management Process* [Video]. YouTube. https://youtu.be/o0U0gwvnhek.

1.7 Conclusion

This chapter provides an overview of strategic management and strategy. Ideas about strategy span many centuries, and modern understanding of strategy borrows from ancient strategies as well as classic military strategies. You should now understand that there are numerous ways to conceptualize the idea of strategy, and that effective strategic management is needed to ensure the long-term success of firms. The study of strategic management provides tools to effectively manage organizations, but it also involves the art of knowing how and when to apply creative thinking. Knowledge of both the art and the science of strategic management is needed to help guide organizations as their strategies emerge and evolve over time. Such tools will also help you effectively chart a course for your career as well as to understand the effective strategic management of the organizations for which you will work.

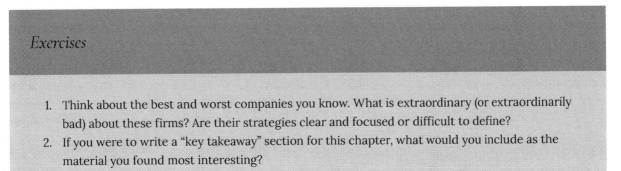

Exercises

1. Think about the best and worst companies you know. What is extraordinary (or extraordinarily bad) about these firms? Are their strategies clear and focused or difficult to define?
2. If you were to write a "key takeaway" section for this chapter, what would you include as the material you found most interesting?

Chapter 2: Assessing Organizational Performance

Learning Objectives

After reading this chapter, you should be able to understand and articulate answers to the following questions:

1. What are organizational vision, mission, values, and goals, and why are they important to organizations?
2. How should executives analyze the performance of their organization?
3. What is competitive advantage and how is it calculated?

2.1 Introduction

The foundation of strategic management is for an organization to answer three questions:

1. Where are we?
2. Where are we going?
3. How are we going to get there?

Organizations answer the first question by assessing their organization. Often this is by looking at financial data, reviewing historical trends, and comparing the financial performance to other benchmarks such as industry averages or competitors' performance. But financial indicators are not the only assessment measures to determine where a company is in relation to the marketplace. Other **organizational performance indicators** are also reviewed, such as quality measures, productivity measures, human resource indicators such as staff satisfaction and retention rates, and customer satisfaction and retention. A multitude of different measures from different perspectives allow a firm to determine how it is doing.

Organizational leadership provides the answer to the second question; where are we going? In collaboration with other stakeholders, leadership sets the **vision** for the firm. The vision is what the organization aspires to be, that big goal it wants to accomplish. The vision is developed within the organization's **mission**: its purpose for being. The vision must also be aligned with the organization's **core values**: the principles that are important as it carries out its mission and vision.

The third question, how are we going to get there, speaks to the heart of strategic management. An organization develops **strategies** to work toward achieving its vision. These are developed after much assessment is performed to determine the best road map to advance the organization in the marketplace.

2.2 Vision, Mission, and Goals

Questions Are Brewing at Starbucks

March 30, 2011, marked the fortieth anniversary of Starbucks's first store opening for business in Seattle, Washington. From its humble beginnings, Starbucks grew to become the largest coffeehouse company in the world while stressing the importance of both financial and social goals. As it created thousands of stores across dozens of countries, the company navigated many interesting periods. The last few years were a particularly fascinating era.

Figure 2.1: Starbucks's global empire includes this store in Seoul, South Korea

In early 2007, Starbucks appeared to be very successful, and its stock was worth more than $35 per share. By 2008, however, the economy was slowing, competition in the coffee business was heating up, and Starbucks's performance had become disappointing. In a stunning reversal of fortune, the firm's stock was worth less than $10 per share by the end of the year. Anxious stockholders wondered whether Starbucks's decline would continue or whether the once high-flying company would return to its winning ways.

Riding to the rescue was Howard Schultz, the charismatic and visionary founder of Starbucks who had stepped down as chief executive officer eight years earlier. Schultz again took the helm and worked to turn the company around by emphasizing its mission statement: "to inspire and nurture the human spirit—one person, one cup and one neighborhood at a time" (Starbucks). About a thousand under-performing stores were shut down permanently. Thousands of other stores closed for a few hours so that baristas could be retrained to make inspiring drinks. Food offerings were revamped to ensure that coffee—not breakfast sandwiches—were the primary aroma that tantalized customers within Starbucks's outlets.

By the time Starbucks's fortieth anniversary arrived, Schultz had led his company to regain excellence, and its stock price was back above $35 per share. In March 2011, Schultz summarized the situation by noting that "over the last three years, we've completely transformed the company, and the health of Starbucks is quite good. But I don't think this is a time to celebrate or run some victory lap. We've got a lot of work to do" (Starbucks, 2011). Schultz retired a second time in 2017 and was replaced by the COO, Kevin Johnson. Starbucks has continued its dominance, opening its 30,000th store in March, 2019, in Shenzhen, China. During the COVID-19 pandemic of 2020, Starbucks and Johnson were praised on how the organization handled the crisis. Phase 1: Mitigate and Contain, was implemented, limiting access to only drive-thru and delivery. Employees were paid whether they worked or not. Then Phase 2: Monitor and Adapt was implemented, with the gradual reopening of stores. The decision to open stores was made locally, not by corporate headquarters. Johnson emphasized the principles of prioritizing the health and well-being of its staff and customers and playing a positive and constructive role with the communities and government officials where they serve.

References

Starbucks. *Our Starbucks mission statement.* (n.d.). http://www.starbucks.com/about-us/company-information/mission-statement.

NPR. (2011, March 28). *Starbucks CEO: Can you 'Get big and stay small'?* http://www.npr.org/2011/03/28/134738487/starbucks-ceo-can-you-get-big-and-stay-small.

Bariso, J. (2020, April 20). *Why Starbucks CEO's Letter to Employees About Covid-19 Wins.* Inc. https://www.inc.com/justin-bariso/starbucks-ceos-letter-to-employees-about-covid-19-is-a-master-class-in-emotional-intelligence.html.

The Importance of Vision

"Vision animates, inspires, transforms purpose into action." – Warren Bennis

Knowledge, skills, and abilities separate effective strategic leaders like Howard Schultz from poor strategic leaders. One of them is the ability to inspire employees to work hard to improve their organization's performance. Effective strategic leaders are able to convince employees to embrace lofty ambitions and move the organization forward. In contrast, poor strategic leaders struggle to rally their people and channel their collective energy in a positive direction.

As the quote from Warren Bennis suggests, a **vision** is one key tool available to executives to inspire the people in an organization (Table 2.1). An organization's vision describes what the organization hopes to become in the future and helps guide its strategies. Well-constructed visions clearly articulate an organization's aspirations. Avon's vision is "to be the company that best understands and satisfies the product, service, and self-fulfillment needs of women—globally." This brief yet powerful statement emphasizes several aims that are important to Avon, including excellence in customer service, empowering women, and the intent to be a worldwide player. Like all good visions, Avon sets a high standard for employees to work collectively toward. Perhaps no vision captures high standards better than that of aluminum maker Alcoa. This firm's very ambitious vision is "to be the best company in the world—in the eyes of our customers, shareholders, communities and people." By making clear their aspirations, Alcoa's executives hope to inspire employees to act in ways that help the firm become the best in the world.

The results of a survey of 1,500 executives illustrates that creating an inspiring vision creates a tremendous challenge for executives. When asked to identify the most important characteristics of effective strategic leaders, 98% of the executives listed "a strong sense of vision" first. Meanwhile, 90% of the executives also expressed serious doubts about their own ability to create a vision (Quigley, 1994). Not surprisingly, many organizations do not have formal visions. Many organizations that do have vision statements find that employees do not embrace and pursue the visions. Having a well-formulated vision employees embrace can therefore give an organization an edge over its rivals.

That aspirational goal of what the company wants to become is the driver for the strategies that are developed. Accomplishing the strategies and goals drives the organization toward achieving its vision. Thus, there should be alignment between the vision of the company, its mission, values, structure, culture, and the strategies its leaders' select. As discussed in later chapters, for example, certain structures are better for achieving organizational objectives.

An organization's vision describes what the organization hopes to become in the future. Visions highlight the values and aspirations that lay at the heart of the organization. Although vision statements have the potential to inspire employees, customers, and other stakeholders, vision statements are relatively rare and good visions are even rarer. Some of the visions being pursued by businesses today are offered below.

Table 2.1 The Big Picture: Organizational Vision

Company	Vision
Alcoa	To be the best company in the world—in the eyes of our customers, shareholders, communities and people.
Avon	To be the company that best understands and satisfies the product, service and self-fulfillment needs of women—globally.
Chevron	To be the global energy company most admired for its people, partnership, and performance.
Google	To provide access to the world's information in one click.
Kraft Heinz Foods	To be the best food company, growing a better world.
Proctor and Gamble	Be, and be recognized as, the best consumer products and services company in the world.

Mission Statements

In working to turn around Starbucks, Howard Schultz sought to renew Starbucks's commitment to its mission statement: "to inspire and nurture the human spirit—one person, one cup, and one neighborhood at a time." A **mission** such as Starbucks's states the reasons for an organization's existence, its purpose. Well-written mission statements effectively capture an organization's identity and provide answers to the fundamental question "Who are we?". While a vision looks to the future, a mission captures the key elements of the organization's past and present (Table 2.2).

Organizations need support from their key stakeholders, such as employees, owners, suppliers, and customers, if they intend to be successful. A mission statement should explain to stakeholders why they should support the organization by making clear what important role or purpose the organization plays in society. Google's mission, for example, is "to organize the world's information and make it universally accessible and useful." Google pursued this mission in its early days by developing a very popular internet search engine. The firm continues to serve its mission through various strategic actions, including offering its internet browser, Google Chrome, to the online community, providing free e-mail via its Gmail service, and making books available online for browsing.

The organization's mission is an umbrella under which all strategic management functions occur. If strategies and goals do not align with the firm's mission, purpose, and vision, they need to be dropped, modified, or the mission needs to be revised.

While a vision describes what an organization desires to become in the future, an organization's mission is grounded in the past and present. A mission outlines the reasons for the organization's existence and explains what role it plays in society. A well-written mission statement captures the organization's identity and helps to answer the fundamental question of "Who are we?". As a practical matter, a mission statement explains to key stakeholders why they should support the organization. The following examples illustrate the connections between organizations and the needs of their key stakeholders.

Table 2.2 Missions

Company	Mission Statement
Harley Davidson	We fulfill dreams through the experiences of motorcycling, by providing to motorcyclists and to the general public an expanding line of motorcycles and branded products and services in selected market segments.
Internal Revenue Service	Provide America's taxpayers top quality service by helping them understand and meet their tax responsibilities and enforce the law with integrity and fairness to all.
Starbucks	To inspire and nurture the human spirit – one person, one cup, and one neighborhood at a time.
Netflix	We promise our customers stellar service, our suppliers a valuable partner, our investors the prospects of sustained profitable growth, and our employees the allure of huge impact.
Nike	To bring inspiration and innovation to every athlete in the world.
Walmart	To save people money so they can live better.

Mission statements are often short and concise. Years ago, mission statements might have been several paragraphs long. The problem that companies encountered was that employees could not remember or verbalize the mission. In the evolution of mission statements, they have become short and easier to remember. Knowing and living their organization's mission helps employees' engagement and satisfaction.

Figure 2.2: *Many consider Abraham Lincoln to have been one of the greatest strategic leaders in modern history.*

One of Abraham Lincoln's best-known statements is that "a house divided against itself cannot stand." This provides a helpful way of thinking about the relationship between vision and mission. Executives ask for trouble if their organization's vision and mission are divided by emphasizing different domains. Some universities, for example, have fallen into this trap. Many large public universities were established in the late 1800s with missions that centered on educating citizens. As the twentieth century unfolded, however, creating scientific knowledge through research became increasingly important to these universities. Many university presidents responded by creating visions centered on building the scientific prestige of their schools. This created a dilemma for professors: should they devote most of their time and energy to teaching students, as the mission required, or on their research studies, as ambitious presidents demanded via their visions? Some universities continue to struggle with this trade-off today and remain houses divided against themselves. In short, an organization is more effective to the extent that its vision and its mission target employees' effort in the same direction.

Pursuing the Vision and Mission through SMART Goals

An organization's vision and mission offer a broad, overall sense of the organization's direction. To work toward achieving these overall aspirations, organizations also need to create goals—narrower targets that should provide clear and tangible guidance to employees as they perform their work on a daily basis. The most effective goals are those that are specific, measurable, attainable, realistic, and time-bound. An easy way to remember these dimensions is to combine the first letter of each into one word: **SMART** (Table 2.3). Employees are put in a good position to succeed to the extent that an organization's goals are SMART.

While missions and visions provide an overall sense of the organization's direction, goals are narrower aims that should provide clear and tangible guidance to employees. The most effective goals are those that are SMART (specific, measurable, attainable , realistic, and time-bound). SMART goals help provide clarity, transparency, and accountability. As detailed below, one SMART goal is Coca-Cola's aim to "improve our water efficiency by 20%, compared with a baseline year."

Table 2.3 Creating SMART Goals

S	**Specific:** Coca-Cola is seeking to improve its water efficiency by a specific amount—20%. In contrast, goals such as "do your best" are vague, making it difficult to decide if a goal is actually reached.
M	**Measurable:** Water efficiency can be calculated, so Coca-Cola is able to track its progress relative to its 20% target. If progress is slow, more resources can be devoted to achieving the goal.
A	**Attainable:** A series of research studies have established that performance is strongest when goals are challenging but attainable. Reaching a 20% improvement will require aggressive work by Coke, but the goal can be reached.
R	**Realistic:** If Coca-Cola's water efficiency goal was 95% improvement, Coca-Cola's employees will probably react with surprise. Reaching a goal must be feasible in order for employees to embrace it. Unrealistic goals make most people give up and basing goals on impossible clichés, such as "give 110%" creates confusion.
T	**Time-bound:** Coca-Cola is seeking to achieve its 20% improvement. Some universities, such as Texas Tech University, provide incentives, including preferred scheduling for students who sign contracts agreeing to graduate on a four-year schedule. Deadlines such as these are motivating and they create accountability.

Many of the principles for effective organizational vision, missions, and goals apply to individuals too. Here are some ideas that might help you think differently about your own aspirations and how you are working to reach them.

Table 2.4 Be SMART: Vision, Mission, Goals, and You

Vision	Young children often have grandiose visions, such as "I want to be the president of the United States." Now that you are in college, what do you aspire to become? Is your education setting the stage for you to reach this vision?
Mission	Is your mission in life simply to accumulate as much wealth as you can? Or do you also place value on your role in a family and as a member of society?
Specific	Do you create explicit rather than vague goals for yourself? This can help you to target your energy toward what is important.
Measurable	Quantifying your goals allows you to track your accomplishments over time and can help reduce stress. For example, meeting a goal of "write a page every day" might prevent panic the night before an important project is due.
Attainable	Creating challenging, but attainable educational goals (e.g. maintaining a 3.5 GPA) is likely to lead to higher performance than minimal goals (e.g., pass all my classes).
Realistic	To better understand your prospects in the job market, consider researching what kinds of jobs are common for your major and experience level.
Time-Bound	Time management is a challenge in today's world. If you tend to procrastinate, setting interim deadlines for yourself might help you to stay on schedule.

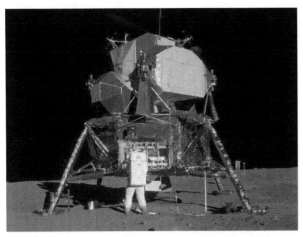

Figure 2.3: Americans landed on the moon eight years after President Kennedy set a moon landing as a key goal for the United States.

The period after an important goal is reached is often overlooked but is critical. This is an opportunity for a strategic decision: will an organization rest on its laurels or will it take on new challenges? The US space program again provides an illustrative example. At the time of the first moon landing, *Time Magazine* asked the leader of the team that built the moon rockets about the future of space exploration. "Given the same energy and dedication that took them to the moon," said Wernher von Braun, "Americans could land on Mars as early as 1982" (Time, 1969). No new goal involving human visits to Mars was embraced, however, and human exploration of space was deemphasized in favor of robotic adventurers. Nearly three decades after von Braun's proposed timeline for reaching Mars expired, President Barack Obama, in 2010. set a goal of creating by 2025 a new space vehicle capable of taking humans beyond the moon and into deep space. This would be followed in the mid-2030s by a flight to orbit Mars as a prelude to landing on Mars (Amos, 2010). Time will tell whether these goals inspire the scientific community and the country in general (Table 2.4).

Corporate Values

In addition to constructing vision and mission statements, firms also develop corporate **value statements**. These are explicit principles that the company endorses and lives by, and expects their employees to embrace. Values related to integrity, diversity, and customer service are often seen on company websites. An information technology company might include innovation as one of its values. Manufacturers may also have sustainability or ecology related values.

Why are values statements important for a firm? They demonstrate to their employees and other stakeholders the important principles that the organization lives by. Employees who do not uphold corporate values may see their employment short-lived at the company. Values also show customers and potential customers what the firm stands for. Some customers may choose a company based on how its values resonate with theirs.

What do values statements have to do with strategic management? An organization should seriously consider their values statement when developing its strategies and goals. If a potential strategy conflicts with one of its values, they need to drop or modify that strategy to ensure the company conforms to their corporate values as they move their organization forward.

Table 2.5 Values Statements from Various Companies

Walmart
Guided by good: service to the customer, respect for the individual, strive for excellence, act with integrity

Harley Davidson Motorcycles
Integrity, be accountable, encourage creativity, inspire teamwork, individuality, and diversity

Facebook
Be bold, Focus on impact, Move fast, Be open, Build social value

Starbucks

- Creating a culture of warmth and belonging, where everyone is welcome.
- Delivering our very best in all we do, holding ourselves accountable for results.
- Acting with courage, challenging the status quo, and finding new ways to grow our company and each other.
- Being present, connecting with transparency, dignity, and respect.

Section Video

A Simple Intro to Mission, Vision, and Values [03:08]

The video for this lesson explains the relationship of mission, vision, values, and strategies/goals.

You can view this video here: https://youtu.be/7mWQh_7fK3U.

Key Takeaway

- Strategic leaders need to ensure that their organizations have four types of aims. A vision states what the organization aspires to become in the future. A mission reflects the organization's past and present by stating why the organization exists and what role it plays in society. Goals are the more specific aims that organizations pursue to reach their visions and missions. The best goals are SMART: specific, measurable, attainable, realistic, and time-bound. Corporate values are key principles that a company endorses and lives by.

References

Amos, J. (2010, April 15). Obama sets Mars goal for America. BBC News. http://news.bbc.co.uk/2/hi/8623691.stm.

National Aeronautics and Space Administration. (n.d.). *Key documents in the history of space policy: 1960s.* http://history.nasa.gov/spdocs.html#1960s.

Quigley, J. V. (1994). Vision: How leaders develop it, share it, and sustain it. *Business Horizons, 37*(5), 37–41.

Time. (1969, July 15). The moon: next, Mars and beyond. Retrieved from http://content.time.com/time/subscriber/article/0,33009,901107,00.html.

Image Credits

Figure 2.1: Fusebok. "Starbucks in Seoul, South Korea" Public Domain. Retrieved from https://commons.wikimedia.org/wiki/File:Starbucks-seoul.JPG.

Figure 2.2: Gardner, Alexander. "Abraham Lincoln" Public Domain. Retrieved from https://commons.wikimedia.org/wiki/Abraham_Lincoln#/media/File:Abraham_Lincoln_O-77_matte_collodion_print.jpg.

Figure 2.3: Armstrong, Neil. "Buzz Aldrin removing the passive seismometer from a compartment in the SEQ bay of the Lunar Lander." Public Domain. Cropped. Retrieved from https://en.wikipedia.org/wiki/File:Apollo_11_Lunar_Lander_-_5927_NASA.jpg.

Video Credits

Flextalk. (2015, June 10). *A simple intro to mission, vision, and values* [Video]. YouTube. https://youtu.be/7mWQh_7fK3U.

2.3 Assessing Organizational Performance

Organizational Performance: A Complex Concept

Organizational performance refers to how well an organization is doing to reach its vision, mission, and goals. Assessing organizational performance is a vital aspect of strategic management. Executives must know how well their organizations are performing to figure out what strategic changes, if any, to make. Performance is a very complex concept, however, and a lot of attention needs to be paid to how it is assessed.

To illustrate this complexity, consider a scenario: suppose that we offered a $10 bet on a coin toss. If it lands on heads, you win $50. If it lands on tails, you lose your $10 bet. If you lost, was the decision a bad one? Well, of course not. You had a 50% chance of winning $50 and a 50% chance of losing $10. In this case, the expected value (EV) of your bet would be $20, ($50 * 50%) – ($10 * 50%). Thus, the decision to bet was a good one, but still led to a poor outcome (or performance). In short, while one can generally expect good decisions to lead to good performance, it is not always the case. The point of this scenario is to highlight that there are situations where good strategies lead to bad outcomes, especially when low probability crises occur. In the case of COVID-19, for example, solid strategies selected several years ago could lead to poor performance because of unexpected conditions.

Two important considerations are (1) **performance measures** and (2) **performance benchmarks** (Figure 2.5). A performance measure is a metric by which an organization's progress can be gauged. Most executives examine measures such as profits, stock price, and sales in an attempt to better understand how well their organizations are competing in the market. But these measures provide just a glimpse of organizational performance. Performance benchmarks are also needed to assess whether an organization is doing well. A performance benchmark is used to make sense of an organization's standing compared to its own or a competitor's financial measures and/or performance indicators. Suppose, for example, that a firm has a profit margin of 20% in 2019. This sounds great on the surface, but suppose that the firm's profit margin in 2018 was 35% and that the average profit margin across all firms in the industry for 2019 was 40%. Viewed relative to these two benchmarks, the firm's 2019 performance is cause for concern.

Figure 2.4: The story of the blind men and the elephant provides a metaphor for understanding the complexities of measuring organizational performance.

Using a variety of performance measures and benchmarks is valuable because different measures and benchmarks provide different information about an organization's functioning. The parable of the blind men and the elephant–popularized in Western cultures through a poem by John Godfrey Saxe in the nineteenth century–is useful for understanding the complexity associated with measuring organizational performance. As the story goes, six blind men set out to "see" what an elephant was like. The first man touched the elephant's side and believed the beast to be like a great wall. The second felt the tusks and thought elephants must be like spears. Feeling the trunk, the third man thought it was a type of snake. Feeling a limb, the fourth man thought it was like a tree trunk. The fifth, examining an ear, thought it was like a fan. The sixth, touching the tail, thought it was like a rope. If the men failed to communicate their different impressions they would have all been partially right but wrong about what ultimately mattered. The point is, an organization must consider organizational performance from various and multiple perspectives to achieve an accurate assessment.

This story parallels the challenge involved in understanding the multidimensional nature of organization performance because different measures and referents may tell a different story about the organization's performance. For example, Fortune 500 lists the largest US firms in terms of sales. These firms are generally not the strongest performers in terms of growth in stock price, however, in part because they are so big that making major improvements is difficult. During the late 1990s, a number of internet-centered businesses enjoyed exceptional growth in sales and stock price but reported losses rather than profits. Many investors in these firms who simply fixated on a single performance measure–sales growth–absorbed heavy losses when the stock market's attention turned to profits and the stock prices of these firms plummeted.

The number of performance measures and referents that are relevant for understanding an organization's performance can be overwhelming. For example, a study of what performance metrics were used within restaurant organizations' annual reports found that 788 different combinations of measures and referents were used within this one industry in a single year (Short & Palmer, 2003). Thus executives need to choose a rich yet limited set of performance measures and referents to focus on.

Table 2.6 How Organizations and Individuals Can Use Financial Performance Measures and Indicators

Types of Measures	Applications for Organizations		Applications for Individuals	
	Key Measure	Key Referent	Key Measure	Key Referent
Liquidity measures: Helpful for understanding if obligations can be paid when due.	Current ratio (Current assets/ Current liabilities)	A ratio of less than 1.0 suggests that the firm does not have enough cash to pay its bills.	Cash in your checking account.	Do you have enough cash to cover your monthly debts?
Leverage measures: Helpful for understanding if debt level is to high. The term leverage refers to the extent to which borrowed money is used.	Debt-to-equity ratio	Competitors' debt-to-equity ratios. The use of debt varies across industries. Auto companies, for example, tend to have high debt-to-equity because they must build massive factories.	Debt-to-income ratio (Monthly debt payments/ Monthly income)	If you have a debt-to-income ratio higher than 40%, you may be on the verge of becoming a credit risk.
Profitability measures: Helpful for understanding how much profit, if any, is really being made.	Net income (income after taxes)	Last year's net income. An increase shows the firm's profits are moving in the right direction.	Net income (income after taxes)	Are you making enough to cover your yearly expenses and save for retirement?

Section Video

What is Organizational Performance? [01:56]

The video for this lesson explains how some organizations assess their organizational performance.

You can view this video here: https://youtu.be/wLXuPgbagJY.

The Balanced Scorecard

To organize performance measures, Professor Robert Kaplan and Professor David Norton of Harvard University developed a tool called the balanced scorecard. Using the scorecard helps managers resist the temptation to fixate on financial measures and instead monitor a diverse set of important measures (Table 2.7). Indeed, the idea behind the framework is to provide a "balance" between financial measures and other measures that are important for understanding organizational activities that lead to sustained, long-term performance. The balanced scorecard recommends that managers gain an overview of the organization's performance by tracking a small number of key measures that collectively reflect four perspectives: (1) financial, (2) customer, (3) internal business process, and (4) staff learning and growth (Kaplan & Norton, 1992).

Because the concept of organizational performance is multidimensional, wise managers realize that understanding organizational performance is like flying a plane. Pilots must be on track in terms of altitude, air speed, and oil pressure and make sure they have enough gas to finish their flight plan. For tracking organizational performance, assessing how the organization is doing financially is just a starting point. The "balanced scorecard" encourages managers to also monitor how well the organization is serving customers, managing internal activities, and setting the stage for future improvements. This provides a fast but comprehensive view of the organization. As shown below, monitoring these four dimensions can also help individuals assess themselves.

Table 2.7 Beyond Profits: Measuring Performance Using the Balanced Scorecard

Scorecard Point	Definition	You could ask yourself...
Financial measures	Such as return on assets and stock price—relate to effectiveness and profits.	How can I improve my personal wealth? Measures might include cash, savings account, and retirement.
Customer measures	Such as number of new or repeat customers and percentage of repeat customers—relate to customer attraction and satisfaction.	How strong is my social network? The number of new contacts you make over time might reflect this dimension.
Internal business process measures	Such as speed at serving a customer and time it takes to create a new product and get it to market—relate to organizational efficiency.	Am I getting better at my current job? Tracking improvements in personal efficiency such as the time needed to complete a task can be helpful.
Learning and growth measures	Such as the average number of new skills learned by each employee every year—relate to the future and emphasize that employee learning is often more important than formal training.	What skills should I develop now for the future? Although the acquisition of new skills is hard to measure, the attainment of specialized licenses or earning of a graduate degree are tangible benchmarks.

Financial Measures

Financial measures of performance relate to organizational effectiveness and profits. Examples include financial ratios such as return on assets, return on equity, and return on investment. Other common financial measures include profits and stock price. Such measures help answer the key question, "How do we look to shareholders?"

Financial performance measures are commonly articulated and emphasized within an organization's annual report to shareholders. To provide context, such measures should be objective and be coupled with meaningful referents, such as the firm's past performance. For example, Starbucks's 2019 annual report highlights the firm's performance in terms of net revenue, operating income, and cash flow over a five-year period.

There are three approaches that organizations use to perform quantitative analysis: financial, market-based, and general.

Financial Analysis: This is basically ratio analysis; being able to make "apple to apple" comparisons between firms or annual trends that account for variable volumes, sales, expenses, and profits. Using ratios allows a direct comparison no matter the size of the firm. Table 2.8 provides basic financial ratios organizations use to compare against benchmarks.

Table 2.8 Key Financial Ratios

RATIO	FORMULA	PURPOSE
Profitability Ratios		
Gross Margin	Gross Profit /Total Revenue	Proportion of revenue related to direct costs (COGS, sales commissions, etc.)
Net Profit Margin	Net Profit /Net Revenue	Profit earned per dollar of revenue
Return on Equity	Net Profit (or Income)/ Shareholder Equity	Profitability in relation to stockholders' equity; i.e. how well you use equity financing
Return on Assets	Net Profit (or Income)/Total Assets	Efficiency in using assets to generate profit
Efficiency Ratios		
Inventory Turnover	COGS /Average Inventory	Efficiency of inventory management
Accounts Receivable Turnover	Net Credit Sales/ Average Acct Rec.	Efficiency of AR management
Leverage Ratio		
Debt Ratio	Total Liabilities/Total Assets	Proportion of assets financed through debt
Liquidity Ratio		
Current Ratio	Current Assets/ Current Liabilities	Ability to pay short term debts with short term assets like cash & inventory
Market Capitalization	Outstanding shares X share price	Market value of the firm

Market-Based Analysis: This analysis helps determine how the firm compares to its competitors in the market. there are two measures to analyze a firm's position in the market:

1. Market Share = Firm's Total Product Revenue / Total Revenue in the industry or market

This measures the percentage of the market that a firm has. For example, if Apple's revenue from selling iPhones is 25% of all the revenue generated from smartphone sales, Apple's market share is 25%.

2. Price-Earnings (PE) Ratio = Stock price / Earnings per Share (EPS)

The Price-Earnings Ration determines how much it costs to invest in the company to receive $1.00 in earnings. For example, if one share of stock costs $10, and it produces $2 annually in earnings, the PE ratio is 5, meaning it costs a $5 investment in this company to receive $1 in earnings. The lower the PE ratio, the better, as far as a simple interpretation goes. However, a higher PE Ratio may indicate the market's belief that the company is a strong performer and will be growing the stock price.

General Quantitative Analysis: There are other types of data sets that can provide useful information. For example, trend analysis is used to determine how much volumes are changing each year, or extrapolate economic data to make predictions. There most likely is industry-specific data to analyze and use as a comparison for firms.

Performance Indicators: As referenced earlier, financial measures alone will not provide sufficient insight into a firm's performance. While financial measures always have operational relevance, other performance indicators often provide strategic insight that may not be evident from the financial picture. This section provides some examples of the other kinds of performance measures helpful in strategic management.

Customer Measures

Customer measures of performance relate to customer attraction, satisfaction, and retention. These measures provide insight to the key question "How do customers see us?" Examples might include the number of new customers, customer satisfaction, and the percentage of repeat customers.

Starbucks realizes the importance of repeat customers and has taken a number of steps to satisfy and to attract regular visitors to their stores. For example, Starbucks rewards regular customers through a rewards program that allows customers to redeem the points they have accumulated for free drinks, bakery items, or merchandise. They also offer all customers free Wi-Fi access (Miller, 2010). Often, firms need external measures about their customers as well. For example, demographic data, taste preferences, or social trends.

Internal Business Process Measures

Internal business process measures of performance relate to organizational efficiency. These measures help answer the key question "What must we excel at?" Examples include the time it takes to manufacture the organization's goods or deliver a service. Another example of this type of measure is the time it takes to create a new product and bring it to market. Productivity and quality data are other measures often targeted for improvement.

Organizations such as Starbucks realize the importance of such efficiency measures for the long-term success of its organization. For this reason, Starbucks carefully examines its processes with the goal of decreasing order fulfillment time. In one example, Starbucks efficiency experts challenged their employees to assemble a Mr. Potato Head to understand how work could be done faster (Jargon, 2009). The aim of this exercise was to help Starbucks employees in general match the speed of the firm's high performers, who boast an average time per order of twenty-five seconds.

Learning and Growth Measures

Learning and growth measures of performance relate to the future. Such measures provide insight to ask the question, "Can we continue to improve and create value?" Learning and growth measures focus on innovation and proceed with an understanding that strategies change over time. Consequently, developing new ways to add value will be needed as the organization continues to adapt to an evolving environment. Employees may need additional training and skills to make a strategy achievable, or the firm may need to hire for the needed skills. An example of a learning and growth measure is the number of new skills learned by employees every year.

One way Starbucks encourages its employees to learn skills that may benefit both the firm and individuals in the future is through its tuition reimbursement program. Employees who have worked with Starbucks for more than a year are eligible. Starbucks hopes that the knowledge acquired while earning a college degree might provide employees with the skills needed to develop innovations that will benefit the company in the future. Another benefit of this program is that it helps Starbucks reward and retain high-achieving employees.

Measuring Performance Using the Triple Bottom Line

Ralph Waldo Emerson once noted, "Doing well is the result of doing good. That's what capitalism is all about." While the balanced scorecard provides a popular framework to help executives understand an organization's performance, other frameworks highlight areas such as social responsibility. One such framework, the triple bottom line, emphasizes the **three P's**: people (making sure that the actions of the organization are socially responsible), planet (making sure organizations act in a way that promotes environmental sustainability), and traditional organization profits. This notion was introduced in the early 1980s but did not attract much attention until the late 1990s.

Social   Environmental   Economic

Figure 2.5: The triple bottom line emphasizes the three Ps of people (social concerns), planet (environmental concerns), and profits (economic concerns).

In the case of Starbucks, the firm has made clear the importance it attaches to the planet by creating an environmental mission statement ("Starbucks is committed to a role of environmental leadership in all facets of our business") in addition to its overall mission (Starbucks, 2011). In terms of the "people" dimension of the triple bottom line, Starbucks strives to purchase coffee beans harvested by farmers who work under humane conditions and are paid reasonable wages. The firm works to be profitable as well.

Key Takeaway

- Organizational performance is a multidimensional concept, and wise managers rely on multiple measures of performance when gauging the success or failure of their organizations. The balanced scorecard provides a tool to help executives gain a general understanding of their organization's current level of achievement across a set of four important dimensions. The triple bottom line provides another tool to help executives focus on performance targets beyond profits alone. This approach stresses the importance of social (people) and environmental (planet) outcomes, as well as profit.

Exercises

1. Given your major, what sets of measures and indicators have you been trained to analyze and value?
2. How might you apply the balanced scorecard framework to measure performance of your college or university?
3. Identify a measurable example of each of the balanced scorecard dimensions other than the examples offered in this section.
4. Identify a mission statement from an organization that emphasizes each of the elements of the triple bottom line.

References

Jargon, J. (2009, August 4). Latest Starbucks buzzword: "Lean" Japanese techniques. *Wall Street Journal*, A1.

Kaplan, R. S., & Norton, D. (1992). The balanced scorecard: Measures that drive performance. *Harvard Business Review*, 70–79.

Miller, C. (2010, June 15). Aiming at rivals, Starbucks will offer free Wi-Fi. *New York Times*, 1B.

Short, J. C., & Palmer, T. B. (2003). Organizational performance referents: An empirical examination of their content and influences. *Organizational Behavior and Human Decision Processes, 90*, 209–224.

Starbucks. (2011). *Our Starbucks mission statement.* http://www.starbucks.com/about-us/company-information/mission-statement.

Image Credits

Figure 2.4: Hanabusa, Itcho. "Blind monks examining an elephant." Public Domain. Retrieved from https://en.wikipedia.org/wiki/File:Blind_monks_examining_an_elephant.jpg.

Video Credits

Word Glossary. (2019, March 18). *What is Organizational Performance?* [Video]. Youtube. https://youtu.be/wLXuPgbagJY.

2.4 Competitive Advantage

While accounting measures and stock market returns provide a sense of how well a firm is performing, these indicators may not be ideal if the intent is to understand which firms perform well systematically over the long term. One limitation of those indicators is that they may reflect random perturbations in market outcomes. A firm may have a stroke of good luck that leads it to capture exceptional profits, even if the strategic position of its business is poor. A firm may also have a stroke of bad luck that leads it to have underwhelming profits, even if the strategic position of its business is healthy. A second limitation of these indicators is that firms are not always attempting to carry profits on their books. For example, there are several publicly traded firms that rarely earn profits but are considered healthy, and even thriving, because they use much of their "would be" profits to invest in further improving their businesses.

At a conceptual level, strategic management scholars are often less concerned with specific accounting and stock market performance indicators and more concerned with the idea of **competitive advantage**. Before offering a formal definition of competitive advantage, it is useful to recall the more familiar concept of economic value creation. Economic value creation (EVC) is the difference between what a customer is willing to pay (WTP) for a product and the cost incurred to produce the product.

$$\textbf{EVC = WTP − Cost}$$

The customer's WTP is also referred to as their reserve price—the maximum they are willing to pay for the product. In this equation, cost reflects the cost incurred by the producer, rather than the cost to the consumer of purchasing the product, which is referred to instead as the price of the product.

Economic value creation may vary across firms. Firms that sell the same product may each incur a different cost of production. Further, consumers may be willing to pay one price when purchasing the good from one firm, but willing to pay another price when purchasing the good from the firm's competitor. This all implies that the economic value created will differ from firm to firm.

With this in mind, we can now say that a firm has a competitive advantage over a competitor if it has a larger economic value creation than that competitor. For example, if we have two firms, A and B, A has a competitive advantage over B if the economic value created by A exceeds the economic value created by B. The magnitude of A's competitive advantage is given by the difference between the economic value created by each firm.

The concept of competitive advantage is useful for several reasons. First, unlike measures such as profits and stock price, competitive advantage does not change based on random perturbations. If a firm's competitive advantage increases, that means that either its economic value creation increased, or its competitor's economic value creation decreased. These changes, in turn, reflect relative shifts in the cost structure, or relative shifts in consumers' willingness to pay. Second, the notion of competitive advantage better reflects the strategic health of firms that reinvest in their business, and therefore are healthy, but do not observe profits. For instance, if firm A earns a profit of $100, but then re-invests $98 of that profit into the business to improve the product, then the accounting profits are $2, but the actual health of the company may have improved because the consumers willingness to pay for the product may have increased. Such a firm would still display a large economic value creation measure, and therefore may still hold a competitive advantage.

Section Video

What is Competitive Advantage? [07:58]

The video for this lesson further explains competitive advantage.

You can view this video here: https://youtu.be/PeCCT7CKpYA.

Video Credits

WolvesandFinance. (2018, February 11). *What is Competitive Advantage?* [Video]. YouTube. https://youtu.be/PeCCT7CKpYA.

2.5 Conclusion

This chapter explains several challenges that executives face in attempting to lead their organizations strategically. Executives must ensure that their organizations have visions, missions, values, and goals in place that help move these organizations forward. Measures and indicators for assessing performance must be thoughtfully chosen. A Balanced Scorecard is a tool that firms can use to measure their progress. When executives succeed at leading strategically, an organization has an excellent chance of gaining a competitive advantage and achieve of success.

Exercises

1. Divide your class into four or eight groups, depending on the size of the class. Assign each group to develop arguments that one of the key issues discussed in this chapter (vision, mission, goals, assessing organizational performance, entrepreneurial orientation) is the most important within organizations. Have each group present their case, and then have the class vote individually for the winner. Which issue won and why?

2. This chapter discussed Howard Schultz and Starbucks on several occasions. Based on your reading of the chapter, how well has Schultz done in dealing with setting a vision, mission, and goals, assessing organizational performance, and entrepreneurial orientation?

3. Write a vision and mission for an organization or firm that you are currently associated with. How could you use the balanced scorecard to assess how well that organization is fulfilling the mission you wrote?

Chapter 3: Evaluating the External Environment

Learning Objectives

After reading this chapter, you should be able to understand and articulate answers to the following questions:

1. What is the macro environment and why is it important to organizations?
2. How is the PESTEL framework used to evaluate the external environment?
3. How is the Porter's Five Forces tool used to perform a competitive analysis of an industry?
4. What are strategic groups and how are they useful to evaluating the competitive environment?

3.1 Introduction

Businesses operate within an external macro-environment that affects the likelihood of their overall success or failure. Forces beyond the control of businesses can hinder the growth of a business or perhaps be harnessed to propel it forward. Strategic management requires that these external and competitive forces be evaluated, so that opportunities may be leveraged and threats may be mitigated as strategies are developed to improve the success of the firm.

This chapter will introduce three tools that help firms assess different perspectives of their competitive environment. The PESTEL framework (Political, Economic, Socio-cultural, Environmental/Ecological, and Legal) evaluates the macro-environment through the evaluation of six external forces. The competitive environment of the industry also must be evaluated through Porter's Five Forces tool. Finally, Strategic Group Mapping helps executives understand how their firm relates to other competitors in the market, and which are their most direct competitors. Once this external analysis is complete, a firm can determine the true strategic issue(s) it faces and can develop strategies to work on strategic issues that move the firm forward toward accomplishing its vision.

Panera Bread: Riding the Trends

Figure 3.1: Panera Bread took advantage of some external forces to expand rapidly.

Founded in 1981 in Boston, Panera Bread was originally a single shop called the Cookie Jar. The following year, its founder, Ron Shaich, merged with Au Bon Pain, a struggling French Bakery in the US. They began to sell soups and fresh sandwiches, at a time when most lunch options were fast food or sit-down restaurants. Shaich sensed two socio-cultural emerging trends in the 1990's. One was the movement toward healthy eating. The other was the public's desire for what would become the "fast casual" restaurant where customers could order at the counter, get their meal quickly, have better food choices than fast food, and dine in an atmosphere conducive to having meetings with friends or business associates. Starbucks helped to stimulate the popularity of the fast casual boom. Shaich sold off Au Bon Pain and focused on building a brand of chain restaurants called Panera Bread.

By 2010 there was a new Panera Bread opening every three days. Staying ahead of the technological forces in the industry, Shaich implemented digital ordering, a loyalty program, and a catering and delivery service. The industry has adopted many of Panera Bread's innovations. By 2017, it had become one of America's most successful restaurant chains and had expanded into Canada. Panera now has over 2000 locations, over 100,000 employees, and its stock is one of the best performers in the industry. Shaick was able to take advantage of emerging trends in the US environment to build a very successful business.

References

Kolhatkar, S. (2018, November). The founder of Panera Bread explains the economic forces that led to Trump. *The New Yorker*. https://www.newyorker.com/business/currency/the-founder-of-panera-bread-explains-the-economic-forces-that-led-to-trump.

Image Credits

3.2 The Relationship between an Organization and its Environment

What Is the Environment?

For any organization, the environment consists of the set of external conditions and forces that have the potential to influence the organization. In the case of Panera Bread, for example, the environment contains its customers, its rivals such as Chipotle and Starbucks, social trends such as the shift in society toward healthier eating, political entities such as the US Congress, and many additional conditions and forces.

It is useful to break the concept of the competitive environment for a business down into two components: the general environment and its industry. The general environment, or macro-environment, includes overall trends and events in society such as social trends, technological trends, demographics, and economic conditions. The industry, or competitive environment, consists of multiple organizations that collectively compete with one another by providing similar goods, services, or both.

Every action that an organization takes, such as raising its prices or launching an advertising campaign, creates some degree of change in the world around it. Most organizations are limited to influencing their industry. Subway's move to cut salt in its sandwiches, for example, may lead other fast-food firms to revisit the amount of salt contained in their products. A few organizations wield such power and influence that they can shape some elements of the general environment. For instance, McDonalds's transition to cage free eggs by 2030 may impact the entire US supply chain for eggs because McDonalds alone purchases approximately 4% of all eggs produced annually, but only 10% of the eggs produced in 2018 were cage free. However, most organizations simply react to major technological trends, for example, the actions of firms such as Intel, Microsoft, and Apple help create these trends. Some aspects of the general environment, such as demographics, simply must be taken as a given by all organizations. Overall, the environment has a far greater influence on most organizations than most organizations have on the environment.

Why Does the Environment Matter?

Understanding the environment that surrounds an organization is important to the executives in charge of the organizations. There are several reasons for this. First, the environment provides resources that an organization needs in order to create goods and services. In the seventeenth century, British poet John Donne famously noted that "no man is an island." Similarly, it is accurate to say that no organization is self-sufficient. As the human body must consume oxygen, food, and water, an organization needs to take in resources such as labor, money, and raw materials from outside its boundaries. Panera Bread, for example, simply would cease to exist without the employees that operate its stores, the suppliers that provide food and other necessary inputs, and the customers who provide Panera Bread with money through purchasing its products. An organization cannot survive without the support of its environment.

Second, the environment is a source of opportunities and threats for an organization. Opportunities are events and trends that create chances to improve an organization's performance level. In the late 1990s, for example, the trends toward obesity in the US and the need for healthy eating helped Panera Bread position itself as a healthy alternative to traditional fast-food restaurants. Threats are events and trends that may undermine an organization's performance. Panera Bread faces a threat from some upstart restaurant chains. Saladworks, for example, offers a variety of salads that contain fewer than five hundred calories. Noodles and Company offers a variety of sandwiches, pasta dishes, and salads that contain fewer than four

Figure 3.2: *Natural disasters devastate many organizations.*

hundred calories. These two firms are much smaller than Panera Bread, but they could grow to become substantial threats to Panera's positioning as a healthy eatery. Panera Bread and other firms must deal with the uncertainty and other impacts of COVID with could threaten this industry for a long period.

Executives also must realize that virtually any environmental trend or event is likely to create opportunities for some organizations and threats for others. This is true even in extreme cases. In addition to horrible human death and suffering, the March 2011 earthquake and tsunami in Japan devastated many organizations, ranging from small businesses that were simply wiped out to corporate giants such as Toyota, whose manufacturing capabilities were undermined. As odd as it may seem, however, these tragic events also opened up significant opportunities for other organizations. The rebuilding of infrastructure and dwellings requires concrete, steel, and other materials. Japanese concrete manufacturers, steelmakers, and construction companies benefited in the wake of this tragedy.

Third, the environment shapes the various strategic decisions that executives make as they attempt to lead their organizations to success. The environment often places important constraints on an organization's goals, for example. A firm that sets a goal of increasing annual sales by 50% might struggle to achieve this goal during an economic recession or if several new competitors enter its market. Environmental conditions also need to be taken into account when examining whether to start doing business in a new country, acquire another company, or launch an innovative product, to name just a few.

Key Takeaway

- An organization's environment is a major consideration in strategic assessment. The environment is the source of resources that the organization needs. It provides opportunities and threats, and it influences the various strategic decisions that executives must make.

Exercises

1. What are the three reasons that the environment matters?
2. Which of these three reasons is most important? Why?
3. Can you identify an environmental trend that no organization can influence?

References

Nowak, S. (2018, October 22). McDonalds announces its making the transition to cage free eggs. *Organic Authority*. https://www.organicauthority.com/buzz-news/mcdonalds-announces-its-making-the-transition-to-cage-free-eggs.

3.3 Evaluating the General Environment

The Elements of the General Environment: PESTEL Analysis

An organization's environment includes factors that it can readily affect as well as factors that largely lay beyond its influence. The latter set of factors are said to exist within the general environment. Executives must track trends and events as they evolve and try to anticipate the implications of these trends and events because the general environment often has a substantial influence on an organization's level of success.

PESTEL analysis is one important tool that executives can rely on to organize factors within the general environment and to identify how these factors influence industries and the firms within them. PESTEL is an acronym, meaning it is an abbreviation formed from the initial letters of other words. PESTEL reflects the names of the six segments of the general environment: (1) political, (2) economic, (3) socio-cultural, (4) technological, (5) environmental, and (6) legal. Wise executives carefully examine each of these six segments to identify major opportunities and threats and then adjust their firms' strategies accordingly (Table 3.1).

Before applying the PESTEL framework, it is important to identify which industry is being evaluated. For example, for using this tool for Panera Bread, what industry is Panera Bread in? If the food service industry is selected, then this includes all types of restaurants, from McDonalds to expensive, five-star restaurants. The food service industry also includes hospital and university cafeterias and catering services. To provide a more accurate assessment for Panera Bread, a smaller segment of the food service industry should be chosen. How about the restaurant industry? This is still too broad. Picking a segment of the restaurant industry, the fast casual restaurant industry, is the most helpful to analyze using PESTEL. To help determine what industry to select, ask "Who does the company directly compete against, head to head?" In this case, Panera Bread competes head to head with other fast casual restaurants. McDonalds, for example, competes head to head with other fast food restaurants in the fast food restaurant industry.

Examining the general environment involves gaining an understanding of key factors and trends in broader society. PESTEL analysis is a popular framework for organizing these factors and trends and isolating how they influence industries and the firms within them. Below we describe each of the six dimensions associated with PESTEL analysis: political, economic, socio-cultural, technological, environmental, and legal.

Table 3.1 PESTEL Framework

P	**Political** factors include elements such as tax policies, changes in trade restrictions and tariffs, and the stability of governments.
E	**Economic** factors include elements such as interest rates, inflation rates, gross domestic product, unemployment rates, levels of disposable income, and the general growth or decline of the economy.
S	**Socio-cultural** factors include trends in demographics such as population size, age, and ethnic mix, as well as cultural trends such as attitudes toward obesity and consumer activism.
T	**Technological** factors include, for example, changes in the rate of new product development, increases in automation, and advancements in service industry delivery.
E	**Environmental** factors, also called ecological factors, include, for example, natural disasters, global warming, pollution, and weather patterns.
L	**Legal** factors include laws involving issues such as employment, health and safety, discrimination, and antitrust.

P is for "Political"

The political segment centers on the role of governments in shaping business. This segment includes elements such as tax policies, changes in trade restrictions and tariffs, and the stability of governments (Table 3.2). Stated differently, the political segment consists of the way that the government is involved in the economy or an industry. Immigration policy is an aspect of the political segment of the general environment that offers important implications for many different organizations. For example, how to approach migrant labor in the United States has been a hotly debated dilemma. Some hospital executives have noted that immigrants lacking legal status put a strain on the healthcare system because these immigrants seldom can pay for medical services, and hospitals by law cannot turn them away from emergency rooms. However, many industries, such as hospitality, construction, and agriculture to name a few, rely heavily on migrant labor in its many forms, so political forces directly impact an industry's ability to thrive.

Examples of several key trends representing political factors in the general environment are illustrated below.

Table 3.2 Political Factors

The extent to which companies developing clean energy sources should be subsidized by the government versus being left on their own to compete with providers of traditional energy sources is currently a hotly contested political issue.
The use of child labor was once commonplace in the United States. Now, firms face political scrutiny when using overseas suppliers that employ child labor.
The word tariff is derived from an Arabic word meaning "fees to be paid." By levying tariffs and implementing other trade restrictions, governments can—to some extent—protect domestic firms from international competition.
The stability of the US government provides a source of confidence for foreign firms who want to do business in the United States. Countries that face frequent regime change and political turmoil have a harder time attracting foreign investments.
One of the most important duties of elected officials in the United States is to debate and set new tax policies.

Figure 3.3: Proposals to provide support for businesses are often featured within political campaigns.

For example, farmers argue that the current US immigration policy is harmful because it impedes their ability to reliably get the work visas necessary each year to employ the critical mass of migrant labor required to effectively and affordably harvest their crops. In particular, if farmers were forced to employ only workers with preexisting legal status, the cost of produce would increase substantially because of a rise in the cost of wages and the inevitable labor shortage to harvest the crops. Restaurant chains such as Panera would pay higher prices for lettuce, tomatoes, and other perishables. As a result, Panera would have to decide whether to absorb these costs or pass them along to customers by charging more for sandwiches. Overall, any changes in immigration policy will have implications for hospitals, farmers, restaurants, and many other industries.

E is for "Economic"

The economic segment centers on the economic conditions within which organizations operate. It includes elements such as interest rates, inflation rates, gross domestic product, unemployment rates, levels of disposable income, and the general growth or decline of the economy (Table 3.3). The world-wide economic crisis of 2020 created by COVID-19 had a tremendous negative effect on a vast array of organizations. Rising unemployment discouraged consumers from purchasing expensive, nonessential goods such as automobiles and television sets. Some businesses that were forced to close drained all their resources and were never able to reopen.

One way to determine if the economic force is strong or weak in an industry is to ask, "If the economy drops, is this industry affected?" If the answer is yes, then the economic force is moderate, if not strong. In the hospital industry, for example, the economic force is weak, as a dropping economy does not have much impact on hospitals. People still need and use healthcare services in a poor economy, paid mostly by insurance.

Examples of several key trends representing economic factors in the general environment are illustrated below.

Table 3.3 Economic Factors

The unemployment rate is the percentage of the labor force actively looking for employment within the last four weeks. During the Great Depression of the 1930s, the United States suffered through an unemployment rate of approximately 25%. In 2020, the unemployment rate hit about 15% due to the COVID-19 pandemic, the highest since the Great Depression (The Washington Post, 2020).

Housing starts is an economic indicator that measures the number of houses, apartments, and condos on which new construction has been started. Because construction involves a wide array of industries–concrete, steel, wood, drywall, plumbing, banks, and many others–housing starts are a carefully watched measure of economic conditions.

Gross domestic product (GDP) refers to the market value of goods and services within a country produced in a given time period and serves as a rough indicator of a country's standard of living. The United States has a larger GDP than China, but China has enjoyed a much higher rate of GDP growth in recent years.

The Federal Reserve System, commonly referred to as "The Fed", is the United States' central banking system. The Fed attempts to strengthen the economy through its decisions, such as setting short-term interest rates.

Discretionary income refers to the amount of money individuals have to spend after all necessary bills are paid. As discretionary income increases, firms such as boutique clothing retailers that sell nonessential goods and services are more likely to prosper.

Some businesses, however, actually prospered during the COVID-19 crisis. Retailers that offer deep discounts, such as Dollar General and Walmart, enjoyed an increase in their customer base as consumers sought to find ways to economize. Grocery stores like Kroger and providers of personal protective equipment (PPE) also saw their sales increase significantly.

Figure 3.4: Decisions about interest rates made by the Federal Reserve create opportunities for some organizations and threats for others.

S is for "Socio-cultural"

A generation ago, ketchup was an essential element of every American pantry and salsa was a relatively unknown product. Today, however, food manufacturers sell more salsa than ketchup in the United States. This change reflects the socio-cultural segment of the general environment. Socio-cultural factors include trends in demographics such as population size, age, and ethnic mix, as well as cultural trends such as attitudes toward obesity and consumer activism (Table 3.4). The exploding popularity of salsa and other Hispanic foods reflects the increasing number of Latinos in the United States, as well as the growing acceptance of Latino food by other ethnic groups.

Examples of several key trends representing social factors in the general environment are illustrated below.

Table 3.4 Socio-cultural Factors

The rise of upscale cupcake outlets reflects a current trend in American eateries: pricey specialty stores are very popular among some consumers.
In the 1800s, most American couples raised many children. Farmers, for example, took this approach because of the high infant mortality rate, and children provided an important source of labor that small, family farms needed in order to operate. Today, most families are smaller.
The obesity rate in America, in 2020 was 40%, up from 30.5% in 2000, due in part to the increasing prevalence of fast-food restaurants and the popularity of sedentary activities such as playing video games (Galvin, 2020).
Hemline theory contends that women's skirt lengths predict stock market increases and declines. The idea was born in the 1920s when economist George Taylor noticed that many women raised their skirts to reveal their silk stockings when times were good, but lowered their skirts to hide the fact that they weren't wearing stockings when times were tough.
The tendency to collect material items while being reluctant to throw them away has led to a rise in self-storage outlets as well as awareness of a hoarding epidemic.

Sometimes changes in the social segment arise from unexpected sources. Before World War II, the American workforce was overwhelmingly male. When millions of men were sent to Europe and Asia to fight in the war, however, organizations had no choice but to rely heavily on female employees. At the time, the attitudes of many executives toward women were appalling. Consider, for example, some of the advice provided to male supervisors of female workers in the July 1943 issue of *Transportation Magazine*:

- Older women who have never contacted the public have a hard time adapting themselves and are inclined to be cantankerous and fussy. It's always well to impress upon older women the importance of friendliness and courtesy.
- General experience indicates that "husky" girls—those who are just a little on the heavy side—are more even tempered and efficient than their underweight sisters.
- Give every girl an adequate number of rest periods during the day. You have to make some allowances for feminine psychology. A girl has more confidence and is more efficient if she can keep her hair tidied, apply fresh lipstick and wash her hands several times a day.

The tremendous contributions of female workers during the war contradicted these awful stereotypes. The main role of women who assembled airplanes, ships, and other war materials was to support the military, of course, but their efforts also changed some male executives' minds about what females could accomplish within organizations if provided with opportunities. When men returned from the war, women were largely displaced from their jobs. Inequities in the workplace are still pervasive today, but modern attitudes among men toward women in the workplace are much more enlightened than they were in 1943. Nevertheless, as a strategic decision maker, it is important to note that socio-cultural trends like these take many decades to change significantly.

The trend toward widespread acceptance of women into the US workforce has created important opportunities for certain organizations. Retailers such as Talbot's and Dillard's developed new markets for selling business attire to women. Subway and other restaurants benefit when the scarceness of time leads dual income families to purchase take-out meals rather than cook at home.

Figure 3.5: Women's immense contributions to the war effort during World War II helped create positive social changes in the ensuing decades.

Figure 3.6: A surprising demographic trend is that both China and India have more than twice as many English-speaking college graduates each year than does the United States.

T is for "Technological"

The technological segment centers on improvements in products and services that are provided by science. Relevant factors include, for example, changes in the rate of new product development, increases in automation, and advancements in service industry delivery (Table 3.5). One key feature of the modern era is the ever-increasing pace of technological innovation. In 1965, Intel co-founder Gordon E. Moore offered an idea that has come to be known as Moore's law. Moore's law suggests that the performance of microcircuit technology roughly doubles every two years. This law has been very accurate in the decades since it was offered.

Examples of several key trends representing technological factors in the general environment are illustrated below.

Table 3.5 Technological Factors

The adoption rate of new technology is closely monitored by market research firms. The internet reached 50 million users in 4 years. To reach the same number of users took 13 years for TV and 38 years for radio.

Online shopping has transformed the retail market. Failure to successfully compete against Amazon has forced long-stable retailers like Sears, JCPennys, KMart, and Neiman Marcus to close stores or shut down all together.

The dramatic changes in the video game industry over the past 25 years highlight the need to constantly adapt to technological factors to maintain market leadership. Once-mighty Atari has given way to current leaders Sony, Nintendo, and Microsoft.

The popularity of smartphones has greatly changed how some businesses operate.

The marketing of many products and services has been transformed because of social media.

One implication of Moore's law is that over time electronic devices can become smaller but also more powerful. This creates important opportunities and threats in a variety of settings. Consider, for example, photography. Just a decade ago, digital cameras were popular and rather inexpensive. With the exception of high-end and action cameras, cell phone cameras have largely replaced digital cameras, which had replaced film cameras the decade before.

Figure 3.7: Moore's law explains how today's iPhone can be one hundred times faster, one hundred times lighter, and ten times less expensive than a "portable" computer built in the 1980s.

E is for "Environmental" or "Ecological"

The environmental segment involves the physical and ecological conditions within which organizations operate. It includes factors such as natural disasters, pollution levels, global warming, and weather patterns (Table 3.6). The threat of pollution, for example, has forced municipalities to treat water supplies with chemicals. These chemicals increase the safety of the water but detract from its taste. This has created opportunities for businesses that provide better-tasting water. Rather than consume cheap but bad-tasting tap water, many consumers purchase bottled water. Global warming has created the need to restrict greenhouse gases by reducing the burning of fossil fuels. The electric car industry is a result of this environmental force. Most all automobile manufacturers have electric cars as part of their product lines.

Examples of several key trends representing environmental/ecological factors in the general environment are illustrated below.

Table 3.6 Environmental Factors

The Subaru automotive plant in Lafayette, Indiana was the first auto manufacturing facility to achieve zero landfill status.
The increased number of solar energy companies and use of solar panels is a direct result of climate change.
Individuals embracing the three Rs of green living—reduce, reuse, recycle—has fueled new business concepts such as Recycle Match, a firm that brings together waste products with businesses that need those materials.
Concern about the environmental effects of burning fossil fuels has contributed to the growing popularity of electric scooters.
The increase in the number of food cooperatives reflects growing interest in sustainable, natural foods that are produced with a high degree of social responsibility.

Figure 3.8: A key trend within the environmental segment is an increasing emphasis on conserving fossil fuels.

As is the case for many companies, bottled water producers not only have benefited from the general environment but also have been threatened by it. Some estimates are that 80% of plastic bottles end up in landfills. This has led some socially conscious consumers to become hostile to bottled water. Meanwhile, water filtration systems offered by Brita and other companies are a cheaper way to obtain clean and tasty water. Such systems also hold considerable appeal for individuals who feel the need to cut personal expenses due to economic conditions. In sum, bottled water producers have been provided opportunities by the environmental segment of the general environment, specifically, the spread of poor-tasting water to combat pollution, but are faced with threats from the socio-cultural segment, the social conscience of some consumers, and the economic segment, the financial concerns of other consumers. The ecological trend toward reducing greenhouse gases and global warming, has also created opportunities for Elon Musk and Tesla on several fronts. Companies that produce solar panels, lithium-ion batteries, and electric cars are ventures Musk has started, leveraging the ecological forces that makes these products more and more desirable.

L is for "Legal"

The legal segment centers on how the courts and laws influence business activity. Examples of important legal factors include employment laws, health and safety regulations, discrimination laws, and antitrust laws (Table 3.7).

Some people confuse the political factors with legal ones. The key distinction is that political factors are related to the interactions and relationship between businesses and the government whereas legal factors are the boundary parameters of business activities. For example, a government policy such as a trade restriction between countries would constitute a political factor, not a legal one. Similarly, a law requiring employees to be paid overtime past 40 hours would be a legal factor, not a political one.

Intellectual property rights are a particularly daunting aspect of the legal segment for many organizations. When a studio such as Pixar produces a movie, a software firm such as Adobe revises a program, or a video game company such as Activision devises a new game, these firms are creating intellectual property. Such firms attempt to make profits by selling copies of their movies, programs, and games to individuals. Piracy of intellectual property—a process wherein illegal copies are made and sold by others—poses a serious threat to such profits. Law enforcement agencies and courts in many countries, including the United States, provide organizations with the necessary legal mechanisms to protect their intellectual property from piracy.

Examples of several key trends representing legal factors in the general environment are illustrated below.

Table 3.7 Legal Factors

Electronic recycling laws are creating opportunities for "green collar jobs." A Missouri law, for example, requires computer electronic equipment manufacturers to develop and implement recycling plans.
The Sherman Antitrust Act of 1890 limits cartels and monopolies in the United States. Senator John Sherman was the principal author of this legislation.
In the United States, it is illegal to discriminate against anyone based on age, race, religion, sex or disability.
The role of the Occupational Safety and Health Administration (OSHA) is to prevent work-related injuries, diseases, and fatalities by enforcing standards for workplace safety and health.
Laws requiring that nutrition information must appear on the packaging of most food products are intended to protect consumers and help them make informed choices.

In other countries, such as China, piracy of intellectual property is quite common. Three other general environment segments play a role in making piracy a major concern. First, in terms of the socio-cultural segment, China is the most populous country in the world. Second, in terms of the economic segment, China's affluence is growing rapidly. Third, in terms of the technological segment, rapid advances in computers and communication have made piracy easier over time. Taken together, these various general environment trends lead piracy to be a major source of angst for firms that rely on intellectual property to deliver profits.

Figure 3.9: A key legal trend in recent years is forcing executives to have greater accountability for corporate misdeeds via laws such as the 2002 Sarbanes-Oxley Act.

- PESTEL is a framework that reflects general environmental factors—political, economic, socio-cultural, technological, environmental, and legal—that can impact an organization either positively or negatively. In many cases, executives can prevent negative outcomes and leverage positive forces by performing a PESTEL analysis to diagnose where in the general environment important opportunities and threats arise.

1. What does each letter of PESTEL mean?
2. Using a recent news article, identify a trend that has a positive and negative implication for a particular industry.
3. Can you identify a general environment trend that has positive implications for nursing homes but negative implications for diaper makers?
4. Are all six elements of PESTEL important to every organization? Why or why not?
5. What is a key trend for each letter of PESTEL and one industry or firm that would be affected by that trend?

References

Earth911. (n.d.). *Plastic recycling facts.* https://earth911.com/earth-watch/the-numbers-on-plastics/#:~:text=Plastics%20recycling%20fast%20facts&text=While%20overall%20recovery%20of%20plastics,of%2037%20percent%20in%202008.

Galvin, G. (2020, February 27). The U.S. obesity rate now tops 40%. *U. S. News and World Report.* https://www.usnews.com/news/healthiest-communities/articles/2020-02-27/us-obesity-rate-passes-40-percent.

Washington Post. (2020, May 8). U.S. unemployment rate soars to 14.7 percent, the worst since the Depression era. *Washington Post.* https://www.washingtonpost.com/business/2020/05/08/april-2020-jobs-report/.

Image Credits

Figure 3.5: Miller, J. Howard. "We Can Do It". Public Domain. Retrieved from https://upload.wikimedia.org/wikipedia/commons/1/12/We_Can_Do_It%21.jpg.

Figure 3.7: Fleser, Casey. "Evolution (34 / 365)." CC BY 2.0. Retrieved from https://flic.kr/p/5XqgCz.

Figure 3.8: Webster, Tony. "Spin Shared Electric Scooters." CC BY 2.0. Cropped. Retrieved from https://www.flickr.com/photos/diversey/46775872844.

3.4 Evaluating the Industry

The Purpose of Five Forces Analysis

Understanding the dynamics that shape how much profit potential exists within an industry is key to knowing how likely a particular firm is to succeed within the industry. There are five key forces that determine the profitability of a particular industry. Taken together, all five forces indicate the attractiveness of an industry. Attractive industries—those with favorable conditions—are more likely to experience higher profitability.

Table 3.8 Porter's Five Forces

Industry Analysis: Porter's Five Forces
Threat of potential entrants are firms that are not currently considered viable competitors in the industry but that may become viable competitors in the future. For example, Tesla Motors' production of electric vehicles poses a threat to displace the traditional powers in the auto industry, and Chinese automakers are rumored to be eyeing the US market.
Bargaining power of suppliers to the auto industry include firms such as Lear Corporation who produces auto interior systems.
Rivalry of industry competitors in the auto industry include firms such as Ford, Fiat Chrysler, and GM.
Bargaining power of buyers are those firms that buy directly from the industry such as automobile dealerships. Automakers also have to pay careful attention to end users, of course, such as individual drivers and rental car agencies.
Threat of substitutes for the auto industry's products include bicycles and mass transit. Luckily for automakers competing in the US market, Americans are notoriously reluctant to embrace these substitutes.

Visit the executive suite of any company and the chances are very high that the chief executive officer and her vice presidents are relying on Five Forces Analysis to understand their industry. Introduced more than thirty years ago by Professor Michael Porter of the Harvard Business School, Five Forces Analysis has long been and remains perhaps the most popular analytical tool in the business world (Table 3.8).

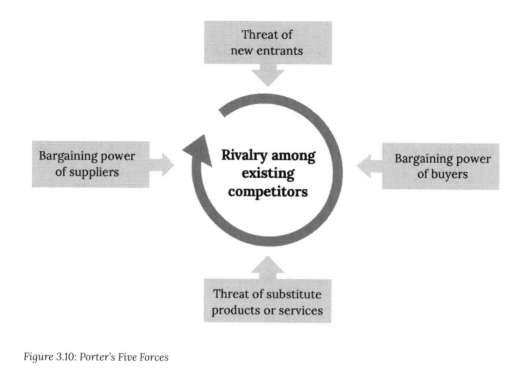

Figure 3.10: Porter's Five Forces

The purpose of Five Forces Analysis is to identify how much profit potential exists in an industry. To do so, Five Forces Analysis considers the interactions among the competitors in an industry, potential new entrants to the industry, substitutes for the industry's offerings, suppliers to the industry, and the industry's buyers (Porter, 1979). If none of these five forces works to undermine profits in the industry, then the profit potential is very strong. If all the forces work to undermine profits, then the profit potential is very weak. Most industries lie somewhere in between these extremes. This could involve, for example, all five forces providing firms with modest help or two forces encouraging profits while the other three undermine profits. Once executives determine how much profit potential exists in an industry, they can then decide what strategic moves to make to be successful. If the situation looks bleak, for example, one possible move is to exit the industry.

The Rivalry among Competitors in an Industry

The competitors in an industry are firms that produce similar products or services. Competitors use a variety of moves such as advertising, new offerings, and price cuts to try to outmaneuver one another to retain existing buyers and to attract new ones. Because competitors seek to serve the same general set of buyers, rivalry can become intense (Table 3.9). Subway faces fierce competition within the restaurant business, for example. This is illustrated by a quote from the man who built McDonald's into a worldwide icon. Former CEO Ray Kroc allegedly once claimed that "if any of my competitors were drowning, I'd stick a hose in their mouth." While this sentiment was (hopefully) just a figure of speech, the announcement in March 2011 that Subway had surpassed McDonald's in terms of numbers of stores, this intense rivalry has led to Subway having 10,000 more stores world-wide than McDonald's in 2020.

High levels of rivalry tend to reduce the profit potential of an industry. A number of characteristics that affect the intensity of the rivalry among competitors are illustrated below.

Table 3.9 Rivalry

Rivalry among existing competitors tends to be high to the extent that...	
Competitors are numerous or are roughly equal in size and power.	No one firm rules the industry, and cutthroat moves are likely as firms jockey for position.
The growth rate of the industry is slow.	A shortage of new customers leads firms to steal each other's customers.
Competitors are not differentiated from each other.	This forces firms to compete based on price rather than based on the uniqueness of their offerings.
Fixed costs in the industry are high.	These costs must be covered, even if it means slashing prices in order to do so.
Exit barriers are high.	Firms must stay and fight rather than leaving the industry gracefully.
Excess capacity exists in the industry.	When too much of a product is available, firms must work hard to earn sales.
Capacity must be expanded in large increments to be efficient.	The high costs of adding these increments needs to be covered.
The product is perishable	Firms need to sell their wares before they spoil and become worthless.

Understanding the intensity of rivalry among an industry's competitors is important because the degree of intensity helps shape the industry's profit potential. Of particular concern is whether firms in an industry compete based on price. When competition is bitter and cutthroat, the prices competitors charge—and their profit margins—tend to go down. If, on the other hand, competitors avoid bitter rivalry, then price wars can be avoided and profit potential increases.

Every industry is unique to some degree, but there are some general characteristics that help to predict the likelihood that fierce rivalry will erupt. Rivalry tends to be fierce, for example, to the extent that the growth rate of demand for the industry's offerings is low (because a lack of new customers forces firms to compete more for existing customers), fixed costs in the industry are high (because firms will fight to have enough customers to cover these costs), competitors are not differentiated from one another (because this forces firms to compete based on price rather than based on the uniqueness of their offerings), and exit barriers in the industry are high (because firms do not have the option of leaving the industry gracefully). Exit barriers can include emotional barriers, such as the bad publicity associated with massive layoffs, or more objective reasons to stay in an industry, such as a desire to recoup considerable costs that might have been previously spent to enter and compete.

Industry concentration is an important aspect of competition in many industries. Industry concentration is the extent to which a small number of firms dominate an industry (Table 3.10). Among circuses, for example, the four largest companies collectively own 89% of the market. Meanwhile, these companies tend to keep their competition rather polite. Their advertising does not lampoon one another, and they do not put on shows in the same city at the same time. This does not guarantee that the circus industry will be profitable; there are four other forces to consider as well as the quality of each firm's strategy. But low levels of rivalry certainly help build the profit potential of the industry.

In contrast, the restaurant industry is fragmented, meaning that the largest rivals control just a small fraction of the business and that a large number of firms are important participants. Rivalry in fragmented industries tends to become bitter and fierce. Quiznos, a chain of sub shops that is roughly 15% the size of Subway, has directed some of its advertising campaigns directly at Subway, including one depicting a fictional sub shop called "Wrong Way" that bore a strong resemblance to Subway.

Within fragmented industries, it is almost inevitable that over time some firms will try to steal customers from other firms, such as by lowering prices, and that any competitive move by one firm will be matched by others. In the wake of Subway's success in offering foot-long subs for $5, for example, Quiznos has matched Subway's price. Such price jockeying is delightful to customers, of course, but it tends to reduce prices, and profit margins) within an industry. Indeed, Quiznos later escalated its attempt to attract budget-minded consumers by introducing a flatbread sandwich that cost only $2. Overall, when choosing strategic moves, Subway's presence in a fragmented industry forces the firm to try to anticipate not only how fellow restaurant giants such as McDonald's and Burger King will react but also how smaller sub shop chains like Quiznos and various regional and local players will respond.

Industry concentration refers to the extent to which large firms dominate an industry. Buyers and suppliers generally have more bargaining power when they are from concentrated industries. This is because the firms that do business with them have fewer options when seeking buyers and suppliers. One popular way to measure industry concentration is via the percentage of total industry output that is produced by the four biggest competitors. Below are examples of industries that have high (80%-100%), medium (50%-79%), and low (below 50%) levels of concentration.

Table 3.10 Industry Concentration

High-Concentration Industries
Circuses (89%) and breakfast cereal manufacturing (85%)

Medium-Concentration Industries
Flight training (52%) and sugar manufacturing (60%)

Low-Concentration or "Fragmented" Industries
Full-service restaurants (9%), Legal services (3%), Truck driving schools (27%), and Telephone call centers (22%)

The Threat of Potential New Entrants to an Industry

Competing within a highly profitable industry is desirable, but it can also attract unwanted attention from outside the industry. Potential new entrants to an industry are firms that do not currently compete in the industry but may in the future (Table 3.11). New entrants tend to reduce the profit potential of an industry by increasing its competitiveness. If, for example, an industry consisting of five firms is entered by two new firms, this means that seven rather than five firms are now trying to attract the same general pool of customers. Thus, executives need to analyze how likely it is that one or more new entrants will enter their industry as part of their effort to understand the profit potential that their industry offers.

Figure 3.11: The entry of chicken burger restaurant Oporto into the United States might hurt hamburger restaurants more than it hurts Subway and other sandwich makers.

New entrants can join the fray within an industry in several different ways. New entrants can be start-up companies created by entrepreneurs, foreign firms that decide to enter a new geographic area, supplier firms that choose to enter their customers' business, or buyer firms that choose to enter their suppliers' business. The likelihood of these four paths being taken varies across industries. Restaurant firms such as Subway, for example, do not need to worry about their buyers entering the industry because they sell directly to individuals, not to firms. It is also unlikely that Subway's suppliers, such as farmers, will make a big splash in the restaurant industry.

On the other hand, entrepreneurs launch new restaurant concepts every year, and one or more of these concepts may evolve into a fearsome competitor. Also, competitors based overseas sometimes enter Subway's core US market. In February 2011, Australia-based Oporto opened its first US store in California (Odell, 2011). Oporto operates more than 130 chicken burger restaurants in its home country. But Oporto didn't survive in the US, and closed its US stores in 2013.

Every industry is unique to some degree, but some general characteristics help to predict the likelihood that new entrants will join an industry. New entry is less likely, for example, to the extent that existing competitors enjoy economies of scale (because new entrants struggle to match incumbents' prices), capital requirements to enter the industry are high (because new entrants struggle to gather enough cash to get started), access to distribution channels is limited (because new entrants struggle to get their offerings to customers), governmental policy discourages new entry, differentiation among existing competitors is high (because each incumbent has a group of loyal customers that enjoy its unique features), switching costs are high (because this discourages customers from buying a new entrant's offerings), expected retaliation from existing competitors is high, and cost advantages independent of size exist.

The Great Wall of China effectively protected China against potential raiders for centuries. The metaphor of a high wall as a defense against potential entrants is a key element in Porter's Five Forces model. Industries with higher barriers to entry are in a safer defensive position than industries with lower barriers. Below we describe several factors that make it difficult for would-be invaders to enter an industry.

Table 3.11 New Entrants

Economies of scale	As the number of customers a firm serves increases, the cost of serving each customer tends to decrease. This is because fixed costs—the expenses the firm must pay, such as the loan payments on an automobile factory—are allocated across a larger number of sales. When the firms in an industry enjoy significant economies of scale, new firms struggle to be able to sell their wares at competitive prices.
Capital requirements	The more expensive it is to enter a business, the less likely a new firm is to attempt to enter it. When these capital requirements are substantial, as in the automobile and many other manufacturing industries, existing competitors have less fear of new firms entering their market. It is simply very difficult to gather up enough cash to enter certain businesses.
Access to distribution channels	The ability to get goods and services to customers can pose a significant challenge to would-be newcomers. In the auto industry, for example, a new firm would struggle to match the network of dealerships enjoyed by Ford, GM, and other automakers.
Government policy	Decisions made by governments can deter or encourage potential new entrants. In 2009, the US government kept GM afloat via a massive infusion of cash. Had GM been left to die instead, this could have opened the door for a new company to enter the industry, perhaps by buying some of GM's factories.
Differentiation	Automakers spend millions of dollars each year on advertising in order to highlight the unique features of their cars. A new entrant would struggle to match the differentiation that years of advertising have created for various brands.
Switching costs	Switching costs endured by consumers are one of the challenges facing the makers of alternative fuel vehicles. A massive number of gas stations and repair shops are in place to support gasoline-powered cars, but few facilities can recharge or fix electric cars. At present, few consumers are willing to live with the significant hassles and inconvenience that arise when purchasing an alternative fuel vehicle.
Expected retaliation	New firms must be concerned about whether current industry members will aggressively respond to them entering the market. If a firm succeeded in entering the automobile business, for example, existing companies might slash their prices in order to keep their market share intact.
Cost advantages independent of size	Proprietary technology, access to raw materials, and desirable geographic location are all examples of cost advantages not directly associated with size and economies of scale. In the auto industry, the decades of engineering experience possessed by the major auto markers is an example of such an advantage. A new entrant would struggle to duplicate this know-how at any price.

The Threat of Substitutes for an Industry's Offerings

Executives need to take stock not only of their direct competition but also of players in other industries that can steal their customers. Substitutes are offerings that differ from the goods and services provided by the competitors in an industry but that fill similar needs to what the industry offers (Table 3.12). How strong of a threat substitutes are depends on how effective substitutes are in serving an industry's customers.

At first glance, it could appear that the satellite television business is a tranquil one because there are only two significant competitors in the US: DIRECTV and DISH Network. These two industry giants, however, face a daunting challenge from substitutes. The closest substitute for satellite television is provided by cable television firms, such as Comcast and Charter Communications. DIRECTV and DISH Network also need to be wary of streaming video services, such as Netflix, and video rental services, such as Redbox. The availability of viable substitutes places stringent limits on what DIRECTV and DISH Network can charge for their services. If the satellite television firms raise their prices, customers will be tempted to obtain video programs from alternative sources. This limits the profit potential of the satellite television business.

In other settings, viable substitutes are not available, and this helps an industry's competitors enjoy profits. Like light bulbs, candles can provide lighting within a home. Few consumers, however, would be willing to use candles instead of light bulbs. Candles simply do not provide as much light as light bulbs. Also, the risk of starting a fire when using candles is far greater than the fire risk of using light bulbs. Because candles are a poor substitute, light bulb makers such as Sylvania and Phillips do not need to fear candle makers stealing their customers and undermining their profits.

Figure 3.12: Few consumers would be willing to substitute candles for light bulbs.

The dividing line between which firms are competitors and which firms offer substitutes is a challenging issue for executives. Most observers would agree that, from Subway's perspective, sandwich maker Quiznos should be considered a competitor and that grocery stores such as Kroger offer a substitute for Subway's offerings. But what about full-service restaurants, such as Ruth's Chris Steak House, and "fast casual" outlets, such as Panera Bread? Whether firms such as these are considered competitors or substitutes depends on how the industry is defined. Under a broad definition–Subway competes in the restaurant business–Ruth's Chris and Panera should be considered competitors. Under a narrower definition–Subway competes in the sandwich business–Panera is a competitor and Ruth's Chris is a substitute. Under a very narrow definition–Subway competes in the sub sandwich business–both Ruth's Chris and Panera provide substitute offerings. Thus clearly defining a firm's industry is an important step for executives who are performing a Five Forces Analysis.

A substitute teacher is a person who fills in for a teacher. Some substitute teachers are almost as good as the "real" teacher while others are woefully inadequate. In business, the competitors in an industry not only must watch each other, they must keep an eye on firms in other industries whose products or services can serve as effective substitutes for their offerings. In some cases, substitutes are so effective that they are said to "disrupt" the industry, meaning they kill most or all industry demand. Below we note a number of effective substitutes for particular industries.

Table 3.12 Substitutes

Substitutes in Different Industries
Cooking at home can be an effective substitute for eating at restaurants, especially in challenging economic times.
Emails and faxes are less expensive substitutes for some of the US Postal Service's offerings. Meanwhile, text messages can serve as substitutes for many emails.
Typewriting classes were once common in schools. But once personal computers and printers became widely accepted, the typewriter industry declined dramatically.
Railroads once held almost a monopoly position on freight transportation. However, the rise of the trucking industry reduced demand for the railroad industry's services.
DIRECTV's commercials compare the firm's offerings not only to what its fellow satellite television provider DISH Network provides but also to the offerings of a close substitute—cable television companies.

The Power of Suppliers to an Industry

Suppliers provide inputs that the firms in an industry need to create the goods and services that they in turn sell to their buyers. A variety of supplies are important to companies, including raw materials, financial resources, and labor (Table 3.13). For restaurant firms such as Subway, key suppliers include such firms as Sysco that bring various foods to their doors, restaurant supply stores that sell kitchen equipment, and employees that provide labor.

The relative bargaining power between an industry's competitors and its suppliers help shape the profit potential of the industry. If suppliers have greater leverage over the competitors than the competitors have over the suppliers, then suppliers can increase their prices over time. This cuts into competitors' profit margins and makes them less likely to be prosperous. On the other hand, if suppliers have less leverage over the competitors than the competitors have over the suppliers, then suppliers may be forced to lower their prices over time. This strengthens competitors' profit margins and makes them more likely to be prosperous. Thus when analyzing the profit potential of their industry, executives must carefully consider whether suppliers have the ability to demand higher prices.

Every industry is unique to some degree, but some general characteristics help to predict the likelihood that suppliers will be powerful relative to the firms to which they sell their goods and services. Suppliers tend to be powerful, for example, to the extent that the suppliers' industry is dominated by a few companies, if it is more concentrated than the industry that it supplies and/or if there is no effective substitute for what the supplier group provides. These circumstances restrict industry competitors' ability to shop around for better prices and put suppliers in a position of strength.

Supplier power is also stronger to the extent that industry members rely heavily on suppliers to be profitable, industry members face high costs when changing suppliers, and suppliers' products are differentiated. Finally, suppliers possess power to the extent that they have the ability to become a new entrant to the industry if they wish. This is a strategy called forward vertical integration. Ford, for example, used a forward vertical integration strategy when it purchased rental car company and Ford customer, Hertz. A difficult financial situation forced Ford to sell Hertz for $5.6 billion 11 years later. But before rental car companies such as Avis and Thrifty drive too hard of a bargain when buying cars from an automaker, their executives should remember that automakers are much bigger firms than are rental car companies. The executives running the automaker might simply decide that they want to enjoy the rental car company's profits themselves and acquire the firm.

A number of characteristics that impact the power of suppliers to a given industry are illustrated below.

Table 3.13 Power of Suppliers

Power of Suppliers	Example
A supplier group is powerful if it is dominated by a few companies or is more concentrated than the industry that it supplies.	The DeBeers Company of South Africa owns the vast majority of diamond mines in the world. This gives the firm great leverage when negotiating with various jewelry producers.
A supplier group is powerful if there is no substitute for what the supplier group provides.	Although artificial diamonds are fine for industrial applications, real diamonds are necessary for jewelry. Any groom who thinks otherwise is playing a risky game indeed.
A supplier group is powerful if industry members rely heavily on suppliers to be profitable.	Computer, cellular phone, and digital appliance manufacturers all rely heavily on suppliers in the microchip manufacturing industry.
A supplier group is powerful if industry members face high costs when changing suppliers.	Most computers installed in university classrooms are PCs. A university that wants to switch to using Apple computers would endure enormous costs in money and labor. This strengthens the position of PC makers a bit when they deal with universities.
A supplier group is powerful if their products are differentiated.	Dolby Laboratories offers top-quality audio systems that are backed by a superb reputation. Firms that make home theater equipment and car stereos have little choice but to buy from Dolby because many consumers simply expect to enjoy Dolby's technology.
A supplier group is powerful if it can credibly threaten to compete (integrate forward) in the industry if motivated.	Before a rental car company drives too hard of a bargain when buying cars from an auto maker, it should remember that Ford used to own Hertz.

Strategy at the Movies

Flash of Genius

When dealing with a large company, a small supplier can get squashed like a bug on a windshield. That is what college professor and inventor Dr. Robert Kearns found out when he invented intermittent windshield wipers in the 1960s and attempted to supply them to Ford Motor Company. As depicted in the 2008 movie *Flash of Genius*, Kearns dreamed of manufacturing the wipers and selling them to Detroit automakers. Rather than buy the wipers from Kearns, Ford replicated the design. An angry Kearns then spent many years trying to hold the firm accountable for infringing on his patent. Kearns eventually won in court, but he paid a terrible personal price along the way, including a nervous breakdown and estrangement from his family. Kearns's lengthy battle with Ford illustrates the concept of bargaining power that is central to Porter's Five Forces model. Even though Kearns created an exceptional new product, he had little leverage when dealing with a massive, well-financed automobile manufacturer.

What did Henry Ford II Steal from a common man | One man fought the might of Ford Motors and won! [01:52]

This video is about Robert Kearns taking on Ford.

You can view this video here: https://youtu.be/iroEVFDZOHI.

The Power of an Industry's Buyers

Buyers purchase the goods and services that the firms in an industry produce (Table 3.14). For Panera Bread and other restaurants, buyers are individual people. In contrast, the buyers for some firms are other firms rather than end users. For Procter & Gamble, for example, buyers are retailers such as Walmart and Target who stock Procter & Gamble's pharmaceuticals, hair care products, pet supplies, cleaning products, and other household goods on their shelves.

Figure 3.13: College students' lack of buyer power in the textbook industry has kept prices high for decades and created frustration for students.

The relative bargaining power between an industry's competitors and its buyers helps shape the profit potential of the industry. If buyers have greater leverage over the competitors than the competitors have over the buyers, then the competitors may be forced to lower their prices over time. This weakens competitors' profit margins and makes them less likely to be prosperous. Walmart furnishes a good example. The mammoth retailer is notorious among manufacturers of goods for demanding lower and lower prices over time (Bianco & Zellner, 2003). In 2008, for example, the firm threatened to stop selling compact discs if record companies did not lower their prices. Walmart has the power to insist on price concessions because its sales volume is huge. Compact discs make up a small portion of Walmart's overall sales, so exiting the market would not hurt Walmart. From the perspective of record companies, however, Walmart is their biggest buyer. If the record companies were to refuse to do business with Walmart, they would miss out on access to a large portion of consumers.

On the other hand, if buyers have less leverage over the competitors than the competitors have over the buyers, then competitors can raise their prices and enjoy greater profits. This description fits the textbook industry quite well. College students are often dismayed to learn that an assigned textbook costs $150 or more. Historically, textbook publishers have been able to charge high prices because buyers had no leverage. A student enrolled in a class must purchase the specific book that the professor has selected. Used copies are sometimes a lower-cost option, but textbook publishers have cleverly worked to undermine the used textbook market by releasing new editions after very short periods of time.

Of course, the presence of a very high profit industry is attractive to potential new entrants. Firms such as, the publisher of this book, have entered the textbook market with lower-priced offerings. Time will tell whether such offerings bring down textbook prices. Like any new entrant, upstarts in the textbook business must prove that they can execute their strategies before they can gain widespread acceptance. Overall, when analyzing the profit potential of their industry, executives must carefully consider whether buyers have the ability to demand lower prices. In the textbook market, buyers do not.

A number of characteristics that impact the power of buyers to a given industry are illustrated below.

Table 3.14 Power of Buyers

Power of Buyers	Example
A buyer group is powerful when there are relatively few buyers compared to the number of firms supplying the industry.	Buyers that purchase a large percentage of the seller's goods and services are more powerful, as Walmart has demonstrated by aggressively negotiating with suppliers over the years.
A buyer group is powerful when the industry's goods or services are standardized or undifferentiated.	Subway can drive a hard bargain when purchasing commodities such as wheat and yeast since both are typically identical to another vendor's.
A buyer group is powerful when they face little or no switching costs in changing vendors.	Circuses can find elephants, clowns, and trapeze artists from any source possible. This allows circus managers to shop around for the best prices.
A buyer group is powerful when the good or service purchased by the buyers represents a high percentage of the buyer's costs, encouraging ongoing searches for lower-priced suppliers.	Most consumers pay little attention to prices when buying toothpaste, but may spend hours exhaustively searching the internet for information on automobile prices.
A buyer group is powerful if it can credibly threaten to compete (integrate backward) in the industry if motivated.	Ford and General Motors are well known for threatening to self-manufacture auto parts if suppliers do not provide goods and services at acceptable prices.
A buyer group is powerful when the good or service purchased by buyer groups is of limited importance to the quality or price of the buyer's offerings.	While stereo systems and tires are components that car buyers may be sensitive to when making a purchase decision, auto manufacturers can purchase glass and spark plugs from any vendor as long as it meets quality standards. This gives automakers leverage when negotiating with glass and spark plugs companies.

Every industry is unique to some degree, but some general characteristics help to predict the likelihood that buyers will be powerful relative to the firms from which they purchase goods and services. Buyers tend to be powerful, for example, to the extent that there are relatively few buyers compared with the number of firms that supply the industry, the industry's goods or services are standardized or undifferentiated, buyers face little or no switching costs in changing vendors, the good or service purchased by the buyers represents a high percentage of the buyer's costs, and the good or service is of limited importance to the quality or price of the buyer's offerings.

Finally, buyers possess power to the extent that they have the ability to become a new entrant to the industry if they wish. This strategy is called backward vertical integration. DIRECTV used to be an important customer of TiVo, the pioneer of digital video recorders. This situation changed, however, when executives at DIRECTV grew weary of their relationship with TiVo. DIRECTV then used a backward vertical integration strategy and started offering DIRECTV-branded digital video recorders. Profits that used to be enjoyed by TiVo were transferred at that point to DIRECTV.

Interpreting the Five Forces

When using Porter's Five Forces tool, it is important to note the strength of each of the five forces that are analyzed. The forces are typically ranked as Strong/High, Moderate/Medium, or Weak/Low. If these competitive forces within an industry are high, then the profit potential in that industry is low. Strong forces indicate high competition for the profits within that industry, making it a less desirable industry to be in. Conversely, if the forces within an industry are generally weak, this indicates a stronger potential for profit and a desirable industry to be in. A mixture of strong and weak forces means there is profit potential, but there exist competitive forces within the industry that can dilute the profit potential. Upon doing Porter's Five Forces Analysis, companies should make an informed decision on entering that market, and how they might compete, given the various strengths of the forces.

The Limitations of Five Forces Analysis

Five Forces Analysis is useful, but it has some limitations too. The description of Five Forces Analysis provided by its creator, Michael Porter, seems to assume that competition is a zero-sum game, meaning that the amount of profit potential in an industry is fixed. One implication is that if a firm is to make more profit, it must take that profit from a rival, a supplier, or a buyer. In some settings, however, collaboration can create a larger pool of profit that benefits everyone involved in the collaboration. In general, collaboration is a possibility that Five Forces Analysis tends to downplay. The relationships among the rivals in an industry, for example, are depicted as adversarial. In reality, these relationships are sometimes adversarial and sometimes collaborative. General Motors and Toyota compete fiercely all around the world, for example, but they also have worked together in joint ventures. Similarly, Five Forces Analysis tends to portray a firm's relationships with its suppliers and buyers as adversarial, but many firms find ways to collaborate with these parties for mutual benefit. Indeed, concepts such as just-in-time inventory systems depend heavily on a firm working as a partner with its suppliers and buyers.

Section Videos

Porter's Five Forces [02:57]

This video for the lesson explains the Porter's Five Forces Model.

You can view this video here: https://youtu.be/_IaBZmBO9RE.

Porter's Five Forces (Tesla Example) [09:51]

This video for the lesson works through the Porter's Five Forces analysis using Tesla as an example.

You can view this video here: https://youtu.be/5F0dI8zaotU.

Key Takeaway

- "How much profit potential exists in our industry?" is a key question for executives. Five Forces Analysis provides an answer to this question. It does this by considering the interactions among the competitors in an industry, potential new entrants to the industry, substitutes for the industry's offerings, suppliers to the industry, and the industry's buyers.

Exercises

1. What are the five forces?
2. Is there an aspect of industry activity that the five forces seems to leave out?
3. Imagine you are the president of your college or university. Which of the five forces would be most important to you? Why?

References

Bianco, B., & Zellner, W. (2003, October). Is Wal-Mart too powerful? *Bloomberg Businessweek.*
https://www.bloomberg.com/news/articles/2003-10-05/is-wal-mart-too-powerful

Odell, K. (2011, February 22). Portuguese-influenced Australian chicken burger chain, Oporto, comes to SoCal.
Eater LA. http://la.eater.com/archives/2011/02/22/
portugueseinfluenced_australian_chicken_burger_chain_oporto_comes_to_socal.php

Porter, M. E. (1979, March–April). How competitive forces shape strategy. *Harvard Business Review*, 137–156.

Image Credits

Figure 3.10: Kindred Grey (2020). "Porter's Five Forces." CC BY-SA 4.0. Retrieved from
https://commons.wikimedia.org/wiki/File:Porter%27s_Five_Forces.png.

Figure 3.11: MDRX. "Oporto drive through menu in Sydney." CC BY-SA 4.0. Cropped. Retrieved from
https://upload.wikimedia.org/wikipedia/commons/3/3e/Oportodrivethrumenu.jpg.

Figure 3.12: Sugeesh. "A candle lit inside an electric bulb." Public Domain. Retrieved from
https://commons.wikimedia.org/wiki/File:Candle_in_Incandescent_light_bulb.png.

Figure 3.13: Grabowska, Karolina. "Person Holding Stack of Books." Pexels License.
Retrieved from https://www.
pexels.com/photo/person-
holding-stack-of-books-4218978
.

Video Credits

Desai, Y. (2017, August 22). *What did Henry Ford II Steal from a common man | One man fought the might of Ford Motors and won!* [Video] YouTube. https://youtu.be/iroEVFDZOHI.

MindToolsVideos. (2018, January 9). *Porter's five forces* [Video]. YouTube. https://youtu.be/_IaBZmB09RE.

Learn to Invest. (2019, July 31). *Porter's 5 forces (Tesla example)* [Video]. YouTube. https://youtu.be/
5F0dI8zaotU.

3.5 Mapping Strategic Groups

Understanding Strategic Groups

The analysis of the strategic groups in an industry can offer important insights to executives. Strategic groups are sets of firms that follow similar strategies to one another (Hunt, 1972; Short et al., 2007). More specifically, a strategic group consists of a set of industry competitors that have similar characteristics to one another but differ in important ways from the members of other groups (Table 3.15).

Understanding the nature of strategic groups within an industry is important for at least three reasons. First, emphasizing the members of a firm's group is helpful because these firms are usually its closest rivals. When assessing their firm's performance and considering strategic moves, the other members of a group are often the best referents for executives to consider. In some cases, one or more strategic groups in the industry are irrelevant. Subway, for example, does not need to worry about competing for customers with the likes of Ruth's Chris Steak House and P. F. Chang's. This is partly because firms confront mobility barriers that make it difficult or illogical for a particular firm to change groups over time. Because Subway is unlikely to offer a gourmet steak as well as the experience offered by fine dining outlets, they can largely ignore the actions taken by firms in that restaurant industry strategic group.

Second, the strategies pursued by firms within other strategic groups highlight alternative paths to success. A firm may be able to borrow an idea from another strategic group and use this idea to improve its situation. During the recession of the late 2000s, mid-quality restaurant chains such as Applebee's and Chili's used a variety of promotions such as coupons and meal combinations to try to attract budget-conscious consumers. Firms such as Subway and Quiznos that already offered low-priced meals still had an inherent price advantage over Applebee's and Chili's, however: there is no tipping expected at the former restaurants, but there is at the latter. It must have been tempting to executives at Applebee's and Chili's to try to expand their appeal to budget-conscious consumers by experimenting with operating formats that do not involve tipping.

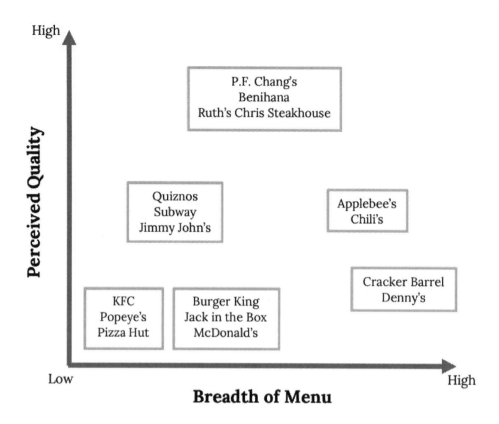

Figure 3.15: Strategic groups are sets of firms that follow similar strategies. Understanding the nature of strategic groups within an industry is important in part because the members of a firm's group are usually that firm's closest rivals. Below we illustrate several strategic groups in the restaurant industry.

Third, the analysis of strategic groups can reveal gaps in the industry that represent untapped opportunities. Within the restaurant business, for example, it appears that no national chain offers both very high quality meals and a very diverse menu. Perhaps the firm that comes the closest to filling this niche is the Cheesecake Factory, a chain of approximately 150 outlets whose menu includes more than 200 lunch, dinner, and dessert items. Ruth's Chris Steak House already offers very high quality food; its executives could consider moving the firm toward offering a very diverse menu as well. This would involve considerable risk, however. Perhaps no national chain offers both very high quality meals and a very diverse menu because doing so is extremely difficult. Nevertheless, examining the strategic groups in an industry with an eye toward untapped opportunities offers executives a chance to consider novel ideas.

Figure 3.16: Mid-quality restaurants do not compete directly with pricey steakhouses, but they might be able to borrow ideas from such venues.

Designing a Strategic Group Map

To develop a strategic group map for an industry, the competitive factors for each of the two axes must be selected. On the vertical axis, price is often the measurement used. A different parameter that further differentiates the members of the industry is chosen for the horizontal axis. For the airline industry, for example, it could be the number of routes flown. It can be the breadth of models offered by each car manufacturer in the automobile industry. The competitive factors should be chosen based on the market characteristics that are to be examined, usually the most important ones.

Once the various firms in the industry are plotted on the strategic group map, the natural groupings of the companies can be determined and circled. The stiffest competition in the industry typically happens within each strategic group. Profitability between each group often varies. It is generally difficult to move from one group to another, as mobility barriers exist hindering the ability of a firm to impact the chosen competitive factors being measured.

Section Video

Strategic Group Mapping [05:42]

The video for this lesson gives further insights and an example of constructing a strategic group map.

You can view this video here: https://youtu.be/CcF3ZMgXQrA.

Key Takeaway

- Examination of the strategic groups in an industry provides a firm's executives with a better understanding of their closest rivals, reveals alternative paths to success, and highlights untapped opportunities.

Exercises

1. What other colleges and universities are probably in your school's strategic group?
2. From what other groups of colleges and universities could your school learn? What specific ideas could be borrowed from these groups?

References

Hunt, M. S. (1972). *Competition in the major home appliance industry 1960–1970*. [Unpublished doctoral dissertation]. Harvard University.

Short, J. C., Ketchen, D. J., Palmer, T., & Hult, G. T. (2007). Firm, strategic group, and industry influences on performance. *Strategic Management Journal*, 28, 147–167.

Image Credits

Figure 3.15: Kindred Grey (2020). "Breadth of menu vs. Quality" CC BY-SA 4.0. Retrieved from https://commons.wikimedia.org/wiki/File:Breadth_of_menu_vs._Quality.png.

Figure 3.16: With wind. "Steak." CC BY-NC 2.0. Cropped. Retrieved from https://flic.kr/p/brpy2C.

Video Credits

ddd9255. (2013, September 1). *Strategic group mapping* [Video]. YouTube. https://youtu.be/CcF3ZMgXQrA.

3.6 Conclusion

This chapter explains several considerations for examining the external environment that executives must monitor to lead their organizations strategically. Executives must be aware of trends and changes in the general environment, as well as the condition of their specific industry, as elements of both have the potential to change considerably over time. While PESTEL analysis provides a useful framework to understand the general environment, Porter's five forces is helpful to make sense of an industry's profit potential and competitive environment. Strategic groups are valuable for understanding close competitors that affect a firm more than other industry members. When executives carefully monitor their organization's environment using these tools, they greatly increase the chances of their organization being successful.

Exercises

1. In groups of four or five, use the PESTEL framework to identify elements from each factor of the general environment that could have a large effect on your future career.
2. Use Porter's five forces analysis to analyze an industry in which you might like to work in the future. Discuss the implications your results may have on the salary potential of jobs in that industry and how that could impact your career plans.

Chapter 4: Evaluating the Internal Environment

Learning Objectives

After reading this chapter, you should be able to understand and articulate answers to the following questions:

1. What is the Resource-Based View and why is it important to organizations?
2. How is the VRIO tool applied to strategic resources?
3. In what ways can intellectual property serve as a value-added resource for organizations?
4. What are isolating mechanisms and how can they contribute to a firm's competitive advantage?
5. How can the Value Chain be applied to achieve a competitive advantage?

4.1 Introduction

In addition to evaluating the external environment of a firm and the industry in which it operates, strategic management requires that a firm conduct an internal assessment of its resources and capabilities. This further helps the firm answer the question "Where are we?" before setting strategies for reaching the goals and vision of the organization. Part of this assessment is the organizational performance evaluation discussed in Chapter 2 that deals primarily with financial and other quantitative information. This helps the firm determine where it is in comparison with its competitors. Next, the firm needs to look inside to see how it can achieve a competitive advantage over its rivals, so customers will buy what the firm has to sell instead of buying from competitors.

One method of internal assessment is using the Resource-Based View. This model examines any resources and/or capabilities of the firm that may provide a competitive advantage. The VRIO framework is used to evaluate each resource or capability to determine what type, if any, of competitive advantage it brings. If a resource or capability cannot be imitated by a competitor, then that resource may create a sustained competitive advantage. Patents or isolating mechanisms can reduce or eliminate temporarily the opportunity for a rival to imitate.

Another tool used for internal assessment is Value Chain Analysis. Each element of a firm's primary and supportive activities are examined to see if it can provide a competitive advantage over its rivals. Weaknesses that are identified can be addressed to improve organizational performance.

Once the external and internal assessments are complete, the firm can use the most relevant information to develop a SWOT analysis and identify the most pressing strategic issue(s) the firm must address, as discussed in Chapter 5.

4.2 Managing Firm Resources

Southwest Airlines: Let Your LUV Flow

Figure 4.1: Southwest Airlines marked forty-seven consecutive profitable years in 2019

In 1971, a new firm named Southwest Airlines opened for business by offering flights between Houston, San Antonio, and its headquarters at Love Field in Dallas. From its initial fleet of three airplanes and three destinations, Southwest has grown to operate hundreds of airplanes in scores of cities. Despite competing in an industry that is infamous for bankruptcies and massive financial losses, Southwest marked its forty-seventh profitable year in a row in 2019.

Why has Southwest succeeded while many other airlines have failed? Historically, the firm has differed from its competitors in a variety of important ways. Most large airlines use a "hub and spoke" system. This type of system routes travelers through a large hub airport on their way from one city to another. Many Delta passengers, for example, end a flight in Atlanta and then take a connecting flight to their actual destination. The inability to travel directly between most pairs of cities adds hours to a traveler's itinerary and increases the chances of luggage being lost. In contrast, Southwest does not have a hub airport; preferring instead to connect cities directly. This makes flying on Southwest attractive to many travelers.

Southwest has also been more efficient than its rivals. While most airlines use a variety of different airplanes, Southwest operates only one type of jet: the Boeing 737. This means that Southwest can service its fleet much more efficiently than can other airlines. Southwest mechanics need only the know-how to fix one type of airplane, for example, while their counterparts with other firms need a working knowledge of multiple planes. Southwest also gains efficiency by not offering seat assignments in advance, unlike its competitors. This makes the boarding process move much faster, meaning that Southwest's jets spend more time in the air transporting customers (and making money) and less time at the gate relative to its rivals' planes.

Organizational culture is the dimension along which Southwest perhaps has differed most from its rivals. The airline industry as a whole suffers from a reputation for mediocre (or worse) service and indifferent (sometimes even surly) employees. In contrast, Southwest enjoys strong loyalty and a sense of teamwork among its employees.

One tangible indicator of this culture is Southwest's stock ticker symbol. Most companies choose stock ticker symbols that evoke their names. Ford's ticker symbol is F, for example, and Walmart's symbol is WMT. When Southwest became a publicly traded company in 1977, executives chose LUV as its ticker symbol. LUV pays a bit of homage to the firm's humble beginnings at Love Field. More important, however, LUV represents the love that executives have created among employees, between employees and the company, and between customers and the company. This "LUV affair" has long been and remains a huge success. As recently as March 2011, for example, Southwest was ranked fourth on Fortune magazine's World's Most Admired Company list.

In early 2020, the US and the world were hit by the coronavirus pandemic. The number of airline passengers dropped by over 90% during the peak months early in the pandemic. Southwest implemented cost saving measures, but still lost $94 million in the first quarter (PRNewswire, 2020). Known for its efficiency, how can Southwest drive down costs to reflect the new reality of less air travel and lower volumes for years to come? Where in its value chain can it not only trim costs but reinvent itself as a more cost effective organization? What resources and capabilities does the airline have to help it re-tool and not only survive the crisis, but come out a sustainable winner for the future?

References

PRNewswire. (2020, April 28). *Southwest reports first quarter 2020 results.* http://investors.southwest.com/news-and-events/news-releases/2020/04-28-2020-110107839.

Image Credits

Figure 4.1: Seeger, Stuart. "A Southwest Airlines Boeing 737 aircraft parked on the tarmac under cloudy skies at Bob Hope Airport in Burbank, California, United States." CC BY 2.0. Cropped. Retrieved from https://upload.wikimedia.org/wikipedia/commons/d/d8/Southwest_737_At_Burbank.jpg.

4.3 Resource-Based View

Figure 4.2: Southwest Airlines's unique organizational culture is reflected in the customization of their aircraft, such as the "Lone Star One" design.

According to resource-based theory, organizations that own "strategic resources" have important competitive advantages over organizations that do not. Some resources, such as cash and trucks, are not considered to be strategic resources because an organization's competitors can readily acquire them. Instead, a resource is strategic to the extent that it is valuable, rare, difficult to imitate, and organized to capture value. Consider how Southwest Airlines's organizational culture serves as a strategic resource.

Table 4.1 Resource-Based View: The Basics

Strategic Resources	Expansion
VALUABLE resources aid in improving the organization's effectiveness and efficiency while neutralizing the opportunities and threats of competitors.	Although the airline industry is extremely competitive, Southwest Airlines's turns a profit virtually every year. One key reason for their success is a legendary organizational culture that inspires employees to do their very best.
RARE resources are those held by few or no other competitors.	Southwest Airlines's culture provides the firm with uniquely strong employee relations in an industry where strikes, layoffs, and poor morale are common.
DIFFICULT-TO-IMITATE resources often involve legally protected intellectual property such as trademarks, patents, or copyrights. Other difficult-to-imitate resources, such as brand names, usually need time to develop fully.	Southwest's culture arose from its very humble beginnings and has evolved across decades. Because of this unusual history, other airlines could not replicate Southwest's culture, regardless of how hard they might try.
ORGANIZED TO CAPTURE VALUE: Having in place the organizational systems, processes, and structure to capitalize on the potential of the resources and capabilities of the firm to provide a competitive advantage.	The influence of Southwest's organizational culture extends to how customers are treated by employees. Executives strongly encourage flight attendants to entertain passengers, like hiding in an overhead compartment. Processes related to passengers are infused with customer service attention and actions.

Important Points to Remember:

1. Resources such as Southwest's culture that reflect all four qualities—valuable, rare, difficult to imitate, and organized to capture value—are ideal because they can create sustained competitive advantages. A resource that has three or less of the qualities can provide an edge in the short term, but competitors can overcome such an advantage eventually.

2. Firms often bundle together multiple resources and strategies (that may not be unique in and of themselves) to create uniquely powerful combinations. Southwest's culture is complemented by approaches that individually could be copied—the airline's emphasis on direct flights, its reliance on one type of plane, and its unique system for passenger boarding—in order to create a unique business model in which effectiveness and efficiency is the envy of competitors.

3. Satisfying only one or two of the valuable, rare, difficult-to-imitate, organized to capture value criteria will likely only lead to competitive parity or a temporary advantage.

Resources and capabilities are the basic building blocks that organizations use to create strategies. These two building blocks are tightly linked—capabilities from using resources over time.

Resources can be divided into two main types: tangible and intangible. While resources refer to what an organization owns, capabilities refer to what the organization can do. More specifically, capabilities refer to the firm's ability to bundle, manage, or otherwise exploit resources in a manner that provides added value and, hopefully, advantage over competitors.

Table 4.2 Resources and Capabilities

Resources
Tangible resources are resources that can be readily seen, touched, and quantified. Physical assets such as a firm's property, plant, and equipment are considered to be tangible resources, as is cash.
Intangible resources are quite difficult to see, touch, or quantify. Intangible resources include, for example, the knowledge and skills of employees, a firm's reputation, and a firm's culture. In a nod to Southwest Airlines' outstanding reputation, the firm ranks eighth in Fortune magazine's 2018 list of the "World's Most Admired Companies."

Capabilities
A dynamic capability exists when a firm is skilled at continually updating its array of capabilities to keep pace with changes in its environment. Coca-Cola, for example, has an uncanny knack for building new brands and products as the soft drink market evolves. Not surprisingly, this firm ranks among the top twelve in Fortune's "World's Most Admired Companies" for 2020.

Resources and Capabilities

The tangibility of a firm's resources is an important consideration within resource-based theory. **Tangible resources** are resources that can be readily seen, touched, and quantified. Physical assets such as a firm's property, plant, and equipment, as well as cash, are considered to be tangible resources. In contrast, **intangible resources** are quite difficult to see, to touch, or to quantify. Intangible resources include, for example, the knowledge and skills of employees, a firm's reputation, brand name, exclusive rights to intellectual property, leadership traits of executives, and a firm's culture. In comparing the two types of resources, intangible resources are more likely to meet the criteria for strategic resources (i.e., valuable, rare, difficult-to-imitate, and organized to capture value) than are tangible resources. Executives who wish to achieve long-term competitive advantages should therefore place a premium on trying to nurture and develop their firms' intangible resources.

Capabilities are another key concept within resource-based theory. An effective way to distinguish resources and capabilities is this: resources refer to what an organization owns, capabilities refer to what the organization can do (Table 4.2). Capabilities tend to arise over time as a firm takes actions that build on its strategic resources. Southwest Airlines, for example, has developed the capability of providing excellent customer service by building on its strong organizational culture. Capabilities are important in part because they are how organizations capture the potential value that resources offer. Customers do not simply send money to an organization because it owns strategic resources. Instead, capabilities are needed to bundle, to manage, and otherwise to exploit resources in a manner that provides value added to customers and creates advantages over competitors.

Some firms develop a dynamic capability. This means that a firm has a unique ability to create new capabilities. Said differently, a firm that enjoys a dynamic capability is skilled at continually updating its array of capabilities to keep pace with changes in its environment. Coca-Cola has an uncanny knack for building new brands and products as the soft-drink market evolves. Not surprisingly, Coca-Cola ranks among the top twelve in Fortune's "World's Most Admired Companies" for 2020.

VRIO: Four Characteristics of Strategic Resources

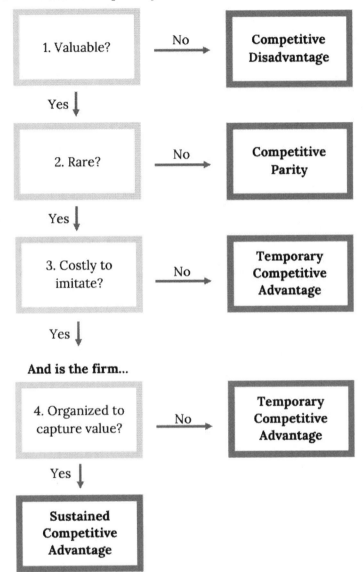

Figure 4.3: The VIRO Framework

Resource-based theory can be confusing because the term resources is used in many different ways within everyday common language. It is important to distinguish **strategic resources** from other resources. To most individuals, cash is an important resource. Tangible goods such as one's car and home are also vital resources.

When analyzing organizations, however, common resources such as cash and vehicles are not considered to be strategic resources. Resources such as cash and vehicles are valuable, of course, but an organization's competitors can readily acquire them. Thus an organization cannot hope to create an enduring competitive advantage around common resources.

Southwest Airlines provides an illustration of resource-based theory in action. Resource-based theory contends that the possession of strategic resources provides an organization with a golden opportunity to develop competitive advantages over its rivals (Table 4.1). These competitive advantages in turn can help the organization enjoy strong profits (Barney, 1991; Wernerfelt, 1981).

A strategic resource is an asset that is valuable, rare, difficult to imitate, and organized to capture value (Barney, 1991; Chi, 1994). A resource is valuable to the extent that it helps a firm create strategies that capitalize on opportunities and ward off threats. Southwest Airlines' culture fits this standard well. Most airlines struggle to be profitable, but Southwest makes money virtually every year. One key reason is a legendary organizational culture that inspires employees to do their very best. This culture is also rare in that strikes, layoffs, and poor morale are common within the airline industry. Southwest embraces a culture of fun for both its customers and employees. Most other airlines do not have this philosophy.

Competitors have a hard time duplicating resources that are difficult to imitate. Some difficult to imitate resources are protected by various legal means, including trademarks, patents, and copyrights. Other resources are hard to copy because they evolve over time and they reflect unique aspects of the firm. Southwest's culture arose from its very humble beginnings. The airline had so little money that at times it had to temporarily "borrow" luggage carts from other airlines and put magnets with the Southwest logo on top of the rivals' logo. Southwest is a "rags to riches" story that has evolved across several decades. Other airlines could not replicate Southwest's culture, regardless of how hard they might try, because of Southwest's unusual history.

A resource is <u>organized to capture value</u> when the firm has organizational systems, processes, and structure in place to capitalize on the resource for a competitive advantage. This may provide bargaining power for the firm in the marketplace. A key benefit of Southwest's culture is that it leads employees to treat customers well, which in turn creates loyalty to Southwest among passengers. This customer loyalty is why many passengers choose Southwest over other airlines.

The key to using the Resource Based View is to evaluate a firm's resources and capabilities using the VRIO framework decision tree.

Note that the decision tree is used to assess resources and capabilities, NOT a firm's products, services, or the firm itself. The evaluation occurs within the industry of the firm being evaluated. Using Southwest Airlines culture as the resource to evaluate with VRIO:

1. Is Southwest's culture valuable? If not, all the effort to develop it is a waste of resources and a competitive disadvantage. If yes, go to number 2.
2. Is Southwest's culture rare within the airline industry? If not, then this resource only provides Southwest competitive parity. It does not help or hurt Southwest competitively. If yes, go to number 3.
3. In the airline industry, is Southwest's culture hard to imitate? If not then culture provides Southwest with a temporary competitive advantage over its rivals, but competitors can imitate it. If yes, go to number 4.

4. Has Southwest organized this resource of culture to capture value? If not, then it still only provides a temporary competitive advantage. If yes, then Southwest's culture is providing a sustained competitive advantage.

For the company culture resource of Southwest Airlines, a yes can be answered for each of the four steps, providing a sustained competitive advantage for this organization. As can be seen from its exceptional organizational performance over many years when compared to other airlines, VRIO shows that company culture is one reason why it is more successful than its competitors.

Figure 4.4 The VRIO Framework Decision Matrix: Southwest's Company Culture

Valuable?	Rare?	Difficult to imitate?	Organized to capture value?	Competitive Advantage
Yes	Yes	Yes	Yes	Sustained Competitive Advantage

As another example, what about Southwest Airlines' capability to arrive on time at a much higher rate than the industry average? What kind of competitive advantage, if any, does this capability provide?

Capability: High on-time arrival

Figure 4.5 VRIO Analysis of On-Time Arrival Capability of Southwest Airlines

Valuable?	Rare?	Difficult to Imitate?	Organized to Capture Value?	Competitive Advantage?
Yes	Yes	No		Temporary Competitive Advantage

In the case of on-time arrival capability, Southwest Airline enjoys a temporary competitive advantage (the third line), but it is not that difficult for rivals to imitate this ability. In working through the decision tree, once a no is obtained, there is no need to continue through the tree.

Ideally, a firm will its own resources, like Southwest's culture, that embrace the four VRIO qualities shown in Table 4.1. If so, these resources can provide not only a competitive advantage but also a sustained competitive advantage—one that will endure over time and help the firm stay successful far into the future. Resources that do not have all four qualities can still be very useful, but they are unlikely to provide long-term advantages. A resource that is valuable and rare but that can be imitated, for example, might provide an edge in the short term, but competitors can eventually overcome such an advantage.

Figure 4.6 VRIO Analysis Worksheet

Resource or Capability	Valuable?	Rare?	Costly to Imitate?	Organized to capture value?	Competitive Implication

Resource-based theory also stresses the merit of an old saying: the whole is greater than the sum of its parts. Specifically, it is important to recognize that strategic resources can be created by taking several strategies and resources that each could be copied and bundling them together in a way that cannot be copied. For example, Southwest's culture is complemented by approaches that individually could be copied–the airline's emphasis on direct flights, its reliance on one type of plane, and its unique system for passenger boarding–to create a unique business model whose performance is without peer in the industry.

On occasion, events in the environment can turn a common resource into a strategic resource. Consider, for example, a very generic commodity: water. Humans simply cannot live without water, so water has inherent value. Also, water cannot be imitated (at least not on a large scale), and no other substance can substitute for the life-sustaining properties of water. Despite having three of the four properties of strategic resources, water in the United States has remained cheap; however, this may be changing. Major cities in hot climates such as Las Vegas, Los Angeles, and Atlanta are confronted by dramatically shrinking water supplies. As water becomes more and more rare, landowners in Maine stand to benefit. Maine has been described as "the Saudi Arabia of water" because its borders contain so much drinkable water. It is not hard to imagine a day when companies in Maine make huge profits by sending giant trucks filled with water south and west or even by building water pipelines to service arid regions.

Strategy at the Movies

That Thing You Do! [02:48]

How can the members of an organization reach success "doing that thing they do"? According to resource-based theory, one possible road to riches is creating–on purpose or by accident–a unique combination of resources. In the 1996 movie *That Thing You Do!*, unwittingly assembling a unique bundle of resources leads a 1960s band called The Wonders to rise from small-town obscurity to the top of the music charts. One resource is lead singer Jimmy Mattingly, who possesses immense musical talent. Another is guitarist Lenny Haise, whose fun attitude reigns in the enigmatic Mattingly. Although not a formal band member, Mattingly's girlfriend Faye provides emotional support to the group and even suggests the group's name. When the band's usual drummer has to miss a gig due to injury, the door is opened for charismatic drummer Guy Patterson, whose energy proves to be the final piece of the puzzle for The Wonders.

Despite Mattingly's objections, Guy spontaneously adds an up-tempo beat to a sleepy ballad called "That Thing You Do!" during a local talent contest. When the talent show audience goes crazy in response, it marks the beginning of a meteoric rise for both the song and the band. Before long, The Wonders perform on television and "That Thing You Do!" is a top-ten hit record. The band's magic vanishes as quickly as it appeared, however. After their bass player joins the Marines, Lenny elopes on a whim, and Jimmy's diva attitude runs amok, the band is finished and Guy is left to "wonder" what might have been. *That Thing You Do!* illustrates that while bundling resources in a unique way can create immense success, preserving and managing these resources over time can be very difficult.

The Wonders- That Thing You Do!

This video is the song "That Thing You Do!" by the Wonders.

You can view this video here: https://youtu.be/BJn-Jl2ZeQU.

Key Takeaway

- Resource-based theory suggests that tangible or intangible resources that are valuable, rare, difficult to imitate, and organized to capture value best position a firm for long-term success. These strategic resources can provide the foundation to develop firm capabilities that can lead to superior performance over time. Capabilities are needed to bundle, to manage, and otherwise to exploit resources in a manner that provides added value to customers and creates advantages over competitors. The VRIO tool can be used to determine if resources or capabilities are valuable, rare, difficult-to-imitate, and organized to capture value, and thereby understand what type of competitive advantage they offer to a firm.

1. What tangible and intangible resources does your favorite restaurant have that might give it a competitive advantage?
2. Do any of the resources or capabilities of your favorite restaurant have the four qualities of resources (VRIO) that lead to success as articulated by resource-based theory?

References

Barney, J. B. (1991). Firm resources and sustained competitive advantage. *Journal of Management, 17,* 99–120.

Chi, T. (1994). Trading in strategic resources: Necessary conditions, transaction cost problems, and choice of exchange structure. *Strategic Management Journal, 15*(4), 271–290.

Wernerfelt, B. (1984). A resource-based view of the firm. *Strategic Management Journal, 5,* 171–180.

Image Credits

Video Credits

4.4 Intellectual Property & Isolating Mechanisms

Intellectual Property

Defining Intellectual Property

The inability of competitors to imitate a strategic resource is a key to leveraging the resource to achieve long-term competitive advantages. Companies are clever, and effective imitation is often very possible. But resources that involve intellectual property reduce or even eliminate this risk. As a result, developing intellectual property is important to many organizations.

Intellectual property refers to creations of the mind, such as inventions, artistic products, and symbols. The four main types of intellectual property are patents, trademarks, copyrights, and trade secrets (Table 4.5). If a piece of intellectual property is also valuable, rare, difficult to imitate, and organized to capture value, it constitutes a strategic resource. Even if a piece of intellectual property does not meet all four criteria for serving as a strategic resource, it can be bundled with other resources and activities to create a resource.

*The term **intellectual property** refers to creations of the mind, such as inventions, artistic products, and symbols. Some forms of intellectual property are protected by law while others can best be defended by surrounding them in secrecy.*

Table 4.5 Intellectual Property

Types of Intellectual Property
Patents protect inventions from direct imitation for a limited period of time. Within the pharmaceutical industry, patents protect the new drugs created by firms such as Merck and Pfizer for up to twenty years. If a new drug gains acceptance in the market, its patent creates a window of opportunity for the patent holder to enjoy excellent profits.
Trademarks are phrases, pictures, names, or symbols used to identify a particular organization. McDonald's golden arches, the phrase "Intel Inside," and the brand name Virginia Tech are examples of trademarks.
Copyrights provide exclusive rights to the creators of original artistic works such as books, movies, songs, and screenplays. Sometimes copyrights are sold and licensed. The late pop star Michael Jackson bought the rights to The Beatles' music catalog and later licensed songs to Target and other companies for use in television advertisements.
Trade secrets refer to formulas, practices, and designs that are central to a firm's business and that remain unknown to competitors. One famous example is the blend of eleven herbs and spices used in Kentucky Fried Chicken's original recipe chicken. KFC protects this secret by having multiple suppliers each produce a portion of the herb and spice blend; no one supplier knows the full recipe.

A variety of formal and informal methods are available to protect a firm's intellectual property from imitation by rivals. Some forms of intellectual property are best protected by legal means, while defending others depends on surrounding them in secrecy. This can be contrasted with Southwest Airlines's well-known culture, which rivals are free to attempt to copy if they wish. Southwest's culture thus is not intellectual property, although some of its complements such as Southwest's logo and unique color schemes are.

Patents

Patents protect inventions from direct imitation for a limited period of time. Some examples and key issues surrounding patents are illustrated below.

Table 4.6 Patents

Examples of Patents
To earn a patent from the US Patent and Trademark Office, an inventor must demonstrate that an invention is new, non obvious, and useful.
Perhaps the greatest inventor in history was Thomas Edison, who was awarded over one thousand patents.
As several different inventors raced to create a workable system for voice transmission over wires, Alexander Graham Bell was awarded a patent for the telephone in 1876.
Apple and Samsung began suing each other in 2011 for patent infringement, with numerous court cases and appeals. The multiple lawsuits were finally settled in 2018, with a jury awarding Apple $539 million (Reuters, 2018).

Patents are legal decrees that protect inventions from direct imitation for a limited period of time (Table 4.6). Obtaining a patent involves navigating a challenging process. To earn a patent from the US Patent and Trademark Office, an inventor must demonstrate that an invention is new, non-obvious, and useful. If the owner of a patent believes that a company or person has infringed on the patent, the owner can sue for damages. Patenting an invention is important because patents can fuel enormous profits. Imagine, for example, the potential for lost profits if the Slinky had not been patented. Shipyard engineer Richard James came up with the idea for the Slinky by accident in 1943 while he was trying to create springs for use in ship instruments. When James accidentally tipped over one of his springs, he noticed that it moved downhill in a captivating way. James spent his free time perfecting the Slinky and then applied for a patent in 1946. To date, more than three hundred million Slinkys have been sold by the company that Richard James and his wife Betty created.

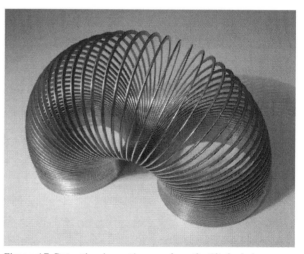

Figure 4.7: Patenting inventions such as the Slinky helps ensure that the invention is protected from imitation.

Trademarks

Trademarks are phrases, pictures, names, or symbols used to identify a particular organization (Table 4.7). Trademarks are important because they help an organization stand out and build an identity in the marketplace. Some trademarks are so iconic that almost all consumers recognize them, including McDonald's golden arches, the Nike swoosh, and Apple's outline of an apple.

Other trademarks help rising companies carve out a unique niche for themselves. For example, French shoe designer Christian Louboutin has trademarked the signature red sole of his designer shoes. Because these shoes sell for many hundreds of dollars via upscale retailers such as Neiman Marcus and Saks Fifth Avenue, competitors would love to copy their look. Thus, legally protecting the distinctive red sole from imitation helps preserve Louboutin's profits.

Trademarks are important to colleges and universities. Schools earn tremendous sums of money through royalties on t-shirts, sweatshirts, hats, backpacks, and other consumer goods sporting their names and logos. On any given day, there are probably several students in your class wearing one or more pieces of clothing featuring your school's insignia; your school benefits every time items like this are sold. Schools' trademarks are easy to counterfeit, however, and the sales of counterfeit goods take money away from colleges and universities. Not surprisingly, many schools fight to protect their trademarks. Virginia Tech filed a lawsuit in 2011 against a new local business called Hokie Real Estate, claiming trademark infringement. Virginia Tech had received a legal trademark for its nickname Hokies. Hokie Real Estate prevailed, as there were a number of other businesses in the locality also using the Hokie name.

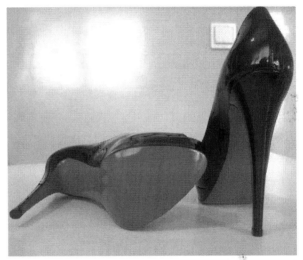

Figure 4.8: *Fashionistas instantly recognize the trademark red sole of Christian Louboutin's high-end shoes.*

An organization's trademarks consist of phrases, pictures, names, or symbols that are closely associated with the organization. Some examples and key issues surrounding trademarks are illustrated below.

Table 4.7 Trademarks

Examples of Trademarks
To be fully protected in the United States, a trademark must be registered with the United States Patent and Trademark Office. A capital R with a circle around it denotes a registered trademark.
As part of the punishment for German aggression during World War I, German drug maker Bayer lost its trademark on "Aspirin" in France, Russia, the United Kingdom, and the United States. Today, Bayer still retains its trademark in Germany, Canada, Mexico and dozens of other countries.
Many small companies use their founders' name as the basis for a trademarked company name.
The distinctive pattern of clothing retailer Burberry Ltd. is an example of a trademark that does not involve words or symbols.

Copyrights

The rights of creators of original artistic works such as books, movies, songs, and screenplays are protected by copyrights. Some examples and key issues surrounding copyrights are illustrated below.

Table 4.8 Copyrights

Examples of Copyrights
Illegal downloads of music are copyright infringements. In spite of laws and increased enforcement, millions of songs are obtained illegally.
Today's cheesy television ads aimed at inventors follow a long tradition of companies offering to help individuals copyright their ideas—for a small fee, of course.
The presence of the copyright symbol tells consumers that they are not allowed to duplicate the product that carries the copyright.
A painting such as Johannes Vermeer's "Girl with a Pearl Earring" enters the public domain (i.e., is not subject to copyright) one hundred years after its creator's death.
When it became apparent that The Verve's 1997 hit single "Bittersweet Symphony" duplicated a Rolling Stones song, The Verve was forced to give up the copyright for the song.

Copyrights provide exclusive rights to the creators of original artistic works such as books, movies, songs, and screenplays for an author's lifetime plus 70 years (Figure 4.8). Sometimes copyrights are sold and licensed. In the late 1960's, Buick thought it had an agreement in place to license the number one hit, "Light My Fire" by The Doors, for a television advertisement until the band's volatile lead singer Jim Morrison loudly protested what he saw as mistreating a work of art. Classic rock by The Beatles has been used in television ads in recent years. After the late pop star Michael Jackson bought the rights to the band's music catalog, he licensed songs to Target and other companies. Some devoted music fans consider such ads to be abominations, perhaps proving the merit of Morrison's protest decades ago.

Figure 4.9: He looks calm here, but the licensing of a copyrighted song for a car commercial enraged rock legend Jim Morrison.

Over time, piracy has become a huge issue for the owners of copyrighted works. In China, millions of pirated DVDs are sold each year, and music piracy is estimated to account for at least 95% of music sales. This piracy deprives movie studios, record labels, and artists of millions of dollars in royalties. In response to the damage piracy has caused, the US government has pressed its Chinese counterpart and other national governments to better enforce copyrights.

Trade Secrets

Trade secrets refer to formulas, practices, and designs that are central to a firm's business and that remain unknown to competitors (Table 4.9). Trade secrets are protected by laws on theft, but once a secret is revealed, it cannot be a secret any longer. This leads firms to rely mainly on silence and privacy rather than the legal system to protect trade secrets.

Trade secrets are formulas, practices, and designs that are central to a firm's business and that remain unknown to competitors. Everyone loves a good mystery, so it is no surprise that legends have arisen around some trade secrets. Some examples and key issues surrounding trade secrets are illustrated below.

Table 4.9 Trade Secrets

Examples of Trade Secrets
Low-end fast food chain Long John Silver's considers its "crumblies" (small bits of fried batter) to be a trade secret, but would anyone really want to solve the mystery?
In 2006, Pepsi was offered a chance to buy a stolen copy of Coca-Cola's secret recipe. An FBI sting was created and the thieves were arrested.
WD-40 was developed to repel water and prevent corrosion, but it was later found to have over two thousand uses. Creating WD-40 took a lot of work: the product's unusual name stands for "Water Displacement, 40th attempt." Despite being created in 1953, the formula for making WD-40 remains unknown outside the company that sells it.
FarmVille creator Zynga alleged in a lawsuit that Disney had lured away Zynga employees to work for Disney and then urged the employees to turn over a secret "playbook" that described Zynga's strategy. The case was settled out of court in late 2010.
In a 1995 episode of the hit comedy Seinfeld, a very successful but mean-spirited restaurateur nicknamed the "Soup Nazi" saw his business collapse when his secret recipes were revealed to customers. Individuals could now make delicious soups at home rather than endure the Soup Nazi's verbal abuse when buying soup.

Some trade secrets have become legendary, perhaps because a mystique arises around the unknown. One famous example is the blend of eleven herbs and spices used in Kentucky Fried Chicken's original recipe chicken. KFC protects this secret by having multiple suppliers each produce a portion of the herb and spice blend; no one supplier knows the full recipe. The formulation of Coca-Cola is also shrouded in mystery. In 2006, Pepsi was approached by shady individuals who were offering a chance to buy a stolen copy of Coca-Cola's secret recipe. Pepsi wisely refused. An FBI sting was used to bring the thieves to justice. The soft-drink industry has other secrets too. Dr Pepper's recipe remains unknown outside the company.

Figure 4.10: *The recipe for Dr Pepper is a secret dating back to the 1880s.*

Although Coke's formula has been the subject of greater speculation, Dr Pepper is actually the original secret soft drink; it was created a year before Coca-Cola.

Section Video

Understanding Intellectual Property (IP) [02:14]

The video for this lesson further explains intellectual property.

You can view this video here: https://youtu.be/UqZJPuyK9VY.

Isolating Mechanisms

The goal of a firm is to have a sustained competitive advantage, whereby a resource or capability of the firm provides a competitive edge for a long time. The length of time a firm can maintain a sustained competitive advantage depends on the industry. A company in a fast-moving industry, such as information technology or fast fashion, may be quite satisfied if they can hold a competitive advantage for a year. A sustained competitive advantage in another type of industry, like feminine hygiene that does not have such frequent changes may last much longer. No firm is able to keep a sustained competitive advantage indefinitely. The competition is always attempting to gain its own competitive advantage.

If a firm can prevent a competitor from imitating the resource or capability that gives it a competitive advantage, it is able to sustain that advantage longer. This strategy is called **isolating mechanisms**. A patent, for example, is a legal way to prevent imitation. Sometimes a competitor is able to "re-engineer" the patented concept by making slight changes, working around the patent to imitate the idea without infringing on the patent. There are other isolating mechanisms a firm may be able to employ to lessen the likelihood of imitation by a competitor. These other isolating mechanisms are Social Complexity, Path Dependence, and Causal Ambiguity.

Social Complexity

The interrelationships within a firm, along with relationships within or across a business process, can be difficult to imitate. For example, key relationships that members of a firm have with a supplier of a key strategic resource create a condition that a competitor cannot duplicate. This **social complexity** creates a barrier to imitation and can prolong a competitive advantage possessed by an organization. Social complexity might arise through certain customer relationships or with key political figures, provided they can help the firm's competitive position. For example, a CEO of a firm in the defense industry may cultivate relationships with key members of Congress that help bring business to that firm, at the expense of the competition (in this example, this might be called collusion, but that is a story for another day, and Chapter 11 on corporate ethics).

Path Dependence

The path that a firm takes over time to achieve the point of a competitive advantage may also provide a barrier to imitation. Decisions made in the past that brought a firm to its current position may make it very difficult for other firms to imitate. The accumulated learning and experience gained along the historical path are not easily duplicated. This **path dependence** can serve as an isolating mechanism to block competitors from gaining the same position in the market. Warby Parker, for example, made a decision early in its development to build relationships with a variety of suppliers and to use the "buy one, give one" strategy, where a pair of glasses is given away to someone in need for every pair sold. This decision and path created loyal suppliers and customers within the online eye wear industry, and a copycat strategy by a competitor would likely be cost prohibitive.

Causal Ambiguity

The third isolating mechanism, **causal ambiguity**, means the reason for achieving a competitive advantage is not apparent. The cause for success is obscure and not understood well. Because the firm itself does not really know why it has achieved success, it is quite difficult for a competitor to replicate it. For example, why does Netflix still enjoy immense popularity in spite of numerous streaming competitors? In 2020 Netflix had a market penetration of 54%, while Amazon Prime is a distant second at 30% (Roxorough, 2019). Is it because they were the first mainline streaming service? Is it related to CEO Reed Hastings? Does content make a big difference? Competitors find it difficult to duplicate Netflix's success model because it is not clear what has caused it.

It was noted earlier in this chapter that intangible resources are usually more valuable than tangible ones in the context of sustained competitive advantage. The reason for this is due, in part, to the isolating mechanisms discussed above. Physical resources tend to be in abundance and are far easier to obtain. So, if two firms have the same physical resources, then there is little to no differentiation. The key distinction that firms can make is how they use those physical resources in their value chain. The intangible resources including skills, knowledge, or brand name used to capitalize on physical resources are far more likely to produce an advantage for firms than simply possessing a physical resource alone. In this way, firms such as Nike can capitalize on marketing and their brand to sell shoes at a premium when their shoes have few physical differences from their competitors. In some cases, a manufacturing facility may very well produce the same product for multiple companies (e.g., t-shirts). In such cases the difference to consumers is the brand.

Key Takeaway

- Intellectual property can serve as a strategic resource for organizations. While some sources of intellectual property such as patents, trademarks, and copyrights can receive special legal protection, trade secrets provide competitive advantages by simply staying hidden from competitors.
- Utilizing isolating mechanisms strategically is a way for organizations to prevent imitation and maintain their competitive advantage.

Exercises

1. What designs for your college or university are protected by trademarks?
2. What type of intellectual property provides the most protection for firms?
3. Why would a firm protect a resource through trade secrets rather than by a formal patent?

References

Reuters. (2018, May 24). Jury awards apple $539 million in Samsung patent case. *The New York Times.* https://www.nytimes.com/2018/05/24/business/apple-samsung-patent-trial.html#:~:text=The%20world's%20top%20smartphone%20rivals,to%20a%20retrial%20over%20damages.

Roxborough, S. (2019, November 13) Netflix dominates global SVOD market, but local services gain ground, study finds. *The Hollywood Reporter.* https://www.hollywoodreporter.com/news/netflix-dominates-global-svod-market-but-local-services-gain-ground-1254438.

Image Credits

Figure 4.7: McLassus, Roger. "Metal slinky." CC BY-SA 3.0. Retrieved from https://upload.wikimedia.org/wikipedia/commons/f/f3/2006-02-04_Metal_spiral.jpg.

Figure 4.8: Arroser. "Christian Louboutin." CC BY-SA 3.0. Retrieved from https://upload.wikimedia.org/wikipedia/commons/6/62/Louboutin_altadama140.jpg.

Figure 4.9: Persson, Jan and Polfoto. "The Doors performing for Danish television in Copenhagen." Public Domain. Retrieved from https://upload.wikimedia.org/wikipedia/commons/1/15/ The_Doors_in_Copenhagen_1968.jpg.

Figure 4.10: Anyjazz65. "Dr. Pepper." CC BY 2.0. Retrieved from https://flic.kr/p/7uDd8e.

Video Credits

Federallabs. (2019, March 27). *Understanding intellectual property (IP)* [Video]. YouTube. https://youtu.be/UqZJPuyK9VY.

4.5 Value Chain

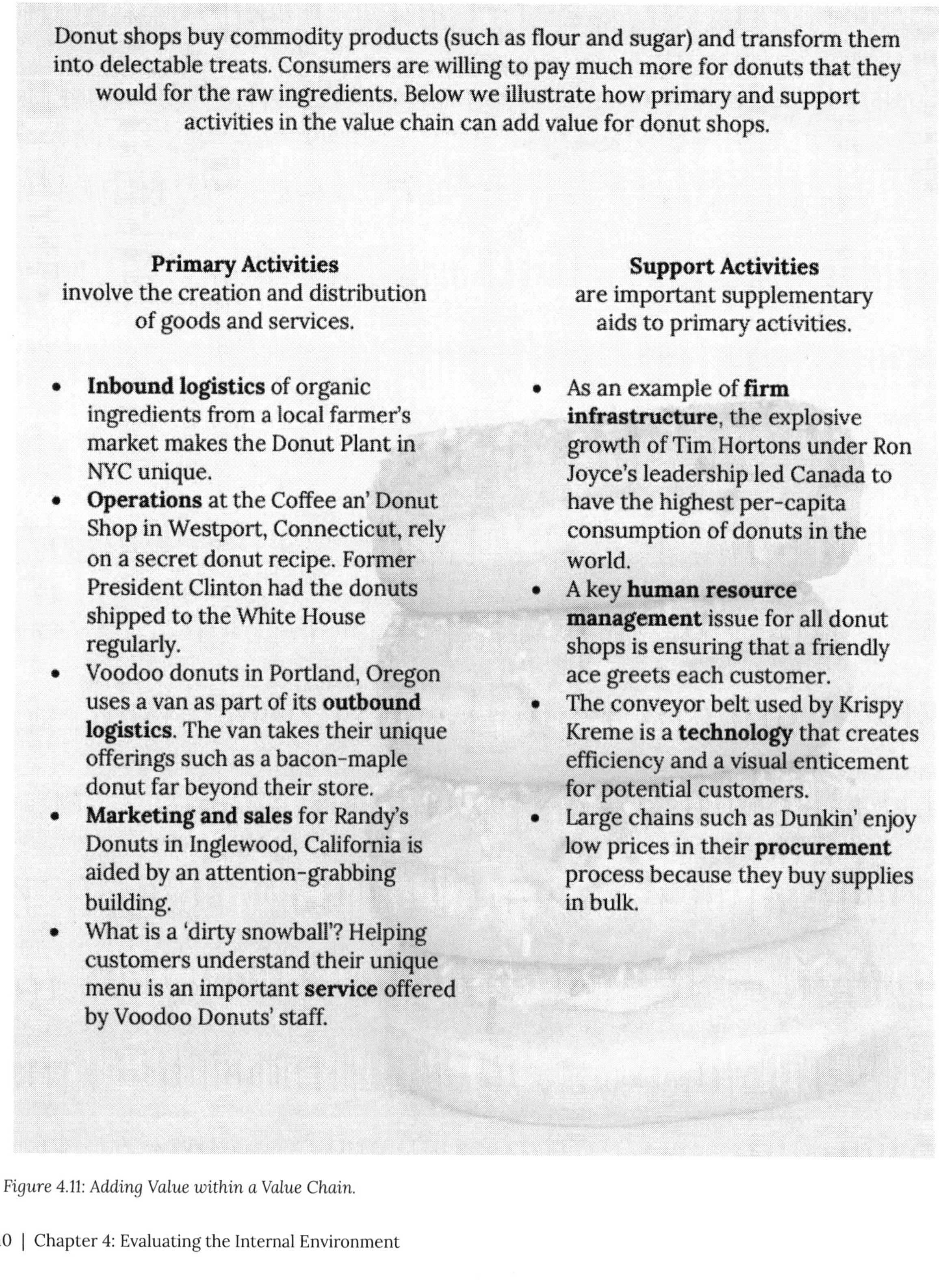

Donut shops buy commodity products (such as flour and sugar) and transform them into delectable treats. Consumers are willing to pay much more for donuts that they would for the raw ingredients. Below we illustrate how primary and support activities in the value chain can add value for donut shops.

Primary Activities
involve the creation and distribution of goods and services.

- **Inbound logistics** of organic ingredients from a local farmer's market makes the Donut Plant in NYC unique.
- **Operations** at the Coffee an' Donut Shop in Westport, Connecticut, rely on a secret donut recipe. Former President Clinton had the donuts shipped to the White House regularly.
- Voodoo donuts in Portland, Oregon uses a van as part of its **outbound logistics**. The van takes their unique offerings such as a bacon-maple donut far beyond their store.
- **Marketing and sales** for Randy's Donuts in Inglewood, California is aided by an attention-grabbing building.
- What is a 'dirty snowball'? Helping customers understand their unique menu is an important **service** offered by Voodoo Donuts' staff.

Support Activities
are important supplementary aids to primary activities.

- As an example of **firm infrastructure**, the explosive growth of Tim Hortons under Ron Joyce's leadership led Canada to have the highest per-capita consumption of donuts in the world.
- A key **human resource management** issue for all donut shops is ensuring that a friendly ace greets each customer.
- The conveyor belt used by Krispy Kreme is a **technology** that creates efficiency and a visual enticement for potential customers.
- Large chains such as Dunkin' enjoy low prices in their **procurement** process because they buy supplies in bulk.

Figure 4.11: Adding Value within a Value Chain.

Elements of the Value Chain

When executives choose strategies, an organization's resources and capabilities should be examined alongside consideration of its **value chain**. A value chain charts the path by which products and services are created and eventually sold to customers (Porter, 1985). The term value chain reflects the fact that, as each step of this path is completed, the product becomes more valuable than it was at the previous step (Table 4.10). Within the lumber business, for example, value is added when a tree is transformed into usable wooden boards; the boards created from a tree can be sold for more money than the price of the tree.

The Value Chain is used as an internal assessment tool to help a firm determine where it might be able to achieve a competitive advantage. In which areas of the primary and secondary activities is the firm particularly strong? Can that activity be leveraged to provide a competitive advantage over its rivals? Resources and/ or capabilities within that activity can be evaluated using the **VRIO framework** to determine what type of competitive advantage they provide. For example, Netflix was the first firm to leverage its technology development support activity to bring high quality movies to customers through streaming. Being the first mover in this industry gave Netflix a foothold and reputation in this industry, and others have not been able to catch up. When using this tool for internal assessment, each activity of the Value Chain should be examined for its potential to achieve a competitive advantage. Conversely, weak activities in the Value Chain are opportunities to improve organizational performance. The overall intent of the Value Chain is to produce a profit margin for the firm.

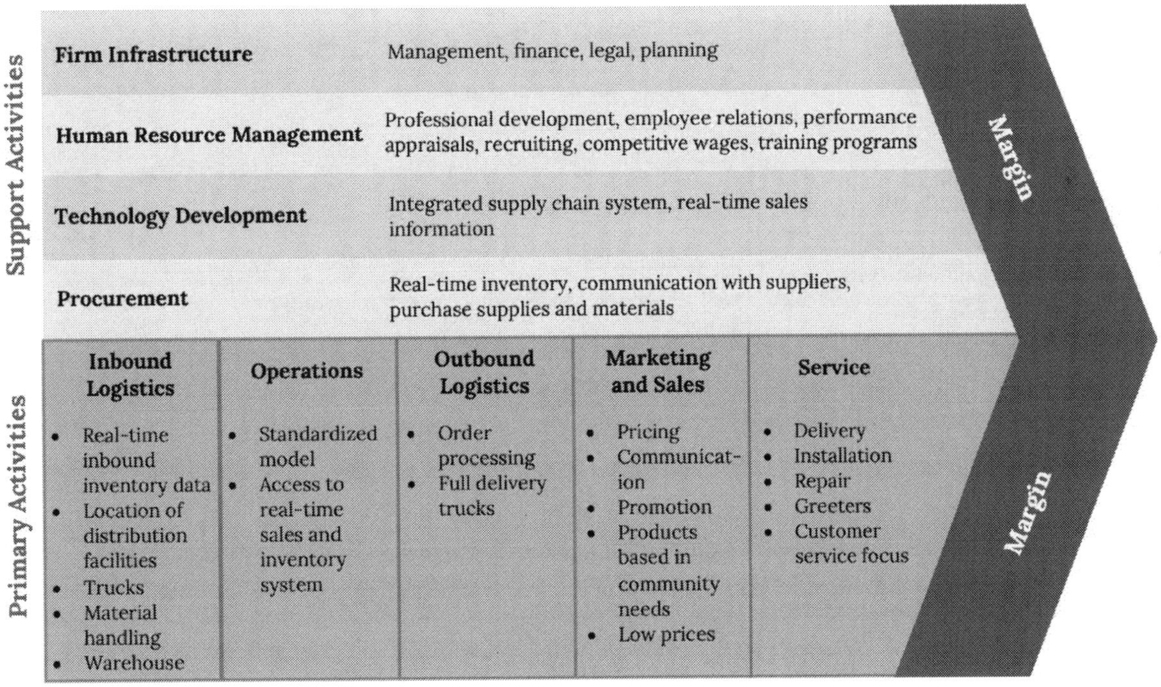

Figure 4.12: The Value Chain

Value chains include both primary and secondary activities. Primary activities are actions that are directly involved in creating and distributing goods and services. Consider a simple illustrative example: doughnut shops. Doughnut shops transform basic commodity products such as flour, sugar, butter, and grease into delectable treats. Value is added through this process because consumers are willing to pay much more for doughnuts than they would be willing to pay for the underlying ingredients.

There are five primary activities. Inbound logistics refers to the arrival of raw materials. Although doughnuts are seen by most consumers as notoriously unhealthy, the Doughnut Plant in New York City has carved out a unique niche for itself by obtaining organic ingredients from a local farmer's market. Operations refers to the actual production process, while outbound logistics tracks the movement of a finished product to customers. Referring back to Southwest Airlines, one of Southwest Airlines' unique capabilities is moving passengers more quickly than its rivals. This advantage in operations is based in part on Southwest's reliance on one type of airplane (which speeds maintenance) and its avoidance of advance seat assignments (which accelerates the passenger boarding process).

Attracting potential customers and convincing them to make purchases is the domain of marketing and sales. For example, people cannot help but notice Randy's Donuts in Inglewood, California, because the building has a giant doughnut on top of it. Finally, service refers to the extent to which a firm provides assistance to their customers. Voodoo Donuts in Portland, Oregon, has developed a clever website (voodoodoughnut.com) that helps customers understand their uniquely named products, such as the Voodoo Doll, the Texas Challenge, the Memphis Mafia, and the Dirty Snowball.

Secondary activities are not directly involved in the evolution of a product, but instead provide important underlying support for primary activities. Firm infrastructure refers to how the firm is organized and led by executives. The effects of this organizing and leadership can be profound. For example, Ron Joyce's leadership of Canadian doughnut shop chain Tim Hortons was so successful that Canadians consume more doughnuts per person than all other countries. In terms of resource-based theory, Joyce's leadership was clearly a valuable and rare resource that helped his firm prosper.

Human resource management is also important. Human resource management involves the recruitment, training, and compensation of employees. A recent research study used data from more than twelve thousand organizations to demonstrate that the knowledge, skills, and abilities of a firm's employees can act as a strategic resource and strongly influence the firm's performance (Crook et al., 2011). Certainly, the unique level of dedication demonstrated by employees at Southwest Airlines has contributed to that firm's excellent performance over several decades.

Technology refers to the use of computerization and telecommunications to support primary activities. Although doughnut making is not a high-tech business, technology plays a variety of roles for doughnut shops, such as allowing customers to pay using credit cards.

Procurement is the process of negotiating for and purchasing raw materials. Large doughnut chains such as Dunkin' and Krispy Kreme can gain cost advantages over their smaller rivals by purchasing flour, sugar, and other ingredients in bulk. Meanwhile, Southwest Airlines has gained an advantage over its rivals by using futures contracts within its procurement process to minimize the effects of rising fuel prices.

Sometimes competitive advantage is achieved from the support activities of a firm as opposed to the primary activities. Superior technology development or human resource management can produce a temporary if not a sustained competitive advantage. A strong research and development arm in a pharmaceutical company can develop medications that are patented and cannot be imitated. Incentives to staff such as those provided by 3M and Google to be creative and develop new products have resulted in a competitive advantage.

Section Video

Strategic Management: Value Chain Analysis [04:41]

The video for this lesson further discusses value chain analysis.

You can view this video here: https://youtu.be/Tpb1fxt9YfU.

Key Takeaway

- The value chain provides a useful tool for managers to examine systematically where value may be added to their organizations. This tool is useful in that it examines key elements in the production of a good or service, as well as areas in which value may be added in support of those primary activities.

Exercises

1. If you were hired as a consultant for your university, what specific element of the value chain would you seek to improve first?
2. What local business in your town could be improved most dramatically by applying the value chain? Would improvements of primary or support activities help to improve this firm most? Could knowledge of strategic supply chain management add further value to this firm?

References

Crook, T. R., Todd, S. Y., Combs, J. G., Woehr, D. J., & Ketchen, D. J. (2011). Does human capital matter? A meta-analysis of the relationship between human capital and firm performance. *Journal of Applied Psychology, 96*(3), 443–456.

Porter, M. E. (1985). *Competitive advantage: Creating and sustaining superior performance.* Free Press.

Image Credits

Figure 4.11: Kindred Grey (2020). "Adding value within a value chain." CC BY NC SA 4.0. Image of donut: Annie Spratt (2016). "Stacked donuts." Public Domain. Retrieved from: https://unsplash.com/photos/AjTclDIadpg Adaptation of Figure 4.10 from Mastering Strategic Management (2015) (CC BY NC SA 4.0). Retrieved from https://open.lib.umn.edu/app/uploads/sites/11/2015/04/9c5437a4d7bfd1ad4b0baa480978c7bd.jpg.

Figure 4.12: Kindred Grey (2020). "The value chain." CC BY NC SA 4.0. Adaptation of Figure 4.11 from Mastering Strategic Management (2015) (CC BY NC SA 4.0). Retrieved from https://open.lib.umn.edu/app/uploads/sites/11/2015/04/b38d1270a489c447e16e30df24d931aa.jpg.

Video Credits

Melissa Schilling. (2020, May 25). Strategic management: *Value chain analysis* [Video]. YouTube. https://youtu.be/Tpb1fxt9YfU.

4.6 Conclusion

This chapter explains key issues that executives face in managing resources to keep their firms competitive. Resource-based theory argues that firms will perform better when they assemble resources that are valuable, rare, difficult-to-imitate, and organized to capture value. When executives can successfully bundle organizational resources into unique capabilities, the firm is more likely to enjoy lasting success. Different forms of intellectual property—which include patents, trademarks, copyrights, and trade secrets—may also serve as strategic resources for firms. Examining a firm's resources can be aided by the value chain, a tool that systematically examines primary and secondary activities in the creation of a good or service.

1. Divide your class into four or eight groups, depending on the size of the class. Each group should search for a patent tied to a successful product, as well as a patent associated with a product that was not a commercial hit. Were there resources tied to the successful organization that the poor performer did not seem to attain?

2. This chapter discussed Southwest Airlines. Based on your reading of the chapter, how well has Southwest done in bundling together the resources recommended by resource-based theory? What theoretical perspective best explains the competitive actions of most firms in the airline industry?

Chapter 5: Synthesis of Strategic Issues and Analysis

5.1 Introduction

5.2 SWOT Framework

5.3 Strategic Issue Identification

5.4 Conclusion

Learning Objectives

After reading this chapter, you should be able to understand and articulate answers to the following questions:

1. How is the SWOT framework developed and used for determining strategic issues and strategies?
2. What is a strategic issue and how is it identified and expressed?

5.1 Introduction

The last three chapters have dealt with assessing organizational performance, external analysis of the industry, and competitive environments of a firm, and analyzing the internal environment of an organization. What happens to all information that is obtained as a result of all these evaluations? The SWOT framework helps to pull the most important information into a format that can then be used in strategic management to determine the strategic issue the firm needs to address and resolve by consolidating a summary of the other analyses into one framework. The SWOT framework is also helpful in the next phase of strategic management, setting strategies.

A strategic issue is the primary matter faced by an organization that must be addressed for the organization to survive, excel, or achieve a major strategic initiative. The strategic issue defines what the organization needs to address and resolve to move the organization forward toward success by analyzing the data and information from the internal and external assessments as presented in the SWOT. Once the strategic issue is defined, strategies can be developed that address and resolve the strategic issue and propel the organization toward accomplishing its vision. The next chapter discusses how basic business level strategies are developed. The development of the firm's strategic issue is discussed in greater detail later in this chapter.

5.2 SWOT Framework

Chess master Bruce Pandolfini has noted the similarities between business and chess. In both arenas, you must understand your own abilities as well as your flaws. You must also know your opponents, try to anticipate their moves, and deal with considerable uncertainty. A very popular management tool that incorporates the idea of understanding the elements internal and external to the firm is SWOT (strengths, weaknesses, opportunities, and threats) analysis. Strengths and weaknesses are assessed by examining the firm, while opportunities and threats refer to external events and trends. These ideas can be applied to individuals too. Below are examples of each element of SWOT analysis for organizations and for individuals who are seeking employment.

Table 5.1 SWOT

SWOT point	Organizational Examples	Individual Examples
Strengths	Having high levels of cash flow gives firms discretion to purchase new equipment if they wish to.	Strong technical and language skills, as well as previous work experience, can help individuals rise above the competition.
Weaknesses	Dubious leadership and CEO scandals have plagued some corporations in recent years.	Poor communication skills keep many job seekers from being hired into sales and supervisory positions.
Opportunities	The high cost of gasoline creates opportunities for substitute products based on alternative energy sources.	The US economy is increasingly services based, suggesting that individuals can enjoy more opportunities in service firms.
Threats	Concerns about worldwide pollution are a threat to petroleum-based products.	A tight job market poses challenges to new graduates.

Porter's Five Forces analysis examines the situation faced by the competitors in an industry. Strategic groups analysis narrows the focus by centering on subsets of these competitors whose strategies are similar. SWOT analysis takes an even narrower focus by centering on an individual firm. Specifically, SWOT analysis is a tool that considers a firm's strengths and weaknesses along with the opportunities and threats that exist in the firm's environment (Table 4.12).

Executives using SWOT analysis compare these internal and external factors to generate ideas about how their firm might become more successful. In general, it is wise to focus on ideas that allow a firm to leverage its strengths, steer clear of or resolve its weaknesses, capitalize on opportunities, and protect itself against threats. For example, untapped overseas

Figure 5.1: *China's huge population and growing wealth makes it an attractive opportunity for Subway and other American restaurant chains.*

markets have presented potentially lucrative opportunities to Subway and other restaurant chains such as McDonald's and KFC. Meanwhile, Subway's strengths include a well-established brand name and a simple business format that can easily be adapted to other cultures. In considering the opportunities offered by overseas markets and Subway's strengths, it is not surprising that entering and expanding in different countries has been a key element of Subway's strategy in recent years. Indeed, Subway in 2020 had operations in 111 nations.

The SWOT framework is developed by synthesizing the information developed from the external, competitive, and internal assessments. The most important information from these assessments is pulled into the SWOT framework. Once complete, the SWOT is helpful in determining the strategic issue facing the organization. SWOT is also beneficial is developing the strategies for the firm.

SWOT analysis is helpful to executives, and it is used within most organizations. Important cautions need to be offered about SWOT analysis, however. First, in laying out each of the four elements of SWOT, internal and external factors should not be confused with each other. It is important not to list strengths as opportunities, for example, if executives are to succeed at matching internal and external concerns during the idea generation process. Internal environment assessment tools such as VRIO and Value Chain Analysis can lead to organizational strengths and weaknesses. Using external environment analysis tools like PESTEL and Porter's Five Forces help to determine opportunities and threats. Second, opportunities should not be confused with strategic moves designed to capitalize on these opportunities. In the case of Subway, it would be a mistake to list "entering new countries" as an opportunity. Instead, untapped markets are the opportunity presented to Subway, and entering those markets is a way for Subway to exploit the opportunity. Finally, and perhaps most important, the results of SWOT analysis should not be overemphasized. SWOT analysis is a relatively simple tool for understanding a firm's situation. As a result, SWOT is best viewed as a brainstorming technique for generating creative ideas, not as a rigorous method for selecting strategies. Thus the ideas produced by SWOT analysis offer a starting point for executives' efforts to craft strategies for their organization, not an ending point. The SWOT framework is also very helpful in determining the strategic issue facing the firm that will need to be addressed and resolved through the strategies that are developed.

Table 5.2 SWOT Analysis for Subway in 2020

Strengths	Weaknesses
• Healthy menu options • Economical pricing • Simple business format	• Limited menu items • High employee turnover • No hamburgers or french fries
Opportunities	Threats
• Untapped international markets • Movement to more healthy eating	• Competitors offering more options • Long-term economic slow-down due to pandemic

In addition to organizations, individuals can benefit from applying SWOT analysis to their personal situation. A college student who is approaching graduation, for example, could lay out her main strengths and weaknesses and the opportunities and threats presented by the environment. Suppose, for instance, that this person enjoys and is good at helping others (a strength) but also has a rather short attention span (a weakness). Meanwhile, opportunities to work at a rehabilitation center or to pursue an advanced degree are available. Our hypothetical student might be wise to pursue a job at the rehabilitation center, where her strength at helping others would be a powerful asset, rather than entering graduate school, where a lot of reading is required and her short attention span could undermine her studies.

Section Video

Business strategy-SWOT analysis [03:08]

The video for this lesson discusses SWOT analysis.

You can view this video here: https://youtu.be/9-NWhwskTO4.

Key Takeaway

- Executives using SWOT analysis compare internal strengths and weaknesses with external opportunities and threats to generate ideas about how their firm might become more successful. Ideas that allow a firm to leverage its strengths, mitigate or resolve its weaknesses, capitalize on opportunities, and protect itself against threats are particularly helpful.

Exercises

1. What do each of the letters in SWOT represent?
2. What are your key strengths, and how might you build your own personal strategies for success around them?

Image Credits

Video Credits

5.3 Strategic Issue Identification

So, what happens in strategic management once all the external and internal analysis is done and the SWOT framework is complete? Is it time to start developing strategies? No, not yet. One more thing needs to happen: defining the strategic issue or issues the firm needs to be sure to address.

What is a **strategic issue**? First, it is an issue, something that needs to be addressed and resolved. Second, it is strategic. It is a long-term issue whose resolution will help move the organization toward its vision. Resolving the strategic issue will have a major impact on the direction and success of the firm (Ambler, 2020). The strategic issue is derived from the facts and data provided by the external and internal analysis and its synthesis through the SWOT framework. The business decision makers do not define the strategic issue(s) at the beginning of the strategic management process, through a hunch or guess, but after the analysis is completed. Once defined, the strategic issue helps drive the strategies that the organization develops and pursues. A strategic issue, when identified correctly and used effectively, becomes the strategic focus of the organization. In this process, more than one strategic issue may surface. Generally, decision makers will condense these into a single statement, or deal with less important strategic issues when establishing strategies or lower order goals.

The word "issue" often connotes a negative situation that a firm may be facing. For example, Southwest Airlines was faced with much lower passenger volumes as a result of the COVID-19 pandemic that started in 2020. However, the Subway example discussed at the beginning of this chapter demonstrates that the strategic issue was framed as capitalizing on an opportunity—how to move into untapped international markets.

Ideally, the strategic issue is reduced to one concise sentence, so that it is easily captured and understood. Amplifying information may be provided to further explain the situation and justify the choice of the strategic issue. Often, the strategic issue starts with the word *how*. In the Southwest Airlines example, the strategic issue could be: "How does Southwest Airlines adjust to long-term, lower passenger volumes and remain the preferred, low-cost leader in the industry?" For Subway, it may have been "How does Subway enter untapped international markets?" Once defined, these companies would develop strategies that move their organization towards its vision, while addressing the strategic issue.

Figure 5.2: The Planning Team

The strategic issue will change over time, as the external, competitive and internal dynamics change. For organizations working through the strategic management process, defining the strategic issue may not be simple. The planning team members may interpret data differently or through the lens of their own perspective. The CFO may see the strategic issue in financial terms, the marketing director as a marketing issue, and the human resources director as an issue with manpower and training. One process organizations can use to determine the strategic issue is for planning team members to study the data from the analysis and each draft and share their idea of the strategic issue. The team then has a process to prioritize these, dropping some, combining some, until they arrive at a consensus on the wording of the strategic issue (Ambler, 2020).

Section Video

Strategic Issues [01:57]

The video for this lesson discusses Strategic Issues.

You can view this video here: https://youtu.be/Zj_dxbJpCqo.

Exercises

1. Suppose internal and external analysis data from Apple show an upcoming slump in sales of desktop and laptop computers and tablets for years to come. What might the strategic issue for Apple be?
2. You are a college senior preparing to graduate in six months. The COVID-19 pandemic has caused massive furloughs and layoffs nationwide. What might be your strategic issue?

References

Ambler, T. E. (2020). *Strategic issues: The pivotal process for strategic success*. The Center for Simplified Strategic Planning, Inc. https://www.cssp.com/CD0799/ProcessForStrategicSuccess/.

Image Credits

Figure 5.2: Morillo, Christina. "People on conference room." Pexels license. Retrieved from https://www.pexels.com/photo/people-on-conference-room-1181427/.

Video Credits

Gregg Learning. (2018, June 9). *Strategic issues* [Video]. YouTube. https://youtu.be/Zj_dxbJpCqo.

5.4 Conclusion

In the analysis stage of the strategic management process, the final phase is to apply the SWOT framework to consolidate a "snapshot" of the internal and external analysis conducted and identify the key strategic issue(s). The SWOT pulls together the important information from the external and internal analysis and the organizational performance assessment and displays it in an organized framework. The strengths and weaknesses are internal to the organization, and the opportunities and threats are external to the firm.

The information and data from the assessments and SWOT are then used to formulate the strategic issue(s). What needs to be addressed and resolved to move the organization forward toward success and its vision? Strategies are then developed that address the resolution of the strategic issue and advance the organization, as discussed in the next chapter.

Chapter 6: Selecting Business-Level Strategies

Learning Objectives

After reading this chapter, you should be able to understand and articulate answers to the following questions:

1. Why is an examination of generic strategies valuable?
2. What are the four main generic strategies?
3. What is a best-cost strategy?
4. What does it mean to be "stuck in the middle"?

6.1 Introduction

Within the strategic management framework, an organization must define and continue to improve its generic, business-level strategy. A generic, business-level strategy is also called its generic competitive strategy, because it defines how a firm competes head-to-head against similar products and services in the marketplace. According to Michael Porter, a firm may pursue one of five generic/competitive business-level strategies. These are broad cost leadership, broad differentiation, focused cost leadership, focused differentiation, and best cost strategies. An important point of distinction is that business level strategies are viewed from the perspective of which consumer(s) are being targeted. It may be tempting to view business-level strategies in terms of the product lines, but the key point is to evaluate the business-level based on to whom the strategy appeals. In this way, a firm can target a broad audience with a single or a few products.

There are two primary decisions in a generic business strategy. Will the intent of the strategy be on a broad or focused target audience, and simultaneously, does the firm organize around a cost or differentiation approach? If selecting a broad cost leadership or broad differentiation strategy, the target market for the product or service is broad, meaning most people who buy within that industry. If the strategy is focused, that target market is narrow, a niche market, and not meant for most people in the industry. A strategy of broad cost leadership offers the lowest price in the market for that product or service. It appeals particularly to price sensitive customers. Firms pursuing a broad differentiation strategy offer something unique that differentiates their product or service from others. Typically this uniqueness adds cost and value to the product or service, allowing the company to charge more. If the strategy is focused cost leadership, then the firm attempts to provide the lowest cost to a narrow, niche target market. Focused differentiation provides unique or differentiated products or services to a narrow, niche target market. The fifth generic business-level strategy is called best cost, where the firm attempts to offer a hybrid of both lower cost and differentiated products or services, combining the two basic strategies. A firm pursuing this strategy must be careful to perform both strategies well, or risk not performing either well, and therefore becoming "stuck in the middle," and losing customers to the competition.

Once a firm establishes its overall generic business-level strategy, the strategic management process helps the firm to continuously improve upon that strategy. The organizational performance, external, and internal assessments, and the development of the strategic issue(s) through the SWOT analysis are then used to plot strategies for the firm to achieve its vision through its business-level strategy.

The Competition Takes Aim at Target

On January 13, 2011, Target Corporation announced its intentions to operate stores outside the United States for the first time. The plan called for Target to enter Canada by purchasing existing leases from a Canadian retailer and then opening 100 to 150 stores in 2013 and 2014 (Target, 2011). The chain already included more than 1,700 stores in forty-nine states. Given the close physical and cultural ties between the United States and Canada, entering the Canadian market seemed to be a logical move for Target.

Figure 6.1: Inside of a Target store

In addition to making its initial move beyond the United States, Target had several other sources of pride. The company claimed that 96% of American consumers recognized its signature logo, surpassing the percentages enjoyed by famous brands such as Apple and Nike. In 2020, Fortune magazine ranked Target twenty-second on its list of the "World's Most Admired Companies." But not all had been well with Target (Fortune, 2020). They pulled out of Canada in 2015 after just two years and $2 billion in losses. Concern also surrounded Target's possible vulnerability to competition within the retail industry (Peterson, 2015). Since its creation in the early 1960s, Target executives had carved out a lucrative position for the firm. Target offers relatively low prices on brand name consumer staples such as cleaning supplies and paper products, but it also offers chic clothing and household goods. This unique combination helps Target to appeal to fairly affluent customers. Perhaps the most tangible reflection of Target's upscale position among large retailers is the tendency of some customers to jokingly pronounce its name as if it were a French boutique: "Tar-zhay."

Target's lucrative position was far from guaranteed, however. Indeed, a variety of competitors seemed to be taking aim at Target. Retail chains such as Kohl's and Old Navy offered fashionable clothing at prices similar to Target's. Discounters like T.J. Maxx, Marshalls, and Ross offered designer clothing and chic household goods for prices that often were lower than Target's. Closeout stores such as Big Lots offered a limited selection of electronics, apparel, and household goods but at deeply discounted prices. All these stores threatened to steal business from Target.

Walmart was perhaps Target's most worrisome competitor. After some struggles in the 2000s, the mammoth retailer's performance was strong enough that it ranked consistently above Target on Fortune's list of the "World's Most Admired Companies" (eighteenth vs. twenty-second in 2020). Walmart also was much bigger than Target. The resulting economies of scale meant that Walmart could undercut Target's prices anytime it desired. Just such a scenario had unfolded before. A few years ago, Walmart's victory in a price war over Kmart led the latter into bankruptcy.

One important difference between Kmart and Target is that Target is viewed by consumers as offering relatively high-quality goods. But this difference might not protect Target. Although Walmart's products tended to lack the chic appeal of Target's, Walmart had begun offering better products during the recession of the late 2000s in an effort to expand its customer base. If Walmart executives chose to match Target's quality while charging lower prices, Target could find itself without a unique appeal for customers. As 2020 continued, a big question loomed: could Target maintain its unique appeal to customers or would the competitive arrows launched by Walmart and others force Target's executives to quiver?

References

Fortune Magazine. (2020). *World's most admired companies*.
https://fortune.com/worlds-most-admired-companies/2020/search/?ordering=asc.

Peterson, H. (2015, January 15). 5 reasons Target failed in Canada. *Business Insider*.
https://www.businessinsider.com/why-target-canada-failed-2015-1.

Target fact card. (2007, January). https://web.archive.org/web/20071128161431/http://sites.target.com/
images/corporate/about/pdfs/corp_factcard_101107.pdf.

Target. (2011, January 13). Target Corporation to acquire interest in Canadian real estate from Zellers Inc., a
subsidiary of Hudson's Bay Company, for $1.825 billion [Press release]. https://investors.target.com/news-
releases/news-release-details/target-corporation-acquire-interest-canadian-real-estate-zellers.

Image Credits

6.2 Understanding Business-Level Strategy through "Generic Strategies"

Why Examine Generic Strategies?

Business-level strategy addresses the question of how a firm will compete in a particular industry (Table 6.1). This seems to be a simple question on the surface, but it is actually quite complex. The reason is that there are a great many possible answers to the question. Consider, for example, the restaurants in your town or city. Chances are that you live fairly close to some combination of McDonald's, Subway, Chili's, Applebee's, Panera Bread Company, dozens of other national brands, and a variety of locally based eateries that have just one location. Each of these restaurants competes using a business model that is at least somewhat unique. When an executive in the restaurant industry analyzes her company and her rivals, she needs to avoid getting distracted by all the nuances of different firm's business-level strategies and losing sight of the big picture.

The solution is to think about business-level strategy in terms of generic strategies. A generic business-level strategy is a general way of positioning a firm within an industry. Focusing on generic strategies allows executives to concentrate on the core elements of firms' business-level strategies. The most popular set of generic strategies is based on the work of Professor Michael Porter of the Harvard Business School and subsequent researchers that have built on Porter's initial ideas (Porter, 1980; Williamson & Zeng, 2009).

Firms compete on two general dimensions—the source of competitive advantage (cost or differentiation) and the scope of operations (broad or narrow). Four possible generic business-level strategies emerge from these decisions. An example of each generic business-level strategy from the retail industry is illustrated below.

Table 6.1 Business-Level Strategies

Competitive Advantage: Cost
Broad Target Market: Walmart's cost leadership strategy depends on attracting a large customer base and keeping prices low by buying massive quantities of goods from suppliers.
Narrow Target Market: In using a focused cost leadership, Dollar General does not offer a full array of consumer goods, but those that it does offer are priced to move.

Competitive Advantage: Differentiation
Broad Target Market: Nordstrom builds its differentiation strategy around offering designer merchandise and providing exceptional service.
Narrow Target Market: Anthropologie follows a focused differentiation strategy by selling unique (and pricey) women's apparel, accessories, and home furnishings.

According to Porter, two competitive dimensions are the keys to business-level strategy. The first dimension is a firm's source of competitive advantage. This dimension involves whether a firm tries to gain an edge on rivals by keeping costs down or by offering something unique in the market. The second dimension is a firms' scope of operations. This dimension involves whether a firm tries to target customers in general or whether it seeks to attract just a narrow segment of customers. Four generic business-level strategies emerge from these decisions: (1) **broad cost leadership**, (2) **broad differentiation**, (3) **focused cost leadership**, and (4) **focused differentiation**. In rare cases, firms are able to offer both low prices and unique features that customers find desirable. These firms are following a **best-cost** strategy. Firms that are not able to offer low prices or appealing unique features are referred to as "**stuck in the middle**."

Understanding the differences that underlie generic strategies is important because different generic strategies offer different value propositions to customers. A firm focusing on cost leadership will have a different value chain configuration than a firm whose strategy focuses on differentiation. For example, marketing and sales for a differentiation strategy often requires extensive effort while some firms that follow cost leadership such as Waffle House are successful with limited marketing efforts. This chapter presents each generic strategy and the "recipe" generally associated with success when using that strategy. When firms follow these recipes, the result can be a strategy that leads to superior performance. But when firms fail to follow logical actions associated with each strategy, the result may be a value proposition configuration that is expensive to implement and that does not satisfy enough customers to be viable.

Figure 6.2: Analyzing generic strategies enhances the understanding of how firms compete at the business level.

Limitations of Generic Strategies

Examining business-level strategy in terms of generic strategies has limitations. Firms that follow a particular generic strategy tend to share certain features. For example, one way that cost leaders generally keep costs low is by not spending much on advertising. Not every cost leader, however, follows this path. While cost leaders such as Waffle House spend very little on advertising, Walmart spends considerable money on print and television advertising despite following a cost leadership strategy. Thus a firm may not match every characteristic that its generic strategy entails. Indeed, depending on the nature of a firm's industry, tweaking the recipe of a generic strategy may be essential to cooking up success.

Section Video

Five Competitive Strategies [02:50]

The video for this lesson explains the five generic strategies and why some work better in some industries or conditions than others.

You can view this video here:
https://www.youtube.com/watch?v=xUW6_Nbe8d0&feature=emb_logo

Key Takeaway

- Business-level strategies examine how firms compete in a given industry. Firms derive such strategies by executives making decisions about whether their source of competitive advantage is based on price or differentiation and whether their scope of operations targets a broad or narrow market.

Exercises

1. What are examples of each generic business-level strategy in the apparel industry?
2. What are the limitations of examining firms in terms of generic strategies?
3. Create a new framework to examine generic strategies using different dimensions than the two offered by Porter's framework. What does your approach offer that Porter's does not?

References

Porter, M. E. (1980). *Competitive strategy: Techniques for analyzing industries and competitors.* Free Press.

Williamson, P. J. & Zeng, M. (2009). Value-for-money strategies for recessionary times. *Harvard Business Review*, 87(3), 66–74. https://hbr.org/2009/03/value-for-money-strategies-for-recessionary-times.

Video Credits

Gregg Learning. (2018, June 11). *Five competitive strategies* [Video]. YouTube. https://www.youtube.com/watch?v=xUW6_Nbe8d0&feature=emb_logo.

6.3 Cost Leadership

Firms that compete based on price and target a broad target market are following a broad cost leadership strategy. Several examples of firms pursuing a broad cost leadership strategy are illustrated below.

Table 6.2 Cost Leadership

Examples of Firms Pursuing a Broad Cost Leadership Strategy
Despite its name, Dunkin' Donuts makes more money selling inexpensive coffee than it does from selling donuts. The coffee is often advertised as costing under a dollar, making Dunkin' Donuts a low-priced alternative to Starbucks.
Supercuts's website makes clear their longstanding cost leadership strategy by noting, "A Supercut is a haircut that has kept people looking their best, while keeping money in their pockets, since 1975."
Payless ShoeSource is a discount retailer that sells inexpensive shoes for men, women, and children. However, they filed for bankruptcy in 2020 and closed all their stores, only operating their overseas stores. Super Shoes survives as a low cost leader.
Little Debbie snack cakes began when O. D. McKee started selling treats for five cents each in the early 1930s. Little Debbie cakes cost a lot more than five cents today, but they remain cheaper than similar offerings from Entenmann's, Tastykake, and other snack cake rivals.

The Nature of the Cost Leadership Strategy

It is tempting to think of cost leaders as companies that sell inferior, poor-quality goods and services for rock-bottom prices. This is not necessarily true, but some companies get this reputation. K-Mart, for example, had been a successful discount department store with a cost leadership strategy. As Walmart competed head to head with K-Mart, however, and offered higher quality products at the same or lower prices than its rivals, K-Mart was doomed. Its reputation for cheap, inferior products and its inability to win a price war with Walmart pushed K-Mart into bankruptcy.

In contrast to firms such as K-Mart, cost leaders can be very successful. A firm following a cost leadership strategy offers products or services with acceptable quality and features to a broad set of customers at a low price (Table 6.2). Super Shoes, for example, sells name-brand shoes at inexpensive prices. Little Debbie snack cakes offer another example. The brand was started in the 1930s when O. D. McKee began selling sugary treats for five cents. Most consumers today would view the quality of Little Debbie cakes as a step below similar offerings from Entenmann's, but enough people believe that they offer acceptable quality that the brand is still around eight decades after its creation.

Perhaps the most famous cost leader is Walmart, which has used a cost leadership strategy to become the largest company in the world. The firm's advertising slogans such as "Always Low Prices" and "Save Money. Live Better" communicate Walmart's emphasis on price slashing to potential customers. Meanwhile, Walmart has the broadest customer base of any firm in the United States. Approximately one hundred million Americans visit a Walmart in a typical week (Zimmerman & Hudson, 2006). Incredibly, this means that roughly one-third of Americans are frequent Walmart customers. This huge customer base includes people from all demographic and social groups within society.

Cost leaders tend to share some important characteristics. The ability to charge low prices and still make a profit is challenging. Cost leaders manage to do so by emphasizing efficiency. At Waffle House restaurants, for example, customers are served cheap eats quickly to keep booths available for later customers. As part of the effort to be efficient, most cost leaders spend little on advertising, market research, or research and development. Waffle House, for example, limits its advertising to billboards along highways. Meanwhile, the simplicity of Waffle House's menu requires little research and development.

Many cost leaders rely on economies of scale to achieve efficiency. **Economies of scale** are created when the costs of offering goods and services decreases as a firm is able to sell more items. This occurs because expenses are distributed across a greater number of items. Walmart spent approximately $3.5 billion on advertising in 2019 (Guttmann, 2019). This is a huge number, but Walmart is so large that its advertising expenses equal just a tiny fraction of its sales. Also, cost leaders are often large companies, which allows them to demand price concessions from their suppliers. Walmart is notorious for squeezing suppliers such as Procter & Gamble to sell goods to Walmart for lower and lower prices over time. The firm passes some of these savings to customers in the form of reduced prices in its stores.

Advantages and Disadvantages of Cost Leadership

Each generic strategy offers advantages that firms can potentially leverage to enhance their success as well as disadvantages that may undermine their success. In the case of cost leadership, one advantage is that cost leaders' emphasis on efficiency makes them well positioned to withstand price competition from rivals (Table 6.3). Kmart's ill-fated attempt to engage Walmart in a price war ended in disaster, in part because Walmart was so efficient in its operations that it could live with smaller profit margins far more easily than Kmart could.

Using a cost leadership strategy offers firms important advantages and disadvantages. Below, table 6.3 illustrates a few examples in relation to entertainment and leisure.

Table 6.3 Executing a Low-Cost Strategy

Advantages
High profits can be enjoyed if a cost leader has a high market share. An example is Kampgrounds of America, a chain of nearly 500 low cost camping franchises in the United States.
Low-cost firms such as many municipal golf courses can withstand price wars because high-priced competitors will not want to compete directly with a more efficient rival.

Disadvantages
If perceptions of quality become too low, business will suffer.
Large volumes of sales are a must because margins are slim.
The need to keep expenses low might lead cost leaders to be late in detecting key environment trends.
Low-cost firms' emphasis on efficiency makes it difficult for them to change quickly if needed.

Beyond existing competitors, a cost leadership strategy also creates benefits relative to potential new entrants. Specifically, the presence of a cost leader in an industry tends to discourage new firms from entering the business because a new firm would struggle to attract customers by undercutting the cost leaders' prices. Thus, a cost leadership strategy helps create barriers to entry that protect the firm—and its existing rivals—from new competition.

In many settings, cost leaders attract a large market share because a large portion of potential customers find paying low prices for goods and services of acceptable quality to be very appealing. This is certainly true for Walmart, for example. The need for efficiency means that cost leaders' profit margins are often slimmer than the margins enjoyed by other firms. However, cost leaders' ability to make a little bit of profit from each of a large number of customers means that the total profits of cost leaders can be substantial.

In some settings, the need for high sales volume is a critical disadvantage of a cost leadership strategy. Highly fragmented markets and markets that involve a

Figure 6.3: Challenging a cost leader in a price war may end up destroying a company.

lot of brand loyalty may not offer much of an opportunity to attract a large segment of customers. In both the soft drink and cigarette industries, for example, customers appear to be willing to pay a little extra to enjoy the brand of their choice. Lower-end brands of soda and cigarettes appeal to a minority of consumers, but famous brands such as Coca-Cola, Pepsi, Marlboro, and Camel still dominate these markets. A related concern is that achieving a high sales volume usually requires significant upfront investments in production and/or distribution capacity. Not every firm is willing and able to make such investments.

Due to the need for cost leaders to have high volumes and slim margins, a focused cost leadership strategy is difficult to achieve. By definition, a focused approach is directed at a narrow, niche segment of the market. This means lower volumes, therefore contrary to the normal cost leadership strategy. An example would be an Hispanic grocery store in Northern Virginia serving the niche market of Hispanics living there, that uses a cost leadership strategy to compete against the other Hispanic grocery stores.

Cost leaders tend to keep their costs low by minimizing advertising, market research, and research and development, but this approach can prove to be expensive in the long run. A relative lack of market research can lead cost leaders to be less skilled than other firms at detecting important environmental changes. Meanwhile, downplaying research and development can slow cost leaders' ability to respond to changes once they are detected. Lagging rivals in terms of detecting and reacting to external shifts can prove to be a deadly combination that leaves cost leaders out of touch with the market and out of answers.

Section Video

Low Cost Strategy [03:20]

The video for this lesson describes the competitive approach of low cost strategy.

You can view this video here:
https://www.youtube.com/watch?v=-C0MQzIb7Y4&feature=emb_logo.

Key Takeaway

- Cost leadership is an effective business-level strategy to the extent that a firm offers low prices, provides satisfactory quality, and attracts enough customers to be profitable.

Exercises

1. What are three industries in which a cost leadership strategy would be difficult to implement?
2. What is your favorite cost leadership restaurant?
3. Name three examples of firms conducting a cost leadership strategy that use no advertising. Should they start advertising? Why or why not?

References

Guttmann, A. (2019, August 9). Walmart: advertising spending 2014-2019. *Statista.* https://www.statista.com/statistics/622029/walmart-ad-spend/.

Zimmerman, A., & Hudson, K. (2006). Managing Wal-Mart: How US-store chief hopes to fix Wal-Mart. *Wall Street Journal. https://www.wsj.com/articles/SB114462756022321371.*

Image Credits

Figure 6.3: Skirvin, Ben. "Closed Sign." CC BY-NC 2.0. Retrieved from https://flic.kr/p/8ScoFg.

Video Credits

Gregg Learning. (2018, June 12). *Low cost strategy* [Video]. YouTube. https://www.youtube.com/watch?v=-C0MQzIb7Y4&feature=emb_logo.

6.4 Differentiation

Firms that compete on uniqueness and target a broad market are following a differentiation strategy. Several examples of firms pursuing a differentiation strategy are illustrated below.

Table 6.4 Differentiation

Examples of Firms Pursuing a Differentiation Strategy
Although salt is a commodity, Morton has differentiated its salt by building a brand around its iconic umbrella girl and its trademark slogan of "When it rains, it pours."
FedEx's former slogan "When it absolutely, positively has to be there overnight" highlights the commitment to very speedy delivery that differentiates them from competitors such as UPS and the US Postal Service.
Offerings such as Hot Wheels cars and the Barbie line of dolls highlight toy maker Mattel's differentiation strategy. Both are updated regularly to reflect current trends and tastes.
Nike differentiates its athletic shoes through its iconic "swoosh" as well as an intense emphasis on product innovation through research and development. Nike also differentiates their athletic brand through their marketing strategy of highlighting social justice issues regardless of potential public controversy.
The Walt Disney Company has developed incomparable customer service standards ("the happiest place on earth") and numerous well-known characters such as Mickey Mouse, the Little Mermaid, and Captain Jack Sparrow that help differentiate their movies, theme parks, and merchandise.

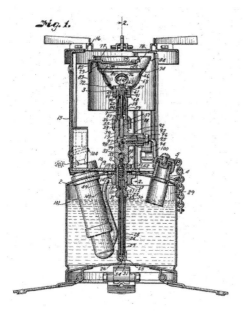

Figure 6.4: Coleman's patented stove captures the essence of a differentiation strategy, since buyers are willing to pay a premium for its reliability.

The Nature of the Differentiation Strategy

A famous cliché contends that "you get what you pay for." This saying captures the essence of a differentiation strategy. A firm following a differentiation strategy attempts to convince customers to pay a premium price for its goods or services by providing unique and desirable features (Table 6.4). The message that such a firm conveys to customers is that you will pay a little bit more for our offerings, but you will receive a good value overall because our offerings provide something special.

In terms of the two competitive dimensions described by Michael Porter, using a differentiation strategy means that a firm is competing based on uniqueness rather than price and is seeking to attract a broad market (Porter, 1980). Coleman camping equipment offers a good example. If camping equipment such as sleeping bags, lanterns, and stoves fail during a camping trip, the result will be, well, unhappy campers. Coleman's sleeping bags, lanterns, and stoves are renowned for their reliability and durability. Cheaper brands are much more likely to have problems. Lovers of the outdoors must pay more to purchase Coleman's goods than they would to obtain lesser brands, but having equipment that you can count on to keep you warm and dry is worth a price premium in the minds of most campers.

Successful use of a differentiation strategy depends on not only offering unique features but also communicating the value of these features to potential customers. As a result, advertising in general and brand building in particular are important to this strategy. Few goods are more basic and generic than table salt. This would seemingly make creating a differentiated brand in the salt business next to impossible. Through clever marketing, however, Morton Salt has done so. Morton has differentiated its salt by building a brand around its iconic umbrella girl and its trademark slogan of "When it rains, it pours." Would the typical consumer be able to tell the difference between Morton Salt and cheaper generic salt in a blind taste test? Not a chance. Yet Morton succeeds in convincing customers to pay a little extra for its salt through its brand-building efforts.

FedEx and Nike are two other companies that have done well at communicating to customers that they provide differentiated offerings. FedEx's former slogan "When it absolutely, positively has to be there overnight" highlights the commitment to speedy delivery that sets the firm apart from competitors such as UPS and the US Postal Service. Nike differentiates its athletic shoes and apparel through its iconic "swoosh" logo as well as an intense emphasis on product innovation through research and development.

Developing a Differentiation Strategy at Express Oil Change

Express Oil Change and Service Centers is a chain of auto repair shops that stretches from Florida to Texas. Based in Birmingham, Alabama, the firm has more than 170 company-owned and franchised locations under its brand. Express Oil Change tries to provide a unique level of service, and the firm is content to let rivals offer cheaper prices. We asked an Express Oil Change executive about his firm (Ketchen & Short, 2010).

Question:

The auto repair and maintenance business is a pretty competitive space. How is Express Oil Change being positioned relative to other firms, such as Super Lube, American LubeFast, and Jiffy Lube?

Figure 6.5: Express Oil Change sets itself apart through superior service and great locations.

Don Larose, Senior Vice President of Franchise Development:

Every good business sector is competitive. The key to our success is to be more convenient and provide a better overall experience for the customer. Express Oil Change and Service Centers outperform the industry significantly in terms of customer transactions per day and store sales, for a host of reasons.

In terms of customer convenience, Express Oil Change is faster than most of our competitors—we do a ten-minute oil change while the customer stays in the car. Mothers with kids in car seats especially enjoy this feature. We also do mechanical work that other quick lube businesses don't do. We change and rotate tires, do brake repairs, air conditioning, tune ups, and others. There is no appointment necessary for many mechanical services like tire rotation and balancing, and checking brakes. So, overall, we are more convenient than most of our competitors.

In terms of staffing our stores, full-time workers are all that we employ. Full-time workers are better trained and typically have less turnover. They therefore have more experience and do better quality work.

We think incentives are very important. We use a payroll system that provides incentives to the store staff on how many cars are serviced each day and on the total sales of the store, rather than on increasing the average transactions by selling the customer items they did not come in for, which is what most of the industry does. We don't sell customers things they don't yet need, like air filters and radiator flushes. We focus on building trust, by acting with integrity, to get the customer to come back and build the daily car count. This philosophy is not a slogan for us. It is how we operate with every customer, in every store, every day.

The placement of our outlets is another key factor. We place our stores in A-caliber retail locations. These are lots that may cost more than our competitors are willing or able to pay. We get what we pay for though; we have approximately 41% higher sales per store than the industry average.

Question:

What is the strangest interaction you've ever had with a potential franchisee?

Larose:

I once had a franchisee candidate in New Jersey respond to a request by us for proof of his liquid assets by bringing to the interview about $100,000 in cash to the meeting. He had it in a bag, with bundles of it wrapped in blue tape. Usually, folks just bring in a copy of a bank or stock statement. Not sure why he had so much cash on hand, literally, and I didn't want to know. He didn't become a franchisee.

A differentiation strategy offers important advantages and disadvantages for firms that adopt it. Below we illustrate a few examples in relation to an often differentiated product—women's handbags.

Table 6.5 Executing a Differentiation Strategy

Advantages
Buyer loyalty is common among handbag buyers. Many individuals enjoy seeing—and being seen with—a designer logo on the products they buy such as the iconic C that is shown on Coach bags.
Chanel enjoys strong margins because their well-known name allows them to charge a premium for their handbags.

Disadvantages
Less expensive bags from retailers such as Target provide enough of a trendy look to satisfy many price-sensitive buyers. These individuals will choose to save their money by avoiding expensive bags from top-end designers.
Imitations may steal customers, such as is common with knock-off handbags sold by street vendors.

Advantages and Disadvantages of Differentiation

Each generic strategy offers advantages that firms can potentially leverage to enjoy strong performance, as well as disadvantages that may damage their performance. In the case of differentiation, a key advantage is that effective differentiation creates an ability to obtain premium prices from customers (Table 6.5). This enables a firm to enjoy strong profit margins. Coca-Cola, for example, currently enjoys a profit margin of approximately 33%, meaning that about 33 cents of every dollar it collects from customers is profit. In comparison, Walmart's cost leadership strategy delivered a margin of under 4% in 2010.

In turn, strong margins mean that the firm does not need to attract huge numbers of customers to have a good overall level of profit. Luckily for Coca-Cola, the firm does attract a great many buyers. Overall, the firm made a profit of just under $9.0 billion on sales of just over $37.3 billion in 2019. Interestingly, Walmart's profits were only 2.4 times higher ($22.0 billion) than Coca-Cola's while its sales volume ($514.4 billion) was 13.8 times higher than Coca-Cola's (Walmart, 2019; Coca Cola, 2019). This comparison of profit margins and overall profit levels illustrates why a differentiation strategy is so attractive to many firms.

To the extent that differentiation remains in place over time, buyer loyalty may be created. Loyal customers are very desirable because they are not price sensitive. In other words, buyer loyalty makes a customer unlikely to switch to another firm's products if that firm tries to steal the customer away through lower prices. Many soda drinkers are fiercely loyal to Coca-Cola's products. Coca-Cola's headquarters are in Atlanta, and loyalty to the firm is especially strong in Georgia and surrounding states. Pepsi and other brands have a hard time convincing loyal Coca-Cola fans to buy their beverages, even when offering deep discounts. This helps keep Coca-Cola's profits high because the firm does not have to match any promotions that its rivals launch to keep its customers.

Meanwhile, Pepsi also has attracted a large set of brand-loyal customers that Coca-Cola struggles to steal. This enhances Pepsi's profits. In contrast, store-brand sodas such as Sam's Choice, which is sold at Walmart, seldom attract loyalty. As a result, they must be offered at very low prices to move from store shelves into shopping carts.

Beyond existing competitors, a differentiation strategy also creates benefits relative to potential new entrants. Specifically, the brand loyalty that customers feel to a differentiated product makes it difficult for a new entrant to lure these customers to adopt its product. A new soda brand, for example, would struggle to take customers away from Coca-Cola or Pepsi. Thus, a differentiation strategy helps create barriers to entry that protect the firm and its industry from new competition.

The big risk when using a differentiation strategy is that customers will not be willing to pay extra to obtain the unique features that a firm is trying to build its strategy around. Department store Dillard's stopped carrying men's sportswear made by Nautica because the seafaring theme of Nautica's brand had lost much of its cache among many men (Kapner, 2007). Because Nautica's uniqueness had eroded, Dillard's believed that space in its stores that Nautica had been occupying could be better allocated to other brands.

In some cases, customers may simply prefer a cheaper alternative. For example, products that imitate the look and feel of offerings from Ray-Ban, Gucci, and Patagonia are attractive to many value-conscious consumers. Firms such as these must work hard at product development and marketing to ensure that enough customers are willing to pay a premium for their goods rather than settling for knockoffs.

In other cases, customers desire the unique features that a firm offers, but competitors are able to imitate the features well enough that they are no longer unique. If this happens, customers have no reason to pay a premium for the firm's offerings. IBM experienced the pain of this scenario when executives tried to follow a differentiation strategy in the personal computer market. The strategy had worked for IBM in other areas. Specifically, IBM had enjoyed a great deal of success in the mainframe computer market by providing superior service and charging customers a premium for their mainframes. A business owner who relied on a mainframe to run her company could not afford to have her mainframe out of operation for long. Meanwhile, few businesses had the skills to fix their own mainframes. IBM's message to customers was that they would pay more for IBM's products but that this was a good investment because when a mainframe needed repairs, IBM would provide faster and better service than its competitors could. The customer would thus be open for business again very quickly after a mainframe failure.

Figure 6.6: Firms following a differentiation strategy must "watch" out for counterfeit goods such as the faux Rolexes shown here.

This positioning failed when IBM used it in the personal computer market. Rivals such as Dell were able to offer service that was just as good as IBM's while also charging lower prices for personal computers than IBM charged. From a customer's perspective, a person would be foolish to pay more for an IBM personal computer since IBM did not offer anything unique. IBM steadily lost market share as a result. IBM's struggles led it to sell its personal computer business to Lenovo. The firm is still successful, however, within the mainframe market where its offerings remain differentiated.

Section Video

Differentiation Strategy [04:28]

The video for this lesson discusses differentiation strategies.

You can view this video here:
https://www.youtube.com/watch?v=NshI_qoaf7g&feature=emb_logo.

Key Takeaway

- Differentiation can be an effective business-level strategy to the extent that a firm offers unique features that convince customers to pay a premium for their goods and services. As with other business-level strategies, there are advantages and disadvantages in pursuing a differentiation strategy.

Exercises

1. What are two industries in which a differentiation strategy would be difficult to implement?
2. What is an example of a differentiated business near your college or university?
3. Name three ways businesses that provide entertainment that might better differentiate their services. How might they do this?

References

Kapner, S. (2007, November 1). Nautica brand losing ground. CNNM*oney*.
http://money.cnn.com/2007/10/31/news/companies/Kapner_Nautica.fortune/index.htm.

Ketchen, D. J., & Short, J. C. (2010). The franchise player: An interview with Don Larose. *Journal of Applied Management and Entrepreneurship, 15*(4), 94–101.

Porter, M. E. (1980). *Competitive strategy: Techniques for analyzing industries and competitors.* Free Press.

The Coca Cola Company. (2019). Form 10K. https://investors.coca-colacompany.com/filings-reports/annual-filings-10-k.

Walmart. (2019). *Earnings release.* https://s2.q4cdn.com/056532643/files/doc_financials/2019/Q4/Q4FY19-Earnings-Release-Final.pdf.

Image Credits

Figure 6.4: Tullis, B.W. – US Patent Office. "Patent drawing for Coleman Model 520 stove – No. 236098." Public Domain. Retrieved from https://en.wikipedia.org/wiki/G.I._pocket_stove#/media/File:Patent_Drawing_for_Coleman_Model_520_Stove.jpg

Figure 6.5: Dystopos. "Express Oil Change." CC BY-NC 2.0. Cropped. Retrieved from https://flic.kr/p/8FYBk.

Figure 6.6: Nino, Gerald. "Counterfeit Rolex watches seized by US CBP." Public Domain. Retrieved from https://commons.wikimedia.org/wiki/File:Patent_Drawing_for_Coleman_Model_520_Stove.jpg.

Video Credits

Gregg Learning. (2018, June 13). *Differentiation strategy* [Video]. YouTube. https://www.youtube.com/watch?v=NshI_qoaf7g&feature=emb_logo.

6.5 Focused Cost Leadership and Focused Differentiation

Companies that use a cost leadership strategy and those that use a differentiation strategy share one important characteristic: both groups try to be attractive to customers in general. These efforts to appeal to broad markets can be contrasted with strategies that involve targeting a relatively narrow niche of potential customers. These latter strategies are known as focus strategies (Porter, 1980).

The Nature of the Focus Cost Leadership Strategy

Figure 6.7: Redbox machines are available nationwide.

Focused cost leadership is the first of two focus strategies. A focused cost leadership strategy requires competing based on price to target a narrow market (Table 6.6). A firm that follows this strategy does not necessarily charge the lowest prices in the industry. Instead, it charges low prices relative to other firms that compete within the target market. Redbox, for example, uses vending machines placed outside grocery stores and other retail outlets to rent DVDs of movies for $1. There are ways to view movies even cheaper, such as through the flat-fee streaming video subscriptions offered by Netflix. But among firms that rent actual DVDs, Redbox offers unparalleled levels of low price and high convenience.

Firms that compete based on price and target a narrow market are following a focused cost leadership strategy. Several examples of firms pursuing a focused cost leadership strategy are illustrated below.

Table 6.6 Focused Cost Leadership

Example of Firms Pursuing a Focused Cost Leadership Strategy
Redbox rents DVDs and video games through vending machines for only $1.
Papa Murphy's targets its inexpensive take-and-bake pizzas at value-conscious families. Because the pizzas are baked at home rather than in the store, Papa Murphy's is permitted to accept food stamps. This allows the firm to attract customers that might not otherwise be able to afford a restaurant-quality pizza.
Claire's nearly 3,000+ locations target young women with inexpensive jewelry, accessories, and ear piercings. The strategy has worked: Claire's has over three thousand locations and has stores in 95% of US shopping malls.
Providing indoor seating creates expenses for fast food restaurants. Checkers Drive In keeps its costs low by not offering indoor seating. Checkers targets drive-thru customers and offers them big burgers at rock-bottom prices.

Another important point is that the nature of the narrow target market varies across firms that use a focused cost leadership strategy. In some cases, the target market is defined by demographics. Claire's, for example, seeks to appeal to young women by selling inexpensive jewelry, accessories, and ear piercings. Claire's use of a focused cost leadership strategy has been very successful; the firm has more than three thousand locations and has stores in 95% of US shopping malls.

In other cases, the target market is defined by the sales channel used to reach customers. Most pizza shops offer sit-down service, delivery, or both. In contrast, Papa Murphy's sells pizzas that customers cook at home. Because these inexpensive pizzas are baked at home rather than in the store, the law allows Papa Murphy's to accept food stamps as payment. This allows Papa Murphy's to attract customers that might not otherwise be able to afford a prepared pizza. In contrast to most fast-food restaurants, Checkers Drive In is a drive-through-only operation. To serve customers quickly, each store has two drive-thru lanes: one on either side of the building. Checkers saves money in a variety of ways by not offering indoor seating to its customers—Checkers's buildings are cheaper to construct, its utility costs are lower, and fewer employees are needed. These savings allow the firm to offer large burgers at very low prices and still remain profitable.

The Nature of the Focused Differentiation Strategy

Focused differentiation is the second of the two focused strategies. A focused differentiation strategy requires offering unique features that fulfill the demands of a narrow market (Table 6.7). As with a focused low-cost strategy, narrow markets are defined in different ways in different settings. Some firms using a focused differentiation strategy concentrate their efforts on a particular sales channel, such as selling over the internet only. Others target particular demographic groups. One example is Breezes Resorts, a company that caters to couples without children. The firm operates seven tropical resorts where vacationers are guaranteed that they will not be annoyed by loud and disruptive children.

Firms that compete based on uniqueness and target a narrow market are following a focused differentiation strategy. Several examples of firms pursuing a focused differentiation strategy are illustrated below.

Table 6.7 Focused Differentiation

Examples of Firms Pursuing a Focused Differentiation Strategy
Whole Foods Market focuses on selling natural and organic products. The supermarket's reputation for high prices has led to a wry nickname—"Whole Paycheck"—but a sizable number of consumers are willing to pay a premium in order to feel better about the food they are buying. Amazon, a broad cost leader, owns Whole Foods.
At Build-A-Bear Workshop, customers enjoy an interactive process of designing and assembling teddy bears. Build-A-Bear customers are willing to pay a premium price because they receive a unique, hands-on experience rather than simply buying a stuffed toy.
You can buy a cinnamon roll cheaper elsewhere, but Cinnabon's pricey pastries are so delicious that sugar-obsessed snackers line up to buy them. Perhaps in a nod to Cinnabon's strategy, the brand is owned by a parent company named Focus Brands.
The dedication of Mercedes-Benz to cutting-edge technology, styling, and safety innovations has made the firm's vehicles prized by those who are wealthy enough to afford them.

While a differentiation strategy involves offering unique features that appeal to a variety of customers, the need to satisfy the desires of a narrow market means that the pursuit of uniqueness is often taken to the proverbial "next level" by firms using a focused differentiation strategy. Thus the unique features provided by firms following a focused differentiation strategy are often specialized.

When it comes to uniqueness, few offerings can top Kopi Luwak coffee beans. High-quality coffee beans often sell for $10 to $15 a pound. In contrast, Kopi Luwak coffee beans sell for hundreds of dollars per pound (Cat's Ass Coffee, n.d.). This price is driven by the rarity of the beans and their rather bizarre nature. As noted in an article in the New York Times, these beans are found in the droppings of the civet, a nocturnal, furry, long-tailed catlike animal that prowls Southeast Asia's coffee-growing lands for the tastiest, ripest coffee cherries. The civet eventually excretes the hard, indigestible innards of the fruit—essentially, incipient coffee beans—though only after they have been fermented in the animal's stomach acids and enzymes to produce a brew described as smooth, chocolaty and devoid of any bitter aftertaste (Onishi, 2010).

Although many consumers consider Kopi Luwak to be disgusting, a relatively small group of coffee enthusiasts has embraced the coffee, making it a profitable product. This illustrates the essence of a focused differentiation strategy—effectively serving the specialized needs of a niche market can create great riches.

Larger niches are served by Whole Foods Market and Mercedes-Benz. Although most grocery stores devote a section of their shelves to natural and organic products, Whole Foods Market works to sell such products exclusively. For customers, the large selection of organic goods comes at a steep price. Indeed, the supermarket's reputation for high prices has led to a wry nickname—"Whole Paycheck"—but a sizable number of consumers are willing to pay a premium to feel better about the food they buy.

Figure 6.8: Janis Joplin's musical tribute to Mercedes-Benz underscores the allure of the brand.

The dedication of Mercedes-Benz to cutting-edge technology, styling, and safety innovations has made the firm's vehicles prized by those who are rich enough to afford them. This appeal has existed for many decades. In 1970, acid-rocker Janis Joplin recorded a song called "Mercedes Benz" that highlighted the automaker's allure.

Since then Mercedes-Benz has used the song in several television commercials. Here is Joplin's song "Mercedes Benz:" https://youtu.be/-H7YULkiLIA

Developing a Focused Differentiation Strategy at Augustino LoPrinzi Guitars and Ukuleles

Augustino LoPrinzi Guitars and Ukuleles in Clearwater, Florida, builds high-end custom instruments. The founder of the company, Augustino LoPrinzi, has been a builder of custom guitars for five decades. While a reasonably good mass-produced guitar can be purchased elsewhere for a few hundred dollars, LoPrinzi's handmade models start at $1,100, and some sell for more than $10,000. The firm's customers have included professional musicians such as Dan Fogelberg, Leo Kottke, Herb Ohta (Ohta-San), Lyle Ritz, Andrés Segovia, and B. J. Thomas. Their instruments can be found at http://www.augustinoloprinzi.com. We asked Augustino about his firm (Short, 2007).

Question:

Were there other entrepreneurial opportunities you considered before you began making guitars?

Augustino Loprinzi:

I originally thought of pursuing a career in commercial art, but I found my true love was in classical guitar building. I was trained by my father to be a barber from a very young age, and after my term in the service, I opened a barbershop.

Question:

What is the most expensive guitar you've ever sold?

Loprinzi:

$17,500.

Question:

How old were you when you started your first business in the guitar industry?

Loprinzi:

I was in my early twenties.

Question:

How did you get your break with more famous customers?

Loprinzi:

I think word of mouth had a lot to do with it.

Advantages and Disadvantages of the Focused Strategies

Each generic strategy offers advantages that firms can potentially leverage to enhance their success as well as disadvantages that may undermine their success. In the case of focus differentiation, one advantage is that very high prices can be charged. Indeed, these firms often price their wares far above what is charged by firms following a differentiation strategy (Table 6.8). Recreational Equipment Inc. (REI), for example, commands a hefty premium for its outdoor sporting goods and clothes that feature name brands, such as The North Face and Marmot. Nat Nast's focused differentiation strategy centers on selling men's silk camp shirts with a 1950s retro flair. These shirts retail for more than $100. Focused cost leaders such as Checkers Drive In do not charge high prices like REI and Nat Nast do, but their low cost structures enable them to enjoy healthy profit margins.

A second advantage of using a focus strategy is that firms often develop tremendous expertise about the goods and services that they offer. In markets such as camping equipment where product knowledge is important, rivals and new entrants may find it difficult to compete with firms following a focus strategy.

Using one of the focus strategies offers firms important advantages and disadvantages. Below we illustrate a few examples in relation to an industry where many different types of focus exist—sporting goods.

Table 6.8 Executing a Focus Strategy

Advantages
High prices can be charged. Recreational Equipment Incorporated (REI), for example, commands a premium for their outdoor sporting goods and clothes that feature name brands such as The North Face and Marmot.
Firms using a focused strategy often develop great expertise about the good or service being sold. Thus, customers may gravitate toward a specialty camping shop in order to learn how to best take advantage of limited vacation time.

Disadvantages
Limited demands exist for specialized goods and services, so every potential sale counts.
The area of focus may be taken over by others or even disappear over time. Many gun stores went out of business after large retailers such as Walmart started carrying an array of firearms.
Other firms may provide an even narrower focus. An outdoor sporting goods store, for example, might lose business to a store that focuses solely on ski apparel because the latter can provide more guidance about how skiers can stay warm and avoid broken bones.

In terms of disadvantages, the limited demand available within a niche can cause problems. First, a firm could find its growth ambitions stymied. Once its target market is being well served, expansion to other markets might be the only way to expand, and this often requires developing a new set of skills. Also, the niche could disappear or be taken over by larger competitors. Many gun stores have struggled and even gone out of business since Walmart and sporting goods stores such as Academy Sports and Bass Pro Shops have started carrying an impressive array of firearms.

Figure 6.9: In contrast to tacky Hawaiian souvenirs, the quality of Kamaka ukuleles makes them a favorite of ukulele phenom Jake Shimabukuro and others who are willing to pay $1,000 or more for a high-end instrument.

Finally, damaging attacks may come not only from larger firms but also from smaller ones that adopt an even narrower focus. A sporting goods store that sells camping, hiking, kayaking, and skiing goods, for example, might lose business to a store that focuses solely on ski apparel because the latter can provide more guidance about how skiers can stay warm and avoid broken bones.

Strategy at the Movies

Zoolander

One man's trash is another man's fashion? That's what fashion mogul Jacobim Mugatu was counting on in the comedy Zoolander. In his continued effort to be the most cutting-edge designer in the fashion industry, Mugatu developed a new line of clothing inspired "by the streetwalkers and hobos that surround us." His new product line, Derelicte, characterized by dresses made of burlap and parking cones and pants made of garbage bags and tin cans, was developed for customers who valued the uniqueness of his...eclectic design. Emphasizing unique products is typical of a company following a differentiation strategy; however, Mugatu targeted a very specific set of customers. Few people would probably be enticed to wear garbage for the sake of fashion. By catering to a niche target market, Mugatu went from a simple differentiation strategy to a focused differentiation. Mugatu's Derelicte campaign in Zoolander is one illustration of how a particular firm might develop a focused differentiation strategy.

Section Video

Focused Strategy [03:47]

The video for this lesson explains that focused strategies concentrate on a narrow segment of the total market.

You can view this video here:
https://www.youtube.com/watch?v=cSMD6MoNeBo&feature=emb_logo.

References

Cat's Ass Coffee. http://www.catsasscoffee.com.

Onishi, N. (2010, April). From dung to coffee brew with no aftertaste. *New York Times.* http://www.nytimes.com/2010/04/18/world/asia/18civetcoffee.html?pagewanted=all.

Porter, M. E. (1980). *Competitive strategy: Techniques for analyzing industries and competitors.* Free Press.

Short, J. C. (2007). A touch of the masters' hands: An interview with Augustino and Donna Loprinzi. *Journal of Applied Management and Entrepreneurship*, 12, 103–109.

Image Credits

Figure 6.9: Surfsupusa. "Jake Shimabukuro performing in Joshua Tree, California in 2007." Public Domain. Retrieved from https://upload.wikimedia.org/wikipedia/commons/f/fc/Jake_Shimabukuro.jpg.

Music Credits

Columbia Records. (1971). Mercedes Benz – Janis Joplin. All Rights Reserved. Provided to YouTube by Sony Music Entertainment. https://youtu.be/-H7YULkiLIA.

Video Credits

Gregg Learning. (2018, June 14). *Focused strategy* [Video]. YouTube. https://www.youtube.com/watch?v=cSMD6MoNeBo&feature=emb_logo.

6.6 Best-Cost Strategy

Firms that charge relatively low prices and offer substantial differentiation are following a best-cost strategy. This strategy is difficult to execute, but it is also potentially very rewarding. Several examples of firms pursuing a best-cost strategy are illustrated below.

Table 6.9 Best-Cost Strategy

Examples of Firms Pursuing a Best-Cost Strategy
Southwest Airlines provides low cost flights to vacation destinations such as San Antonio, San Diego, and Orlando. While many airlines make passengers feel like cattle loaded onto a truck, Southwest creates fun by, for example, getting children excited about visiting Sea World when they see this custom Shamu plane design.
Target offers extremely competitive prices, but the firm also differentiates itself from other discount retailers by carrying products from trendy designers such as Michael Graves, Isaac Mizrahi, Fiorruci, and Universal Thread.
Chipotle Mexican Grill relies on organic ingredients to create very tasty burritos that are sold at prices comparable to those of fast-food restaurants. When noon arrives, many hungry people prefer to spend their lunch dollars on a top-shelf burrito rather than a greasy burger combo meal.
Pabst Blue Ribbon is offered at an extremely low price and its taste (or lack thereof) is comparable to other inexpensive beers. PBR enjoys brand loyalty, however, due to its high name recognition. The frequent appearance of PBR's well-known logo on signs, t-shirts, and other merchandise has helped make PBR an enduring favorite among beer consumers with light wallets.

The Challenge of Following a Best-Cost Strategy

Some executives are not content to have their firms compete based on offering low prices or unique features. They want it all! Firms that charge relatively low prices and offer substantial differentiation are following a best-cost strategy (Table 6.9). This strategy is difficult to execute in part because creating unique features and communicating to customers why these features are useful generally raises a firm's costs of doing business. Product development and advertising can both be quite expensive. However, firms that manage to implement an effective best-cost strategy are often very successful.

Target appears to be following a best-cost strategy. The firm charges prices that are relatively low among retailers while at the same time attracting trend-conscious consumers by carrying products from famous designers, such as Michael Graves, Isaac Mizrahi, Fiorucci, Universal Thread, and others. This is a lucrative position for Target, but the position is under attack from all sides. Cost leader Walmart charges lower prices than Target. This makes Walmart a constant threat to steal the thriftiest of Target's customers. Focus differentiators such as Anthropologie that specialize in trendy clothing and home furnishings can take business from Target in those areas. Deep discounters such as T. J. Maxx and Marshalls offer another viable alternative to shoppers because they offer designer clothes and furnishings at closeout prices. A firm such as Target that uses a best-cost strategy also opens itself up to a wider variety of potentially lethal rivals.

Developing a Best-Cost Strategy at Plain Ivey Jane

According to government statistics, women are 60% less likely than men to become entrepreneurs. Meanwhile, succeeding within the specialty fashion retailing market is notoriously difficult. These trends do not worry Sarah Reeves, a young entrepreneur and 2007 graduate of Auburn University who is rapidly becoming a key player within the Austin, Texas, retail scene by offering high-end fashion at low prices.

Figure 6.10: The success recent college graduates have as entrepreneurs have may inspire other recent graduates to become entrepreneurs.

Sarah describes Plain Ivey Jane as "the go-to place for women who want to elevate their wardrobes. We offer high end designer names at a discount, and the new overstocked apparel is handpicked from over 70 different brands to offer exactly what Austin needs at a price every girl can afford. To pair with your fabulous new wardrobe, Plain Ivey Jane carries accessories from undiscovered local artisans." We asked Reeves to discuss her firm (Ketchen & Short).

Question:

Can you tell us a little about your Plain Ivey Jane concept?

Sarah Reeves, Owner:

Plain Ivey Jane sells overstock from Anthropologie, Urban Outfitters, Bloomingdales, and other high-end and small designers. Although I buy from the same designers as the big and famous retailers, our dresses and accessories are sold at a fraction of their prices.

Question:

What differentiates your boutique from competitors?

Reeves:

I'm one of the lowest-priced retailers in the shopping district that people in Austin call the Second Street area. My niche in the fashion retailing business is that my merchandise is overstock from great brands. There's maybe one other business in Austin that sells overstock. What makes my concept different is that it has the feel of a high-end retail store versus a basement feel of the typical discount retailer.

Question:

Do have a lot of regular customers?

Reeves:

Yes. Once people find out what I offer, they're in here all the time. I see the same group of people every few months, but getting in new faces is the challenge. I think a lot of people walk by and assume that our clothes are expensive, but nothing could be further from the truth.

Question:

Were you fearful of starting your own business so young?

Reeves:

No, I figured this was a great time since I had nothing to lose. I thought getting it out of my system now was a good idea, and it was a good time since I was able to get a great deal on my lease. With the downturn in the economy, the time was right for my lower-priced strategy.

Question:

What would you say is the biggest key to success for a small business?

Reeves:

Flexibility. Rolling with the punches and definitely the ability to follow up with people. I thought that people who owned their own business must know what they are doing, but many people don't. At this point, I prefer to do everything myself. At least I can blame myself when things go wrong.

Another key is networking with other small-business owners. A lot of the other boutique owners nearby have become close friends. I learn what works for them and what might possibly apply to my concept.

Many firms would like to use a best cost strategy but struggle to meet the strategy's dual requirements of charging low prices and providing differentiation features. One way to help make the best cost strategy a reality is to use a business model that slashes fixed costs. Amazon.com, for example, can charge low prices in part because it does not have to absorb the overhead involved in operating stores. Similarly, some talented chefs are pursuing a best cost strategy by operating food trucks and thereby avoiding the overhead required to run a restaurant such as rent and utilities. Several examples are illustrated below.

Table 6.10 Driving toward a Best-Cost Strategy

Driving toward a Best-Cost Strategy by Reducing Overhead
For about the same price as a Subway or Jimmy John's sandwich, Counter Culture in Austin, Texas, provides vegan offerings such as their Garbanzo "Tuna" sandwich.
PBJ's offer unique sandwiches with organic peanut butter at the heart of many of their creations. The traditional PB and J is a staple nationwide, but customers will travel far to get the "Hot Hood" with Challah bread, black cherry jam, jalapeño, applewood-smoked bacon, and PBJ's peanut butter for only $5.50.
Owners Kahala and Kat founded Ninja Plate Lunch in Portland, Oregon, to offer large portions of delectable Hawaiian foods such as pulled pork for only around $5.
In the smash hit graphic novel *Tales of Garçon: The Franchise Players*, the Tapas Taxi takes the concept of a cheap taxi ride to a new level by also offering passengers a variety of "tapas." These Spanish snacks are top shelf, of course!

Pursuing the Best-Cost Strategy through a Low-Overhead Business Model

One route toward a best-cost strategy is for a firm to adopt a business model whose fixed costs and overhead are very low relative to the costs that competitors are absorbing (Table 6.10). The internet has helped make this possible for some firms. Amazon, for example, can charge low prices in part because it does not have to endure the expenses that firms such as Walmart and Target do in operating many hundreds of stores. Meanwhile, Amazon offers an unmatched variety of goods. This combination has made Amazon the unquestioned leader in e-commerce.

Another example is Netflix. This firm is able to offer customers a far greater variety of movies and charge lower prices than video rental stores by conducting all its business over the internet and via mail. Netflix's best-cost strategy has been so successful that $10,000 invested in the firm's stock in May 2006 was worth more than $1,050,000 in May 2020, fourteen years later (Forbes, 2020).

Moving toward a best-cost strategy by dramatically reducing expenses is also possible for firms that cannot rely on the internet as a sales channel. Owning a restaurant requires significant overhead costs, such as rent and utilities. Some talented chefs are escaping these costs by taking their food to the streets. Food trucks that serve high-end specialty dishes at very economical prices are becoming a popular trend in cities around the country. In Portland, Oregon, a food truck called the Viking Soul Food offers Norwegian food at low prices. Another Portland food truck is The Good and Evil Wrap Company, whose unique and inexpensive wraps center on specialty foods. Beyond keeping costs low, the mobility of food trucks offers important advantages over a traditional restaurant. Some food trucks set up outside big-city nightclubs, for example, to sell party goers a late-night snack before they head home.

Figure 6.11: Hey Cupcake! in Austin, Texas, is a low-overhead bakery that has become a delicious success.

A best cost strategy offers some important advantages and disadvantages.

Table 6.11 Executing a Best Cost Strategy

Advantages	Disadvantages
Best cost can attract both the cost-conscientious buyer and one looking for better quality than the low cost leader.	Trying to achieve best cost can result in not having low enough prices to attract the cost-conscious buyer.
Best cost can also result in the best value for the buyer.	Neither achieving a low enough price nor sufficient differentiation can result in accomplishing neither, and getting "stuck in the middle."

Key Takeaway

- A best-cost strategy can be an effective business-level strategy to the extent that a firm offers differentiated goods and services at relatively low prices.

Exercises

1. What is an example of an industry in which you think a best-cost strategy could be successful? How would you differentiate a company to achieve success in this industry?
2. What is an example of a firm following a best-cost strategy near your college or university?

References

Ketchen, D. J., & Short, J. C. Forthcoming. The discount diva: An interview with Sarah Reeves. *Journal of Applied Management and Entrepreneurship.*

Forbes. (n.d.). *Netflix (NFLX)*. [Infographic]. https://www.forbes.com/companies/netflix/#bf246018541f.

Image Credits

Figure 6.10: Mentadgt. "Two Women Looking and Pointing at Macbook Laptop." Pexels license. Retrieved from https://www.pexels.com/photo/two-women-looking-and-pointing-at-macbook-laptop-1569076.

Figure 6.11: Bench, Evan. "Hey Cupcake!" CC BY 2.0. Retrieved from https://flic.kr/p/5W7uPu.

Video Credits

Gregg Learning. (2018, June 15). *Best-Cost provider strategy* [Video]. YouTube. https://www.youtube.com/watch?v=zOaMXfFHzwQ&feature=emb_logo.

6.7 Stuck in the Middle

A firm is said to be stuck in the middle if it does not offer features that are unique enough to convince customers to buy its offerings and its prices are too high to effectively compete based on price. Firms that are stuck in the middle generally perform poorly because they lack a clear market or competitive pricing. Several examples of such firms are illustrated below.

Table 6.12 Stuck in the Middle

Examples of Firms that are Stuck in the Middle
Arby's signature roast beef sandwiches are neither cheaper than other fast food nor are they standouts in taste.
Sears and their famous catalog once dominated US retailing, but the failure to cultivate customers among newer generations and prices that are higher than those of rivals have severely wounded the company. Sears filed for bankruptcy in 2018.
Electronics retailer Circuit City found itself squeezed by the superior service offered by rival Best Buy and the cheaper prices charged on electronics by Walmart and Target. Headquartered in Richmond, Virginia, the firm went bankrupt in 2009 after sixty years in business.
Kmart's "Blue Light Specials" that alert shoppers to a deeply discounted item reflect the firm's long-running effort to be a cost leader. But emerging on the losing end of a price war with Walmart sent the firm into bankruptcy. Struggling to survive, it has closed most of its stores.

Stuck in the Middle: Neither Inexpensive nor Differentiated

Some firms fail to effectively pursue one of the generic strategies. A firm is said to be stuck in the middle if it does not offer features that are unique enough to convince customers to buy its offerings, and its prices are too high to compete effectively based on price (Table 6.11). Arby's appears to be a good example. Arby's signature roast beef sandwiches are neither cheaper than other fast-food sandwiches nor standouts in taste. Firms that are stuck in the middle generally perform poorly because they lack a clear market or competitive pricing.

Doing Everything Means Doing Nothing Well

Michael Porter has noted that strategy is as much about executives deciding what a firm is not going to do as it is about deciding what the firm is going to do (Porter, 1996). In other words, a firm's business-level strategy should not involve trying to serve the varied needs of different segments of customers in an industry. No firm could possibly pull this off.

Figure 6.12: This illustration from 1887 captures the lesson of Aesop's fable "The Miller, His Son, and Their Ass"—a lesson that executives need to follow.

The fable, *The Miller, His Son, and Their Ass*, told by the ancient Greek storyteller Aesop helps illustrate this idea. In this tale, a miller and his son were driving their ass (donkey) to market for sale. They soon encountered a group of girls who mocked them for walking instead of riding. The father then told his son to ride the animal. Not long after, father and son overheard a man claim that young people had no respect for the elderly. On hearing this opinion, the father told the boy to dismount the animal and he began to ride. They progressed a short distance farther and met a company of women and children. Several of the women suggested that it was both ridiculous and lazy for the father to ride while the young son was forced to walk alone; once again the two changed positions. Another bystander suggested that they could not believe that the man was the owner of the beast, judging from the way it was weighed down. In fact, it would make more sense for the man and his son to carry the ass. On hearing this, the father and his son tied the animal's legs together and carried it on a pole. As they crossed a bridge near town, the townspeople began to gather and laugh at the unorthodox sight. The noise and the chaos frightened the beast, leading it to thrash around until it tumbled into the river. With tongue in cheek, we note that the moral of the story is that if you try to please everyone, you may lose your ass (Short & Ketchen, 2005).

Getting Outmaneuvered by Competitors

In many cases, firms become stuck in the middle not because executives fail to arrive at a well-defined strategy but because firms are simply outmaneuvered by their rivals. After six decades as an electronics retailer, Circuit City went out of business in 2009. The firm had simply lost its appeal to customers. Rival electronics retailer

Best Buy offered comparable prices to Circuit City's prices, but the former offered much better customer service. Meanwhile, the service offered by discount retailers such as Walmart and Target on electronics was no better than Circuit City's, but their prices were better.

The results were predictable–customers who made electronics purchases based on the service they received went to Best Buy, and value-driven buyers patronized Walmart and Target. Circuit City's demise was probably inevitable because it lacked a competitive advantage within the electronics business. Although Target was on the winning end of this battle, Target executives need to worry that their firm could become stuck in the middle between Walmart's better prices on one side and the trendiness of specialty shops on the other.

IBM's personal computer business offers another example. IBM tried to position its personal computers via a differentiation strategy. In particular, IBM's personal computers were offered at high prices, and the firm promised to offer excellent service to customers in return. Unfortunately for IBM, rivals such as Dell were able to provide equal levels of service while selling computers at lower prices. Nothing made IBM's computers stand out from the crowd, and the firm eventually exited the business.

Figure 6.13: Netflix and Redbox have left video rental stores such as Movie Gallery and Blockbuster stuck in the middle. Blockbuster filed for bankruptcy in late 2010.

At its peak in the mid-2000's, Blockbuster operated approximately 9,000 video rental stores. By 2010, the firm filed for bankruptcy. This rapid demise can be traced to the firm becoming outmaneuvered by Netflix. When Netflix began offering inexpensive DVD rentals through the mail, customers defected in droves from Blockbuster and other video rental stores such as Movie Gallery. Netflix customers were delighted by the firm's low prices, vast selection, the convenience of not having to visit a store to select and return videos, and were among the first to transition to streaming movies. The low price strategy of RedBox also hurt the firm.

Blockbuster was stuck in the middle—its prices were higher than those of Redbox and Netflix, and Netflix's service was superior. Once individuals lacked a compelling reason to be Blockbuster customers, the firm's fate was sealed. As of 2020 Blockbuster operated one store!

Key Takeaway

- When executing a business-level strategy, a firm must not become stuck in the middle between viable generic business-level strategies by neither offering unique features nor competitive pricing.

Exercises

1. What is an example of a firm that you would consider to be "stuck in the middle"? What would your advice be to the executives in charge of this firm?
2. Research a company that has gone bankrupt or otherwise stopped operations in the past decade because their strategy was "stuck in the middle" of otherwise viable generic business-level strategies. Could its demise have been prevented?

References

Porter, M. E. (1996). What is strategy? *Harvard Business Review*, reprint 96608.

Short, J. C., & Ketchen, D. J. (2005). Using classic literature to teach timeless truths: An illustration using Aesop's fables to teach strategic management. *Journal of Management Education, 29*(6), 816–832.

Image Credits

Figure 6.12: Crane, Walter. "Illustration for 'The Man That Pleased None.'" Public Domain. Retrieved from https://upload.wikimedia.org/wikipedia/commons/a/a5/Can%27t_please_everyone2.jpg.

Figure 6.13: Stu pendousmat. "A Blockbuster location in Moncton." CC BY-SA 3.0. Retrieved from https://upload.wikimedia.org/wikipedia/commons/3/35/BlockbusterMoncton.JPG.

6.8 Conclusion

This chapter explains generic business-level strategies that executives select to keep their firms competitive. Executives must select their firm's source of competitive advantage by choosing to compete based on low-cost versus more expensive features that differentiate their firm from competitors. In addition, targeting either a narrow or broad market helps firms further understand their customer base. Based on these choices, firms will follow broad cost leadership, broad differentiation, focused cost leadership, or focused differentiation strategies. Another potentially viable business strategy, best cost, exists when firms offer relatively low prices while still managing to differentiate their goods or services on some important value-added aspects. All firms pursuing a best cost strategy can fall victim to being "stuck in the middle" by not offering unique features or competitive prices.

Exercises

1. Divide your class into four or eight groups, depending on the size of the class. Each group should select a different industry. Find examples of each generic business-level strategy for your industry. Discuss which strategy seems to be the most successful in your selected industry.
2. This chapter discussed Target and other retailers. If you were assigned to turn around a struggling retailer such as Kmart, what actions would you take to revive the company?

Chapter 7: Innovation Strategies

Learning Objectives

After reading this chapter, you should be able to understand and articulate answers to the following questions:

1. What is Entrepreneurial Orientation?
2. Why should companies innovate?
3. What are the four types of innovation?
4. What are the four stages of the product life cycle and crossing the chasm?
5. What are the ways firms might cooperate with their competitors?

7.1 Introduction

A firm's philosophy toward innovation greatly impacts the business-level/competitive strategies that it pursues. Having an entrepreneurial orientation stimulates a firm toward innovation, improving its products and services and launching new product lines. Innovation can open new markets for a company, and being the first mover to launch a new product or service can be an advantage over competitors, but not always. There are four types of innovation that depend on if existing or new markets are reached or if existing or new technology is used. Firms may also find it advantageous to cooperate at certain levels, such as through a joint venture, strategic alliance, merger, acquisition co-location, or co-opetition.

Innovation is important in strategic management. A firm must be improving its products and services or developing new ones to stay competitive. Business level strategy will not be able to sustain any competitive advantage by sitting still. As firms implement corporate and international strategies, discussed in the next two chapters, cooperative and co-opetition measures help companies obtain resources and capabilities needed to innovate and enter new markets.

7.2 Entrepreneurial Orientation

A famous Nike slogan encourages people to "just do it!" For people and organizations that have developed an entrepreneurial orientation (EO), "just do it!" is a way of life. While often associated with starting new ventures, an EO can be very valuable to established organizations as well. Below we describe each of the three characteristics associated with an EO: innovativeness, proactiveness, and risk-taking.

An additional two characteristics were later added—competitive aggressiveness and autonomy. However, these two dimensions of EO have been subject to much debate and are omitted for the purposes of this text.

Table 7.1 Understanding Entrepreneurial Orientation

Term	Definition	Example
Innovativeness	The tendency to pursue novel ideas, creative processes, and experimentation.	3M has built its business around its mission statement: to solve unsolved problems innovatively. 3M employs over 7,000 researchers and more than 118,000 patents as of 2019, adding more than 4,000 patents annually. 3M's innovativeness has led it to develop thousands of products (such as Post-it notes and Scotch tape) that are sold in almost 200 countries.
Proactiveness	The tendency to anticipate and act on future opportunities rather than rely solely on existing products and services.	Proactive Communications Inc. lives up to its name by focusing on emerging and unusual opportunities. The firm embraces contracts in war zones and natural disaster areas that are often avoided by other telecommunications firms.
Risk Taking	The tendency to take bold actions rather than being cautious.	Richard Brandson's launching of Virgin Galactic—a company that plans to offer suborbital space flights to commercial passengers—reflects his love of high-risk, high-reward ventures.

The Value of Thinking and Acting Entrepreneurially

When asked to think of an entrepreneur, people typically offer examples such as Elon Musk, Oprah Winfrey, Jeff Bezos, Kylie Jenner, and Mark Zuckerberg —individuals who have started their own successful businesses from the bottom up that generated a lasting impact on society. But entrepreneurial thinking and doing are not limited to those who begin in their garage with a new idea, financed by family members or personal savings. Some people in large organizations are filled with passion for a new idea, spend their time championing a new product or service, work with key players in the organization to build a constituency, and then find ways to acquire the needed resources to bring the idea to fruition.

Entrepreneurship within an organization is called intrapreneurship. Companies often grow by offering new services or launching new products. Rather than acquire another company that provides that product or service, they develop it themselves. This is a method of strategy implementation called internal development. To maximize opportunities for intrapreneurship, companies need employees with a high entrepreneurial orientation.

Thinking and behaving entrepreneurially can help a person's career as well. Some enterprising individuals successfully navigate through the environments of their respective organizations and maximize their own career prospects by identifying and seizing new opportunities (Table 7.1) (Certo et al., 2009).

Section Video

The relationship between entrepreneurial orientation and organizational performance [01:02]

The video for this lesson discusses the relationship between entrepreneurial orientation and organizational performance.

You can view this video here: https://youtu.be/Iru7IBqc3Vk.

In the 1730s, Richard Cantillon used the French term entrepreneur, or literally "undertaker," referring to those who undertake self-employment while also accepting an uncertain return. In subsequent years, entrepreneurs have also been referred to as innovators of new ideas (Thomas Edison), individuals who find and promote new combinations of factors of production (Bill Gates' bundling of Microsoft's products), and those who exploit opportunistic ideas to expand small enterprises (Mark Zuckerberg at Facebook). The common elements of these conceptions of entrepreneurs are that they do something new and that some individuals can make something out of opportunities that others cannot.

Entrepreneurial orientation (EO) is a key concept when executives are crafting strategies in the hopes of doing something new and exploiting opportunities that other organizations cannot exploit. EO refers to the processes, practices, and decision-making styles of organizations that act entrepreneurially (Lumpkin & Dess, 1996). Any organization's level of EO can be understood by examining how it stacks up relative to three dimensions: (1) innovativeness, (2) proactiveness, (3) and risk taking. These dimensions are also relevant to individuals.

Entrepreneurial orientation (EO) is measured at both the organizational and the individual levels. The characteristics of an entrepreneurial company noted in Table 7.1 also apply to individuals. Those individuals who are less risk averse, innovative thinkers, and competitive tend to have a higher EO and greater success at starting a business. Online EO assessment tools exist for those wishing to determine their EO. It is important to note that EO is not only related to high tech start-ups. Starting a lawn care business or a beauty shop are very valid and necessary entrepreneurial ventures, and will have a better chance of success if an entrepreneur possesses a higher EO.

Figure 7.1: *As a college student, Michael Dell demonstrated an entrepreneurial orientation by starting a computer-upgrading business in his dorm room. He later founded Dell Inc.*

Innovativeness

Innovativeness is the tendency to pursue creativity and experimentation. Some innovations build on existing skills to create incremental improvements, while more radical innovations require brand-new skills and may make existing skills obsolete. Either way, innovativeness is aimed at developing new products, services, and processes. Those organizations that are successful in their innovation efforts tend to enjoy stronger performance than those that do not.

Figure 7.2: *Ben & Jerry's displays innovativeness by developing a series of offbeat and creative flavors over time.*

Known for efficient service, FedEx has introduced its Smart Package, which allows both shippers and recipients to monitor package location, temperature, and humidity. This type of innovation is a welcome addition to FedEx's lineup for those in the business of shipping delicate goods, such as human organs. How do firms generate these types of new ideas that meet customers' complex needs? Perennial innovators 3M and Google have found a few possible answers. 3M sends nine thousand of its technical personnel in thirty-four countries into customers' workplaces to experience firsthand the kinds of problems customers encounter each day. Google's two most popular features of its Gmail, thread sorting and unlimited e-mail archiving, were first suggested by an engineer who was fed up with his own e-mail woes. Both 3M and Google allow employees to use a portion of their work time on projects of their own choosing with the goal of creating new innovations for the company. This latter example illustrates how multiple EO dimensions—in this case, autonomy and innovativeness—can reinforce one another.

Proactiveness

Proactiveness is the tendency to anticipate and act on future needs rather than reacting to events after they unfold. A proactive organization is one that adopts an opportunity-seeking perspective. Such organizations act in advance of shifting market demand and are often either the first to enter new markets or "fast followers" that improve on the initial efforts of first movers.

Consider Proactive Communications, an aptly named small firm in Killeen, Texas. From its beginnings in 2001, this firm has provided communications in hostile environments, such as Iraq and areas impacted by Hurricane Katrina. Being proactive in this case means being willing to don a military helmet or sleep outdoors—activities often avoided by other telecommunications firms. By embracing opportunities that others fear, Proactive's executives have carved out a lucrative niche in a world that is technologically, environmentally, and politically turbulent (Choi, 2008).

Risk Taking

Risk taking refers to the tendency to engage in bold rather than cautious actions. Starbucks, for example, made a risky move when it introduced a new instant coffee called VIA Ready Brew. Instant coffee has long been viewed by many coffee drinkers as a bland drink, but Starbucks decided that the opportunity to distribute its product in a different format was worth the risk of associating its brand name with instant coffee.

Although a common belief about entrepreneurs is that they are chronic risk takers, research suggests that entrepreneurs do not perceive their actions as risky; most take action only after using planning and forecasting to reduce uncertainty (Simon et al., 2000). However, uncertainty seldom can be fully eliminated. A few years ago, Jeroen van der Veer, CEO of Royal Dutch Shell PLC, entered a risky energy deal in Russia's Far East. At the time, van der Veer conceded that it was too early to know whether the move would be successful (Certo et al., 2008). Just six months later, however, customers in Japan, Korea, and the United States had purchased all the natural gas expected to be produced there for the next twenty years. If political instabilities in Russia and challenges in pipeline construction do not dampen returns, Shell stands to post a hefty profit from its 27.5% stake in the venture.

Building an Entrepreneurial Orientation

Steps can be taken by executives to develop a stronger entrepreneurial orientation throughout an organization and by individuals to become more entrepreneurial themselves. For executives, it is important to design organizational systems and policies to reflect the three dimensions of EO. As an example, how an organization's compensation systems encourage or discourage these dimensions should be considered. Is taking sensible risks rewarded through raises and bonuses, regardless of whether the risks pay off, for example, or does the compensation system penalize risk taking? Other organizational characteristics such as corporate debt level may influence EO. Do corporate debt levels help or impede innovativeness? Is debt structured in such a way as to encourage risk taking? These are key questions for executives to consider.

Examination of some performance measures can assist executives in assessing EO within their organizations. To understand how the organization develops and reinforces autonomy, for example, top executives can administer employee satisfaction surveys and monitor employee turnover rates. Organizations that effectively develop autonomy should foster a work environment with high levels of employee satisfaction and low levels of turnover. Innovativeness can be gauged by considering how many new products or services the organization has developed in the last year and how many patents the firm has obtained.

Similarly, individuals should consider whether their attitudes and behaviors are consistent with the three dimensions of EO. Is an employee making decisions that focus on competitors? Does the employee provide executives with new ideas for products or processes that might create value for the organization? Is the employee making proactive as opposed to reactive decisions? Each of these questions will aid employees in understanding how they can help to support EO within their organizations.

Section Video

Entrepreneurial Orientation [02:39]

The video for this lesson explains the importance of entrepreneurial orientation.

You can view this video here: https://youtu.be/L6MqD5Hhs2U.

Key Takeaway

- Building an entrepreneurial orientation can be valuable to organizations and individuals alike in identifying and seizing new opportunities. Entrepreneurial orientation consists of three dimensions: (1) innovativeness, (2) proactiveness, and (3) risk taking.

References

Certo, S. T., Connelly, B., & Tihanyi, L. (2008). Managers and their not-so-rational decisions. *Business Horizons*, 51(2), 113–119.

Certo, S. T., Moss, T. W., & Short, J. C. (2009). Entrepreneurial orientation: An applied perspective. *Business Horizons*, 52, 319–324.

Choi, A. S. (2008, April 16). PCI builds telecommunications in Iraq. *Bloomberg Businessweek*. https://www.bloomberg.com/news/articles/2008-04-15/pci-builds-telecommunications-in-iraq.

Lumpkin, G. T., & Dess, G. G. (1996). Clarifying the entrepreneurial orientation construct and linking it to performance. *Academy of Management Review*, 21, 135–172.

Simon, M., Houghton, S. M., & Aquino, K. (2000). Cognitive biases, risk perception, and venture formation: How individuals decide to start companies. *Journal of Business Venturing*, 14, 113–134.

Image Credits

Video Credits

The Oxford Review. (2018, December 16). *The relationship between entrepreneurial orientation and organisational performance* [Video]. YouTube. https://youtu.be/Iru7IBqc3Vk.

Tarlan Golkar. (2020, April 28). *Entrepreneurial orientation* [Video]. YouTube. https://youtu.be/L6MqD5Hhs2U.

7.3 Why Innovate?

Innovate to Capture Markets

Innovation can be a key strategy to stay ahead of the competition. Firms who sit still, perhaps satisfied with their success, will find themselves outsmarted and left behind, with the competition winning over their customers. An innovation strategy coupled with an entrepreneurial orientation will help keep customers buying.

Automobile manufacturers have used this strategy of innovation for years. Every year, a new innovation of nearly all car models comes out in the fall season. The new year's model may look a little sleeker, have some safety improvements, or be connected to the internet. These innovations entice consumers to sell their existing car to have the latest look or technology. Cell phone manufacturers do the same thing, coming out with a new model almost annually, with more memory, a faster processor, a better camera, etc. Where would Apple be today if they stopped with the iPhone 7? Drug manufacturers are always innovating by doing research to find the next medication to slow Alzheimers or cure skin cancer.

Figure 7.3: Apple's iPhone has continued to boast new features since its initial release in 2007.

Innovation is usually the strategy of new startup IT companies. A new software program is developed or a new way to do interactive video games can meet a need or provide a service that consumers want. It is the innovation strategy that propels the organization forward. This is not to discount the need for a business-level/competitive strategy such as focused differentiation, as the firm still needs to determine their business-level strategy and optimize it. Often a differentiation strategy, broad or focused, can be used for a new, innovative product or service and priced high, because the competitors are few or none.

Joseph Addison, an eighteenth century poet, is often credited with coining the phrase "He who hesitates is lost."

This proverb is especially meaningful in today's business world. It is easy for executives to become paralyzed by the dizzying array of competitive and cooperative moves available to them. Given the fast-paced nature of most industries today, hesitation can lead to disaster. Some observers have suggested that competition in many settings has transformed into hyper-competition, which involves very rapid and unpredictable moves and countermoves that can undermine competitive advantages. Under such conditions, it is often better to make a reasonable move quickly rather than hoping to uncover the perfect move through extensive and time-consuming analysis.

The importance of continuous learning also contributes to the value of adopting a "get moving" mentality. Success in business often depends on executives learning from a series of competitive and cooperative moves, not on selecting ideal moves. In some circumstances, advantages can be created by taking decisive action, even if the decision is based on incomplete information.

Blue Ocean Strategy

It is best to win without fighting. – Sun-Tzu, The Art of War

A **blue ocean strategy** involves creating a new, untapped market rather than competing with rivals in an existing market (Kim & Mauborgne, 2004). This strategy follows the approach recommended by the ancient master of strategy Sun-Tzu in the quote above. Instead of trying to outmaneuver its competition, a firm using a blue ocean strategy tries to make the competition irrelevant (Table 7.2). Baseball legend Wee Willie Keeler offered a similar idea when asked how to become a better hitter: "Hit 'em where they ain't." In other words, hit the baseball where there are no fielders rather than trying to overwhelm the fielders with a ball hit directly at them.

Nintendo openly acknowledges following a blue ocean strategy in its efforts to invent new markets. Perrin Kaplan, Nintendo's former vice president of marketing and corporate affairs for Nintendo of America noted in an interview, "We're making games that are expanding our base of consumers in Japan and America. Yes, those who've always played games are still playing, but we've got people who've never played to start loving it with titles like Nintendogs, Animal Crossing and Brain Games. These games are blue ocean in action" (Rosmarin, 2006). Other examples of companies creating new markets include FedEx's invention of the fast-shipping business and eBay's invention of online auctions.

Firms that create blue oceans experience a temporary competitive advantage. How long "temporary competitive advantage lasts" in a blue ocean strategy depends on the particular combination of internal and external factors that create the opportunity in the first place. Needless to say, the more successful a company is with a blue ocean strategy, the more attention they will receive from potential competitors who want to get into a position to benefit from those same advantages.

It's a big ocean out there! When pursuing a blue ocean strategy, executives try to create and exploit vast untapped markets rather than competing directly with rivals. See several examples of firms following a blue ocean strategy below.

Table 7.2 Blue Ocean Strategy

Examples of Firms Following a Blue Ocean Strategy
The interactive features of Nintendo's Wii transformed playing video games from a hobby for the hardcore gamers into a treasured family event.
Coffee shops were once the domain of old men, insomniacs, and chain-smoking urban hipsters. By reinventing coffee shops, Starbucks made the $4 latte a must-have item for college students, business people, and soccer moms.
At a time when cars were only for the wealthy, Henry Ford envisioned cars that were affordable to the typical American. Ford priced his vehicles so that his assembly line workers could afford them.
eBay's invention of online auctions extended the auction experience—and the chance to buy that rare Elvis plate—to anyone with internet access.
Golf can be frustrating to even skilled players. Callaway's creation of the Big Bertha club with an oversized head made golf appealing to a whole new set of weekend warriors.
A classy, affordable wine for novice wine drinkers? Casella wines (maker of Yellow Tail) steered clear of wine snobs and sommeliers and instead created fun and simple tastes for the masses.

Key Takeaway

- Firms must continually innovate to stay ahead of the competition. Blue ocean strategy is one way that innovation can capture new markets.

Exercises

1. Find a key trend from the general environment and develop a blue ocean strategy that might capitalize on that trend.

References

Kim, W. C., & Mauborgne, R. (2004, October). Blue ocean strategy. *Harvard Business Review*, 76–85.

Rosmarin, R. (2006, February 7). Nintendo's new look. *Forbes*. Retrieved from http://www.forbes.com/2006/02/07/xbox-ps3-revolution-cx_rr_0207nintendo.html.

7.4 Types of Innovation

Being a First Mover: Advantages and Disadvantages

The idea of first mover advantage borrows from military strategy. For example, Confederate general Nathan Beford Forrest's attack plan was simply stated as "git thar fustest with the mostest."

When confronted by a poisonous snake, should you strike first or wait for the serpent to make a move? Each option has advantages and disadvantages. In business, being a first mover might allow a firm to "rattle its rivals, but a first move might also attract the "venom" of skeptical customers. Below are examples of successful—and not so successful—first movers.

Table 7.3 First Mover Advantage

First Move Successes	First Move Failures
At a time when using most personal computers required memorizing obscure commands, Apple pioneered a user-friendly interface. The firm gained a reputation as an innovator that persists today.	Netscape's web browser was a first mover that was popular in the 1990s, but nearly extinct by 2002 with the advent of Microsoft's competitive offering—Internet Explorer.
Following World War II, Japan's economy laid in ruin. Ibuka Masaru used this backdrop to build a company that would be the first in Japan to create tape recorders and transistors radios. The company he pioneered—Sony—has now been a fierce electronics competitor for over a half century.	Not all of Apple's first moves were triumphs. The firm's disastrous attempt to pioneer the personal digital assistant market through its "Newton" created a loss of around one-hundred million dollars.

A famous cliché contends that "the early bird gets the worm." Applied to the business world, the cliché suggests that certain benefits are available to a first mover into a market that will not be available to later entrants. A first-mover advantage exists when making the initial move into a market allows a firm to establish a dominant position that other firms struggle to overcome (Table 7.3). For example, Apple's creation of a user-friendly, small computer in the early 1980s helped fuel a reputation for creativity and innovation that persists today. Kentucky Fried Chicken (KFC) was able to develop a strong bond with Chinese officials by being the first Western restaurant chain to enter China. Today, KFC is the leading Western fast-food chain in this rapidly growing market. Genentech's early development of biotechnology allowed it to overcome many of the pharmaceutical industry's traditional entry barriers such as financial capital and distribution networks and become a profitable firm. Decisions to be first movers helped all three of these firms to be successful in their respective industries (Ketchen et al., 2004).

On the other hand, a first mover cannot be sure that customers will embrace its offering, making a first move inherently risky. Apple's attempt to pioneer the personal digital assistant market, through its Newton, was a financial disaster. The first mover also bears the costs of developing the product and educating customers. Others may learn from the first mover's successes and failures, allowing them to cheaply copy or improve the product. Sony, Samsung, and others have built on Apple's knowledge and creation of Airpods to offer competing products. In many industries, knowledge diffusion and public-information requirements make such imitation increasingly easy.

One caution is that first movers must be willing to commit sufficient resources to follow through on their pioneering efforts. RCA and Westinghouse were the first firms to develop active-matrix LCD display technology for flat computer screens, but their executives did not provide the resources needed to sustain the products spawned by this technology. Today, these firms are not even players in this important business segment that supplies screens for notebook computers, camcorders, medical instruments, and many other products.

To date, the evidence is mixed regarding whether being a first mover leads to success. One research study of 1,226 businesses over a fifty-five-year period found that first movers typically enjoy an advantage over rivals for about a decade, but other studies have suggested that first moving offers little or no advantages.

Perhaps the best question that executives can ask themselves when deciding whether to be a first mover is, how will this move provide my firm with a sustainable competitive advantage? First moves that build on strategic resources such as patented technology are difficult for rivals to imitate and thus are likely to succeed. For example, Pfizer enjoyed a monopoly in the erectile dysfunction market for five years with its patented drug Viagra before two rival products (Cialis and Levitra) were developed by other pharmaceutical firms. Despite facing stiff competition, Viagra continues to raise about $1.9 billion in sales for Pfizer annually.

In contrast, E-Trade Group's creation of the portable mortgage seemed doomed to fail because it did not leverage strategic resources. This innovation allowed customers to keep an existing mortgage when they move to a new home. Bigger banks could easily copy the portable mortgage if it gained customer acceptance, undermining E-Trade's ability to profit from its first move.

Incremental Innovation

Innovation can be classified into four types:

1. Incremental Innovation
2. Disruptive Innovation
3. Architectural Innovation
4. Radical Innovation

The type of innovation is dependent on two factors:

1. Market – does the innovation create a new market, or address the existing market?
2. Technology – does the innovation use a new technology or an existing technology?

Figure 7.4 illustrates the four types of innovation.

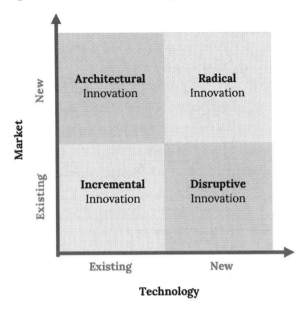

Figure 7.4: Types of Innovation

Incremental innovation can be described as making improvements on an existing product or service. The improvements are based on using existing technology and are directed at the existing market. In the automobile industry, the improvements made each year to the newest model of car are incremental innovations. No new markets are formed, and existing technology is used to make the car better. Some other examples of incremental innovation are presented in Table 7.4

Incremental innovation occurs when the innovation uses existing technology to improve a product or service that addresses the existing market.

Table 7.4 Incremental Innovation

Incremental Innovation Examples
Each new version of Apple's iPhone that comes out is typically incremental innovation. iPhone features such as the camera and processor are tweaked to make an improvement over the previous model.
When Gillette went from a single razor blade to a double blade, to now up to six blades, no new markets were created, as the same consumers are buying the blades. There was no new technology involved, so this is incremental innovation.
Residential washers and dryers have been transitioning from top-loading to side-loading, and can handle larger loads. This incremental innovation used existing technology and created no new markets, but stimulated demand for more purchasers at higher prices.

Disruptive Innovation

Some firms have the opportunity to shake up their industry by introducing a disruptive innovation–an innovation that conflicts with, and threatens to replace, traditional approaches to competing within an industry (Table 7.5). Disruptive innovation occurs when a new product or service engages the existing market with a new technology. The iPad has proved to be a disruptive innovation since its introduction by Apple in 2010. Many individuals quickly abandoned clunky laptop computers in favor of the sleek tablet format offered by the iPad. And as a first mover, Apple was able to claim a large share of the market.

Disruptive innovations occur when firms introduce offerings that are so unique and superior that they threaten to replace traditional approaches. Existing markets are disrupted by new technology. Sometimes a disruption is so significant that it may create a "blue ocean" by finding a new market while disrupting an existing one, but this is not typically the case. A number of disruptive innovations are illustrated below.

Table 7.5 Shaking the Market with Disruptive Innovations

Disruptive Innovation Examples
Tablet computers disrupted laptop sales due to their versatility and portability. Reading books can be awkward on traditional computers, but user-friendly devices such as iPad, Nook, and Kindle are popular platforms for aggressive textbook publishers.
Many stores that relied on compact disc sales went under when downloadable digital media disrupted the music industry. Years earlier, CDs supplanted vinyl albums and cassette tapes due to their superior durability and quality. Music subscriptions such as Spotify and Apple Music are new technologies that are replacing downloads. What new technology will replace subscriptions?
Digital cameras disrupted the photography industry by offering instant gratification and eliminating the cost of getting film developed. Excellent cameras on cell phones have since disrupted the digital camera industry.
The emergence of personal computers disrupted the dominance of mainframes and made it possible for everyone to have a computer in their home.
LED lights are a newer technology that have been disrupting and replacing incandescent lights by selling to the existing market.

The iPad story is unusual because most disruptive innovations are not overnight sensations. Typically, a small group of customers embrace a disruptive innovation as early adopters and then a critical mass of customers builds over time. An example is digital cameras. Few photographers embraced digital cameras initially because they took pictures slowly and offered poor picture quality relative to traditional film cameras. As digital cameras improved, they gradually won over almost everyone that takes pictures. Executives who are deciding whether to pursue a disruptive innovation must first make sure that their firm can sustain itself during an initial period of slow growth.

Architectural Innovation

Architectural innovation occurs when new products or services use existing technology to create new markets and/or new consumers that did not purchase that item before. For example, the smart watch used existing cell phone technology and was repackaged into a watch. This opened up a new market of purchasers by repackaging an existing technology. Typically, firms alter the architecture of the product to create a new product that opens up sales to new markets. Table 7.5 provides more examples.

Firms can innovate by using and adapting existing technology to create new products or services that address new markets and consumers. This type of innovation is called Architectural Innovation, since the architecture of a product is changed to create a new product to reach new markets.

Table 7.6 Architectural Innovation

Architectural Innovation Examples
Peloton, maker of home exercise bicycles, packages the already existent bicycle, internet, and communications technologies to create new consumers who otherwise would not buy an exercise bike.
Some firms have leveraged solar cell technology to produce small outdoor ground lighting. This created a whole new group of consumers who decorate their yards with these environmentally friendly lights.
Copiers used to be large and expensive machines purchased only for large offices. Canon and others reconfigured these copiers to be small and usable on desktops, creating a whole new market of people buying personal copier/printers.

Radical Innovation

When new products or services are developed using new technology that open up new markets, the result is called radical innovation. The airplane is a good example of a radical innovation. It used an entirely new aeronautical technology to open up a whole new market for people traveling. Traveling across the country was unthinkable for most people, when it would take weeks to go from New York to San Francisco by car or train. Table 7.6 provides more examples of radical innovation.

Innovation that uses new technology to reach new consumers is radical innovation. Firms who are successful with a new product of service using radical innovation may then employ a strategy of incremental innovation to continually improve the product or service and generate more sales.

Table 7.7 Radical Innovation

Radical Innovation Examples
Pharmaceutical researchers often produce a new product that is radical innovation. They come up with a new combination of chemicals to treat a medical condition that attracts new buyers. Aricept, a new medication co-marketed by Eisai and Pfizer that helps treat the symptoms of Alzheimer's disease, has opened new markets.
Apple's Airpods can be considered a radical innovation. Apple developed an earpiece that could use wireless technology to receive Bluetooth signals. Now we see people with Airpods in their ears when before they would not have been using wired earphones nearly as much.
The Magnetic Resonance Imaging (MRI) machine uses electro-magnetic forces instead of x-rays to produce images internal to the body. This new technology generated a brand new market for hospitals to buy these machines for new diagnostic capabilities.

Footholds

Footholds are useful for rock climbers looking for sure footing to ascend a difficult mountain, as well as firms hoping to gain positions in new markets. In business, a foothold is a small position that a firm intentionally establishes within a market in which it does not yet compete. Examples of the use of footholds are illustrated below.

Table 7.8 Footholds

Foothold Examples
Swedish furniture seller IKEA opens just a single store when entering a new country, such as their first store in Japan. This foothold is used as a showcase to establish IKEA's brand; more stores are opened once brand recognition is gained in the country.
Pharmaceutical giant Merck obtained a foothold by purchasing SmartCells Inc.,–a company developing a possible new diabetes treatment.
The foothold concept also applies to warfare. Many armies establish new positions in geographic territories that they have not previously occupied. The Allied Forces used Normandy, France, as their foothold to advance on German forces during World War II.

Similarly, some organizations find it valuable to establish footholds in certain markets. Within the context of business, a **foothold** is a small position that a firm intentionally establishes within a market in which it does not yet compete (Upson et al., 2012). Swedish furniture seller IKEA is a firm that relies on footholds. When IKEA enters a new country, it opens just one store. This store is then used as a showcase to establish IKEA's brand. Once IKEA gains brand recognition in a country, more stores are established (Hambrick & Fredrickson, 2005).

Pharmaceutical giants such as Merck often obtain footholds in emerging areas of medicine. In December 2010, for example, Merck purchased SmartCells Inc., a company that was developing a possible new treatment for diabetes. In May 2011, Merck acquired an equity stake in BeiGene Ltd., a Chinese firm that was developing novel cancer treatments and detection methods. Competitive moves such as these offer Merck relatively low-cost platforms from which it can expand if clinical studies reveal that the treatments are effective.

Key Takeaway

- Being the first mover can provide a firm a competitive advantage, but competitors who wait may be the ultimate winners.
- There are four types of innovation that firms employ to increase their strength in the marketplace.

1. Provide an example of a product that, if invented, would work as a disruptive innovation. How widespread would be the appeal of this product?
2. How would you propose to develop a new foothold if your goal was to compete in the fashion industry?

References

Hambrick, D. C., & Fredrickson, J. W. (2005). Are you sure you have a strategy? *Academy of Management Executive, 19*, 51–62.

Johnson, S. (2010, September 25) The genius of the tinkerer. *Wall Street Journal.* http://online.wsj.com/article/SB10001424052748703989304575503730101860838.html.

Ketchen, D. J., Snow, C., & Street, V. (2004). Improving firm performance by matching strategic decision making processes to competitive dynamics. *Academy of Management Executive, 19*(4), 29–43.

Monster Mini Golf, KISS Mini Golf to rock Las Vegas this fall [Press release]. (2011, April 28). Monster Mini Golf website: https://monsterminigolf.com/locations/kiss-las-vegas/?apppush.

Rosmarin, R. (2006, February 7). Nintendo's new look. *Forbes.* http://www.forbes.com/2006/02/07/xbox-ps3-revolution-cx_rr_0207nintendo.html.

Turisas. (n.d.). http://www.turisas.com/site/.

Upson, J., Ketchen, D. J., Connelly, B., & Ranft, A. (2012). Competitor analysis and foothold moves. *Academy of Management Journal 55*(1), 93–110.

Image Credits

7.5 Implementing Innovation

Product Life Cycle and Crossing the Chasm

When innovation creates a new product, it typically goes through four stages within the marketplace. This is true whether it is a high-tech product like a new video game system or a more mundane product like a laundry detergent. The four stages are:

1. Introduction: The product is launched, with the hopes that it catches on. Sales are low.
2. Growth: The product catches on, and sales increase with time. Competitors jump in, but the rivalry among competitors is not really strong yet, and there are plenty of sales for all.
3. Maturity: Sales begin to level out, growth slows, and competition increases. Shake-out occurs, with some competitors leaving the market or being acquired by others.
4. Decline: Sales start declining. More consolidation occurs, with firms looking for exit strategies. A few firms remain.

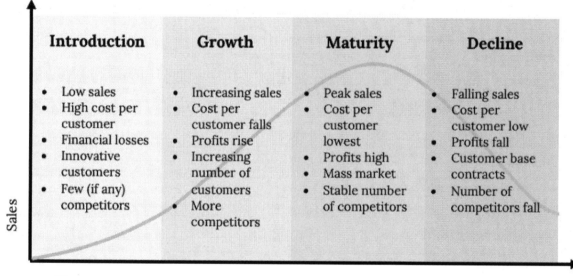

Figure 7.5: Product Life Cycle

Figure 7.5 illustrates these four stages over time. To prevent the decline of their product after the maturity stage, firms will often "relaunch" their product with a new and improved model. Innovation again plays a role, making improvements to the product, so that consumers will purchase the latest model. Prime examples of incremental innovation strategy are Apple's iPhone and car manufacturers, such as Ford and Toyota. In essence, the new model starts the product life cycle all over again. Figure 7.6 illustrates this concept.

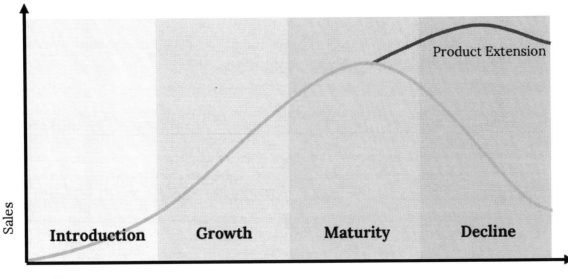

Figure 7.6: Product Life Cycle Extension

Profits generated during the product life cycle also usually follow a traditional pattern. During the research and development phase of the product, the firm is investing funds into the product, generating a negative profit. Losses continue during the introduction phase, when sales are low and marketing expenses are high. Firms tend to recoup their investment in R&D and marketing during the growth phase, with maximum profits at the beginning of the maturity phase. Once competition heats up in the maturity phase, price competition kicks in, and lower prices mean lower profits. Figure 7.7 illustrates the profits during the four phases of the product life cycle.

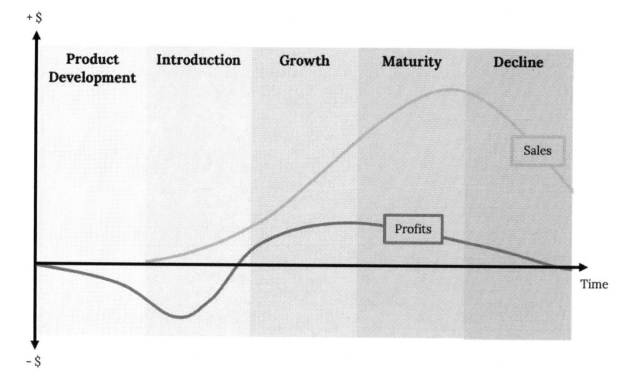

Figure 7.7: Profits During the Product Life Cycle

Another phenomenon that occurs in the innovation process with new technology is called "crossing the chasm." When a new technology is launched, often there are technology innovators/enthusiasts who will purchase the new technology to check it out. A few more, called early adopters, will also want to try out the new product. But how does the firm get the product into the mainstream market? How do they get it to catch on? This can often be challenging. Can the product make the leap to the mainstream? This is called "crossing the chasm," and often requires a different marketing approach.

Figure 7.6 illustrates this concept, breaking down the market into customer segments. Innovators and early adopters make up about 15% of the market. Firms must determine a business strategy for each segment of the market. If they cannot convince the early majority to buy their product, the product fails. Google Glass is an example of a product that did not cross the chasm. Eyeglasses connected to the internet were quite an innovative product, projecting internet sites in front of the eyes, or allowing the wearer to take pictures. Its true usefulness, however, was questionable, and aside from some early adopters, it failed.

Where is the electric car in this technology adoption life cycle? The purchase of electric cars has certainly been growing. Have they crossed the chasm? In 2019, approximately 2.2% of all car sales were electric plug-in vehicles (Coran, 2019). Electric vehicles still need to cross the chasm. The lack of charging stations across the nation and concern for running out of battery are limiting factors preventing the electric vehicle from selling to the early majority.

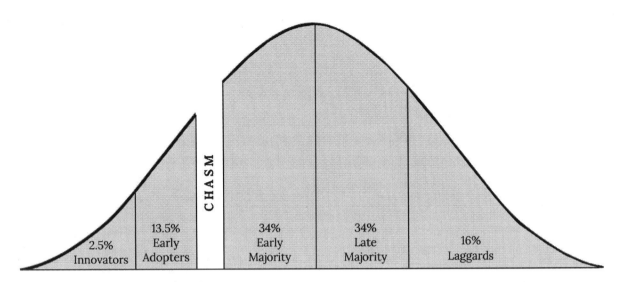

Figure 7.8: Technology Adoption Life Cycle

Making Cooperative Moves

Franklin Roosevelt once quipped, "Competition has been shown to be useful up to a certain point and no further, but cooperation, which is the thing we must strive for today, begins where competition leaves off." We illustrate four commonly used cooperative moves used by firms below.

Table 7.9 Making Cooperative Moves

Joint Ventures	Joint ventures involve two or more organizations that contribute to the creation of a new entity. For example, Hong Kong Disneyland is a joint venture between the government of Hong Kong and the Walt Disney Company. While the park consists of Disney mainstays such as Main Street, USA, Fantasyland, Adventureland, and Tomorrowland, the park also incorporates elements of Chinese culture such as adherence to the rules of Feng Shui—a set of aesthetic design principles believed to promote positive energy.
Strategic Alliances	Strategic alliances are cooperative arrangements governed by contract between two or more organizations that do not involve creating new entities. For example, a strategic alliance between Merck and PAREXEL International Corporation was formed with the goal of collaborating on biotechnology efforts known as biosimilars—a term used to describe subsequent versions of innovative drugs.
Mergers and Acquisitions	Mergers and Acquisitions combine two organizations into one. Mergers typically occur between like-size firms. Sprint and T-Mobile merged to create a stronger force in the wireless communications industry. Acquisitions usually are done by larger companies acquiring smaller ones, as when Google acquired Fitbit.

In addition to competitive moves, firms can benefit from cooperating with one another. Cooperative moves such as forming joint ventures and strategic alliances may allow firms to enjoy successes that might not otherwise be reached (Table 7.9). This is because cooperation enables firms to share rather than duplicate resources and to learn from one another's strengths. Firms that enter cooperative relationships take on risks, however, including the loss of control over operations, possible transfer of valuable secrets to other firms, and possibly being taken advantage of by partners (Ketchen et al., 2004).

Joint Ventures

A **joint venture** is a cooperative arrangement that involves two or more organizations with each contributing to the creation of a new entity. The partners in a joint venture share decision-making authority, control of the operation, and any profits that the joint venture earns.

Sometimes two firms create a joint venture to deal with a shared opportunity. A joint venture was created between Merck and Sun Pharmaceutical Industries Ltd., an Indian pharmaceutical company. The purpose of the joint venture was to create and sell generic drugs in developing countries. In a press release, a top executive at Sun stressed that each side has important strengths to contribute: "This joint venture reinforces [Sun's] strategy of partnering to launch products using our highly innovative delivery technologies around the world. Merck has an unrivaled reputation as a world leading, innovative, research-driven pharmaceutical company" (Merck, 2011). Both firms contributed executives to the new organization, reflecting the shared decision making and control involved in joint ventures.

In other cases, a joint venture is designed to counter a shared threat. Brewers SABMiller and Molson Coors Brewing Company created a joint venture called MillerCoors that combines the firms' beer operations in the United States. Miller and Coors found it useful to join their US forces to better compete against their giant rival Anheuser-Busch, while the two parent companies still remain separate. The joint venture controls a wide array of brands, including Miller Lite, Coors Light, Blue Moon Belgian White, Coors Banquet, Foster's, Henry Weinhard's, Icehouse, Keystone Premium, Leinenkugel's, Killian's Irish Red, Miller Genuine Draft, Miller High Life, Milwaukee's Best, Molson Canadian, Peroni Nastro Azzurro, Pilsner Urquell, and Red Dog. This diverse portfolio makes MillerCoors a more potent adversary for Anheuser-Busch than either Miller or Coors would be on their own.

Strategic Alliances

A **strategic alliance** is a cooperative arrangement between two or more organizations that does not involve the creation of a new entity. For example, Twitter formed a strategic alliance with Yahoo! Japan. The alliance involved relevant Tweets appearing within various functions offered by Yahoo! Japan (Rao, 2011). The alliance simply involves the two firms collaborating through a contractual relationship as opposed to creating a new entity together.

The pharmaceutical industry is the location of many strategic alliances. In another example, Merck and PAREXEL International Corporation engaged in a strategic alliance. Within this alliance, the two companies collaborate on biotechnology efforts known as biosimilars. This alliance could be quite important to Merck

Figure 7.9: ExxonMobil, a merger of Exxon and Mobil oil companies

because the global market for biosimilars has been predicted to rise significantly (PRWeb, 2011).

Mergers and Acquisitions

Another way for firms to cooperate to the advantage of both firms and their stockholders is through **mergers**. Two firms decide to combine into one entity, often gaining strength in the market. The merger of T-Mobile and Sprint is a prime example. As the number three and four players in the wireless communications industry, combining forces makes the new firm a much stronger competitor against AT&T and Verizon. Sometimes both firms' identities remain in the name of the new company, such as with the merger of Exxon and Mobil oil companies to ExxonMobil. At other times, only one of the firm's names remains, or a new name is selected for the merged companies.

Whereas mergers typically occur with like-size companies, **acquisitions** are usually done by the larger firm acquiring the smaller firm. The end result is basically the same, with two companies combining into one. Sometimes the acquired firm is absorbed into the acquiring company, but sometime it retains its identity. Besides combining the strengths of both organizations with the intent of having a stronger performing company, mergers and acquisitions reduce the number of competitors in the industry.

Mergers and acquisitions are not without risk, however. According to a Harvard Business Review report, the failure rate of mergers and acquisitions is between 70% – 90% (Lakelet Capital, 2019). Often, the enthusiasm of the perceived benefits of the merger overshadow the challenges of adapting two organizational cultures into one, the total costs of the venture, and/or dealing with different technical systems. Also, an acquisition is a quick way to increase firm revenues, a metric that may incentivize CEOs to acquire another firm without adequate due diligence, creating an agency problem, which is discussed in Chapter 11 on ethics.

Internal Development

Another method to expand a firm is through **internal development.** If a firm wants to add a new product or service line, rather than acquire that expertise by buying a company, the firm can develop that capability themselves. Although this is more of a competitive rather than a cooperative move, this is where a firm's strength of entrepreneurial orientation (EO) comes into play, and when intrapreneurship is important. Instead of acquiring Fitbit, Google could have developed this wearable technology internally by hiring those with the expertise and paying for the research and development for product development to enter this market.

Key Takeaways

- New products and services typically follow a predictable product life cycle, and must be able to "cross the chasm" to attract buyers beyond the early adopters.
- Sometimes it is advantageous for a firm to make a cooperative move with a competitor, with strategies such as a joint venture, strategic alliance, merger, or acquisition. Internal development is also a method to add innovative capability.

Exercises

1. What are examples of firms that "relaunch" their products once in the maturity stage of the product life cycle?
2. Why might local restaurants not be in the position to respond to large franchises or chains? What can local restaurants do to avoid being ruined by chain restaurants?
3. How could a family jewelry store use one of the cooperative moves mentioned in this section?? What type of organization might be a good cooperative partner for a family jewelry store?
4. What are some reasons why a merger between Ford and Volkswagen might fail?

References

Coran, M. (2019, December 6). 2019 was the year electric cars grew up. Quartz. https://qz.com/1762465/2019-was-the-year-electric-cars-grew-up/#:~:text=Electric%20vehicles%20(EVs)%20grabbed%202.2,new%20models%20hit%20the%20road.

Ketchen, D. J., Snow, C., & Street, V. (2004). Improving firm performance by matching strategic decision making processes to competitive dynamics. *Academy of Management Executive, 19*(4) 29-43.

Lakelet Capital. (2019, June 15). Reasons shy mergers & acquisitions fail and succeed. https://lakeletcapital.com/reasons-why-mergers-acquisitions-fail-and-succeed/#:~:text=According%20to%20collated%20research%20and,70%20percent%20and%2090%20percent.

Merck & Co., Inc., and Sun Pharma establish joint venture to develop and commercialize novel formulations and combinations of medicines in emerging markets [Press release]. 2011, April 11. Merck website. Retrieved from https://web.archive.org/web/20110608025556/http://www.merck.com/licensing/our-partnership/sun-partnership.html.

PRWeb, Global biosimilars market to reach US$4.8 billion by 2015, according to a new report by Global Industry Analysts, Inc. [Press release]. 2011, February 15. PRWeb website. Retrieved from http://www.prweb.com/releases/biosimilars/human_growth _hormone/prweb8131268.htm.

Rao, L. 2011, June 14. Twitter announces "strategic alliance" with Yahoo Japan [Blog post]. Techcrunch website. Retrieved from http://www.techcrunch.com/2011/06/14/twitter-announces-firehose-partnership-with-yahoo-japan.

Ritson, M. (2009, October). Should you launch a fighter brand? *Harvard Business Review*, 65–81.

Image Credits

Figure 7.5: Kindred Grey (2020). "Product Life Cycle." CC BY-SA 4.0. Retrieved from https://commons.wikimedia.org/wiki/File:Product_Life_Cycle.png. Adapted from https://marketing-insider.eu/wp-content/uploads/2017/07/Characteristics-of-the-Product-Life-Cycle-Stages-and-their-Marketing-Implications.png.

Figure 7.6: Kindred Grey (2020). "Product Extension and the product life cycle." CC BY-SA 4.0. Retrieved from https://commons.wikimedia.org/wiki/File:Product_Extension_and_the_product_life_cycle.png. Adapted from https://marketing-insider.eu/wp-content/uploads/2017/07/Characteristics-of-the-Product-Life-Cycle-Stages-and-their-Marketing-Implications.png.

Figure 7.7: Kindred Grey (2020). "Difference between profits and sales." CC BY-SA 4.0. Retrieved from https://commons.wikimedia.org/wiki/File:Difference_between_profits_and_sales.png. Adapted from https://marketing-insider.eu/wp-content/uploads/2017/07/Characteristics-of-the-Product-Life-Cycle-Stages-and-their-Marketing-Implications.png.

Figure 7.8: Kindred Grey (2020). "Technology adoption life cycle – breaking the chasm." CC BY-SA 4.0. Retrieved from https://commons.wikimedia.org/wiki/File:Technology_adoption_life_cycle_-_breaking_the_chasm.png. Adapted from http://www.themarketingstudent.com/wp-content/uploads/2017/04/chasm-adoption-lifecycle.jpeg.

Figure 7.9: Unknown Author. "ExxonMobil logo." Public Domain, Trademarked logo. Retrieved from https://commons.wikimedia.org/wiki/File:ExxonMobil_Logo.svg.

7.6 Responding to Innovation in the Market

Executives in many markets must cope with a rapid-fire barrage of attacks from rivals, such as head-to-head advertising campaigns, price cuts, and attempts to grab key customers. If a firm is going to respond to a competitor's move, doing so quickly is important. If there is a long delay between an attack and a response, this generally provides the attacker with an edge. For example, PepsiCo made the mistake of waiting fifteen months to copy Coca-Cola's introduction of Vanilla Coke. In the interim, Vanilla Coke carved out a significant market niche.

In contrast, fast responses tend to prevent such an edge. Pepsi's announcement of a mid-calorie cola introduction was quickly followed by a similar announcement by Coke, signaling that Coke would not allow this niche to be dominated by its longtime rival. Thus, as former General Electric CEO Jack Welch noted in his autobiography, success in most competitive rivalries "is less a function of grandiose predictions than it is a result of being able to respond rapidly to real changes as they occur. That's why strategy has to be dynamic and anticipatory."

So...We Meet Again

Multi-point competition adds complexity to decisions about whether to respond to a rival's moves. With multi-point competition, a firm faces the same rival in more than one market. Cigarette makers R. J. Reynolds (RJR) and Philip Morris, for example, square off not only in the United States, but also in many countries around the world. When a firm has one or more multi-point competitors, executives must realize that a competitive move in a market can have effects not only within that market, but also within others. When RJR started using lower-priced cigarette brands in the United States to gain customers, Philip Morris responded in two ways. The first response was cutting prices in the United States to protect its market share. This started a price war that ultimately hurt both companies. Second, Philip Morris started building market share in Eastern Europe where RJR had been establishing a strong position. This combination of moves forced RJR to protect its market share in the United States and neglect Eastern Europe.

If rivals are able to establish mutual forbearance, then multi-point competition can help them be successful. Mutual forbearance occurs when rivals do not act aggressively because each recognizes that the other can retaliate in multiple markets. Southwest Airlines and United Airlines compete in some, but not all markets. United announced plans to form a new division that would move into some of Southwest's other routes. Southwest CEO Herb Kelleher publicly threatened to retaliate in several shared markets. United then backed down, and Southwest had no reason to attack. The result was better performance for both firms. Similarly, in hindsight, both RJR and Philip Morris probably would have been more profitable had RJR not tried to steal market share in the first place. Thus, recognizing and acting on potential forbearance can lead to better performance through firms not competing away their profits, while failure to do so can be costly.

Responding to a Disruptive Innovation

When a rival introduces a disruptive innovation that conflicts with the industry's current competitive practices, such as the emergence of online stock trading, executives choose from among three main responses. First, executives may believe that the innovation will not replace established offerings entirely and thus, may choose to focus on their traditional modes of business while ignoring the disruption. For example, many traditional bookstores such as Barnes & Noble did not consider book sales on Amazon to be a competitive threat until Amazon began to take market share from them. Second, a firm can counter the challenge by attacking along a different dimension. For example, Apple responded to the direct sales of cheap computers by Dell and Gateway by adding power and versatility to its products. The third possible response is to simply match the competitor's move. Merrill Lynch, for example, confronted online trading by forming its own Internet-based unit. Here the firm risks cannibalizing its traditional business, but executives may find that their response attracts an entirely new segment of customers.

Fighting Brands: Get Ready to Rumble

A firm's success can be undermined when a competitor tries to lure away its customers by charging lower prices for its goods or services. Such a scenario is especially scary if the quality of the competitor's offerings is reasonably comparable to the firm's. One possible response would be for the firm to lower its prices to prevent customers from abandoning it. This can be effective in the short term, but it creates a long-term problem. Specifically, the firm will have trouble increasing its prices back to their original level in the future because charging lower prices for a time will devalue the firm's brand and make customers question why they should accept price increases.

The creation of a fighting brand is a move that can prevent this problem. A **fighting brand** is a lower-end brand that a firm introduces to try to protect the firm's market share without damaging the firm's existing brands. In the late 1980s, General Motors (GM) was troubled by the extent to which the sales of small, inexpensive Japanese cars were growing in the United States. GM wanted to recapture lost sales, but it did not want to harm its existing brands, such as Chevrolet, Buick, and Cadillac, by putting their names on low-end cars. GM's solution was to sell small, inexpensive cars under a new brand: Geo.

Interestingly, several of Geo's models were produced in joint ventures between GM and the same Japanese automakers that the Geo brand was created to fight. A sedan called the Prizm was built side by side with the Toyota Corolla by the New United Motor Manufacturing Incorporated (NUMMI), a factory co-owned by GM and Toyota. The two cars were virtually identical except for minor cosmetic differences. A smaller car (the Metro) and a compact sport utility vehicle (the Tracker) were produced by a joint venture between GM and Suzuki. By 1998, the US car market revolved around higher-quality vehicles, and the low-end Geo brand was discontinued.

Figure 7.10: The Geo brand was known for its low price and good gas mileage, not for its styling.

Some fighting brands are rather short lived. Merck's failed attempt to protect market share in Germany by creating a fighting brand is an example. Zocor, a treatment for high cholesterol, was set to lose its German patent in 2003. Merck tried to keep its high profit margin for Zocor intact until the patent expired as well as preparing for the inevitable competition with generic drugmakers by creating a lower-priced brand, Zocor MSD. Once the patent expired, however, the new brand was not priced low enough to keep customers from switching to generics. Merck soon abandoned the Zocor MSD brand (Ritson, 2009).

Two major airlines experienced similar futility. In response to the growing success of discount airlines such as Southwest, AirTran, Jet Blue, and Frontier, both United Airlines and Delta Airlines created fighting brands. United launched Ted in 2004 and discontinued it in 2009. Delta's Song had an even shorter existence. It started in 2003 and ended in 2006. Southwest's acquisition of AirTran in 2011 created a large airline that may make United and Delta lament that they were not able to make their own discount brands successful.

Despite these missteps, the use of fighting brands is a time-tested competitive move. For example, very successful fighting brands were launched forty years apart by Anheuser-Busch and Intel. After Anheuser-Busch increased the prices charged by its existing brands in the mid-1950s (Budweiser and Michelob), smaller brewers started gaining market share. In response, Anheuser-Busch created a lower-priced brand: Busch. The new brand won back the market share that had been lost and remains an important part of Anheuser-Busch's brand portfolio today. In the late 1990s, silicon chipmaker Advanced Micro Devices (AMD) started undercutting the prices charged by industry leader Intel. Intel responded by creating the Celeron brand of silicon chips, a brand that has preserved Intel's market share without undermining profits. Wise strategic moves such as the creation of the Celeron brand help explain why Intel ranks thirty-second on Fortune magazine's list of the "World's Most Admired Corporations." Meanwhile, Anheuser-Busch is the second most admired beverage firm, ranking behind Coca-Cola.

Table 7.10 Co-location and Co-opetition

Co-location	Co-location refers to a situation when goods and services offered under different brands are located very close to each other. Noting one common example of co-location, a comedian once joked that La Quinta was Spanish for "Next to Denny's." Both hotels and restaurants are often co-located alongside freeway exits to allow numerous choices for road-weary travelers.
Co-opetition	Co-opetition is a term that refers to the blending of competition and cooperation between two firms. Toyota and General Motors' creation of jointly owned New United Motor Manufacturing incorporated (NUMMI) allowed for collaboration on automobile designs while Toyota and GM continued to compete for market share worldwide. The NUMMI experience also inspired the comedy Gung Ho.

Co-location

Co-location occurs when goods and services offered under different brands are located close to one another. In many cities, for example, theaters and art galleries are clustered together in one neighborhood. Auto malls that contain several different car dealerships are found in many areas. Restaurants and hotels are often located near one another as well. "Big Box Stores" like Target. Staples, Best Buy, Lowes, etc., are almost always found clustered together with other retailers. By providing customers with a variety of choices, a set of co-located firms can attract a bigger set of customers collectively than the sum that could be attracted to individual locations. If a desired play is sold out, a restaurant overcrowded, or a hotel overbooked, many customers simply patronize another firm in the area.

Because of these benefits, savvy executives in some firms co-locate their own brands. The industry that Brinker International competes within is revealed by its stock ticker symbol: EAT. This firm often sites outlets of the multiple restaurant chains it owns on the same street. Marriott's Courtyard and Fairfield Inn often sit side by side. Yum! Brands takes this clustering strategy one step further by locating more than one of its brands—A&W, Long John Silver's, Taco Bell, Kentucky Fried Chicken, and Pizza Hut—within a single store.

Co-opetition

Although competition and cooperation are usually viewed as separate processes, the concept of co-opetition highlights a complex interaction that is becoming increasingly popular in many industries. Ray Noorda, the founder of software firm Novell, coined the term to refer to a blending of competition and cooperation between two firms. For example, drug manufacturers Merck and Roche are rivals in some markets, but the firms are working together to

Figure 7.11: Yum! Co-located brands

develop tests to detect cancer and to promote a hepatitis treatment. NEC, a Japanese electronics company, has three different relationships with Hewlett-Packard Co.: customer, supplier, and competitor. Some units of each company work cooperatively with the other company, while other units are direct competitors. NEC and Hewlett-Packard could be described as "frienemies"—part friends and part enemies.

Toyota and General Motors provide a well-known example of co-opetition. In terms of cooperation, Toyota and GM vehicles were produced side by side for many years at the jointly owned New United Motor Manufacturing Incorporated (NUMMI) in Fremont, California. While Honda and Nissan used wholly owned plants to begin producing cars in the United States, NUMMI offered Toyota a lower-risk means of entering the US market. This entry mode was desirable to Toyota because its top executives were not confident that Japanese-style management would work in the United States. Meanwhile, the venture offered GM the chance to learn Japanese management and production techniques—skills that were later used in GM's facilities. NUMMI offered both companies economies of scale in manufacturing and the chance to collaborate on automobile designs.

Meanwhile, Toyota and GM compete for market share around the world. In recent years, the firms have been the world's two largest automakers, and they have traded the top spot over time.

In their book titled, not surprisingly, Co-opetition, A. M. Brandenberger and B. J. Nalebuff suggest that cooperation is generally best suited for "creating a pie," while competition is best suited for "dividing it up" (Brandenberger & Nalebuff, 1996). In other words, firms tend to cooperate in activities located far in the value chain from customers, while competition generally occurs close to customers. The NUMMI example illustrates this tendency—GM and Toyota worked together on design and manufacturing but worked separately on distribution, sales, and marketing. Similarly, a research study focused on Scandinavian firms found that, in the mining equipment industry, firms cooperated in material development, but they competed in product development and marketing. In the brewing industry, firms worked together on the return of used bottles but not in distribution (Bengtsson & Kock, 2000).

Section Video

Innovation Strategy [04:16]

The video for this lesson explains innovation strategy.

You can view this video here: https://youtu.be/B-tY6citUHw.

Key Takeaway

- Cooperating with other firms is sometimes a more lucrative and beneficial approach than directly attacking competing firms.

1. Divide your class into four or eight groups, depending on the size of the class. Each group should select a different industry. Find examples of competitive and cooperative moves that you would recommend if hired as a consultant for a firm in that industry.
2. What types of cooperative moves could your college or university use to partner with local, national, and international businesses? What benefits and risks would be created by making these moves?
3. If a new alternative fuel was found in the auto industry, what are two ways existing car manufacturers might respond to this disruptive innovation?
4. How might a firm such as Apple computers use a fighting brand?

References

Bengtsson, M., & Kock, S. (2000). "Coopetition" in business networks—to cooperate and compete simultaneously. *Industrial Marketing Management*, 29(5), 411–426.

Brandenberger, A. M., & Nalebuff, B. J. (1996). *Co-opetition*. New York, NY: Doubleday.

Ritson, M. (2009, October). Should you launch a fighter brand? *Harvard Business Review*, 65–81.

Image Credits

Figure 7.10: Rutger van der Maar (2014). "Geo Prizm." CC BY 2.0. Retrieved from https://flic.kr/p/ooQzaF.

Figure 7.11: Cantnot. "Older design of Taco Bell restaurant currently in use, adjacent to sister Yum Brands restaurant KFC, near Burlington." Public Domain. Retrieved from https://en.wikipedia.org/wiki/File:TBOldDesign.JPG.

Video Credits

Kuczmarski Innovation. (2016, May 17). *Innovation strategy* [Video]. YouTube. https://youtu.be/B-tY6citUHw.

7.7 Conclusion

This chapter explains how innovation impacts strategy development. An entrepreneurial orientation helps a firm develop and implement new innovations. Being the first mover can present advantages, but is not without the risk of competitors learning from the first mover and eventually beating them. Executives may also choose a more conservative route by establishing a foothold within an area that can serve as a launching point or by avoiding existing competitors overall by using a blue ocean strategy. There are four types of innovation: incremental, disruptive, architectural, and radical. New products typically follow a predictable product life cycle with four stages: introduction, growth, maturity, and decline. Firms often use incremental innovation to re-launch products with improved features, starting the product life cycle over again. New products and services must "cross the chasm" to get them into the mainstream. Firms may cooperate with competitors through joint ventures, strategic alliances, mergers, and acquisitions, or through co-location and co-opetition. Executives may also react to competitive attacks by using fighting brands. All of these efforts by firms are part of the strategic management process that executives must respond to if they want their companies to be successful.

Exercises

1. Divide your class into four or eight groups, depending on the size of the class. Each group should think of one example for each of the four types of innovation: Incremental, Architectural, Radical, and Disruptive. Report out to the class.
2. Divide your class into four or eight groups, depending on the size of the class. Each group should think of one product or service that launched but did not "cross the chasm." Report out to the class.

Chapter 8: Selecting Corporate-Level Strategies

Learning Objectives

After reading this chapter, you should be able to understand and articulate answers to the following questions:

1. What is corporate-level strategy and how does it differ from business-level strategy?
2. What is vertical integration and what benefits can it provide?
3. What are the three types of diversification and when should they be used?
4. What are four methods that a firm can use to implement its corporate strategy?
5. Why and how might a firm retrench or restructure?
6. What is portfolio planning and why is it useful?

8.1 Introduction

The preceding chapters focused on generic business-level, also referred to as generic competitive strategy: how firms compete head-to-head on products and services they offer. The intent is to develop strategies that provide a competitive advantage, so that buyers will purchase what a business has to offer instead of purchasing from a competitor. However, there are three types of strategy: business-level, corporate-level, and international strategy.

In this chapter, the focus is on corporate-level strategy. Corporate-level strategy is a paradigm shift from business-level strategy. It asks: what businesses should the firm be in, and how can being in those businesses create synergy and improve performance? Diversification is the key in corporate strategy. There are several ways that a corporate diversification strategy can be implemented that will be examined here. The third and final type of strategy following business-level and corporate-level strategies is international strategy, which will be discussed in the next chapter.

8.2 Corporate-Level Strategy Defined

What's the Big Picture at Disney?

Figure 8.1: *Walt Disney remains a worldwide icon five decades after his death.*

Disney's *Avengers: Endgame* movie, released in 2019, was Disney's highest grossing movie of all time. With revenues of over $2 billion, it is one of seven Disney movies to gross over $1 billion. *Frozen II* was the highest grossing animated movie at $1.37 billion (Clark, 2020).

Although Walt Disney was a visionary, even he would have struggled to imagine such enormous numbers when his company was created. In 1923, Disney Brothers Cartoon Studio was started by Walt and his brother Roy in their uncle's garage. The fledgling company gained momentum in 1928 when a character was invented that still plays a central role for Disney today—Mickey Mouse. Disney expanded beyond short cartoons to make its first feature film, *Snow White and the Seven Dwarves*, in 1937.

Following a string of legendary films such as *Pinocchio* (1940), *Fantasia* (1940), *Bambi* (1942), and *Cinderella* (1950), Walt Disney began to diversify his empire. His company developed a television series for the American Broadcasting Company (ABC) in 1954 and opened the Disneyland theme park in 1955. Shortly before its opening, the theme park was featured on the television show to expose the American public to Walt's innovative ideas. One of the hosts of that episode was Ronald Reagan, who twenty-five years later became president of the United States. A larger theme park, Walt Disney World, was opened in Orlando in 1971. Roy Disney died just two months after Disney World opened; his brother Walt had passed in 1966 while planning the creation of the Orlando facility.

The Walt Disney Company began a series of acquisitions in 1993 with the purchase of movie studio Miramax Pictures. ABC was acquired in 1996, along with its very successful sports broadcasting company, ESPN. Two other important acquisitions were made during the following decade. Pixar Studios was purchased in 2006 for $7.4 billion (Stewart, 2011). This strategic move brought a very creative and successful animation company under Disney's control. Three years later, Marvel Entertainment was acquired for $4.24 billion. Marvel was attractive because of its vast roster of popular characters, including Iron Man, the X-Men, the Incredible Hulk, the Fantastic Four, and Captain America. In addition to featuring these characters in movies, Disney could build attractions around them within its theme parks.

With annual revenues in excess of $38 billion, The Walt Disney Company was the largest media conglomerate in the world by 2010. It was active in four key industries. Disney's theme parks included not only its American locations but also joint ventures in France and Hong Kong. A park in Shanghai, China opened in 2016. The theme park business accounted for 28% of Disney's revenues.

Disney's presence in the television industry, including ABC, ESPN, Disney Channel, and ten television stations, accounted for 45% of revenues. Disney's original business, filmed entertainment, accounted for 18% of revenue. Merchandise licensing was responsible for 7% of revenue. This segment of the business included children's books, video games, and 350 stores spread across North American, Europe, and Japan. The remaining 2% of revenues were derived from interactive online technologies. Much of this revenue was derived from Playdom, an online gaming company that Disney acquired in 2010.

Disney continued with more acquisitions, buying Lucasfilm in 2012, Maker Studios in 2015, BAMTech in 2017, and 21st Century Fox in 2019. With the exception of 2017, when there was a slight revenue decline, Disney's revenues have shown consistent, strong growth (Macrotrends, n.d.). Can Disney maintain this trend? Is Disney getting too large to manage effectively? With the COVID-19 pandemic of 2020 shutting down many of Disney's business lines temporarily, should Disney diversify into other industries, and not be so dependent on the entertainment industry for its future success?

Business-level strategy deals directly with how a firm competes in the marketplace. How does the firm get buyers to purchase their products and services as opposed to those of their competitors? Corporate-level strategy considers issues at a broader level of analysis. The word "corporate" does not refer to the legal entity of a corporation, but to the level of strategy higher than direct head-to-head competition. Any size firm can develop corporate-level strategy. The owner of a McDonald's franchise can pursue a corporate strategy, as can the owner of a local plumbing company.

Figure 8.2: Will John Lassiter, Pixar's chief creative officer, be prevented from making more quirky films like Up! by parent company Disney?

Corporate Strategy –Specifies actions taken by the firm to gain a competitive advantage by selecting and managing a group of different businesses in several industries and/or product markets.

In corporate-level strategy, executives seek to answer two basic questions, and then three more detailed questions.

A. What business(es) should we be in?

B. How should we manage the portfolio to achieve synergy/create value?

With respect to the first question A above, what business(es) should we be in, firms must ask:

1. In what stage of the industry value chain should we participate?
2. What range of products and services should we offer?
3. Where geographically should we compete?

All three of these questions should be answered within the context of question B above, how can synergy be achieved?

Synergy in the business context means the cooperation or interaction of two or more business units so that they perform more effectively together than they would if independent. For example, if a larger company acquires a similar smaller company, some of the administrative overhead expenses such as accounting or human resources can be combined and operate more efficiently. Another synergy produced is overall reduced marketing expenses since they can market their products together.

The foundational issue in corporate-level strategy is diversification: how can the organization diversify, and in doing so, create synergy? Diversification can address geographic questions, such as how Disney established theme parks in France, Japan, and China. Also, moving a firm into other industries, outside the home industry, is another way to diversify. Warren Buffet's company Berkshire Hathaway owns businesses as diverse as real estate, insurance, and a railroad. Additionally, a firm may expand into business areas within its value chain, by acquiring suppliers upstream in the supply chain or distributors or retailers downstream. For example, when Disney launched its streaming service Disney+, it diversified downstream in its value chain to control and provide an outlet for the movie content it produced.

The executives in charge of a firm such as The Walt Disney Company must decide whether to remain within their present domains or venture into new ones. In Disney's case, the firm has expanded from its original business (films) and into television, theme parks, cruise lines, and several others. In contrast, many firms never expand beyond their initial choice of industry. Disney executives could consider further diversifying geographically, diversifying into additional industries, and diversifying deeper into its value chain, for example, by acquiring some of its suppliers. In all these considerations, Disney needs to evaluate if and how synergy can be produced.

References

Clark, T. (2020, January 15). The 7 Disney movies of 2019 that made over $1 billion at the box office. *Business Insider*.
https://www.businessinsider.com/disney-movies-with-1-billion-at-box-office-2019-8

Macrotrends. (n.d.). *Disney revenue 2006-2020 | DIS*.
https://www.macrotrends.net/stocks/charts/DIS/disney/revenue.

Standard and Poors. (n.d.) Walt Disney Company. https://www.standardandpoors.com.

Stewart, J. B. (2011, June). A collision of creativity and cash. *New York Times*. http://www.nytimes.com/2011/07/02/business/02stewart.html.

Image Credits

8.3 Diversification

There are a variety of reasons a company may consider diversification. Diversification strategies can help mitigate the risk of a company operating in only one industry. If an industry experiences issues or slows down, being in other industries can help soften the impact. Companies can also diversify within their own industry. There are three types of diversification:

1. **Related Diversification** –Diversifying into business lines in the same industry; Volkswagen acquiring Audi is an example.
2. **Unrelated Diversification** –Diversifying into new industries, such as Amazon entering the grocery store business with its purchase of Whole Foods.
3. **Geographic Diversification** –Operating in various geographic markets, which is the corporate strategy of Starbucks, Target, and KFC.

In all three diversification strategies, the goal is to achieve synergy. How can the firm operate more efficiently and effectively through its diversification efforts?

Three Tests for Diversification

A proposed diversification move must first answer three questions to determine if it should be accepted or rejected (Porter, 1987).

1. How attractive is the industry that a firm is considering entering? Unless the industry has strong profit potential,

entering it may be very risky. Porter's Five Forces Analysis can help with this assessment.

2. How much will it cost to enter the industry? Executives need to be sure that their firm can recoup the expenses that it absorbs in diversifying. When Philip Morris bought 7Up, it paid four times what 7Up was actually worth. Making up these costs proved to be impossible and 7Up was sold less than 10 years later.

3. Will the new unit and the firm be better off? Unless at least one side gains a competitive advantage, diversification should be avoided. In the case of Philip Morris and 7Up, for example, neither side benefited significantly from joining together.

Related Diversification

Related diversification occurs when a firm moves into a new industry that has important similarities with the firm's existing industry or industries (Figure 8.1). Because films and television are both aspects of entertainment, Disney's purchase of ABC is an example of related diversification. Some firms that engage in related diversification aim to develop and exploit a core competency to become more successful. A **core competency** is a skill set that is difficult for competitors to imitate, can be leveraged in different businesses, and contributes to the benefits enjoyed by customers within each business (Prahalad & Hamel, 1990). For example, Newell Rubbermaid is skilled at identifying under-performing brands and integrating them into their three business groups: (1) home and family, (2) office products, and (3) tools, hardware, and commercial products.

Estee Lauder was a pioneer in the cosmetics industry. Estee Lauder summarized her zest for business by noting, "I have never worked a day in my life without selling. If I believe in something, I sell it, and I sell it hard." The company that bears her name has used related diversification and other growth strategies to create over two dozen brands of cosmetics, perfume, skin care, and hair care products. Below we illustrate some of the products that make up the Lauder empire.

Prescriptives offers customizable cosmetics that provide an exact match to the customer's skin tone.

The Lauder empire includes a number of license agreements such as with Donna Karan's **DKNY** Be Delicious perfume.

Smashbox, acquired in 2010, is the cosmetics line of a premier photo studio founded by the great-grandsons of Hollywood cosmetics legend Max Factor.

Estee Lauder's **Sensuous** is one of the perfumes marketed under the Lauder name.

Bumble and bumble provides salon-quality shampoo, conditioner, and other hair care products.

Clinique was the first high-end, allergy-tested, dermatologist-recommended cosmetics brand.

Bobbi Brown (namesake of the celebrated makeup artist) focuses on teaching women to be their own makeup artists.

M.A.C. (Makeup Art Cosmetics) products were originally designed for professional makeup artists but are now available to consumers worldwide.

Aveda's line of high-end botanical spa products was acquired in 1997.

Figure 8.3: Estee Lauder exemplifies related diversification with their ventures into skincare, makeup, and hair care products.

Honda Motor Company provides a good example of leveraging a core competency through related diversification. Although Honda is best known for its cars and trucks, the company actually started out in the motorcycle business. Through competing in this business, Honda developed a unique ability to build small and reliable engines. When executives decided to diversify into the automobile industry, Honda was successful in part because it leveraged this ability within its new business. Honda also applied its engine-building skills in the all-terrain vehicle, lawn mower, and boat motor industries.

Sometimes the benefits of related diversification that executives hope to enjoy are never achieved. Both soft drinks and cigarettes are products that consumers do not need. Companies must convince consumers to buy these products through marketing activities such as branding and advertising. Thus, on the surface, the acquisition of 7Up by Philip Morris seemed to offer the potential for Philip Morris to take its existing marketing skills and apply them within a new industry. Unfortunately, the possible benefits to 7Up never materialized.

Figure 8.4: Honda's related diversification strategy has taken the firm into several businesses, including boat motors.

Unrelated Diversification

"Don't put all your eggs in one basket" is often a good motto for individual investors. By building a portfolio of stocks, an investor can minimize the chances of suffering a huge loss. Some executives take a similar approach. Rather than trying to develop synergy across businesses, they seek greater financial stability for their firms by owning an array of companies. Warren Buffett's Berkshire Hathaway has long enjoyed strong performance by purchasing companies and improving how they are run. Below we illustrate some of the different groups in their very diversified portfolio of firms.

Table 8.1 Unrelated Diversification at Berkshire Hathaway

Berkshire's insurance group includes firms such as General Reinsurance Corporation and GEICO. They maintain capital strength at exceptionally high levels, which gives them an advantage even a caveman could understand.	Berkshire's financial health is also fueled by utilities and energy companies that are part of the MidAmerican Energy Holdings Company.	Their apparel businesses include well-known names such as Fruit of the Loom and Justin Brands.
Building companies include Acme Building Brands, makers of the famous brick, as well as paint company Benjamin Moore & Co.	FlightSafety International Inc. is a Berkshire firm that engages in high-tech training for aircraft and ship operators.	Retail holdings include a number of furniture businesses such as R.C. Willey Home Furnishings, Star Furniture Company, and Jordan's Furniture, Inc.
Hungry for more businesses to manage, Berkshire acquired The Pampered Chef, Ltd.—the largest direct kitchen tools seller—in 2002.	Buffett had a sweet tooth for See's Candies, whom he purchased from the See's family in 1972.	Shareholders were all on board for the purchase of the Burlington Northern Santa Fe Corporation railroad in 2009.

Why would a soft-drink company buy a movie studio? It's hard to imagine the logic behind such a move, but Coca-Cola did just this when it purchased Columbia Pictures for $750 million. This is a good example of unrelated diversification, which occurs when a firm enters an industry that lacks any important similarities with the firm's existing industry or industries (Table 8.1). Luckily for Coca-Cola, its investment paid off—Columbia was sold to Sony for $3.4 billion just seven years later.

Most unrelated diversification efforts, however, do not have happy endings. Harley-Davidson, for example, once tried to sell Harley-branded bottled water. Starbucks tried to diversify into offering Starbucks-branded furniture. Both efforts were disasters. Although Harley-Davidson and Starbucks both enjoy iconic brands, these strategic resources simply did not transfer effectively to the bottled water and furniture businesses.

A different example, lighter firm Zippo tried to avoid this scenario. According to CEO Geoffrey Booth, the Zippo lighter is viewed by consumers as a "rugged, durable, made in America, iconic" brand (Associated Press, 2011). This brand has fueled ninety years of success for the firm. But the future of the lighter business is bleak. This downward trend is likely to continue as smoking becomes less and less attractive in many countries. To save their company, Zippo executives want to diversify.

In particular, Zippo wants to follow a path blazed by Eddie Bauer and Victorinox Swiss Army Brands Inc. The rugged outdoors image of Eddie Bauer's clothing brand has been used effectively to sell sport utility vehicles made by Ford. The high-quality image of Swiss Army knives has been used to sell Swiss Army–branded luggage and watches. As of 2020, Zippo has diversified into pocket knives, money clips, pocket flashlights, key holders, writing instruments, and tape measures. Trying to figure out which of these diversification options would be winners, such as the Eddie Bauer-edition Ford Explorer, and which would be losers, such as Harley-branded bottled water, was a key challenge facing Zippo executives.

Figure 8.5: The durability of Zippo's products is illustrated by this lighter, which still works despite being made in 1968.

Geographic Diversification

Firms may also diversify through expanding geographically. Big box stores such as Target and Best Buy use this strategy. Starbucks and KFC have found success with international expansion as well as domestic expansion. Synergy is developed in several ways. Many of the administrative functions such as logistics, procurement, human resources, and legal can be consolidated at the corporate level, so they do not need to be duplicated at each location. New store development is also made easier. Having already developed new stores, the firm can establish a process that it has learned from previously establishing stores, and can implement this best practice to efficiently build out, equip, and supply new stores.

Horizontal Integration: Mergers and Acquisitions

Horizontal integration refers to pursuing a diversification strategy by acquiring or merging with a rival. The term merger is generally used when two similarly sized firms are integrated into a single entity. In an acquisition, a larger firm purchases and absorbs a smaller firm. Examples of each are illustrated below..

Table 8.2 Horizontal Integration

Horizontal Integration Examples
ExxonMobil is a direct descendant of John D. Rockefeller's Standard Oil Company. It was formed by the 1999 merger of Exxon and Mobil. As in many mergers, the new company name combines the old company names.
Starbucks acquired competitor Seattle's Best Coffee—which had a presence in Borders Bookstores and Subway Restaurants—in order to target a more working-class audience without diluting the Starbucks brand.
Bill Hewlett and Dave Packard formed Hewlett-Packard in a garage after graduating from Stanford in 1935. HP has pursued horizontal integration through a merger with Compaq computers and the acquisition of Palm, a digital personal assistant. Both failed miserably.
DaimlerChrysler was formed in 1998 when Chrysler entered into what was billed as a "merger of equals" with Germany's Daimler-Benz AG. The marriage failed, with billions of dollars in losses, and Chrysler is currently owned by Italian automaker Fiat.
There tend to be many of mergers in the banking industry. Recently, BB&T merged with SunTrust Banks and adopted the new name Truist Financial Corp.
The merger of wireless carriers Sprint and T-Mobile combined the number three and four companies in the market. The new company name dropped Sprint and operates under the name T-Mobile.

Rather than rely on their own efforts, some firms try to expand their presence in an industry by acquiring or merging with one of their rivals. This strategic move is known as **horizontal integration** (Table 8.2). An acquisition takes place when one company purchases another company. Generally, the acquired company is smaller than the firm that purchases it. A merger joins two companies into one. Mergers typically involve similarly sized companies. Disney was much bigger than Miramax and Pixar when it joined with these firms, thus these two horizontal integration moves are considered to be acquisitions.

Horizontal integration can be attractive for several reasons. In many cases, horizontal integration is aimed at lowering costs by achieving greater economies of scale. This was the reasoning behind several mergers of large oil companies, including BP and Amoco in 1998, Exxon and Mobil in 1999, and Chevron and Texaco in 2001. Oil exploration and refining is expensive. Executives in charge of each of these six corporations believed that greater efficiency could be achieved by combining forces with a former rival. Considering horizontal integration alongside Porter's Five Forces model highlights that such moves also reduce the intensity of rivalry in an industry and thereby make the industry more profitable.

Some purchased firms are attractive because they own strategic resources such as valuable brand names. Acquiring Tasty Baking was appealing to Flowers Foods, for example, because the name Tastykake is well known for quality in heavily populated areas of the northeastern United States. Some purchased firms have market share that is attractive. Part of the motivation behind Southwest Airlines' purchase of AirTran was that AirTran had a significant share of the airline business in cities—especially Atlanta, home of the world's busiest airport—that Southwest had not yet entered. Rather than build a presence from nothing in Atlanta, Southwest executives believed that buying a position was prudent.

Figure 8.6: The combination of UFC and Strikeforce into one company may accelerate the growing popularity of mixed martial arts.

Horizontal integration can also provide access to new distribution channels. Some observers were puzzled when Zuffa, the parent company of the Ultimate Fighting Championship (UFC), purchased rival mixed martial arts (MMA) promotion Strikeforce. UFC had such a dominant position within MMA that Strikeforce seemed to add very little for Zuffa. Unlike UFC, Strikeforce had gained exposure on network television through broadcasts on CBS and its partner Showtime. Thus, acquiring Strikeforce might help Zuffa gain mainstream exposure of its product (Wagenheim, 2011).

Despite the potential benefits of mergers and acquisitions, their financial results often are very disappointing. One study found that more than 60% of mergers and acquisitions erode shareholder wealth while fewer than one in six increases shareholder wealth (Henry, 2002). Some of these moves struggle because the cultures of the two companies cannot be meshed. Other acquisitions fail because the buyer pays more for a target company than that company is worth and the buyer never earns back the premium it paid.

In the end, between 70% to 90% of mergers fail, according to a Harvard Business Review study, often at huge losses (Lakelet Capital, 2009). For example, Mattel purchased The Learning Company in 1999 for $3.6 billion and sold it a year later for $430 million—12% of the original purchase price. Similarly, Daimler-Benz bought Chrysler in 1998 for $37 billion. When the acquisition was undone in 2007, Daimler recouped only $1.5 billion worth of value—a mere 4% of what it paid. Thus, executives need to be cautious when considering using horizontal integration.

Vertical Integration Strategies

When pursuing a **vertical integration** strategy, a firm gets involved in new portions of the value chain (Table 8.3). This approach can be very attractive when a firm's suppliers or buyers have too much power over the firm and are becoming increasingly profitable at the firm's expense. By entering the domain of a supplier or a buyer, executives can reduce or eliminate the leverage that the supplier or buyer has over the firm. Considering vertical integration alongside Porter's five forces model highlights that such moves can create greater profit potential. Firms can pursue vertical integration on their own, such as when Apple opened stores bearing its brand, or through a merger or acquisition, such as when eBay purchased PayPal.

In the late 1800s, Carnegie Steel Company was a pioneer in the use of vertical integration. The firm controlled the iron mines that provided the key ingredient in steel, the coal mines that provided the fuel for steel making, the railroads that transported raw material to steel mills, and the steel mills themselves. Having control over all elements of the production process ensured the stability and quality of key inputs. By using vertical integration, Carnegie Steel achieved levels of efficiency never before seen in the steel industry.

When using vertical integration, firms get involved in different elements of the value chain. This concept gets top billing at American Apparel, a firm that describes its business model as "vertically integrated manufacturing." The elements of their integrated process for designing, manufacturing, wholesaling, and selling basic T-shirts, underwear, leggings, dresses, and other clothing and accessories for men, women, children, and dogs is illustrated below.

Table 8.3 Vertical Integration at American Apparel

American Apparel Vertical Integration
Backward Vertical Integration – entering a supplier's business—is evident as all clothing design is done in-house—often using employees as models.
Manufacturing is conducted in an 800,000 square foot factory in downtown Los Angeles.
Ironically, it was a Canadian named Dov Charney who founded American Apparel in 1989.
The vertical integration process allows the company to keep pace with the fast-moving world of fashion. It takes just a couple of weeks to go from idea to retail floor.
Forward Vertical Integration – American Apparel uses forward vertical integration—entering a buyer's business—by operating 250 plus company-owned stores worldwide.

Today, oil companies are among the most vertically integrated firms. Firms such as ExxonMobil and ConocoPhillips can be involved in all stages of the value chain, including crude oil exploration, drilling for oil, shipping oil to refineries, refining crude oil into products such as gasoline, distributing fuel to gas stations, and operating gas stations.

The risk of not being vertically integrated is illustrated by the 2010 Deepwater Horizon oil spill in the Gulf of Mexico. Although the US government held BP responsible for the disaster, BP cast at least some of the blame on drilling rig owner Transocean and two other suppliers: Halliburton Energy Services (which created the cement casing for the rig on the ocean floor) and Cameron International Corporation (which had sold Transocean blowout prevention equipment that failed to prevent the disaster). In April 2011, BP sued these three firms for what it viewed as their roles in the oil spill.

Vertical integration also creates risks. Venturing into new portions of the value chain can take a firm into very different businesses. A lumberyard that started building houses, for example, would find that the skills it developed in the lumber business have very limited value to home construction. Such a firm would be better off selling lumber to contractors.

Vertical integration can also create complacency. Consider, for example, a situation in which an aluminum company is purchased by a can company. People within the aluminum company may believe that they do not need to worry about doing a good job because the can company is guaranteed to use their products. Some companies try to avoid this problem by forcing their subsidiary to compete with outside suppliers, but this undermines the reason for purchasing the subsidiary in the first place.

Figure 8.7: The 2010 explosion of the Deepwater Horizon oil rig cost eleven lives and released nearly five million barrels of crude oil into the Gulf of Mexico.

Backward Vertical Integration

A **backward vertical integration** strategy involves a firm moving back along the value chain and entering a supplier's business. Some firms use this strategy when executives are concerned that a supplier has too much power over their firms. In the early days of the automobile business, Ford Motor Company created subsidiaries that provided key inputs to vehicles such as rubber, glass, and metal. This approach ensured that Ford would not be hurt by suppliers holding out for higher prices or providing materials of inferior quality.

Figure 8.8: To ensure high quality, Ford relied heavily on backward vertical integration in the early days of the automobile industry.

Although backward vertical integration is usually discussed within the context of manufacturing businesses, such as steel making and the auto industry, this strategy is also available to firms such as Disney that compete within the entertainment sector. ESPN is a key element of Disney's operations within the television business. Rather than depend on outside production companies to provide talk shows and movies centered on sports, ESPN created its own production company. ESPN Films is a subsidiary of ESPN that was created in 2001. ESPN Films has created many of ESPN's best-known programs, including *Around the Horn* and *The Dance* documentary. By owning its own production company, ESPN can ensure that it has a steady flow of programs that meet its needs.

Forward Vertical Integration

A **forward vertical integration** strategy involves a firm moving further down the value chain to enter a buyer's business. Disney has pursued forward vertical integration by operating more than three hundred retail stores that sell merchandise based on Disney's characters and movies. This allows Disney to capture profits that would otherwise be enjoyed by another store. Each time a *Frozen* book bag is sold through a Disney store, the firm makes a little more profit than it would if the same book bag were sold by a retailer such as Target.

Forward vertical integration also can be useful for neutralizing the effect of powerful buyers. Rental car agencies are able to insist on low prices for the vehicles they buy from automakers because they purchase thousands of cars. If one automaker stubbornly tries to charge high prices, a rental car agency can simply buy cars from a more accommodating automaker. It is perhaps not surprising that Ford purchased Hertz Corporation, the world's biggest rental car agency, in 1994. This ensured that Hertz would not drive too hard of a bargain when buying Ford vehicles. By 2005, selling vehicles to rental car companies had become less important to Ford and Ford was struggling financially. The firm then reversed its forward vertical integration strategy by selling Hertz.

Figure 8.9: *The massive number of cars purchased by rental car agencies makes forward vertical integration a tempting strategy for automakers.*

eBay's purchase of PayPal and Apple's creation of Apple Stores are two examples of forward vertical integration. Despite its enormous success, one concern for eBay is that many individuals avoid eBay because they are nervous about buying and selling goods online with strangers. PayPal addressed this problem by serving, in exchange for a fee, as an intermediary between online buyers and sellers. eBay's acquisition of PayPal signaled to potential customers that their online transactions were completely safe—eBay was now not only the place where business took place but eBay also protected buyers and sellers from being ripped off.

Apple's ownership of its own branded stores set the firm apart from computer makers such as Hewlett-Packard, Dell, and Lenovo that only distribute their products through retailers like Best Buy and Office Depot. Employees at Best Buy and Office Depot are likely to know only a little bit about each of the various brands their store carries. In contrast, Apple's stores are popular in part because store employees are experts about Apple products. They can therefore provide customers with accurate and insightful advice about purchases and repairs. This is an important advantage that has been created through forward vertical integration.

- Diversification strategies involve a firm stepping beyond its existing industries and entering a new value chain. Generally, related diversification (entering a new industry that has important similarities with a firm's existing industries) is wiser than unrelated diversification (entering a new industry that lacks such similarities). Geographic diversification is another strategy to drive synergy.
- A horizontal diversification strategy involves trying to compete successfully within a single industry.
- Mergers and acquisitions are popular moves for executing a concentration strategy, but executives need to be cautious about horizontal integration because the results are often poor.
- Vertical integration occurs when a firm gets involved in new portions of the value chain. By entering the domain of a supplier (backward vertical integration) or a buyer (forward vertical integration), executives can reduce or eliminate the leverage that the supplier or buyer has over the firm.

Exercises

1. Studies have shown that executives' pay increases when their firms get larger. What role, if any, do you think executive pay plays in diversification decisions? Is this an ethical issue?
2. Identify a firm that has recently engaged in diversification. Search the firm's website to identify executives' rationale for diversifying. Do you find the reasoning to be convincing? Why or why not?
3. Suppose the president of your college or university decided to merge with or acquire another school. What schools would be good candidates for this horizontal integration move? Would the move be a success?
4. Given that so many mergers and acquisitions fail, why do you think that executives keep making horizontal integration moves?
5. Identify a well-known company that does not use backward or forward vertical integration. Why do you believe that the firm's executives have avoided these strategies?
6. Some universities have used vertical integration by creating their own publishing companies. The Harvard Business Press is perhaps the best-known example. Are there other ways that a university might vertically integrate? If so, what benefits might this create?

References

Henry, D. (2002, October 14). Mergers: Why most big deals don't pay off. *Business Week*, 60–70.

Lakelet Capital. (2009, June 15). *Reasons why mergers & acquisitions fail and succeed.* https://lakeletcapital.com/reasons-why-mergers-acquisitions-fail-and-succeed.

Porter, M. E. (1987). From competitive advantage to corporate strategy. *Harvard Business Review*, 65(3), 102–121. https://hbr.org/1987/05/from-competitive-advantage-to-corporate-strategy.

Prahalad, C. K., & Hamel, G. (1990). The core competencies of the corporation. *Harvard Business Review*, 86(1), 79–91. https://hbr.org/1990/05/the-core-competence-of-the-corporation.

Associated Press. (2011, March 21). Zippo's burning ambition lies in retail expansion. *The Daily Journal*. https://www.smdailyjournal.com/business/zippo-s-burning-ambition-lies-in-retail-expansion/article_80c8ef2e-4495-5823-8e02-9bff74109b2f.html.

Wagenheim, J. (2011, March 12). UFC buys out Strikeforce in another step toward global domination. *Sports Illustrated*. https://www.si.com/more-sports/2011/03/13/strikeforce-purchased.

Image Credits

Figure 8.9: Keiows, Laitr. "Parking lot at HAA Kobe." CC BY 3.0. Retrieved from https://en.wikipedia.org/wiki/Auto_auction#/media/File:Parking_lot_at_HAA_Kobe.jpg.

8.4 Implementing Corporate Strategy

Once a firm decides which corporate strategy to pursue, it must implement that strategy successfully. As noted earlier, many attempts to diversify end in failure. Executing a good implementation plan successfully is key.

There are various ways that a firm can implement their corporate diversification strategy. These are:

- Internal Development
- Strategic Alliance
- Joint Venture
- Merger and Acquisition

Internal Development

When deciding what business to be in, sometimes an organization chooses **internal development**. Internal development means the company develops and launches the new business themselves. To do this, the firm should have a strong entrepreneurial orientation, as this implementation method is the same process as starting a new business. A firm may select this method if they have sufficient resources and capabilities within the firm or can hire the expertise and knowledge to develop this new business unit and achieve the marketing and sales required to be successful. Internal development has been the implementation method of choice for Apple's corporate strategy. Apple has used internal development to enter new markets. Apple moved from the computer industry to the music industry with iPod and Apple music and then into the smartphone industry by developing internal capabilities and resources. This is a very costly and time-intensive strategy, but as is evident with Apple, it can be extremely lucrative and create many competitive benefits.

Strategic Alliance

A firm might implement their corporate strategy by working with another firm, even if that firm is a competitor. A **strategic alliance** is a mutually beneficial relationship between two organizations, usually governed through a contractual agreement. The firms may agree to share expertise or knowledge, resources, supply chain activities, distribution channels, research and development, etc.. Often money changes hands as one company provides what the other company needs. T-Mobile and Nokia entered into a strategic alliance in 2018, where for a fee, Nokia helped T-Mobile develop its 5G network. Barnes & Noble and Starbucks have a strategic alliance whereby

Starbucks puts their coffee shops inside of the Barnes & Noble bookstores. In all these examples, an alliance was beneficial for both companies.

Joint Venture

Similar to a strategic alliance, two or more companies form a **joint venture** when they "birth" a third company, and the joint venture partners are shared owners of the new firm. With a joint venture, a new company is always formed. The ownership arrangement can vary as to how much each partner owns and how much each partner has control. Typically, profits of the new company are shared according to the ownership percentages. Joint ventures can work well, even among competitors, when each partner brings something of value to the venture that the other partner could use. US airplane manufacturer Boeing created a joint venture with the Brazilian aircraft manufacturer of smaller commercial jets Embraer to start a third company that will get Boeing into the smaller passenger planes market. Boeing owns 80% of the company, and Embraer 20% (AP News, 2019).

Mergers and Acquisitions

A common method for firms to diversify is through mergers and acquisitions. A **merger** is between two companies of similar size and are less common. **Acquisitions** occur when one company buys another. Typically, a larger company acquires a smaller one. Mergers and acquisitions (M & A) may occur between competitors, which reduces the competition in the market. In this situation, the M & A is an example of related diversification and horizontal integration. T-Mobile's merger with Sprint is an example. Firms might acquire other companies in their value chain to give them more control within the industry. Moving into their suppliers' industry is backward integration, and buying companies in industries they sell to is forward integration. Forward integration is illustrated by Apple establishing Apple Stores and having direct involvement in the retail market. One way to diversify by acquisitions is through unrelated diversification. Unrelated diversification occurs when one company purchases another company that is located in an industry the first company is not involved in. An example of this strategy is Berkshire Hathaway owning companies in industries as diverse as insurance and railroads.

References

AP News. (2019, February 26). *Embraer shareholders approve jet joint venture with Boeing.* https://apnews.com/590254a4075f4e9580258e829862a1a7.

8.5 Strategies for Getting Smaller

"In what industry or industries should our firm compete?" is the central question addressed by corporate-level strategy. In some cases, the answer that executives arrive at involves exiting one or more industries.

Retrenchment

In the early twentieth century, many military battles were fought in a series of parallel trenches. If an attacking army advanced enough to force a defending army to abandon a trench, the defenders would move back to the next trench and try to refortify their position. This small retreat was preferable to losing the battle entirely. Trench warfare inspired the business term retrenchment. Firms following a retrenchment strategy shrink one or more of their business units. Much like an army under attack, firms using this strategy hope to make just a small retreat rather than losing a battle for survival. It is also commonly referred to as "downsizing" or "right-sizing."

Figure 8.10: The term retrenchment has its origins in trench warfare, which is shown in this World War I photo taken in France.

Retrenchment is often accomplished through laying off employees. For example, South African grocery store chain Pick n Pay announced plans to release more than 3,000 of its estimated 36,000 workers. Just over a month earlier, South African officials had approved Walmart's acquisition of a leading local retailer called Massmart. Rivalry in the South African grocery business seemed likely to become more fierce, and Pick n Pay executives needed to cut costs for their firm to remain competitive.

A Pick n Pay executive explained the layoffs by noting that "the decision was not taken lightly but was required to ensure the viability of the retail business and its employees into the future" (Chilwane, 2011). This is a common rationale for retrenchment—by shrinking the size of a firm, executives hope that the firm can survive as a profitable enterprise. Without becoming smaller and more cost effective, Pick n Pay and other firms that use retrenchment can risk total failure. This strategy was particularly evident during the COVID-19 pandemic of 2020. Many organizations shrank temporarily with hopes of surviving until the economy opened up again. Some did survive, and unfortunately, some did not.

Restructuring

Spin-offs occur when businesses create a new firm from a piece of their operations. Because some diversified firms are too complex for investors to understand, breaking them up can create wealth by resulting in greater stock market valuations. Spinning off a company also reduces management layers, which can lower costs and speed up decision making. Below we describe a variety of firms that were created as spin-offs.

Table 8.4 Spin Offs

Examples of Spin Offs
There are 17 billion of Freescale Semiconductor's chips in use around the world. The firm was spun-off from Motorola.
Toyota started in the car business, right? Wrong. The firm was spun-off in the 1930s from Toyoda Automatic Loom Works—a company that produced commercial weaving looms.
Delphi Automotive—an automotive parts company headquartered in Troy, Michigan—is a spin-off from General Motors.
Guidant Corporation—a spin-off from Eli Lilly—designs and manufacturers artificial pacemakers, defibrillators, stents, and other heart-helpful medical products.

Executives sometimes decide that bolder moves than retrenchment are needed for their firms to be successful in the future. Divestment refers to selling off part of a firm's operations. In some cases, divestment reverses a forward vertical integration strategy, such as when Ford sold Hertz. Divestment can also be used to reverse backward vertical integration. General Motors (GM), for example, turned a parts supplier called Delphi Automotive Systems Corporation from a GM subsidiary into an independent firm. This was done via a spin-off, which involves creating a new company whose stock is owned by investors (Table 8.4). GM stockholders received 0.69893 shares of Delphi for every share of stock they owned in GM. A stockholder who owned 100 shares of GM received 69 shares of the new company plus a small cash payment in lieu of a fractional share.

Divestment also serves as a means to undo diversification strategies. Divestment can be especially appealing to executives in charge of firms that have engaged in unrelated diversification. Investors often struggle to understand the complexity of diversified firms, and this can result in relatively poor performance by the stocks of such firms. This is known as a **diversification discount.** Executives sometimes attempt to unlock hidden shareholder value by breaking up diversified companies.

Figure 8.11: Fortune Brands hopes to unlock hidden shareholder value by divesting unrelated brands such as Masterlock.

Sometimes diversified companies find themselves in a situation where, instead of synergy, they are experiencing increased inefficiency and increased costs. In this case, the value of the individual businesses are worth more separately than when part of the conglomerate. This can happen when an organization grows too large, with too many layers of management, and too top heavy. This situation is called a diversification discount. General Electric is a good example of this phenomenon. GE made everything from light bulbs, to washing machines, to jet engines, to CAT, scanners, to large power systems, and had engaged in operating a financial institution, GE Capital, that provided loans to companies. When the recession of 2008-2009 hit, GE Capital was left holding a lot of unpaid debt, and drove the GE stock price down. GE began to get out of the financing business, along with a number of its other business lines. It trimmed down to a much smaller organization that was not so complicated to manage in order to survive.

Fortune Brands provides another good example. Surprisingly, this company does not own Fortune magazine, but it has been involved in a diverse set of industries. The firm consisted of three businesses: spirits (including Jim Beam and Maker's Mark), household goods (including Masterlock and Moen Faucets), and golf equipment (including Titleist clubs and balls as well as FootJoy shoes). Fortune Brand's CEO announced a plan to separate the three businesses to "maximize long-term value for our shareholders and to create exciting opportunities within our businesses" (Dalal, et. al., 2011). Fortune Brands took the first step toward overcoming the diversification discount when it reached an agreement to sell its golf business to Fila. Later plans to spin off the home products business were announced.

Executives are sometimes forced to admit that the operations that they want to abandon have no value. If selling off part of a business is not possible, the best option may be liquidation. This involves simply shutting down portions of a firm's operations, often at a tremendous financial loss. GM has done this by scrapping its Geo, Saturn, Oldsmobile, and Pontiac brands. Ford followed this approach by shutting down its Mercury brand. Such moves are painful because massive investments are written off, but becoming "leaner and meaner" may save a company from total ruin.

Key Takeaway

- Executives sometimes need to reduce the size of their firms to maximize the chances of success. This can involve fairly modest steps such as retrenchment or more profound restructuring strategies.

Exercises

1. Should Disney consider using retrenchment or restructuring? Why or why not?
2. Given how much information is readily available about companies, why do you think investors still struggle to analyze diversified companies?

References

Chilwane, L. (2011, July 7). Pick n pay to retrench. *The New Age.*
http://www.thenewage.co.za/22462-1025-53-Pick_n_Pay_to_retrench.

Dala, M & Thomas, D. (2011, May 20). Fortune Brands to sell Titleist and FootJoy to S. Korea's Fila. *Reuters.*
https://www.reuters.com/article/fila-fortunebrands-idUSL4E7GK20A20110520.

8.6 Portfolio Planning and Corporate-Level Strategy

Executives in charge of firms involved in many different businesses must figure out how to manage such portfolios. General Electric (GE), for example, competed in a very wide variety of industries, including financial services, insurance, television, theme parks, electricity generation, lightbulbs, robotics, medical equipment, railroad locomotives, and aircraft jet engines. When leading a company such as GE, executives must decide which units to grow, which ones to shrink, and which ones to abandon.

Portfolio planning can be a useful tool. Portfolio planning is a process that helps executives assess their firms' prospects for success within each of its industries, offers suggestions about what to do within each industry, and provides ideas for how to allocate resources across industries. Portfolio planning first gained widespread attention in the 1970s, and it remains a popular tool among executives today.

The Boston Consulting Group Matrix

The Boston Consulting Group (BCG) Matrix is the best-known approach to portfolio planning (Table 8.5). Using the matrix requires a firm's businesses to be categorized as high or low along two dimensions: its share of the market and the growth rate of its industry. The BCG Matrix has four quadrants or categories:

- Cash Cows: High market share units within slow-growing industries are called cash cows. Because their industries have bleak prospects, profits from cash cows should not be invested back into cash cows but rather diverted to more promising businesses.
- Dogs: Low market share units within slow-growing industries are called dogs. These units are good candidates for divestment.
- Stars: High market share units within fast-growing industries are called stars. These units have bright prospects and thus are good candidates for growth.
- Question Marks: Finally, low-market-share units within fast-growing industries are called question marks. Executives must decide whether to build these units into stars, hold them, or to divest them.

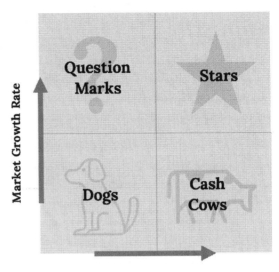

Figure 8.12: BCG Matrix

Figure 8.12 shows how the BCG Matrix is laid out. The various business units that a company has are plotted on the matrix. Once plotted, decisions can be made about the portfolio of businesses the company operates, such as where more investment would be beneficial, and which units may be candidates to divest.

The Boston Consulting Group matrix is the best-known approach to portfolio planning—assessing a firm's prospects for success within the industries in which it competes. The matrix categorizes businesses as high or low along two dimensions—the firm's market share in each industry and the growth rate of each industry. Suggestions are then offered about how to approach each industry.

Table 8.5 The Boston Consulting Group Matrix

	Low Relative Market Share	High Relative Market Share
High Industry Growth Rate	Question marks should be resolved by executives by deciding whether to foster or sell these units.	Stars should be funded and encouraged to grow.
Low Industry Growth Rate	It sounds mean, but dogs should be sold if possible and abandoned if necessary.	Cash cows should be "milked" to supply funds to more promising businesses.

To use the BCG Matrix, the company needs to know the market share for each of its business lines and the relative growth rate. It is important to set the scales on both axes so that the midpoints are roughly in the middle of the range of the market share and growth rates of the business units. Once the axes are set, the business units are plotted on the matrix relative to each other. Figure 8.14 shows a BCG Matrix for the Coca-Cola company and its various products. Notice that sometimes the market share axis is reversed, as it is in Figure 8.12.

Figure 8.13: Owning a puppy is fun, but companies may want to avoid owning units that are considered to be dogs.

Sometimes a third dimension is plotted on the BCG Matrix, using the size of the circle. The circle sizes might represent the business units' proportion of total company revenues or proportion of total company profit generated. This added dimension can assist in decision making regarding the business units. For example, if a business unit in the Dog quadrant also represents 40% of the company's revenue and 35% of its profit, divesting it would mean a significant downsizing of the company with implications for many other support functions.

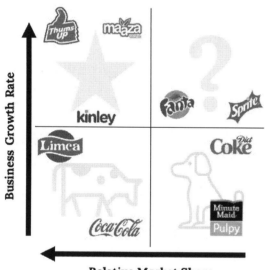

Figure 8.14: BCG Matrix of Coca-Cola

Once plotted, company leadership can evaluate its portfolio and make decisions on how to optimize its company. For example, in Figure 8.13, the two products in the Cash Cow quadrant have little opportunity for growth, given the socio-cultural force toward more healthy foods. Since they already have a high market share, it may be best to use their profits to invest in other business lines with more growth and market share potential. The products in the Question Marks and Dogs categories also are impacted by the trend toward healthy eating, so investment there is questionable. Usually, if investment in Question Marks can result in greater market share, it can be a wise move. Dogs are sometimes considered for divestment, however, Diet Coke has such high revenues and profit margins, divesting it would have a negative impact on the company. Investing in the Stars, where Kinley water products leverage the trend toward healthy beverages, and Thumbs Up is booming in India, would be a good decision.

Limitations to Portfolio Planning

Although portfolio planning is a useful tool, this tool has important limitations. First, portfolio planning oversimplifies the reality of competition by focusing on just two dimensions when analyzing a company's operations within an industry. Many dimensions are important to consider when making strategic decisions, not just two. Second, portfolio planning can create motivational problems among employees. For example, if workers know that their firm's executives believe in the BCG Matrix and that their subsidiary is classified as a dog, then they may give up any hope for the future. Similarly, workers within cash cow units could become dismayed once they realize that the profits that they help create will be diverted to boost other areas of the firm. Third, portfolio planning does not help identify new opportunities. Because this tool only deals with existing businesses, it cannot reveal what new industries a firm should consider entering.

Key Takeaway

- Portfolio planning is a useful tool for analyzing a firm's various business units, but this tool has limitations. The BCG matrix is one of the most widely used approaches to portfolio planning.

Exercises

1. Is market share a good dimension to use when analyzing the prospects of a business? Why or why not?
2. What might executives do to keep employees within dog units motivated and focused on their jobs?

Image Credits

Figure 8.12: Kindred Grey (2020). "The BCG Matrix." CC BY-SA 4.0. Retrieved from: https://commons.wikimedia.org/wiki/File:The_BCG_Matrix.png.

Figure 8.13: Kriz, Jonathan. "Puppy." CC BY 2.0. Retrieved from https://flic.kr/p/8SUChJ.

Figure 8.14: Kindred Grey (2020). "BCG Matrix examples with CocaCola." CC BY-SA 4.0. Retrieved from: https://commons.wikimedia.org/wiki/File:BCG_Matrix_examples_with_CocaCola.png Adapted from: https://image.slidesharecdn.com/cokers-151203095234-lva1-app6892/95/coke-15-638.jpg?cb=1449136402.

8.7 Conclusion

This chapter explains corporate-level strategy. Executives grappling with corporate-level strategy must decide in what industry or industries their firms will compete. Many of the possible answers to this question involve diversification, which can be related, unrelated, or geographic. Integration involves expanding into new stages of the value chain. Backward integration occurs when a firm enters a supplier's business while forward vertical integration occurs when a firm enters a customer's business. Firms implement their corporate diversification strategies through internal development, strategic alliances, joint ventures, mergers and acquisitions. Sometimes being smart about corporate-level strategy requires shrinking the firm through retrenchment or restructuring. Finally, portfolio planning using the BCG Matrix can be useful for analyzing firms that participate in a wide variety of industries or business lines.

Exercises

1. Divide your class into four or eight groups, depending on the size of the class. Each group should create a new portfolio planning technique by selecting two dimensions along which companies can be analyzed. Allow each group three to five minutes to present its approach to the class. Discuss which portfolio planning technique seems to offer the best insights.

Chapter 9: Competing in International Markets

Learning Objectives

After reading this chapter, you should be able to understand and articulate answers to the following questions:

1. What are the main benefits and risks of competing in international markets?
2. What is the "diamond model," and how does it help explain why some firms compete better in international markets than others?
3. How does the CAGE framework help a firm predict its degree of success in doing business in another country?
4. What are the four global strategies that firms can adopt, and what are the two pressures that define these strategies?
5. What methods of entry are available to firms that seek to compete in international markets?

9.1 Introduction

International strategy is the third and final type of strategy presented in this textbook. The first, generic business-level/competitive strategy, is how companies directly compete with rivals on their products and services. Corporate strategy is how a firm might diversify to compete in other industries or expand geographically to reduce risk and grow profits. In international strategy, a firm may desire to expand by entering into new foreign markets or to lower its costs. There are advantages and opportunities when going international, but it is not without risks. There are several tools that firms use to help them assess their potential success when their strategic management process points them abroad. Firms will need to determine which one of four international strategies will work best and which method to enter another country. Some US companies have found great success going international, while others have struggled or failed.

9.2 Advantages and Disadvantages of Competing in International Markets

Kia Picks Up Speed

On June 2, 2011, South Korean automaker Kia announced plans for a major expansion of its American production facility. Capacity at Kia Motors Manufacturing Georgia Inc. (KMMG) was slated to expand 20% from 300,000 to 360,000 vehicles per year. In addition to the crossover utility vehicle Sorento, the plant would begin making a sedan named the Optima in September 2011. The expansion of the plant was estimated to cost $100 million and was expected to create 1,000 new jobs (Sands, 2011).

Figure 9.1: Kia is enjoying accelerated growth within the global automobile industry.

This ambitious growth was made possible by Kia's superb performance in the US market. KMMG had started building vehicles less than two years earlier after being constructed for a cost of $1 billion. In 2010, yearly sales in the United States climbed above 350,000 vehicles. Kia's overall share of the US market increased in 2010 for the sixteenth consecutive year. In May 2011, Kia sold more than 48,000 cars and trucks in the United States, an increase of more than 53% from May 2010 sales levels. The Optima led the way with a whopping 210% increase in sales.

Kia was not the only beneficiary of its success. KMMG's location of West Point, Georgia, had been economically devastated when its homegrown textile company, WestPoint Home, shut down its local factories to take advantage of lower labor prices overseas. Following a fierce competition with towns in Mississippi, Kentucky, and other states, West Point was selected in 2006 as the site of Kia's first US manufacturing facility. To win the plant, state and local authorities offered Kia more than $400 million worth of incentives, including tax breaks, free land, and infrastructure creation. This kind of governmental inducement has become commonplace when states lure new businesses to a region. This practice is also an example of "corporate welfare."

Georgia's return on this investment included two thousand new jobs at the plant as well as hundreds of jobs at suppliers that set up shop to support KMMG. The neighboring state of Alabama benefited from KMMG's success too. As of June 2011, nearly sixty companies spread across twenty-three Alabama counties supplied parts or services to KMMG (Kent, 2011).

Figure 9.2: Workers in Georgia build Cadenzass for South Korea–based Kia.

The name "Kia" means to arise or come up out of Asia (Kia, n.d.). This name is very appropriate; Kia rose from humble beginnings as a maker of bicycle parts in 1944 to become a global player in the automobile industry. As of 2011, Kia was producing more than 2.1 million vehicles per year in eight countries. Kias were sold in 172 countries. Kia employed more than 44,000 people and enjoyed annual revenues in excess of $20 billion. Fellow South Korean automaker Hyundai owned just over 33% of Kia, and the two firms strengthened each other through collaboration. When taking all of these facts into consideration, Kia's slogan–"The Power to Surprise"–had to make its rivals wonder what surprises the Korean upstart might have in store for them next.

As Kia's experience illustrates, international business is a huge segment of the world's economic activity. Amazingly, current projections suggest that, within a few years, the total dollar value of trade across national borders will be greater than the total dollar value of trade within all of the world's countries combined. One driver of the rapid growth of internal business over the past two decades has been the opening up of large economies such as China and Russia that had been mostly closed off to outside investors.

International strategy is determining how to do business outside the borders of a firm's home country. International business has opened up significantly in the last few decades. This has been due to lower trade barriers, improved communications, more efficient shipping via ship and airplane, and the internet. Many US companies have shifted their manufacturing and supply chain activities abroad, where labor is cheaper and overall costs are reduced, even with the additional costs of shipping. The COVID-19 pandemic of 2020 illustrated some issues that emerge when an economy, such as with the US, becomes dependent on other countries for the materials it uses for its final products. During the pandemic, the capacity for global supply chains to meet the sharp increase in demand for paper goods, cleaning supplies, as well as for medications and other medical equipment and supplies, was immediately strained.

International strategy for a firm can be somewhat minimal, such as procuring needed supply chain resources for manufacturing a product in the home country, to an expanded role, like exporting products for sale in other countries, to full manufacturing subsidiaries such as the Kia example in the US. There are multiple reasons why a firm would go international, and also multiple advantages and disadvantages.

The domestication of the camel by Arabian travelers fueled two early examples of international trade: spices and silk. Today, camels have been replaced by airplanes, trains, and ships, and international trade is more alluring than ever. Here are three key reasons why executives are enticed to enter new markets.

Table 9.1 Why Compete in New Markets?

Access to new customers	China's population is roughly four times as large as that of the United States. While political, cultural, and economic differences add danger to trade with China, the immense size of the Chinese market appeals to American firms.
Lowering costs	Access to cheaper raw materials and labor have led to considerable outsourcing and offshoring. Call centers in India have become so sophisticated that many Indian customer service representatives take extensive language training to learn regional US dialects.
Diversification of business risk	Business risk refers to the risk of an operation failing. Competing in multiple markets allows this risk to be spread out among many economies and customers. Coca-Cola, for example, has a presence in over 200 markets worldwide.

The United States enjoys the world's largest economy. As an illustration of the power of the American economy, consider that in 2018, the economy of just one state—California—was the fifth largest in the world. If it were a country, it would rank between Germany and the United Kingdom (CBS News, 2018). The size of the US economy has led American commerce to be very much intertwined with international markets. In fact, it is fair to say that every business is affected by international markets to some degree. Tiny businesses such as individual convenience stores and clothing boutiques sell products that are imported from abroad. Meanwhile, corporate goliaths such as General Motors (GM), Coca-Cola, and Microsoft conduct a great volume of business overseas.

Access to New Customers

Perhaps the most obvious reason to compete in international markets is gaining access to new customers. Although the United States enjoys the largest economy in the world, it accounts for only about 5% of the world's population. Selling goods and services to the other 95% of people on the planet can be very appealing, especially for companies whose industry within their home market is saturated (Table 9.1).

Few companies have a stronger "All-American" identity than McDonald's. Yet McDonald's is increasingly reliant on sales outside the United States. In 2006, the United States accounted for 34% of McDonald's revenue, while Europe accounted for 32% and 14% was generated across Asia, the Middle East, and Africa. By 2011, Europe was McDonald's biggest source of revenue (40%), the US share had fallen to 32%, and the collective contribution of Asia, the Middle East, and Africa had jumped to 23%. By 2019, McDonald's US percent of total revenue had grown to 41% (Statista, 2019). With less than half of its sales being generated in its home country, McDonald's is truly a global powerhouse.

China and India have been attractive markets to US firms. The countries are the two most populous in the world. Both nations have growing middle classes, which means they have been building infrastructures, like education and transportation systems, that support increased purchasing power. In other words, individuals in these countries can buy goods and services that are not merely necessities of life. This trend has created tremendous opportunities for some firms. In 2019, for example, GM sold more vehicles in China than it sold in the United States (3.1 million vs. 2.9 million). This gap has continued from at least 2010. (Reuters, 2020).

Figure 9.3: Levi's jeans are appreciated by customers worldwide, as shown by this balloon featured at the Putrajaya International Hot Air Balloon Fiesta held in Malaysia.

Lowering Costs

Many firms that compete in international markets hope to gain cost advantages. If a firm can increase its sales volume by entering a new country, for example, it may attain **economies of scale** that lower its per unit production costs. Going international also has implications for dealing with suppliers. The growth of overseas expansion leads many businesses to purchase supplies in greater numbers. This can provide a firm with stronger leverage when negotiating prices with its suppliers.

Offshoring has become a popular yet controversial means for trying to reduce costs. Offshoring involves relocating a business activity to another country. Many American companies have closed down operations at home in favor of creating new operations in countries such as China and India that offer cheaper labor. While offshoring can reduce a firm's costs of doing business, the job losses in the firm's home country can devastate local communities. For example, West Point, Georgia, lost approximately 16,000 jobs in the 1990s and 2000s as local textile factories were shut down in favor of offshoring (Copeland, 2010). Fortunately for the town, Kia's decision to locate its first US factory in West Point has improved the economy in the past few years. In another example, Fortune Brands saved $45 million a year by relocating several factories to Mexico, but the employee count in just one of the affected US plants dropped from 1,160 to 350.

A growing number of US companies are finding that offshoring is not providing the benefits they had expected. This has led to a new phenomenon known as **reshoring**, whereby jobs that had been sent overseas are returning home. In some cases, the quality provided by workers overseas is not good enough. Carbonite, a seller of computer backup services, found that its call center in Boston was providing much stronger customer satisfaction than its call center in India. The Boston operation's higher rating was attained even though it handled the more challenging customer complaints. As a result, Carbonite shifted 250 call center jobs back to the United States.

Figure 9.4: Concerns about customer service are leading some American firms to shift their call centers back to the United States.

In other cases, the expected cost savings have not materialized. NCR had been making ATMs and self-service checkout systems in China, Hungary, and Brazil. These machines can weigh more than a ton, and NCR found that shipping them from overseas plants back to the United States was extremely expensive. NCR hired 500 workers to start making the ATMs and checkout systems at a plant in Columbus, Georgia, adding 370 more jobs (Isidore, 2011). Similarly, Apple, General Motors, Boeing, and Ford had brought back thousands of jobs each to the US from abroad by 2019 (Monroe Engineering, 2018).

Diversification of Business Risk

A familiar cliché warns "don't put all of your eggs in one basket." Applied to business, this cliché suggests that it is dangerous for a firm to operate in only one country. Business risk refers to the potential that an operation might fail. If a firm is completely dependent on one country, negative events in that country could ruin the firm. Just like spreading one's eggs into multiple baskets reduces the chances that all eggs will be broken, business risk is reduced when a firm is involved in multiple countries.

Consider, for example, natural disasters such as the earthquakes and tsunami that hit Japan in 2011. If Japanese automakers such as Toyota, Nissan, and Honda sold cars only in their home country, the financial consequences could have been grave. Because these firms operate in many countries, however, they were protected from being ruined by events in Japan. In other words, these firms diversified their business risk by not being overly dependent on their Japanese operations.

American cigarette companies such as Philip Morris and R. J. Reynolds are challenged by trends within the United States and Europe. Tobacco use in these areas is declining as more laws are passed that ban smoking in public areas and in restaurants. In response, cigarette makers are attempting to increase their operations within countries where smoking remains popular to remain profitable over time.

For example, Philip Morris spent $5.2 billion to purchase a controlling interest in Indonesian cigarette maker Sampoerna. This was the biggest acquisition ever in Indonesia by a foreign company. Tapping into Indonesia's population of approximately 230 million people was attractive to Philip Morris in part because nearly two-thirds of men are smokers, and smoking among women is on the rise. At the time, Indonesia was

Figure 9.5: Firms can reduce business risk by competing in a variety of international markets. For example, the ampm convenience store chain has locations in the United States, Mexico, Brazil, and Japan.

the fifth-largest tobacco market in the world, trailing only China, the United States, Russia, and Japan. To appeal to local preferences for cigarettes flavored with cloves, Philip Morris introduced a variety of its signature Marlboro brand called Marlboro Mix 9 that includes cloves in its formulation (The Two Malcontents, 2007).

The use of **PESTEL** can be a valuable tool in assessing the risk for a firm considering international diversification. Analyzing the industry within the target country could provide valuable insights on whether to enter that market or not. For example, if Apple were to consider shifting some of its product manufacturing to India, what do the PESTEL forces reveal for the Indian IT industry?

Table 9.2 PESTEL Analysis of the IT Industry in India

Political	Moderate, positive & negative: Stable government, democracy, international companies highly regulated
Economical	Strong, positive: Low cost labor, IT has strong growth
Socio-cultural	Strong, positive: Many speak English, strong STEM education
Technological	Strong, positive: Strong growth
Ecological	Weak
Legal	Moderate, negative: Highly regulated

In conclusion, a PESTEL analysis reveals that overall it would be a positive move for Apple to do manufacturing in India, but will need to comply with many laws and regulations.

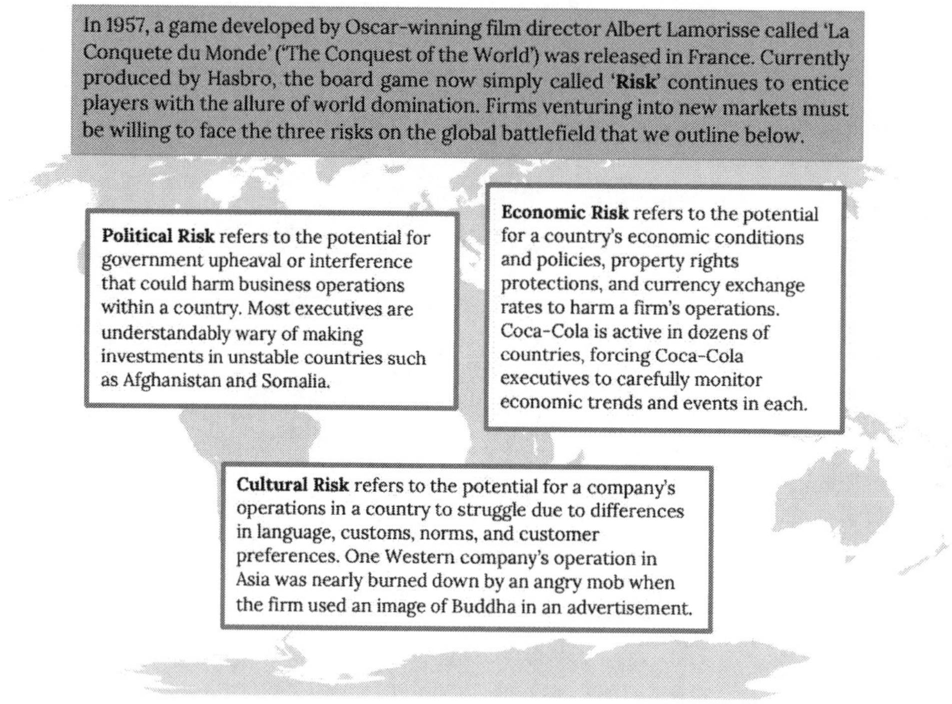

In 1957, a game developed by Oscar-winning film director Albert Lamorisse called 'La Conquete du Monde' ('The Conquest of the World') was released in France. Currently produced by Hasbro, the board game now simply called **'Risk'** continues to entice players with the allure of world domination. Firms venturing into new markets must be willing to face the three risks on the global battlefield that we outline below.

Political Risk refers to the potential for government upheaval or interference that could harm business operations within a country. Most executives are understandably wary of making investments in unstable countries such as Afghanistan and Somalia.

Economic Risk refers to the potential for a country's economic conditions and policies, property rights protections, and currency exchange rates to harm a firm's operations. Coca-Cola is active in dozens of countries, forcing Coca-Cola executives to carefully monitor economic trends and events in each.

Cultural Risk refers to the potential for a company's operations in a country to struggle due to differences in language, customs, norms, and customer preferences. One Western company's operation in Asia was nearly burned down by an angry mob when the firm used an image of Buddha in an advertisement.

Figure 9.6: Entering New Markets: Worth the Risk?

Political Risk

Although competing in international markets offers important potential benefits, such as access to new customers, the opportunity to lower costs, and the diversification of business risk, going overseas also poses daunting challenges. **Political risk** refers to the potential for government upheaval or interference with business to harm an operation within a country (Figure 9.1). For example, the term "Arab Spring" has been used to refer to a series of uprisings in 2011 within countries such as Tunisia, Egypt, Libya, Bahrain, Syria, and Yemen. Unstable governments associated with such demonstrations and uprisings make it difficult for firms to plan for the future. Over time, a government could become increasingly hostile to foreign businesses by imposing new taxes and new regulations. In extreme cases, a firm's assets in a country are seized by the national government. This process is called nationalization. In recent years, for example, Venezuela has nationalized foreign-controlled operations in the oil, cement, steel, and glass industries. US oil companies were expelled from the country.

Countries with the highest levels of political risk tend to be those whose governments are so unstable that few foreign companies are willing to enter them because of the potential for physical violence and harm to life or property. High levels of political risk are also present, however, in several of the world's important emerging economies, including India, the Philippines, and Indonesia. This creates a dilemma for firms in that these risky settings also offer enormous growth opportunities. Firms can choose to concentrate their efforts in countries such as Canada, Australia, South Korea, and Japan that have very low levels of political risk, but opportunities in such settings are often more modest (Kostigen, 2011).

Economic Risk

Economic risk refers to the potential for a country's economic conditions and policies, property rights protections, and currency exchange rates to harm a firm's operations within a country. Executives who lead companies that do business in many different countries have to take stock of these various dimensions and try to anticipate how the dimensions will affect their companies. Because economies are unpredictable, economic risk presents executives with tremendous challenges.

Figure 9.7: President Hugo Chavez of Venezuela nationalized the oil industry, expelling US oil companies.

Figure 9.8: Economic risk involves many complex and daunting elements.

Consider, for example, Kia's operations in Europe., Kia reported increased sales in ten European countries relative to the prior year. The firm enjoyed a 62% year-to-year increase in Slovakia, 58% in Austria, 50% in Gibraltar, 49% in Sweden, 43% in Poland, 24% in Germany, 21% in the United Kingdom, 13% in the Czech Republic, 6% in Belgium, and 3% in Italy (Kia, 2020). As Kia's executives planned for the future, they needed to wonder how economic conditions would influence Kia's future performance in Europe. If inflation and interest rates were to increase in a particular country, this would make it more difficult for consumers to purchase new Kias. If currency exchange rates were to change such that the euro became weaker relative to the South Korean won, this would make a Kia more expensive for European buyers.

Cultural Risk

Cultural risk refers to the potential for a company's operations in a country to struggle because of differences in language, customs, norms, and customer preferences (Table 9.2). The history of business is full of colorful examples of cultural differences undermining companies. For example, a laundry detergent company was surprised by its poor sales in the Middle East. Executives believed that their product was being skillfully promoted using print advertisements that showed dirty clothing on the left, a box of detergent in the middle, and clean clothing on the right. A simple and effective message, right? Not exactly. Unlike English and other Western languages, the languages used in the Middle East, such as Hebrew and Arabic, involve reading from right to left. To consumers, the implication of the detergent ads was that the product could be used to take clean clothes and make them dirty. Not surprisingly, few boxes of the detergent were sold before this cultural blunder was discovered.

The phrase "When in Rome, do as the Romans do" is used to encourage travelers to embrace local customs. An important part of fitting in is avoiding behaviors that locals consider offensive. Below we illustrate a number of activities that would go largely unnoticed in the United States but could raise concerns in other countries.

Table 9.3 Cultural Risk: When in Rome

Examples of Cultural Risk
If you want to signal "Check please!" to catch the attention of your garçon in France and Belgium, remember that snapping your fingers is vulgar there.
Provocative dress is embraced by many Americans, but many people in Muslim countries consider a woman's clothing to be inappropriate if it reveals anything besides the face and hands.
Do you pride yourself on your punctuality? You may be wasting your time in Latin American countries, where the locals tend to be about 20 minutes behind schedule.
Do not eat with your left hand in India or Malaysia. That hand is associated with unclean activities reserved for the bathroom.
In many Asian and Arabian countries, showing the sole of your shoe is considered rude.
If everything is OK when you're in Brazil, avoid making the "OK" hand signal. It's the equivalent to giving someone the middle finger.
Do not clean your plate in China. Leaving food on the plate indicates the host was so generous that the meal could not be finished.
In Japan, direct eye contact is viewed as impolite.

A refrigerator manufacturer experienced poor sales in the Middle East because of another cultural difference. The firm used a photo of an open refrigerator in its print ads to demonstrate the large amount of storage offered by the appliance. Unfortunately, the photo prominently featured pork, a type of meat that is not eaten by the Jews and Muslims who make up most of the area's population (Ricks, 1993). To get a sense of consumers' reactions, imagine if you saw a refrigerator ad that showed meat from a horse or a dog. You would likely be disgusted. In some parts of the world, however, horse and dog meat are accepted parts of diets. Firms must take cultural differences such as these into account when competing in international markets.

Cultural differences can cause problems even when the cultures involved are very similar and share the same language. RecycleBank is an American firm that specializes in creating programs that reward people for recycling, similar to airlines' frequent-flyer programs. When RecycleBank expanded its operations into the United Kingdom, executives at RecycleBank became offended when the British press referred to RecycleBank's rewards program as a "scheme." Their concern was unwarranted, however. The word scheme implies sneakiness when used in the United States, but a scheme simply means a service in the United Kingdom (Maltby, 2010). Differences in the meaning of English words between the United States and the United Kingdom are also vexing (Table 9.4).

Cultural differences rooted in language—even across English-speaking countries—can affect how firms do business internationally. Below we provide a few examples.

Table 9.4 Watch Your Language

Cultural Differences in Language
Book and movie titles are often changed in different markets to appeal to different cultural sensibilities. For example, British author J.K. Rowling's Harry Potter and the Philosopher's Stone was changed to Harry Potter and the Sorcerer's Stone in the United States because of the belief that American children would find a philosopher to be boring.
Moms in the states can be seen walking with strollers in their neighborhoods, while "mums" in Ireland and the United Kingdom keep their children moving in a buggy.
In India, you are more likely to hear "no problem" than "no" as Indian nationals avoid the disappointment associated with using the word no.
The area of a car called a trunk in America is known as the boot in England.
Wondering what it means when a British friend asks, "What's under your bonnet?" Open the hood of your car to offer an answer.
While Americans look for a flashlight when power goes out, a torch is the preferred term for those outside of North America.
Urban legend says that the Chevrolet Nova did not do well in Spanish speaking countries because the name translates as "no go." The truth is that the car sold well in both Mexico and Venezuela.

Key Takeaway

- Competing in international markets involves important opportunities and daunting threats. The opportunities include access to new customers, lowering costs, and diversification of business risk. The threats include political risk, economic risk, and cultural risk.

Exercises

1. Is offshoring ethical or unethical? Why?
2. Do you expect reshoring to become more popular in the years ahead? Why or why not?
3. Have you ever seen an advertisement that was culturally offensive? Why do you think that companies are sometimes slow to realize that their ads will offend people?

References

CBS News. (2018, May 4). *California now has the world's 5th largest economy.* https://www.cbsnews.com/news/california-now-has-the-worlds-5th-largest-economy/.

Copeland, L. (2010, March 25). Kia breathes life into old Georgia textile mill town. *USA Today.* http://www.usatoday.com/news/nation/2010-03-24-boomtown_N.htm.

Isidore, C. (2011, June 17). Made in USA: Overseas jobs come home. *CNNMoney.* http://money.cnn.com/2011/06/17/news/economy/made_in_usa/index.htm.

Kent, D. (2011, June 19). Kia production in Georgia helping companies across Alabama. *al.com.* http://blog.al.com/businessnews/2011/06/kia_production_in_georgia_help.html.

Kia. (n.d.). *Frequently asked questions.* Kia.com. http://www.kia.com/#/faq/.

Kia. (2020, September 7). *Kia sales climb strongly in 10 countries in May* [Press release]. Kia website. http://www.kia-press.com/press/corporate/20090605-kia%20sales%20climb%20strongly%20in%2010%20countries.aspx.

Kostigen, T. (2011, February 25). Beware: The world's riskiest countries. Market Watch. *Wall Street Journal.* http://www.marketwatch.com/story/beware-the-worlds-riskiest-countries-2011-02-25.

Maltby, E. (2010, January 19). Expanding abroad? Avoid cultural gaffes. *Wall Street Journal.* https://www.wsj.com/articles/SB10001424052748703657604575005511903147960.

Monroe Engineering. (2018, July 8). *Study reveals which manufacturing companies are reshoring the most jobs.* https://monroeengineering.com/blog/study-reveals-which-manufacturing-companies-are-reshoring-the-most-jobs/.

Reuters. (2020, January 6). *GM's China sales drop for second year on weak economy.* https://www.reuters.com/article/us-gm-china/gms-2019-china-sales-drop-for-second-year-on-weak-economy-idUSKBN1Z606D.

Ricks, D. A. (1993). *Blunders in international business*. Cambridge, MA: Blackwell.

Sands, P. (2011, June 2). *Kia Motors Manufacturing Georgia begins expansion projects to support increased volume beginning in 2012*. Kia.com. https://www.kmmgusa.com/kia-motors-manufacturing-georgia-begins-expansion-projects-to-support-increased-volume-beginning-in-2012.

Statista. (2019). *Revenue of McDonald's corporation worldwide in 2019, by region*. https://www.statista.com/statistics/219453/revenue-of-the-mcdonalds-corporation-by-geographic-region/.

The Two Malcontents. (2007, July 3). *Clove-flavored Marlboro now in Indonesia*. http://www.the-two-malcontents.com/2007/07/clove-flavored-marlboro- now-in-indonesia.

Image Credits

9.3 CAGE Framework

Doing business abroad is fraught with peril. Even Target failed when it opened stores in Canada—a move that one would think was easy. A firm must assess the risks and the likelihood of success before taking the leap. One way to do this is to analyze the political, economic, and cultural risks discussed earlier in this chapter. Another tool to assist in this evaluation is the CAGE framework.

The CAGE framework (Mariadoss, 2017) helps a firm gauge the distance that the target country is from the firm's home country on four dimensions. The greater the distance or difference, the more risk exists and the less opportunity there is for success.

The four CAGE dimensions are:

- Cultural Distance
- Administrative Distance
- Geographic Distance
- Economic Distance

Cultural Distance: This refers to the differences of cultures between the target and home countries. The history of relationships between nations provides one source of explanation for the closeness (similarity) or distance (difference) between cultures. For instance, many countries suffered under the domination of imperial rule during colonial times with effects that are evident in their contemporary culture and influencing national relationships. For example, as a former colony of Great Britain, there is a smaller cultural distance between the US and the United Kingdom than there is between the US and Spain. However, this is not always the case. Western European countries have a significant cultural distance with many Asian countries despite having colonized many of those same territories. Therefore, history provides a partial insight into cultural distance.

Societal customs and values also play a key role in cultural distance. Language differences also increase or decrease cultural distance. At first glance, it would appear that the US and India would have a large cultural distance, but this is reduced because much of business in India is conducted in English, and both countries were colonies of Great Britain.

Administrative Distance: The legal and political systems of the home and target countries determine the administrative distance between the two. In countries where the political systems are different, for example, democracy versus communism, there is a greater distance and more uncertainty. Different laws between countries can make compliance and doing business more difficult. For example, in some countries, laws governing contract compliance are not enforced. In some nations if a buyer fails to make payment for purchases, the seller can sue, but it may take years before a court will even hear the case. Also, labor laws can be quite different among nations. In the Dominican Republic, for instance, companies are required to pay employees a thirteenth month of salary at the end of the year, as a bonus. Alternatively, some nations protect the civil rights of people who fall within protected categories in the US (e.g., age, race, sex, class, gender, sexual orientation, etc.), but other nations may not. This raises particularly tricky questions for firms who must abide by US laws, but seek to expand abroad,

Geographic Distance: The literal physical distance between the home and target country are a key consideration of this dimension. The more miles the countries are apart, the longer and more costly it is to go there or to ship from one to the other. But mileage is not the only factor. The ease of communication between countries is another. Advances in telephone and internet communications have made this almost a non-issue in most countries. However, when two countries are twelve time zones apart, like the US and China, communication can be hampered when work schedules are twelve hours out of sync. Geographic distance can also be affected by the infrastructure of a country in other ways other than communication and internet capabilities. For example, Haiti is physically close to the US, but its lack of adequate port facilities make it a poor target for outsourcing manufacturing.

Economic Distance: International business between two countries is also impacted by the differences in their economic factors. The greater the differences in the two economies, the more difficult it is to be successful. One way to measure the difference is by GDP per capita. Countries with a similar GDP per capita have a greater opportunity for success. If the purchasing power and disposable income of the target country are quite different from the home country, working in the target country is more challenging.

Suppose Chipotle believes there are great opportunities if they go international. Executives have narrowed the countries down to two—Canada and Spain. Canada made the list because they are close and more like the US. But Spain has 10 million more inhabitants, is not spread out like Canada is, and Spaniards should have a great attraction to Chipotle's menu, since it's Mexican cuisine. The CAGE framework can be used to help make a decision. The four dimensions for each country are measured on a 10 point scale, with the higher numbers indicating greater distance. Therefore, the country with the lower score is the better choice. Table 9.5 illustrates the process.

Table 9.5 Using the CAGE Framework: Canada vs Spain for Chipotle

	C Cultural	A Administrative	G Geographic	E Economic	Total
Canada	**3** Oh, there is the French speaking part of Canada	**2** Parliamentarian with Prime Minister vs US	**2** Very close, but cities very spread out	**2** About the same except for currency	9
Spain	**7** Language difference, and they don't eat much Mexican food	**5** Member of EU, similar to US, some laws different	**5** Easy 6 hour plane flight, 6 hour time difference.	**6** US GDP per capita twice Spain's.	23

As can be seen from the CAGE scores, the Chipotle executives' hunches about Spain proved incorrect, and Canada is the best location to first go international.

Section Video

CAGE Framework for International Trade-Global Matters [02:24]

The video for this lesson discusses the CAGE framework and how it can be used to evaluate international trade opportunities.

You can view this video here: https://youtu.be/7FpUJaG7uMk.

Key Takeaway

- Success with implementing an international strategy starts with selecting the correct country to enter. Using the CAGE framework allows a firm to compare target countries to help make this critical decision. Understanding the distance between the home country and the target country as it relates to differences in culture, administrative functions, geographic barriers, and economic disparities will assist the firm in making the best decision.

Exercises

1. Tesla wants to explore going into Europe or South America, and has narrowed down the countries to Germany or Chile. Use the CAGE framework to decide which would be the better choice.
2. Divide up into groups of 4 or 8 and discuss some of the cultural differences that exist across countries that cultural distance shows should be taken into consideration. Report out.

References

Mariadoss, B. J. (2017). Global Market Opporttnity Assessment – Cage Analysis. *Core principles of international marketing* [Pressbooks edition]. CC BY NC SA 3.0. Washington State University. https://opentext.wsu.edu/mktg360/chapter/6-3-selecting-target-markets-and-target-market-strategies.

Video Credits

Carlson School of Management. (2015, March 12). *Pankaj Ghemawat: CAGE framework for international trade – global matters* [Video]. YouTube. https://youtu.be/7FpUJaG7uMk.

9.4 Types of International Strategies

A firm that has operations in more than one country is known as a **multinational corporation** (MNC). The largest MNCs are major players within the international arena. Walmart's annual worldwide sales, for example, are larger than the dollar value of the entire economies of Austria, Norway, and Saudi Arabia. Although Walmart tends to be viewed as an American retailer, the firm earns 35% of its revenues outside the United States. Walmart owns significant numbers of stores in Mexico, Central America, Brazil, Japan, the United Kingdom, Canada, Chile, Botswana, and Argentina. Walmart also participates in joint ventures in China and India. Even more modestly sized MNCs are still very powerful. If Kia were a country, its current sales level of approximately $21 billion would place it in the top 100 among the more than 180 nations in the world.

Multinationals such as Kia and Walmart must choose an international strategy to guide their efforts in various countries. There are four main international strategies available:

1. International
2. Multi-domestic
3. Global
4. Transnational

(Figure 9.2). Each strategy involves a different approach to trying to be sensitive to (1) costs and efficiencies on one hand and trying to be responsive to (2) variation in customer preferences and market conditions across nations. Responding or not responding to these two pressures of cost and local cultural conditions determines which of the four types of international strategies will be pursued.

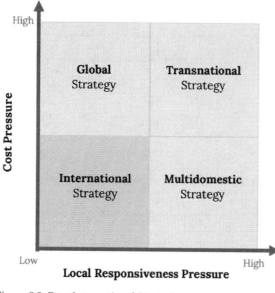

High

Cost Pressure

Low

Global
Strategy

Transnational
Strategy

International
Strategy

Multidomestic
Strategy

Local Responsiveness Pressure

Low   High

Figure 9.9: Four International Strategies

International Strategy

Firms pursuing an international strategy are neither concerned about costs nor adapting to the local cultural conditions. They attempt to sell their products internationally with little to no change. When Harley Davidson sells motorcycles abroad, they do not need to lower their prices or adapt the bike to local motorcycle standards. People in other countries buy a Harley particularly because it is different from the local motorcycles. Buyers want the American look and the sound and power of a Harley, and will pay for that differentiation. Belgium chocolate exporters do not lower their price when exporting to the American market to compete with Hershey's, nor do they adapt their product to American tastes. They use an international strategy. Starbucks and Rolex watches are other examples of firms pursuing the international strategy.

Multi-Domestic Strategy

A firm using a multi-domestic strategy does not focus on cost or efficiency but emphasizes responsiveness to local requirements within each of its markets. Rather than trying to force all of its American-made shows on viewers around the globe, Netflix customizes the programming that is shown on its channels within dozens of countries, including New Zealand, Portugal, Pakistan, and India. Similarly, food company H. J. Heinz adapts its products to match local preferences. Because some Indians will not eat garlic and onion, for example, Heinz offers them a version of its signature ketchup that does not include these two ingredients. Outback Steakhouse uses the multi-domestic strategy in the multiple countries where it operates, adapting to local eating preferences but not lowering prices significantly.

Figure 9.10: Baked beans flavored with curry? This H. J. Heinz product is very popular in the United Kingdom.

Global Strategy

A firm using a global strategy sacrifices responsiveness to local requirements within each of its markets in favor of emphasizing lower costs and better efficiency. This strategy is the complete opposite of a multi-domestic strategy. Some minor modifications to products and services may be made in various markets, but a global strategy stresses the need to gain low costs and economies of scale by offering essentially the same products or services in each market.

Microsoft, for example, offers the same software programs around the world but adjusts the programs to match local languages. Similarly, consumer goods maker Procter & Gamble attempts to gain efficiency by creating global brands whenever possible. Global strategies also can be very effective for firms whose product or service is largely hidden from the customer's view, such as silicon chip maker Intel. Lenovo also uses this strategy. For such firms, variance in local preferences is not very important, but pricing is.

Transnational Strategy

A firm using a transnational strategy seeks a middle ground between a multi-domestic strategy and a global strategy. Such a firm tries to balance the desire for lower costs and efficiency with the need to adjust to local preferences within various countries. For example, large fast-food chains such as McDonald's and Kentucky Fried Chicken (KFC) rely on the same brand names and the same core menu items around the world. These firms make some concessions to local tastes too. In France, for example, wine can be purchased at McDonald's. This approach makes sense for McDonald's because wine is a central element of French diets. In Saudi Arabia, McDonalds serves a McArabia Chicken sandwich, and its breakfast menu features no pork products like ham, bacon, or sausage.

Section Video

Global Strategies [02:45]

The video for this lesson discusses global strategy options.

You can view this video here: https://youtu.be/83rBbT5Qq_E.

Image Credits

Figure 9.9: Kindred Grey (2020). "Cost pressure v. Local responsiveness pressure." CC BY-SA 4.0. Retrieved from: https://commons.wikimedia.org/wiki/File:Cost_pressure_v._Local_responsiveness_pressure.png.

Figure 9.10: AtelierJoly. "Curried Beans." CC BY-SA 3.0. Cropped. Retrieved from https://commons.wikimedia.org/wiki/File:Curry_Beanz.jpg.

Video Credits

pb venkat. (2015, May 14). *Global strategies* [Video]. YouTube. https://youtu.be/83rBbT5Qq_E.

9.5 Drivers of Success and Failure When Competing in International Markets

The title of a book written by newspaper columnist Thomas Friedman attracted a great deal of attention when the book was released in 2005. In *The World Is Flat: A Brief History of the 21st Century*, Friedman argued that technological advances and increased interconnectedness is leveling the competitive playing field between developed and emerging countries. This means that companies exist in a "flat world" because economies across the globe are converging on a single integrated global system (Friedman, 2005). For executives, a key implication is that a firm being based in a particular country is ceasing to be an advantage or disadvantage.

While Friedman's notion of business becoming a flat world is flashy and attention grabbing, it does not match reality. Research studies conducted since 2005 have found that some firms enjoy advantages based on their country of origin while others suffer disadvantages. A powerful framework for understanding how likely it is that firms based in a particular country will be successful when competing in international markets was provided by Professor Michael Porter of the Harvard Business School (Porter, 1990). The framework is formally known as "the determinants of national advantage," but it is often referred to more simply as "the diamond model" because of its shape (Table 9.6).

Diamonds may be a country's best friend. Around half of the world's diamonds are mined in South Africa, giving that country a unique advantage in the global diamond industry. Porter's Determinants of National Advantage (often referred to as the diamond model) includes four key dimensions that help explain why firms located in certain countries are more successful than others in particular industries.

Table 9.6 Porter's Diamond Model of National Advantage

Strategy, Structure, and Rivalry	The United States has an overall trade deficit, but it enjoys a trade surplus within the service sector. Fierce domestic competition in industries such as hotels and restaurants has helped make American firms such as Marriott and Subway important players on the world stage.
Factor Conditions	The inputs present in a country shape a firm's global competitiveness. The rapid growth of Chinese manufacturers has been fueled by the availability of cheap labor.
Demand Conditions	Fussy domestic customers help firms prepare for the global arena. Japanese firms must create excellent goods to meet Japanese consumers' high expectations about quality, aesthetics, and reliability.
Related and Supporting Industries	Firms benefit when their domestic suppliers and other complementary industries are developed and helpful. Italy's fashion industry is enhanced by the abundance of fine Italian leather and well-known designers.

According to the model, the ability of the firms in an industry whose origin is in a particular country (e.g., South Korean automakers or Italian shoemakers) to be successful in the international arena is shaped by four factors:

1. Their home country's demand conditions
2. Their home country's factor conditions
3. Related and supporting industries within their home country
4. Strategy, structure, and rivalry among their domestic competitors

Demand Conditions

Within the diamond model, demand conditions refer to the nature of domestic customers (Table 9.7). It is tempting to believe that firms benefit when their domestic customers are perfectly willing to purchase inferior products. This would be a faulty belief! Instead, firms benefit when their domestic customers have high expectations.

Japanese consumers are known for insisting on very high levels of quality, aesthetics, and reliability. Japanese automakers such as Honda, Toyota, and Nissan reap rewards from this situation. These firms have to work hard to satisfy their domestic buyers. Living up to lofty quality standards at home prepares these firms to offer high-quality products when competing in international markets. In contrast, French car buyers do not stand out as particularly fussy. It is probably not a coincidence that French automakers Renault and Peugeot have struggled to gain traction within the global auto industry.

Figure 9.11: Japanese firms must deliver very high quality to meet the expectations of Japanese consumers.

Within the diamond model, demand conditions refer to the nature of domestic customers. Below we provide examples from the worldwide auto industry that illustrate how domestic customers influence firms' ability to compete in the global arena.

Table 9.7 Demand Conditions

Demand Condition Examples
Japanese consumers insist on very high levels of quality, aesthetics, and reliability. This forces Honda, Toyota, and Nissan to rise to a difficult challenge as well as preparing them to dominate internationally.
Because French car buyers are not particularly picky, Renault and Peugeot have not been forced to excel in their home market. Not surprisingly, they have struggled to gain traction within the global auto industry.
Germans place value on the concept of fahrvergnügen, which means "driving pleasure." Customers around the globe experience driving pleasure when purchasing cars from BMW, Mercedes-Benz, Porsche, and Volkswagen.
The Italian fascination with styling is evident in luxury car brands such as Alfa Romeo, Ferrari, Lamborghini, and Maserati.
To many Americans, bigger is better. This attitude is captured in the large SUVs like the Suburban. When gas prices go down, sales of these hunkers go up.

Demand conditions also help to explain why German automakers such as Porsche, Mercedes-Benz, and BMW create excellent luxury and high-performance vehicles. German consumers value superb engineering. While a car is simply a means of transportation in some cultures, Germans place value on the concept of fahrvergnügen, which means "driving pleasure." Meanwhile, demand for fast cars is high in Germany because the country has built nearly eight thousand miles of superhighways known as autobahns. No speed limits for cars are enforced on more than half of the eight thousand miles. Many Germans enjoy driving at 150 miles per hour or more, and German automakers must build cars capable of safely reaching and maintaining such speeds. When these companies compete in the international arena, the engineering and performance of their vehicles stand out.

Factor Conditions

Factor conditions refer to the nature of raw material and other inputs that firms need to create goods and services (Table 9.8). Examples include land, labor, capital markets, and infrastructure. Firms benefit when they have good access to factor conditions and face challenges when they do not. Companies based in the United States, for example, are able to draw on plentiful natural resources, a skilled labor force, highly developed transportation systems, and sophisticated capital markets to be successful. The dramatic growth of Chinese manufacturers in recent years has been fueled in part by the availability of cheap labor.

The factor conditions in a country serve as the basic building blocks of doing business within the country. Below are examples of how important factor conditions have provided competitive advantages for firms based in certain different countries.

Table 9.8 Factor Conditions

Land	Russia has the greatest land mass of any country in the world and it enjoys vast oil deposits. This abundance of natural resources has helped Russia's petroleum industry become one of the largest in the world.
Labor	India is the seventh largest country in terms of land mass, but its population size is second only to China. Because India graduates more English speakers annually than the United States, it should come as no surprise that Indian firms have gained ground in the international arena within industries that rely on engineering and computer skills.
Capital	The capital market in the United States is one of the largest and most sophisticated in the world. This has helped American companies fund expansion and innovation over time, making them better prepared for international competition.
Entrepreneurial Ability	Entrepreneurial ability creates national wealth when entrepreneurs develop new innovations that support key industries. Denmark's low start-up costs and high research and development spending have fueled success in industries such as pharmaceuticals and medical equipment.

In some cases, overcoming disadvantages in factor conditions leads companies to develop unique skills. Japan is a relatively small island nation with little room to spare. This situation has led Japanese firms to be pioneers in the efficient use of warehouse space through systems such as just-in-time inventory management (JIT). Rather than storing large amounts of parts and material, JIT management conserves space—and lowers costs—by requiring inputs to a production process to arrive at the moment they are needed. Their use of JIT management has given Japanese manufacturers an advantage when they compete in international markets.

Figure 9.12: American furniture makers benefit from the abundance of high-quality lumber in the United States.

Related and Supporting Industries

The Beatles' legendary songwriting team of Lennon and McCartney once wrote that they got by "with a little help from my friends." In Porter's diamond model, the presence of strong friends in the form of related and supporting industries is one of the keys to national advantage. We provide examples of American industries that excel internationally due in part to help from supporting industries.

Table 9.9 Related and Supporting Industries

Related and Supporting Industries
A very strong agriculture business helps support the cattle industry—which accounted for approximately $8.33 billion dollars worth of exports in 2018.
Excellent steel makers and engine manufacturers support the production of one of America's most lucrative exports—commercial aircraft.
The pharmaceutical industry benefits from the research skills possessed by university-affiliated hospitals.
America's excellent performing arts schools such as the Juilliard School cultivate the talents of world-famous American performers.

Could Italian shoemakers create some of the world's best shoes if Italian leather makers were not among the world's best? Possibly, but it would be much more difficult. The concept of related and supporting industries refers to the extent to which firms' domestic suppliers and other complementary industries are developed and helpful (Table 9.9). Italian shoemakers such as Salvatore Ferragamo, Prada, Gucci, and Versace benefit from the availability of top-quality leather within their home country. If these shoemakers needed to rely on imported leather, they would lose flexibility and speed.

The auto industry is a setting where related and supporting industries are very important. Electronics are key components of modern vehicles. South Korean automakers Kia and Hyundai can leverage the excellent electronics provided by South Korean firms Samsung and LG. Similarly, Honda, Nissan, and Toyota are able to draw on the skills of Sony and other Japanese electronics firms. Unfortunately, for French automakers Renault and Peugeot, no French electronics firms are standouts in the international arena. This situation makes it difficult for Renault and Peugeot to integrate electronics into their vehicles as effectively as their South Korean and Japanese rivals.

Figure 9.13: Fine Italian shoes, such as those found at the famous Via Montenapoleone in Milan, are usually made of fine Italian leather.

In extreme cases, the poor condition of related and supporting industries can undermine an operation. Otabo LLC, a small custom shoe company, was forced to shut down its Florida factory as it struggled to find technicians that had the skills needed to fix its shoe making machines. Meanwhile, there are very few suppliers of shoelaces, soles, eyelets, and other components in the United States because about 99% of the shoes purchased in the United States are imported, mostly from China. The few available suppliers were unwilling to create the small batches of customized materials that Otabo wanted. In the end, the American factory simply could not get access to many of the supplies needed to create shoes (Aeppel, 2008). Production was shifted to China, where all the needed supplies can be found easily and cheaply.

Firm Strategy, Structure, and Rivalry

The concept of firm strategy, structure, and rivalry within the diamond model refers to how challenging it is to survive domestic competition. When domestic competition is fierce, the survivors are well prepared for the international arena. Below we offer examples of some of the most renowned exports that have resulted from the intense competition in domestic markets.

Table 9.10 Strategy, Structure, and Rivalry

Successful Export Examples
Cuban cigar brands such as Chiba are treasured by cigar aficionados around the globe. Despite US trade sanctions, cigars remain a leading export from Cuba.
Belgian firms produce over 200 million tons of chocolate each year. Brands that prosper despite this domestic competition stand out when they compete overseas.
Say "domo arigato" (Thank you very much) to the Japanese electronics industry, where competitors Seiko, Sony, Hitachi, and others push each other to bring smiles to the faces of consumers wanting a new watch, camera, video game system, or robot.
Over one million weavers work in Iran's Persian rug industry. Part of the magic behind these world-famous carpets is that excellence is needed in order to fly above a crowded domestic market.
German breweries produce over five thousand brands of beer. With this high level of domestic rivalry, it is not surprising that German beers excel worldwide.
US movie studios have collectively dominated the global scene since the days of Charlie Chaplin and other silent-film stars.

The concept of firm strategy, structure, and rivalry refers to how challenging it is to survive domestic competition (Table 9.10). The Olympics offer a good analogy for illustrating the positive aspects of very challenging domestic situations. If the competition to make a national team in gymnastics is fierce, the gymnasts who make the team will have been pushed to stretch their abilities and performance. In contrast, gymnasts who faced few contenders in their quest to make a national team will not have been tested with the same level of intensity. When the two types meet at the Olympics, the gymnasts who overcame huge hurdles to make their national teams are likely to have an edge over athletes from countries with few skilled gymnasts.

Figure 9.14: *Succeeding despite difficult domestic competition prepares firms to expand their kingdoms into international markets.*

Companies that have survived intense rivalry within their home markets are likely to have developed strategies and structures that will facilitate their success when they compete in international markets. Hyundai and Kia had to keep pace with each other within the South Korean market before expanding overseas. The leading Japanese automakers, Honda, Nissan, and Toyota, have had to compete not only with one another but also with smaller yet still potent domestic firms such as Isuzu, Mazda, Mitsubishi, Subaru, and Suzuki. In both examples, the need to navigate potent domestic rivals has helped firms later become fearsome international players.

If, in contrast, domestic competition is fairly light, a company may enjoy admirable profits within its home market. However, the lack of being pushed by rivals will likely mean that the firm struggles to reach its potential in creativity and innovation. This undermines the firm's ability to compete overseas and makes it vulnerable to foreign entry into its home market. Because neither Renault nor Peugeot has been a remarkable innovator historically, these French automakers have enjoyed fairly gentle domestic competition. Once the auto industry became a global competition, however, these firms found themselves trailing their Asian rivals.

Section Video

Porter's Diamond explained with an example [03:07]

The video for this lesson explains the Porter's Diamond framework by using an example.

You can view this video here: https://youtu.be/NM5Lwj-RZ34.

Key Takeaway

- The likelihood that a firm will succeed when it competes in international markets is shaped by four aspects of its domestic market: (1) demand conditions; (2) factor conditions; (3) related and supporting industries; and (4) strategy, structure, and rivalry among its domestic competitors.

Exercises

1. Which of the four elements of the diamond model do you believe has the strongest influence on a firm's fate when it competes in international markets?
2. Automakers in China and India have yet to compete on the world stage. Based on the diamond model, would these firms be likely to succeed or fail within the global auto industry?

References

Aeppel, T. (2008, March 3). US shoe factory finds supplies are Achilles' heel. *Wall Street Journal.* http://online.wsj.com/article/SB120450124543206313.html.

Friedman, T. L. (2005). *The world is flat: A brief history of the 21st century.* Farrar, Straus and Giroux.

Porter, M. E. (1990). *The competitive advantage of nations.* Free Press.

Image Credits

Figure 9.11: Bantersnaps. "Men's Black and White Suit Photo." Public Domain. Retrieved from https://unsplash.com/photos/dLHIkzxN8sM.

Figure 9.12: Francis Eatherington. "Seneca Lumber spraying herbicides."
CC BY-NC 2.0. Retrieved from https://www.flickr.com/photos/umpquawild/13517864965/.

Figure 9.13: Warburg. "Shop." CC BY-SA 3.0. Retrieved from https://en.wikipedia.org/wiki/File:Milan_Montenapoleone_16.JPG.

Figure 9.14: Chrisloader. "Burger King Branch, Leicester Square, London, UK." CC BY-SA 3.0. Retrieved from https://en.wikipedia.org/wiki/File:Leicester_Square_Burger_King.jpg.

Video Credits

Simply-ptrn. (2015, November 29). *Ep 1: Porter's Diamond explained with an example* [Video]. YouTube. https://youtu.be/NM5Lwj-RZ34.

9.6 Options for Competing in International Markets

French philosopher Michel de Montaigne once quipped that marriage is "a market which has nothing free but the entrance." When trying to match their goods and services with the promise of love from a new market, executives have multiple entry options—but they should carefully consider each, lest the romance be short-lived.

Table 9.11 Market Entry Options

Exporting	Exporting involves creating goods at home and then shipping them to another country. Civilian aircraft are a top-ten US export to countries such as Japan, China, Germany, Italy, and France that want to make their skies friendlier for travel.
Licensing	Licensing involves granting a foreign company the right to create a company's product in exchange for a fee. This option is frequently used in manufacturing industries, such as when Coca-Cola licenses their secret formulas to local bottlers (without revealing the formulas, of course).
Franchising	Franchising involves "renting" a firm's brand name and business processes to local entrepreneurs. Curves International has used franchising to bulk up its fitness empire to include over thirty countries.
Joint Venture	In a joint venture, two or more organizations each contribute to the creation of a new entity. In a strategic alliance, firms work together cooperatively without forming a new organization. Global Nuclear Fuel Co.—a collaboration among General Electric, Toshiba Corporation, and Hitachi Limited—is an example of a joint venture.
Acquisition/Wholly owned Subsidiary	Acquisition/wholly owned subsidiary is when a firm acquires a business operation in a foreign country. The firm fully owns the acquired company. Intel established IPLS—a wholly owned subsidiary in Ireland—to facilitate and manage its research throughout the "Emerald Isle." Smithfield Foods, the world's largest producer of pork products and located in Virginia, was acquired by a Chinese company for nearly $5 million.
Greenfield/Wholly owned subsidiary	Greenfield/wholly owned subsidiary is when a company enters a foreign country and buys property and constructs their business. This could be a manufacturer building a plant, or a retailer building a store, as opposed to acquiring an existing one. BMW used this approach to build its car manufacturing plant in South Carolina.

When the executives in charge of a firm decide to enter a new country, they must decide how to enter the country. There are six basic options available: (1) exporting, (2) licensing, (3) franchising, (4) creating a joint venture or strategic alliance (5) acquisition/creating a wholly owned subsidiary, and (6) greenfield/wholly owned subsidiary (Table 9.11). These options vary in terms of how much control a firm has over its operation, how much risk is involved, and what share of the operation's profits the firm gets to keep.

It is important to note that these options are not exclusively for implementing international strategy. As discussed in Chapter 8, all but exporting are also methods to accomplish corporate strategies in their domestic markets to diversify their portfolio.

As shown in Figure 9.3, there are trade-offs in the selection of the method of entry to another country. These variables are:

- The amount of risk
- The degree of control and ownership
- The potential for profit

Exporting provides the least amount of risk, but also the least amount of control and profit potential. Moving from exporting at one end of the continuum to greenfield on the other end, the amount of risk increases, as does the degree of control/ownership and the potential to make more profit. The most risky method to enter into another country is greenfield, when the investment is high in acquiring land and building facilities, without the advantage of taking over an existing company. However, the venture is totally under the control of the entering company and the profit potential is the highest, although riskiest, as noted.

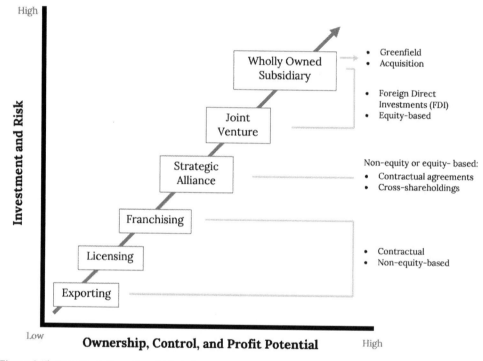

Figure 9.15: Entering International Markets

Exporting

Exporting involves creating goods within a firm's home country and then shipping them to another country. Once the goods reach foreign shores, the exporter's role is over. A local firm then sells the goods to local customers. Many firms that expand overseas start out as exporters because exporting offers a low-cost method to find out whether a firm's products are appealing to customers in other lands. Some Asian automakers, for example, first entered the US market through exporting. Small firms may rely on exporting because it is a low-cost and lower risk option.

Once a firm's products are found to be viable in a particular country, exporting often becomes undesirable. A firm that exports its goods loses control of them once they are turned over to a local firm for sale locally. This local distributor may treat customers poorly and thereby damage the firm's brand. Also, an exporter only makes money when it sells its goods at wholesale prices to a local firm, not when end users buy the goods. Executives may want their firm to enjoy the profits that are made when products are sold to individual customers rather than a local distributor.

Figure 9.16: Exporting often relies on huge cargo ships, such as this one docked in Cyprus.

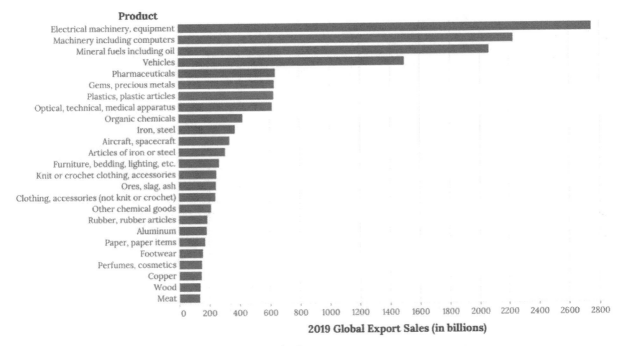

Figure 9.17: What gets exported from one country to another?

Licensing

While franchising is an option within service industries, licensing is most frequently used in manufacturing industries. Licensing involves granting a foreign company the right to create a company's product within a foreign country in exchange for a fee. These relationships often center on patented technology. A firm that grants a license avoids absorbing a lot of costs, but its profits are limited to the fees that it collects from the local firm. The firm also loses some control over how its technology is used.

A historical example involving licensing illustrates how rapidly events can change within the international arena. By the time Japan surrendered to the United States and its Allies in 1945, World War II had crippled the country's industrial infrastructure. In response to this problem, Japanese firms imported a great deal of technology, especially from American firms. When the Korean War broke out in the early 1950s, the American military relied on Jeeps made in Japan using licensed technology. In just a few years, a mortal enemy had become a valuable ally.

Strategy at the Movies

Gung Ho

Can American workers survive under Japanese management? Although this sounds like the premise for a bad reality TV show, the question was a legitimate consideration for General Motors (GM) and Toyota in the early 1980s. GM was struggling at the time to compete with the inexpensive, reliable, and fuel-efficient cars produced by Japanese firms. Meanwhile, Toyota was worried that the US government would limit the number of foreign cars that could be imported. To address these issues, these companies worked together to reopen a defunct GM plant in Fremont, California in 1984 that would manufacture both companies' automobiles in one facility. The plant had been the worst performer in the GM system; however, under Toyota's management, the New United Motor Manufacturing Incorporated (NUMMI) plant became the best factory associated with GM—using the same workers as before! Despite NUMMI's eventual success, the joint production plant experienced significant growing pains stemming from the cultural differences between Japanese managers and American workers.

Figure 9.18: Assembly line at car factory in South Korea.

The NUMMI story inspired the 1986 movie *Gung Ho* in which a closed automobile manufacturing plant in Hadleyville, Pennsylvania, was reopened by Japanese car company Assan Motors. While Assan Motors and the workers of Hadleyville were both excited about the venture, neither was prepared for the differences between the two cultures. For example, Japanese workers feel personally ashamed when they make a mistake. When manager Oishi Kazihiro failed to meet production targets, he was punished with "ribbons of shame" and forced to apologize to his employees for letting them down. In contrast, American workers were presented in the film as likely to reject management authority, prone to fighting at work, and not opposed to taking shortcuts.

When Assan Motors' executives attempted to institute morning calisthenics and insisted that employees work late without overtime pay, the American workers challenged these policies and eventually walked off the production line. Assan Motors' near failure was the result of differences in cultural norms and values. *Gung Ho* illustrates the value of understanding and bridging cultural differences to facilitate successful cross-cultural collaboration, value that was realized in real life by NUMMI.

Franchising

Franchising is a popular way for firms to grow internationally. Below are examples of US-based franchises that are successful worldwide.

Table 9.12 Franchising: A Leading American Export

Successful US-based Franchises
In many Asian countries, McDonald's franchises offer side dishes such as rice alongside its signature French fries.
If you grow tired of strudel while in Germany, remember that Dunkin' Donuts has over 3,200 stores in 36 countries outside of the United States.
Legend says that the first sandwich was created when John Montagu, the fourth Earl of Sandwich, ordered meat tucked between bread so he could play cards and eat at the same time. The sandwich remains popular in Europe, where Subway boasts over one thousand franchised restaurants.
All KFCs in Japan prominently feature a statue of KFC's founder Colonel Sanders.
If a franchised store in Norway was open during the age of the Vikings, its slogan may have been "Thank Asgard for 7-11."

Franchising has been used by many firms that compete in service industries to develop a worldwide presence (Table 9.12). Subway, The UPS Store, and Hilton Hotels are just a few of the firms that have done so. Franchising involves an organization (called a franchiser) granting the right to use its brand name, products, and processes to other organizations (known as franchisees) in exchange for an up-front payment (a franchise fee) and a percentage of franchisees' revenues (a royalty fee).

Figure 9.19: *Firms should own a thoroughly proven business model before franchising in other countries.*

Franchising is an attractive way to enter foreign markets because it requires little financial investment by the franchiser. Indeed, local franchisees must pay the vast majority of the expenses associated with getting their businesses up and running. On the downside, the decision to franchise means that a firm will get to enjoy only a small portion of the profits made under its brand name. Also, local franchisees may behave in ways that the franchiser does not approve. For example, KFC was angered by some of its franchisees in Asia when they started selling fish dishes without KFC's approval. It is often difficult to fix such problems because laws in many countries are stacked in favor of local businesses. Last, franchises are only successful if franchisees are provided with a simple and effective business model. Executives thus need to avoid expanding internationally through franchising until their formula has been perfected.

Joint Ventures and Strategic Alliances

Within each market entry option described earlier, a firm either maintains strong control of operations (wholly owned subsidiary) or it turns most control over to a local firm (exporting, franchising, and licensing). In some cases, however, executives find it beneficial to work closely with one or more local partners in a joint venture or a strategic alliance. In a joint venture, two or more organizations each contribute to the creation of a new entity. In a strategic alliance, firms work together cooperatively, but no new organization is formed. In both cases, the firm and its local partner or partners share decision-making authority, control of the operation, and any profits that the relationship creates.

Joint ventures and strategic alliances are especially attractive when a firm believes that working closely with locals will provide important knowledge about local conditions, facilitate acceptance of their involvement by government officials, or both. In the late 1980s, China was a difficult market for American businesses to enter. Executives at KFC saw China as an attractive country because chicken is a key element of Chinese diets. After considering the various options for entering China with its first restaurant, KFC decided to create a joint venture with three local organizations. KFC owned 51% of the venture; having more than half of the operation was advantageous in case disagreements arose. A Chinese bank owned 25%, the local tourist bureau owned 14%, and the final 10% was owned by a local chicken producer that would supply the restaurant with its signature food item.

Having these three local partners helped KFC navigate the cumbersome regulatory process that was in place and allowed the American firm to withstand the scrutiny of wary Chinese officials. Despite these advantages, it still took more than a year for the store to be built and approved. Once open in 1987, however, KFC was an instant success in China. As China's economy gradually became more and more open, KFC was a major beneficiary. By the end of 1997, KFC operated 191 restaurants in 50 Chinese cities. By the start of 2019, there were approximately 5,000 KFCs spread across 1,100 Chinese cities. Roughly 90% of these restaurants are wholly owned subsidiaries of KFC—a stark indication of how much doing business in China has changed over the past twenty-five years.

Figure 9.20: As of early 2011, KFC was opening a new store in China every eighteen hours on average.

Creating a Wholly Owned Subsidiary: Acquisition and Greenfield

In international strategy, a wholly owned subsidiary is a business operation in a foreign country that a firm fully owns. A firm can develop a wholly owned subsidiary through a greenfield venture, meaning that the firm creates the entire operation itself. This usually means building and operating the facility. Another possibility is purchasing an existing operation from a local company or another foreign operator.

Regardless of whether a firm builds a wholly owned subsidiary "from scratch" or acquires an existing company, having a wholly owned subsidiary can be attractive because the firm maintains complete control over the operation, and gets to keep all of the profits that the operation makes. A wholly owned subsidiary can be quite risky, however, because the firm must pay all of the expenses required to set it up and operate it. Kia, for example, spent $1 billion to build its US factory. Many firms are reluctant to spend such sums in more volatile countries because they fear that they may never recoup their investments.

Section Videos

Global Market Entry Strategy [02:00]

The video for this lesson provides a short explanation of mode of entry to other countries.

You can view this video here: https://youtu.be/a5UaXsYV1aw.

A level Business Revision-Entering International Markets [08:25]

The second video for this lesson is longer, but a more thorough explanation of mode of entry to other countries.

You can view this video here: https://youtu.be/SGoGJEe-ERk.

Key Takeaway

- When entering a new country, executives can choose exporting, licensing, franchising, creating a joint venture or strategic alliance, and creating a wholly owned subsidiary through greenfield or acquisition. The key issues of how much control a firm has over its operation, how much risk is involved, and what share of the operation's profits the firm gets to keep all vary across these options. Along the continuum from exporting to wholly owned subsidiary, risk, control, and profit potential are least with exporting and highest with the wholly owned subsidiary.

Exercises

1. Do you believe that KFC would have been so successful in China today if executives had tried to make their first store a wholly owned subsidiary? Why or why not?
2. The typical joint venture only lasts a few years. Why might joint ventures dissolve so quickly?

Image Credits

Figure 9.15: Kindred Grey (2020). "Entering International Markets." CC BY-SA 4.0. Retrieved from https://commons.wikimedia.org/wiki/File:Entering_International_Markets.png.

Figure 9.16: Mar-Law. Cargo Ship in Channel. CC BY-NC 2.0. Retrieved from https://www.flickr.com/photos/seenlikethis/3032668425/ Edited photo to add brightness.

Figure 9.17: Kindred Grey (2020). "2019 World Exports by Product." CC BY-SA 4.0. Retrieved from https://commons.wikimedia.org/wiki/File:2019_World_Exports_by_Product.png. Data retrieved from https://en.wikipedia.org/wiki/International_trade.

Figure 9.18: Anonyme. "Assembly line at Hyundai Motor Company's car factory in Ulsan, South Korea." CC BY 2.5. Retrieved from https://commons.wikimedia.org/wiki/File:Hyundai_car_assembly_line.jpg.

Figure 9.20: Juxun, Chen. "KFC Restaraunt in China." CC BY-SA 3.0. Retrieved from https://commons.wikimedia.org/wiki/File:Kfc_of_china.jpg.

Video Credits

Lyana Lan. (2014, November 21). *Global market entry strategy* [Video]. YouTube. https://youtu.be/a5UaXsYV1aw.

TakingtheBiz. (2020, March 2). *A level business revision-entering international markets* [Video]. YouTube. https://youtu.be/SGoGJEe-ERk.

9.7 Conclusion

This chapter explains competition in international markets. Executives must consider the benefits and risks of competing internationally when making decisions about whether to expand overseas. Using the CAGE framework helps firms decide the cultural, administrative, geographic, and economic distance between the home and target country. Executives also need to determine the likelihood that their firms will succeed when they compete in international markets by examining demand conditions, factor conditions, related and supporting industries, strategy, structure, and rivalry among its domestic competitors. When a firm does venture overseas, a decision must be made about whether its international strategy will be international, multi-domestic, global, or transnational. Finally, when leading a firm to enter a new market, executives can choose to manage the operation via exporting, licensing, franchising, creating a joint venture or strategic alliance, and creating a wholly owned subsidiary through greenfield or acquisition.

1. Divide your class into four or eight groups, depending on the size of the class. Each group should select a different industry. Find examples of each international strategy for your industry. Discuss which strategy seems to be the most successful in your selected industry.

2. This chapter discussed Kia and other automakers. If you were assigned to turn around a struggling automaker such as General Motors or Chrysler, what actions would you take to revive the company's prospects within the global auto industry?

Chapter 10: Executing Strategy through Organizational Design

Learning Objectives

After reading this chapter, you should be able to understand and articulate answers to the following questions:

1. Why is a firm's organizational structure important?
2. What are the basic building blocks of organizational structure?
3. What are strategic advantages and disadvantages of each organizational structure type?
4. What are the different forms of control and when should they be used?
5. What are the key legal forms of business, and what implications does the choice of a business form have for organizational structure?

10.1 Introduction

With an understanding of developing business-level, corporate level, and international strategies, firms must execute their strategies to be successful. The way a firm organizes itself is critical to its ability to implement strategy. This chapter addresses why organizational structure is important to achieving a firm's strategic goals—which types of structures are deployed by firms, what control systems are used by firms, and what are the options for establishing a legal entity. These organizational decisions should support and align with an organization's mission, vision, and values to ensure ethical as well as strategic outcomes. The role of social responsibility and ethics in a corporate setting will be discussed in detail in the next and final chapter.

The word executing used in this chapter's title has two distinct meanings. These meanings were cleverly intertwined in a quip by John McKay. McKay had the misfortune to be the head coach of a hapless professional football team. In one game, McKay's offensive unit played particularly poorly. When McKay was asked after the game what he thought of his offensive unit's execution, he wryly responded, "I am in favor of it."

In the context of business, execution refers to how well a firm such as GE implements the strategies that executives create for it. This involves the creation and operation of both an appropriate organizational structure with an aligned organizational control process. Executives who skillfully orchestrate structure and control are likely to lead their firms to greater levels of success. In contrast, those executives who fail to do so are likely to be viewed by stakeholders such as employees and owners in much the same way McKay viewed his offense: worthy of execution.

10.2 Why Organizational Design?

Can Oil Well Services Fuel Success for General Electric?

In the spring of 2010 the Deepwater Horizon fire and oil spill in the Gulf of Mexico occurred. It resulted in 11 deaths, 17 injuries, and millions of barrels of oil contaminating the Gulf and US shoreline. As a result of this disaster, General Electric (GE) saw an opportunity. In February 2011, General Electric reached an agreement to acquire the well-support division of John Wood Group PLC for $2.8 billion. This was GE's third acquisition of a company that provides services to oil wells in only five months. In October 2010, GE added the deepwater exploration capabilities of Wellstream Holdings PLC for $1.3 billion. In December 2010, part and equipment maker Dresser was acquired for $3 billion. By spending more than $7 billion on these acquisitions, GE executives made it clear that they had big plans within the oil well services business.

Figure 10.1: General Electric's logo has changed little since its creation in the 1890s, but the company had grown to become the sixth largest in the United States before its downfall.

While many executives would struggle to integrate three new companies into their firms, experts expected GE's leaders to smoothly execute the transitions. In describing the acquisition of John Wood Group PLC, for example, one Wall Street analyst noted, "This is a nice bolt-on deal for GE" (Layne, 2011). In other words, this analyst believed that John Wood Group PLC could be seamlessly added to GE's corporate empire. The way that GE was organized fueled this belief.

GE's organizational structure includes six divisions, each devoted to specific product categories: (1) Energy (the most profitable division), (2) Capital (the largest division), (3) Home & Business Solutions, (4) Healthcare, (5) Aviation, and (6) Transportation. Within the Energy division, there are three subdivisions: (1) Oil & Gas, (2) Power & Water, and (3) Energy Services. Rather than having the entire organization involved with integrating John Wood Group PLC, Wellstream Holdings PLC, and Dresser into GE, these three newly acquired companies would simply be added to the Oil & Gas subdivisions within the Energy division.

In addition to the six product divisions, GE also had a division devoted to Global Growth & Operations. This division was responsible for all sales of GE products and services outside the United States. The Global Growth & Operations division was very important to GE's future. Indeed, GE's CEO Jeffrey Immelt expected that countries other than the United States will account for 60% of GE's sales in the future, up from 53% in 2010. To maximize GE's ability to respond to local needs, the Global Growth & Operations was further divided into twelve geographic regions: China, India, Southeast Asia, Latin/South America, Russia, Canada, Australia, the Middle East, Africa, Germany, Europe, and Japan (GE News Center, 2010).

Finally, like many large companies, GE also provided some centralized services to support all its units. These support areas included public relations, business development, legal, global research, human resources, and finance. By having entire units of the organization devoted to these functional areas, GE hoped not only to minimize expenses but also to create consistency across divisions.

Growing concerns about the environmental effects of drilling, for example, made it likely that GE's oil well services operations would need the help of GE's public relations and legal departments in the future. Other important questions about GE's acquisitions remained open as well. In particular, would the organizational cultures of John Wood Group PLC, Wellstream Holdings PLC, and Dresser mesh with the culture of GE? Most acquisitions in the business world fail to deliver the results that executives expect, and the incompatibility of organizational cultures is one reason why.

This General Electric example highlights several concepts regarding the strategic role decisions about the organization. First, how large, complex organizations organize themselves impact how they accomplish their mission. Also, assessing the external environment can open up organizational opportunities. Third, how the acquisition and then integration of companies into the home firm can be challenging. And fourth, in hindsight, investing in the fossil fuel industry at a time of rising energy renewables was a strategic mistake. Since this time, GE has sold off many of its business lines for billions of dollars, and the downsized company is nowhere near the powerhouse it was a decade ago. GE is still struggling due to the strategic errors in a number of the industries it was involved in.

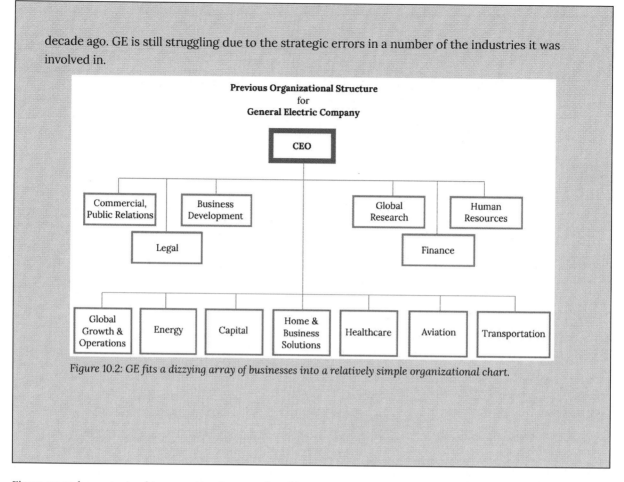

Figure 10.2: GE fits a dizzying array of businesses into a relatively simple organizational chart.

Firms must be organized in an optimal way to be able to compete and accomplish its mission. As noted in an earlier chapter, the external and competitive environments cannot be ignored. A firm must find the best "fit" to deal with the business environment and maximize its internal resources, capabilities, and core competencies. This organizational fit will determine its performance. It is unique to each organization; it is not "one size fits all."

The business-level strategy that a firm selects impacts the organizational structure, with some structures better suited for certain strategies. There are trade-offs with each structure. The structure influences the firm's ability to respond quickly to outside forces, its adaptability, resource efficiency, and accountability.

Walmart uses a functional organizational structure (described later in this chapter) because it is the best design to support a low cost strategy operating in a stable environment. A functional structure allows for excellent resource efficiency, but the trade off is a reduction in its adaptability and responsiveness to external forces (Harvard).

References

GE News Center. (2010, November 8). *GE names vice chairman John Rice to lead GE Global Growth & Operations* [Press release]. https://www.ge.com/news/press-releases/ge-names-vice-chairman-john-rice-lead-ge-global-growth-operations-0.

Layne, R. (2011, February 14). *GE agrees to buy $2.8 billion oil-service unit; shares surge*. Bloomsberg. https://www.bloomberg.com/news/articles/2011-02-14/ge-spending-spree-adds-2-8-billion-john-wood-oil-service-unit.

Image Credits

10.3 The Basic Building Blocks of Organizational Structure

Legendary football coach Vince Lombardi once noted, "The achievements of an organization are the results of the combined effort of each individual." Understanding how people can be most efficiently organized is the basis for modern management thought, and the building blocks of organizational structure are illustrated below.

Table 10.1 The Building Blocks of Organizational Structure

Division of Labor	**Division of labor** is a process of splitting up a task into a series of smaller tasks, each of which is performed by a specialist. In ancient Greece, historian Xenophon wrote about the division of labor in shoe making: one person cut out the shoes, another sewed the uppers together, and a third person assembled the parts.
Organizational Chart	An **organizational chart** is a diagram that depicts a firm's structure.
Informal Linkages	**Informal linkages** are unofficial relationships such as friendships that do not appear in organizational charts. Examples are two department heads that build a relationship for better collaboration between their departments, a mentor relationship, or an experienced staff member taking a new employee "under their wing" to help them get off to a good start at the company.
Vertical Linkages	**Vertical linkages** tie supervisors and subordinates together. These linkages show the lines of responsibility through which a supervisor delegates authority to subordinates, oversees their activities, evaluates their performance, and guides them toward improvement.
Horizontal Linkages	**Horizontal linkages** are formal relationships between equals in an organization. They often take the form of committees and task forces.
Unity of Command	Employees may receive conflicting guidance about how to do their jobs if they work in a situation where multiple bosses are present. This problem can be avoided by following the **unity of command** principle, which states that each person should only report directly to one supervisor.

Division of Labor

General Electric (GE), although downsized, still offers an array of products and services, including power generation, jet engines, medical equipment, and renewable energy. One way that GE could produce its jet engines would be to have individual employees work on one jet engine at a time from start to finish. However, this would be very inefficient so GE and most other organizations avoid this approach. Instead, organizations rely on division of labor when creating their products (Table 10.1). Division of labor is a process of splitting up a task (such as the creation of jet engines) into a series of smaller tasks, each of which is performed by a specialist.

Illustrated below is one of the oldest recorded stories from about 4300 years ago that is relevant to the design of modern organizations.

Table 10.2 Hierarchy of Authority

Hierarchy of Authority Example: Moses	
After fleeing Egypt, Moses found himself as the sole judge of the entire Hebrew population. This was a daunting task because estimates suggest the population may have exceeded one million people.	Moses's father-in-law, Jethro, warned Moses that he would wear himself out if he tried to handle such a heavy load alone.
Jethro offered Moses some practical advice. He told Moses that he should teach the people decrees and laws in an effort to minimize trouble and act as an example to demonstrate how the people live and the duties they were to perform.	Rather than handling all judging himself, Moses should appoint capable and trustworthy officials over groups of thousands, hundreds, fifties, and tens. These men would serve as judges for the people at all times, and only the most difficult cases would be brought to Moses.

This is perhaps the first recorded example of a clear **hierarchy of authority**—an arrangement of individuals based on rank. A similar idea is used today in the US justice system where there are lower courts for easy-to-resolve cases and the Supreme Court only handles the most difficult cases.

The leaders at the top of organizations have long known that division of labor can improve efficiency. Thousands of years ago, for example, Moses's creation of a hierarchy of authority by delegating responsibility to other judges offered perhaps the earliest known example (Table 10.2). In the eighteenth century, Adam Smith's book *The Wealth of Nations* quantified the tremendous advantages that division of labor offered for a pin factory. If a worker performed all the various steps involved in making pins himself, he could make about twenty pins per day. By breaking the process into multiple steps, however, 10 workers could make 48,000 pins a day. In other words, the pin factory was a staggering 240 times more productive than it would have been without relying on division of labor. In the early twentieth century, Smith's ideas strongly influenced Henry Ford and other industrial pioneers who sought to create efficient organizations.

Figure 10.3: Division of labor allowed eighteenth century pin factories to dramatically increase their efficiency.

While division of labor fuels efficiency, it also creates a challenge—figuring out how to coordinate different tasks and the people who perform them. The solution is organizational structure, which is defined as the process by which tasks are assigned and grouped together with formal reporting relationships. Creating a structure that effectively coordinates a firm's activities increases the firm's likelihood of success. Meanwhile, a structure that does not match well with a firm's needs undermines the firm's chances of prosperity.

Figure 10.4: Division of labor was central to Henry Ford's development of assembly lines in his automobile factory. Ford noted, "Nothing is particularly hard if you divide it into small jobs."

Vertical and Horizontal Linkages

Most organizations use a diagram called an organizational chart to depict their structure. These organizational charts show how firms' structures are built using two basic building blocks: vertical linkages and horizontal linkages. Vertical linkages tie supervisors and subordinates together. These linkages show the lines of responsibility through which a supervisor delegates authority to subordinates, oversees their activities, evaluates their performance, and guides them toward improvement when necessary. Every supervisor except for the person at the very top of the organizational chart also serves as a subordinate to someone else. In the typical business school, for example, a department chair supervises a set of professors. The department chair in turn is a subordinate of the dean.

Most executives rely on the unity of command principle when mapping out the vertical linkages in an organizational structure. This principle states that each person should only report directly to one supervisor. If employees have multiple bosses, they may receive conflicting guidance about how to do their jobs. The unity of command principle helps organizations to avoid such confusion. In the case of GE, for example, the head of the Energy division reports only to the chief executive officer. If problems were to arise with executing the strategic move discussed in this chapter's opening vignette, joining the John Wood Group PLC with GE's Energy division, the head of the Energy division would look to the chief executive officer for guidance.

Horizontal linkages are relationships between equals in an organization. These linkages are often called committees, task forces, or teams. Horizontal linkages are important when close coordination is needed across different segments of an organization. For example, most business schools revise their undergraduate curriculum every five or so years to ensure that students are receiving an education that matches the needs of current business conditions. Typically, a committee consisting of at least one professor from every academic area (such as management, marketing, accounting, and finance) will be appointed to perform this task. This approach helps ensure that all aspects of business are represented appropriately in the new curriculum.

Figure 10.5: Committee meetings can be boring, but they are often vital for coordinating efforts across departments.

The organic grocery store chain Whole Foods Market, owned by Amazon, is a company that relies heavily on horizontal linkages. As noted on their website:

> At Whole Foods Market we recognize the importance of smaller tribal groupings to maximize familiarity and trust. We organize our stores and company into a variety of interlocking teams. Most teams have between 6 and 100 Team Members and the larger teams are divided further into a variety of sub-teams. The leaders of each team are also members of the Store Leadership Team and the Store Team Leaders are members of the Regional Leadership Team. This interlocking team structure continues all the way upwards to the Executive Team at the highest level of the company (Mackey, 2010).

This emphasis on teams is intended to develop trust throughout the organization, as well as to make full use of the talents and creativity possessed by every employee.

Informal Linkages

Informal linkages refer to unofficial relationships such as personal friendships, rivalries, and politics. In the long-running comedy series *The Simpsons*, Homer Simpson is a low-level, low-performing employee at a nuclear power plant. In one episode, Homer gains power and influence with the plant's owner, Montgomery Burns, which far exceeds Homer's meager position in the organization chart, because Mr. Burns desperately wants to be a member of the bowling team that Homer captains. Homer tries to use his newfound influence for his own personal gain and, naturally, the organization as a whole suffers. Informal linkages such as this one do not appear in organizational charts, but they nevertheless can have (and often do have) a significant influence on how firms operate.

Section Video

Organizational Design and Structure [02:44]

The video for this lesson explains the process of organizational design and its structure.

You can view this video here: https://youtu.be/Y4vEos6xuks.

Key Takeaway

- The concept of division of labor (dividing organizational activities into smaller tasks) lies at the heart of the study of organizational structure. Understanding vertical, horizontal, and informal linkages helps managers to organize better the different individuals and job functions within a firm.

Exercises

1. How is division of labor used when training college or university football teams? Do you think you could use a different division of labor and achieve more efficiency?
2. What are some formal and informal linkages that you have encountered at your college or university? What informal linkages have you observed in the workplace?

References

Mackey, J. (2010, March 9). *Creating the high trust organization*. Whole Foods Market. https://www.wholefoodsmarket.com/tips-and-ideas/archive/creating-high-trust-organization.

Image Credits

Figure 10.4: Ford Company. "1913 photograph Ford company, USA." Public Domain. Retrieved from https://en.wikipedia.org/wiki/File:A-line1913.jpg.

Figure 10.5: Christina @ wocintechchat.com (2019). CC-BY SA 2.0. Cropped. Retrieved from https://unsplash.com/photos/rg1y72eKw6o.

Video Credits

Gregg Learning. (2019, January 10). *Organizational design and structure* [Video]. YouTube. https://youtu.be/Y4vEos6xuks.

10.4 Creating an Organizational Structure

Within most firms, executives rely on vertical and horizontal linkages to create a structure that they hope will match the needs of their firm's strategy. Four types of structures are available to executives:

1. Functional
2. Multi-divisional
3. Matrix
4. Boundaryless

Like snowflakes, however, no two organizational structures are exactly alike. When creating a structure for their firm, executives will take one of these types and adapt it to fit the firm's unique circumstances. As they do this, executives must realize that the choice of structure will influence their firm's strategy in the future. Once a structure is created, it constrains future strategic moves. If a firm's structure is designed to maximize efficiency, for example, the firm may lack the flexibility needed to react quickly to exploit new opportunities.

Executives rely on vertical and horizontal linkages to create a structure that they hope will match the firm's needs. While no two organizational structures are exactly alike, four general types of structures are available to executives: functional, multi-divisional, matrix, and boundaryless.

Table 10.3 Common Organizational Structures

Functional Structure	Within a functional structure, employees are divided into departments that each handle activities related to a functional area of the business, such as marketing, production, human resources, information technology, and customer service.
Multi-divisional Structure	In this type of structure, employees are divided into departments based on product areas and/or geographic regions. General Electric, for example, had six product divisions: Energy, Capital, Home & Business Solutions, Healthcare, Aviation, and Transportation.
Matrix Structure	The matrix structure can be thought of as a hybrid between functional and divisional structures. Complex organizations or firms that engage in projects of limited duration may use a matrix structure where employees can be put on different teams to maximize creativity and idea flow.
Boundaryless Structure	The boundaryless organization is flat, with decentralized decision making and the use of many cross-functional teams. This structure works well in knowledge industries such as IT, where responsiveness to changing environmental and competitive forces must be quick.

Functional Structure

Organizations become more complex as they grow, and this can require more formal division of labor and a strong emphasis on hierarchy and vertical links.

Functional structures rely on a division of labor whereby groups of people handle activities related to a specific function of the overall business. Illustrated are functional structures in action within two types of organizations that commonly use them.

Table 10.4 Functional Structure

Grocery Store Functions	Spa Functions
Grocery stockers often work at night to make sure shelves stay full during the day.	Some spa employees manicure fingernails, a practice that is over four thousand years old. Many also provide pedicures, a service whose popularity has nearly doubled in the recent past.
Pharmacists' specialized training allows them to command pay that can exceed $55 an hour.	Compared to other spa functions, little training is required of a tanning bed operator–although the ability to tell time may help.
Bakers wake up early to give shoppers their daily bread.	Almost anyone can buy a shotgun or parent a child without any training, but every state requires a license in order to cut hair.
Bagging groceries requires a friendly personality as well as knowing that eggs should not go on the bottom.	Cucumber masks are usually applied by a skincare specialist who has taken a professional training program.
Folks that work checkout aisles should be trusted to handle cash.	The license required of massage therapists in many states ensures that spa visits end happily.
The creation of produce, deli, and butcher departments provides an efficient way to divide a grocery store physically as well as functionally.	

Within a functional structure, employees are divided into departments that each handle activities related to a functional area of the business, such as marketing, production, human resources, information technology, and customer service (Table 10.4). Each of these five areas would be headed up by a manager who coordinates all activities related to her functional area. Everyone in a company that works on marketing the company's products, for example, would report to the manager of the marketing department. The marketing managers and the managers in charge of the other four areas in turn would report to the chief executive officer.

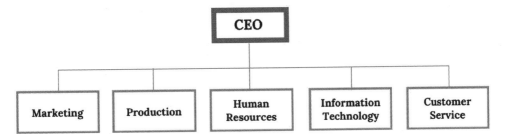

Figure 10.6: An example of a functional structure

Using a functional structure creates advantages and disadvantages. An important benefit of adopting a functional structure is that each person tends to learn a great deal about his or her particular function. By being placed in a department that consists entirely of marketing professionals, an individual has a great opportunity to become an expert in marketing. Thus a functional structure tends to create highly skilled specialists. Second, grouping everyone that serves a particular function into one department tends to keep costs low and to create efficiency. Also, because all the people in a particular department share the same background training, they tend to get along with one another. In other words, conflicts within departments are more rare.

Using a functional structure also has a significant downside: executing strategic changes can be very slow when compared with other structures. Suppose, for example, that a textbook publisher decides to introduce a new form of textbook that includes "scratch and sniff" photos that let students smell various products in addition to reading about them. If the publisher is organized using a functional structure, every department in the organization will have to be intimately involved in the creation of the new textbooks. Because the new product lies outside each department's routines, it may become lost in the proverbial shuffle. And unfortunately for the books' authors, the publication process will be halted whenever a functional area does not live up to its responsibilities in a timely manner. More generally, because functional structures are slow to execute change, they tend to work best for organizations that offer narrow and stable product lines.

The specific functional departments that appear in an organizational chart vary across organizations that use functional structures. In the example offered earlier in this section, a firm was divided into five functional areas: (1) marketing, (2) production, (3) human resources, (4) information technology, and (5) customer service. In the TV show *The Office*, a different approach to a functional structure is used at the Scranton, Pennsylvania, branch of Dunder Mifflin. The branch was divided into six functional areas: (1) sales, (2) warehouse, (3) quality control, (4) customer service, (5) human resources, and (6) accounting. A functional structure was a good fit for the branch at the time because its product line was limited to just selling office paper.

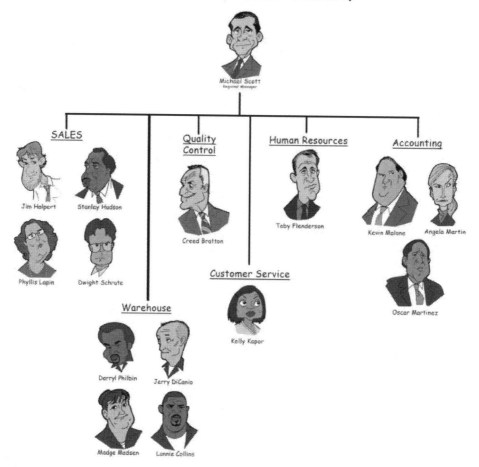

Dunder Mifflin (Functional Structure)

Michael Scott
Regional Manager

SALES — Jim Halpert, Stanley Hudson, Phyllis Lapin, Dwight Schrute

Quality Control — Creed Bratton

Human Resources — Toby Flenderson

Accounting — Kevin Malone, Angela Martin, Oscar Martinez

Customer Service — Kelly Kapor

Warehouse — Darryl Philbin, Jerry DiCanio, Madge Madsen, Lonnie Collins

Figure 10.7: The Scranton branch of Dunder Mifflin may be a dysfunctional organization, but it relies on a functional structure.

Multi-Divisional Structure

Many organizations offer a wide variety of products and services. Some of these organizations sell their offerings across an array of geographic regions. These approaches require firms to be very responsive to customers' needs. Yet, as noted, functional structures tend to be fairly slow to change. As a result, many firms abandon the use of a functional structure as their offerings expand. Often the new choice is a multi-divisional structure. In this type of structure, employees are divided into departments based on product areas and/or geographic regions.

General Electric (GE) is an example of a company organized this way. As shown in the organization chart that accompanies this chapter's opening vignette, most of the company's employees belonged to one of six product divisions (Energy, Capital, Home & Business Solutions, Health Care, Aviation, and Transportation) or to a division that is devoted to all GE's operations outside the United States (Global Growth & Operations).

A big advantage of a multi-divisional structure is that it allows a firm to act quickly. When GE makes a strategic move such as acquiring the well-support division of John Wood Group PLC, only the relevant division (in this case, Energy, needs to be involved in integrating the new unit into GE's hierarchy. In contrast, if GE were organized using a functional structure, the transition would be much slower because all the divisions in the company would need to be involved. A multi-divisional structure also helps an organization to better serve customers' needs. For example, GE's Capital division started to make real-estate loans after exiting that market during the financial crisis of the late 2000s (Jacobius, 2011). Because one division of GE handled all the firm's loans, the wisdom and skill needed to decide when to re-enter real-estate lending was easily accessible.

Of course, empowering divisions to act quickly can backfire if people in those divisions take actions that do not fit with the company's overall strategy. McDonald's experienced this kind of situation. In particular, the French division of McDonald's ran a surprising advertisement in a magazine called *Femme Actuelle*. The ad included a quote from a nutritionist that asserted children should not eat at a McDonald's more than once per week. Executives at McDonald's headquarters in suburban Chicago were concerned about the message sent to their customers, of course, and they made it clear that they strongly disagreed with the nutritionist.

Another downside of multi divisional structures is that they tend to be more costly to operate than functional structures. While a functional structure offers the opportunity to gain efficiency by having just one department handle all activities in an area, such as marketing, a firm using a multi-divisional structure needs to have marketing units within each of its divisions. In GE's case, for example, each of its seven divisions must develop marketing skills. Absorbing the extra expenses that are created reduces a firm's profit margin. Often a multi-divisional firm will employ a functional structure within each of its divisions.

Figure 10.8: Problems can be created when delegating lots of authority to local divisions. McDonald's top executives were angered when an ad by their French division suggested that children should only eat at their restaurants once a week.

GE's organizational chart highlights a way that firms can reduce some of these expenses: the centralization of some functional services. As shown in the organizational chart, departments devoted to important aspects of public relations, business development, legal, global research, human resources, and finance are maintained centrally to provide services to the six product divisions and the geographic division. By consolidating some human resource activities in one location, for example, GE creates efficiency and saves money.

An additional benefit of such moves is that consistency is created across divisions. For example, the Coca-Cola Company created an Office of Sustainability to coordinate sustainability initiatives across the entire company. Bea Perez was named Coca-Cola's chief sustainability officer and was put in charge of the Office of Sustainability. At the time, Coca-Cola's chief executive officer Muhtar Kent noted that Coca-Cola had "made significant progress with our sustainability initiatives, but our current approach needs focus and better integration" (Coca-Cola Company, 2011). In other words, a department devoted to creating consistency across Coca-Cola's sustainability efforts was needed for Coca-Cola to meet its sustainability goals.

Matrix Structure

Within functional and multi-divisional structures, vertical linkages between bosses and subordinates define most of the elements. Matrix structures, in contrast, rely heavily on horizontal relationships (Ketchen & Short, 2011). In particular, these structures create cross-functional teams that each work on a different project. This offers several benefits: maximizing the organization's flexibility, enhancing communication across functional lines, and creating a spirit of teamwork and collaboration. A matrix structure can also help develop new managers. In particular, a person without managerial experience can be put in charge of a relatively small project as a test to see whether the person has a talent for leading others.

Using a matrix structure can create difficulties too. One concern is that a matrix structure violates the unity of command principle, because each employee is assigned multiple bosses. Specifically, any given individual reports to a functional area supervisor as well as one or more project supervisors. This creates confusion for employees because they are left unsure about who should be giving them direction. Violating the unity of command principle also creates opportunities for unsavory employees to avoid responsibility by claiming to each supervisor that a different supervisor is currently depending on their efforts.

The potential for conflicts arising between project managers within a matrix structure is another concern. Chances are that students have had some classes with professors who are excellent speakers, while being forced to suffer through a semester of incomprehensible lectures in other classes. This mix of experiences reflects a fundamental reality of management: in any organization, some workers are more talented and motivated than others. Within a matrix structure, each project manager, naturally, will want the best people in the company assigned to their project because their boss evaluates these managers based on how well their projects perform. Because the best people are a scarce resource, infighting and politics can easily flare up around which people are assigned to each project.

Given these problems, not every organization is a good candidate to use a matrix structure. Organizations such as information technology, engineering, and consulting firms that need to maximize their flexibility to service projects of limited duration can benefit from the use of a matrix. Matrix structures are also used to organize research and development departments within many large corporations. In each of these settings, the benefits of organizing around teams are so great that they often outweigh the risks of doing so.

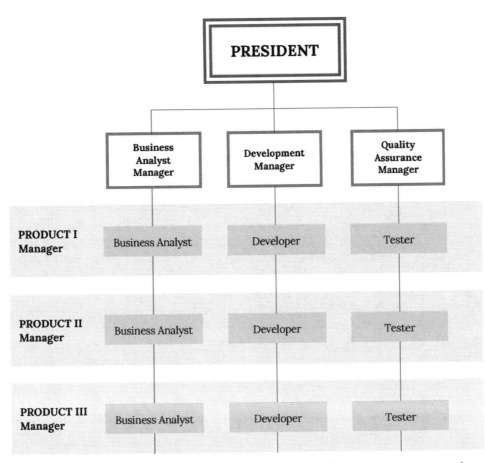

Figure 10.9: *You won't need to choose between a red pill and a blue pill within a matrix structure, but you will have multiple bosses.*

The matrix structure works well for other complex organizations that are not project based. These can be set up on a permanent basis and fit well for firms with multiple locations. This works particularly well for standardizing processes and policies across the various units of the firm. For example, a manufacturer with five plants spread out across the Southeast United States can use this structure to standardize finance and accounting, production, supply chain, marketing, and logistics. Each of these functional areas has a vice-president in charge of that function and reports to the CEO. However, each function in each plant has a manager who reports both to the functional VP and to the plant manager. The matrix structure is best suited for firms implementing a related diversification corporate strategy in complex environments where responding quickly to external forces is important.

Sentara Healthcare is a hospital system that operates 13 hospitals in Virginia. This organization uses a matrix structure to provide consistency and standardization of policies, procedures, supplies, and equipment across its hospitals. The diagram below illustrates how the reporting structure goes both vertically and horizontally. This allows for standardization of the major functions across the hospital system. For example, the emergency rooms in all hospitals use the same medical equipment, the same computer systems, and the same processes and paperwork, so nurses can easily work in any hospital without having to be retrained. Efficiency is improved, best practices are implemented across the system easier, and volume discounts by purchasing identical supplies and equipment for all the emergency departments saves money.

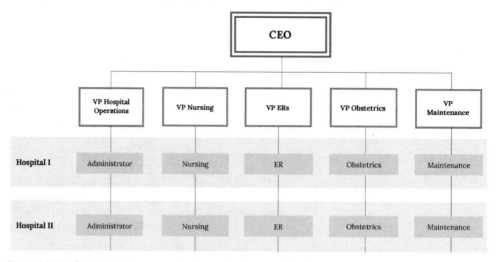

Figure 10.10: A hospital system organizational structure: matrix structure

Strategy at the Movies

Office Space

How much work can a man accomplish with eight bosses breathing down his neck? For Peter Gibbons, an employee at information technology firm Initech in the movie Office Space, the answer was zero. Initech's use of a matrix structure meant that each employee had multiple bosses, each representing a different aspect of Initech's business. High-tech firms often use a matrix structure to gain the flexibility needed to manage multiple projects simultaneously. Successfully using a matrix structure requires excellent communication among various managers—however, excellence that Initech could not reach. When Gibbons forgot to put the appropriate cover sheet on his TPS report, each of his eight bosses—and a parade of his coworkers—admonished him. This fiasco and others led to Gibbons to become cynical about his job.

Simpler organizational structures can be equally frustrating. Joanna, a waitress at nearby restaurant Chotchkie's, had only one manager—a stark contrast to Gibbons's eight bosses. Unfortunately,

Joanna's manager had an unhealthy obsession with the "flair" (colorful buttons and pins) used by employees to enliven their uniforms. A series of mixed messages about the restaurant's policy on flair led Joanna to emphatically proclaim–both verbally and nonverbally–her disdain for the manager. She then quit her job and stormed out of the restaurant.

Office Space illustrates the importance of organizational design decisions to an organization's culture and to employees' motivation levels. A matrix structure can facilitate resource sharing and collaboration but may also create complicated working relationships and impose excessive stress on employees. Chotchkie's organizational structure involved simpler working relationships, but these relationships were strained beyond the breaking point by a manager's eccentricities. In a more general sense, Office Space shows that all organizational structures involve a series of trade-offs that must be carefully managed.

Figure 10.11: Within a poorly organized firm like Initech, simply keeping possession of a treasured stapler is a challenge.

Boundaryless Organizations

Most organizational charts show clear divisions and boundaries between different units. The value of a much different approach was highlighted by former GE CEO Jack Welch when he created the term boundaryless organization. A boundaryless organization is one that removes the usual barriers between parts of the organization as well as barriers between the organization and others (Askenas, et. al., 1995). Eliminating all internal and external barriers is not possible, of course, but making progress toward being boundaryless can help an organization become more flexible and responsive. One example is W. L. Gore, a maker of fabrics, medical implants, industrial sealants, filtration systems, and consumer products. This firm avoids organizational charts, management layers, and supervisors despite having approximately 9,000 employees across 30 countries. Rather than granting formal titles to certain people, leaders with W. L. Gore emerge based on performance, and they attract followers to their ideas over time. As one employee noted, "We vote with our feet. If you call a meeting, and people show up, you're a leader" (Hamel, 2007).

Boundaryless organizations work best in knowledge industries, such as information technology and communications firms. They are characterized by the frequent use of cross-functional teams and decision-making that is highly decentralized. These organizations rely heavily on loose boundaries and the informal linkages mentioned earlier in this chapter. The boundaryless structure lends itself well to the free-rein leadership style where the external environment changes quickly, and for executing innovation strategies.

An illustration of how removing barriers can be valuable has its roots in a very unfortunate event. During Hurricane Katrina in 2005, rescue efforts were hampered by a lack of coordination between responders from the National Guard (who are controlled by state governments) and from active-duty military units (who are controlled by federal authorities). According to one National Guard officer, "It was just like a solid wall was between the two entities" (Elliott, 2011). Efforts were needlessly duplicated in some geographic areas while attention to other areas was delayed or inadequate. For example, poor coordination caused the evacuation of

Figure 10.12: *The boundaryless approach to structure embraced by W.L. Gore drives the kind of creative thinking that led to their most famous product, GORE-TEX.*

thousands of people from the New Orleans Superdome to be delayed by a full day. The results were immense human suffering and numerous fatalities.

Figure 10.13: *In 2005, boundaries between organizations hampered rescue efforts following Hurricane Katrina.*

To avoid similar problems from arising in the future, barriers between the National Guard and active-duty military units are being bridged by special military officers called dual-status commanders. These individuals will be empowered to lead both types of units during a disaster recovery effort, helping to ensure that all areas receive the attention they need in a timely manner.

Reasons for Changing an Organization's Structure

Creating an organizational structure is not a one time activity. Executives must revisit an organization's structure over time and make changes to it if certain danger signs arise. For example, a structure might need to be adjusted if decisions with the organization are being made too slowly or if the organization is performing poorly. Both these problems plagued Sears Holdings leading executives to reorganize the company.

Sears's new structure organized the firm around five types of divisions: (1) operating businesses (such as clothing, appliances, and electronics), (2) support units (certain functional areas such as marketing and finance), (3) brands (which focus on nurturing the firm's various brands such as Lands' End, Joe Boxer, Craftsman, and Kenmore), (4) online, and (5) real estate. At the time, Sears's chairman Edward S. Lampert noted that "by creating smaller focused teams that are clearly responsible for their units, we [will] increase autonomy and accountability, create greater ownership and enable faster, better decisions" (Jones, 2008). Unfortunately, structural changes cannot cure all a company's ills. Sears's stock was worth just over half what it had been worth five years earlier and it continues to close stores into 2020.

Sometimes structures become too complex and need to be simplified. Many observers believe that this description fits Cisco. The company's CEO, John Chambers, moved Cisco away from a hierarchical emphasis toward a focus on horizontal linkages. Before, Cisco had four types of such linkages. For any given project, a small team of people reported to one of 47 boards. The boards averaged 14 members each. Forty-three of these boards each reported to one of 12 councils. Each council also averaged 14 members. The councils reported to an operating committee consisting of Chambers and 15 other top executives. Four of the 47 boards bypassed the councils and reported directly to the operating committee. These arrangements are so complex and time consuming that some top executives spend 30% of their work hours serving on more than 10 of the boards and councils, as well as the operating committee.

Figure 10.14: Although it was created to emphasize the need for unity among the American colonies, this famous 1754 graphic by Ben Franklin also illustrates a fundamental truth about structure: If the parts that make up a firm do not work together, the firm is likely to fail.

Because it competes in fast-changing high-tech markets, Cisco needed to be able to make competitive moves quickly. The firm's complex structural arrangements were preventing this. A competitor, Hewlett-Packard (HP), started promoting a warranty service that provided free support and upgrades within the computer network switches market. Because Cisco's response to this initiative had to work its way through multiple committees, the firm did not take prompt action. During the delay, Cisco's share of the market dropped as customers embraced HP's warranty. This problem and others created by Cisco's overly complex structure were so severe that one columnist wondered aloud "has Cisco's John Chambers lost his mind?" (Blodget, 2009). Finally, Chambers reversed course and decided to return Cisco to a more traditional structure while reducing the firm's workforce by 9%. Since the implementation of these structural changes, Cisco's stock price more than doubled.

Section Video

Organizational Structure [04:49]

The video for this lesson explains organizational structure.

You can view this video here: https://youtu.be/zUd0UNHyy60.

Key Takeaway

- Executives must select among the four types of structure (functional, multi-divisional, matrix, and boundaryless) available to organize operations. Each structure has unique advantages, and the selection of structures involves a series of trade-offs.

Exercises

1. What type of structure best describes the organization of your college or university? What led you to reach your conclusion?
2. The movie *Office Space* illustrates two types of structures. What are some other scenes or themes from movies that provide examples or insights relevant to understanding organizational structure?

References

Askenas, R., Ulrich, D., Jick, T., & Kerr, S. (1995). *The boundaryless organization: Breaking down the chains of organizational structure*. Jossey-Bass.

Blodget, H. (2009, August 6). *Has Cisco's John Chambers lost his mind?* Business Insider. http://www.businessinsider.com/henry-blodget-has-ciscos-john- chambers-lost-his-mind-2009-8.

Coca-Cola Company. (2011, May 19). The Coca-Cola Company names Bea Perez chief sustainability officer. *CSRwire.* https://www.csrwire.com/press_releases/32250-The-Coca-Cola-Company-Names-Beatriz-Perez-Chief-Sustainability-Officer.

Elliott, D. (2011, July 3). *New type of commander may avoid Katrina-like chaos.* NBC News.com. http://www.nbcnews.com/id/43625625/ns/us_news-life/t/new-type-commander-may-avoid-katrina-like-chaos.

Hamel, G. (2007, September 27). *What Google, Whole Foods do best.* CNNMoney. https://money.cnn.com/2007/09/26/news/companies/management_hamel.fortune/index.htm.

Jacobius, A. (2011, July 25). GE Capital slowly moving back into lending waters. *Pensions & Investments.* http://www.pionline.com/article/20110725/PRINTSUB/110729949.

Jones, S. (2008, January 23). Sears separates businesses. *Chicago Tribune.* https://www.chicagotribune.com/news/ct-xpm-2008-01-23-0801231605-story.html.

Ketchen, D. J., & Short, J. C. (2011). Separating fads from facts: Lessons from "the good, the fad, and the ugly." *Business Horizons,* 54, 17–22.

Image Credits

Figure 10.6: Kindred Grey (2020). "Example of Simple Organizational Structure." CC BY-SA 4.0. Retrieved from https://commons.wikimedia.org/wiki/File:Example_of_Simple_Organizational_Structure.png.

Figure 10.8: Alfonsina Blyde. Everything to See You Smile. CC BY-NC-ND 2.0. Retrieved from https://www.flickr.com/photos/alfon18/2503400459/.

Figure 10.9: Kindred Grey (2020). "Product Manager Organizational Structure." CC BY-SA 4.0. Retrieved from https://commons.wikimedia.org/wiki/File:Product_Manager_Organizational_Structure.png.

Figure 10.10: Kindred Grey (2020). "Hospital System Organizational Structure." CC BY-SA 4.0. Retrieved from https://commons.wikimedia.org/wiki/File:Hospital_System_Organizational_Structure.png.

Figure 10.11: Mrschimpf. "A picture of a Swingline 747 stapler." Cropped. Public Domain. Retrieved from https://en.wikipedia.org/wiki/Talk%3AOffice_Space#/media/File:Swingline_747.png.

Figure 10.12: Adifansnet. "adidas_Men's_Winter Story_OT-Tech-Gore-Tex Hooded Jacket_E95062." CC BY-SA 2.0. Retrieved from https://flic.kr/p/6DvjAX.

Figure 10.13: Niemi, Kyle. "New Orleans, Louisiana in the aftermath of Hurricane Katrina, showing Interstate 10 at West End Boulevard, looking towards Lake Pontchartrain." Public Domain. Retrieved from https://en.wikipedia.org/wiki/File:KatrinaNewOrleansFlooded_edit2.jpg.

Figure 10.14: Franklin, Benjamin. "Join or Die." Public Domain. Retrieved from https://commons.wikimedia.org/wiki/File:Benjamin_Franklin_-_Join_or_Die.jpg.

Video Credits

Communication Coach Alex Lyon. (2018, January 7). *Organizational structure* [Video]. YouTube. https://youtu.be/zUd0UNHyy60.

10.5 Creating Organizational Control Systems

In addition to creating an appropriate organizational structure, effectively executing strategy depends on the skillful use of organizational control systems. Executives create strategies trying to achieve their organization's vision, mission, and goals. Organizational control systems allow executives to track how well the organization is performing, identify areas of concern, and then take action to address the concerns. Three basic types of control systems are available to executives: (1) output control, (2) behavioral control, and (3) clan control. Different organizations emphasize different types of control, but most organizations use a mix of all three types.

Output Control

Stephen Covey said "start with the end in mind." Output control is one way decision makers put this into practice. **Output control** focuses on measurable results within an organization. Examples from the business world include the number of hits a website receives per day, the number of microwave ovens an assembly line produces per week, and the number of vehicles a car salesman sells per month (Table 10.5). In each of these cases, executives must decide what level of performance is acceptable, communicate expectations to the relevant employees, track whether performance meets expectations, and then make any needed changes. In an ironic example, a group of post office workers in Pensacola, Florida, were once disappointed to learn that their paychecks had been lost—by the US Postal Service. The corrective action was simple: they started receiving their pay via direct deposit rather than through the mail.

Many times the stakes are much higher. Delta Airlines was forced to face some facts as part of its use of output control. Data gathered by the federal government revealed that only 77.4% of Delta's flights had arrived on time during the year. This performance led Delta to rank dead last among the major US airlines and fifteenth out of 18 total carriers (Yamanouchi, 2011a). In response, Delta took important corrective steps. In particular, the airline added to its ability to service airplanes and provided more customer service training for its employees.

These changes and others paid off. For the second quarter of the following year, Delta enjoyed a $198 million profit, despite having to absorb a $1 billion increase in its fuel costs due to rising prices (Yamanouchi, 2011b).

Outcome controls assess measurable production and other tangible results. Often output controls emphasize "bottom-line" performance. We illustrate some outcome controls found in organizations below.

Table 10.5 Output Controls

Output Control Examples
Because real estate agents are paid a percentage of the selling price when a house sells, the number of dollars generated in houses sold is an important metric. Many realty offices have designations like "five million dollar club" to recognize very productive realtors.
Grade point averages provide a tangible means for employers and graduate schools to compare students.
In the classic movie *Elf*, the main character Buddy leaves Santa's workshop when the number of Etch-A-Sketch toys he produces is nearly 900 units lower than the standard pace.
To earn tenure in a research-focused business school, a professor's output generally must include publishing numerous high-quality articles at reputable scholarly journals.
Within restaurants, servers can increase a key output—amount of tips received—by providing customers with fast, friendly, and high-quality service.

Output control also plays a big part in the college experience. For example, test scores and grade point averages are good examples of output measures. If you perform badly on a test, a student might take corrective action by studying harder or by studying in a group for the next test. At most colleges and universities, a student is put on academic probation when his grade point average drops below a certain level. If the student's performance does not improve, he may be removed from his major and even dismissed. On the positive side, output measures can trigger rewards too. A very high grade point average can lead to placement on the dean's list and graduating with honors.

Figure 10.15: While most scholarships require a high GPA, comedian David Letterman created a scholarship for a "C" student at Ball State University. Ball State later named a new communications and media building after its very famous alumnus.

The balanced scorecard discussed in an earlier chapter is an output measure used by firms to track their progress toward achieving performance goals and strategies. Sometimes an output measure may have unintended consequences and produce the opposite impact desired. For example, if the sales team in a firm is rewarded based only on individual sales totals, sales people may not cooperate, collaborate, or help each other. They may even attempt to sabotage each other in their quest to achieve first place in sales for the period. Organizations must take care in how employees and managers are incentivized.

Behavioral Control

Behavioral controls dictate the actions of individuals. Such controls often emphasize rules and procedures. Some behavioral controls found in organizations are illustrated below.

Table 10.6 Behavioral Controls

Behavioral Control Examples
No shoes, no shirt, no paycheck. Many food service companies have strict attire requirements to make sure employees are in compliance with the rules of the Food and Drug Administration and those of local health departments.
Casual Fridays provide a welcome break in offices that enforce strict dress codes.
Many businesses require that checks are signed by two people. This prevents a dishonest employee from embezzling money.
In a classroom setting, grading attendance is a behavioral control designed to force students to show up for class. This can be very helpful because research shows that attendance is positively related to grades. Unfortunately, there are no behavioral controls that force professors' lectures to be interesting.
Gotta go? Be careful to not take too much time at certain auto factories, where bathroom breaks are monitored in an effort to cut costs. Some employees of US firms are limited to 46 minutes of bathroom time per shift, while Japanese automakers allow their American employees only 30 minutes per shift.

Figure 10.16: *Although some behavioral controls are intended for employees and not customers, following them is beneficial to everyone.*

While output control focuses on results, **behavioral control** focuses on controlling the actions that ultimately lead to results. In particular, various rules and procedures are used to standardize or to dictate behavior (Table 10.6). In most states, for example, signs are posted in restaurant bathrooms reminding employees that they must wash their hands before returning to work. To try to prevent employee theft, many firms require direct deposit for paychecks. And as an extreme example, some automobile factories and meat processing plants dictate to workers how many minutes they can spend in restrooms during their work shift.

Behavioral control also plays a significant role in the college experience. An illustrative (although perhaps unpleasant) example is penalizing students for not attending class. Instructors grade attendance to control students' behavior; specifically, to motivate students to attend class. Meanwhile, student's exert some control over an instructor's future behavior through their student evaluation measures at the end of the semester. .

Outside the classroom, behavioral control is a major factor within college athletic programs. The National Collegiate Athletic Association (NCAA) governs college athletics using an enormous set of rules, policies, and procedures. The NCAA's rule book on behavior is so complex that virtually all coaches violate its rules at one time or another. Critics suggest that the behavioral controls instituted by the NCAA have reached an absurd level. Despite this example, some degree of behavioral control is needed within virtually all organizations to ensure a productive work environment for all employees.

While a firm may have many mechanisms within its behavioral control system, the priority given to a particular set of control mechanisms can be influenced by the external environment. The Supreme Court ruling (June 2020) on LGBTQ workplace protections coupled with parallel outrage regarding social justice issues facing Black, Indigenous, and other People of Color (BIPOC) have an impact on firm decision-making. As a result, firms have been focused to pay more addition to making public statements on racial injustice while making changes to the existing (or absent) practices ensuring enforcement of anti-discrimination and equity policies. These changes may result in new prioritization within organizational behavior control systems. For example, in 2020 NASCAR banned the presence of the Confederate flag at its race venues following national demonstrations against white supremacy.

Creating an effective reward structure is key to effectively managing behavior because people tend to focus their efforts on the rewarded behaviors. Problems can arise when people are rewarded for behaviors that seem positive on the surface but that can actually undermine organizational goals under some circumstances. For example, restaurant servers are highly motivated to serve their tables quickly because doing so can increase their tips. But if a server devotes all his or her attention to providing fast service, other tasks that are vital to running a restaurant, such as communicating effectively with managers, host staff, chefs, and other servers, may suffer. Managers need to be aware of such trade-offs and strive to align rewards with behaviors. For example, waitstaff who consistently behave as team players could be assigned to the most desirable and lucrative shifts, such as nights and weekends.

Clan Control

Rather than measuring results (as in outcome control) or dictating behavior (as in behavioral control), clan control relies on shared traditions, expectations, values, and norms to lead people to work toward the good of their organization. Some of the most interesting and unusual examples of clan control are found on college campuses. Below we illustrate a few striking examples that help build school spirit and loyalty.

Table 10.7 Clan Controls

Clan Controls
Roughly one-quarter of Brandeis University's student body gets adorned in paint—and nothing else—at the annual Liquid Latex event.
No matter how you slice it, the Toast Toss seems strange to outsiders. University of Pennsylvania students fling the breakfast staple into the air after the third quarter of home football games.
Students at Texas Tech University honor the school's Southwest heritage by throwing tortillas at sporting events.

Instead of measuring results (as in outcome control) or dictating behavior (as in behavioral control), clan control is an informal type of control. Specifically, **clan control** relies on shared traditions, expectations, values, and norms to lead people to work toward the good of their organization (Table 10.7). Clan control is often used heavily in settings where creativity is vital, such as many high-tech businesses. In these companies, output is tough to dictate, and many rules are not appropriate. The creativity of a research scientist would be likely to be stifled, for example, if she were given a quota of patents that she must meet each year (output control) or if a strict dress code were enforced (behavioral control).

Figure 10.17: As part of the team-building effort at Google, new employees are known as Noogles and are given a propeller hat to wear.

Google is a firm that relies on clan control to be successful. Employees are permitted to spend 20% of their workweek on their own innovative projects. The company offers an "ideas mailing list" for employees to submit new ideas and to comment on others' ideas. Google executives routinely make themselves available two to three times per week for employees to visit with them to present their ideas. These informal meetings have generated a number of innovations, including personalized home pages and Google News, which might otherwise have never been adopted. Another illustration is when NASCAR banned the Confederate flag, all the race car drivers and crews walked the racetrack at Talladega, Alabama, in a powerful support of the ban.

Some executives look to clan control to improve the performance of struggling organizations. In Florida, officials became fed up with complaints about surly clerks within the state's driver's license offices. The solution was to look for help with training employees from two companies that are well-known for friendly, engaged employees and excellent customer service. The first was The Walt Disney Company, which offers world-famous hospitality at its Orlando theme parks. The second was regional supermarket chain Publix, a firm whose motto stressed that "shopping is a pleasure" in its stores. The goal of the training was to build the sort of positive team spirit Disney and Publix enjoy. The state's highway safety director summarized the need for clan control when noting that "we've just got to change a little culture out there" (Bousquet, 2005).

Clan control is also important on many college campuses. Philanthropic and social organizations such as clubs, fraternities, and sororities often revolve around shared values and team spirit. More broadly, many campuses have treasured traditions that bind alumni together across generations. Purdue University, for example, proudly owns the world's largest drum. The drum is beaten loudly before home football games to fire up the crowd. After athletic victories, Auburn University students throw rolls of toilet paper into campus oak trees. At Virginia Tech, their spirit of service as modeled in their motto "That I May Serve" leads them to hold the largest Relay for Life fundraising event on a university campus year after year. These examples and thousands of others spread across the country's colleges and universities help students feel like they belong to something special.

Management Fads: Out of Control?

The emergence and disappearance of fads appears to be a predictable aspect of modern society. A fad arises when some element of culture—such as fashion, a toy, or a hairstyle—becomes enthusiastically embraced by a group of people. Fads also seem to be a predictable aspect of the business world. Below we illustrate several fads that executives have latched onto in an effort to improve their organizations' control systems.

Table 10.8 Managing Management Fads

Management by Objectives	A supervisor and an employee create a series of goals that provide structure and motivation for the employee. A huge set of studies shows that setting challenging but attainable goals leads to good performance, but not every aspect of work can be captured by a goal.
Sensitivity Training	Free-flowing group discussions are used to lead individuals toward greater understanding of themselves and others. Because a "mob mentality" can take over a group, sensitivity training too often degenerates into hostility and humiliation.
Quality Circles	Volunteer employee groups developed to brainstorm new methods or processes to improve quality. Quality is important, but managers face trade-offs among quality, cost, flexibility, and speed. A singular obsession with quality sacrifices too much along other dimensions.
Strong Culture	Fueled by 1982's In Search of Excellence and fascination with Japanese management systems, having a strong culture became viewed as crucial to organizational success. Within a few years, many of the "excellent" companies highlighted in the book had fallen on hard times. However, firms such as Disney continue to gain competitive advantage through their strong cultures.

Don't chase the latest management fads. The situation dictates which approach best accomplishes the team's mission. -Colin Powell

The emergence and disappearance of fads appears to be a predictable aspect of modern society. A fad arises when some element of popular culture becomes enthusiastically embraced by a group of people. Over the past few decades, for example, fashion fads have included leisure suits (1970s), "Members Only" jackets (1980s), platform shoes (1990s), Crocs (2000s), and torn jeans (2010s). Ironically, the reason a fad arises is also usually the cause of its demise. The uniqueness (or even outrageousness) of a fashion, toy, or hairstyle creates "buzz" and publicity but also ensures that its appeal is only temporary (Ketchen & Short, 2011).

Fads also seem to be a predictable aspect of the business world (Table 10.8 "Managing Management Fads"). As with cultural fads, many provocative business ideas go through a life cycle of creating buzz, captivating a group of enthusiastic adherents, and then giving way to the next fad. Bookstore shelves offer a seemingly endless supply of popular management books whose premises range from the intriguing to the absurd. Within the topic of leadership, for example, various books promise to reveal the "leadership secrets" of an eclectic array of famous individuals such as Jesus Christ, Hillary Clinton, Attila the Hun, and Santa Claus.

Beyond the striking similarities between cultural and business fads, there are also important differences. Most cultural fads are harmless, and they rarely create any long-term problems for those that embrace them. In contrast, embracing business fads could lead executives to make bad decisions. As our quote from Colin Powell suggests, relying on sound business practices is much more likely to help executives to execute their organization's strategy than are generic words of wisdom from Old St. Nick.

Many management fads have been closely tied to organizational control systems. For example, one of the best-known fads was an attempt to use output control to improve performance. Management by Objectives (MBO) is a process wherein managers and employees work together to create goals. These goals guide employees' behaviors and serve as the benchmarks for assessing their performance. Following the presentation of MBO in Peter Drucker's 1954 book *The Practice of Management*, many executives embraced the process as a cure-all for organizational problems and challenges.

Like many fads, however, MBO became a good idea run amok. Companies that attempted to create an objective for every aspect of employees' activities eventually discovered that this was unrealistic. The creation of explicit goals can conflict with activities involving tacit knowledge about the organization. Intangible notions such as "providing excellent customer service," "treating people right," and "going the extra mile" are central to many organizations' success, but these notions are difficult if not impossible to quantify. Thus, in some cases, getting employees to embrace certain values and other aspects of clan control is more effective than MBO.

Quality circles were a second fad that built on the notion of behavioral control. Quality circles began in Japan in the 1960s and were first introduced in the United States in 1972. A quality circle is a formal group of employees that meets regularly to brainstorm solutions to organizational problems. As the name "quality circle" suggests, identifying behaviors that would improve the quality of products and the operations management processes that create the products was the formal charge of many quality circles.

While the quality circle fad depicted quality as the key driver of productivity, it quickly became apparent that this perspective was too narrow. Instead, quality is just one of four critical dimensions of the production process; speed, cost, and flexibility are also vital. Maximizing any one of these four dimensions often results in a product that simply cannot satisfy customers' needs. Many products with perfect quality, for example, would be created too slowly and at too great a cost to compete in the market effectively. Thus trade-offs among quality, speed, cost, and flexibility are inevitable.

Improving clan control was the aim of sensitivity-training groups (or T-groups) that were used in many organizations in the 1960s. This fad involved gatherings of approximately eight to fifteen white people openly discussing their emotions, feelings, beliefs, and biases about workplace issues. In stark contrast to the rigid nature of MBO, the T-group involved free-flowing conversations led by a facilitator. These discussions were thought to lead individuals to greater understanding of themselves and others. The anticipated results were more enlightened workers and a greater spirit of teamwork.

Research on social psychology has found that groups are often far crueler than individuals. Unfortunately, this meant that the candid nature of T-group discussions could easily degenerate into accusations and humiliation. Eventually, the T-group fad gave way to recognition that creating potentially hurtful situations has no place within an organization. Hints of the softer side of T-groups can still be observed in modern team-building fads, however. Perhaps the best known is the "trust game," which claims to build trust between employees by having individuals fall backward and depend on their coworkers to catch them.

Improving clan control was the basis for the fascination with organizational culture that was all the rage in the 1980s. This fad was fueled by a best-selling 1982 book titled *In Search of Excellence: Lessons from America's Best-Run Companies*. Authors Tom Peters and Robert Waterman studied companies that they viewed as stellar performers and distilled eight similarities that were shared across the companies. Most of the similarities, including staying "close to the customer" and "productivity through people," arose from powerful corporate cultures. The book quickly became an international sensation; more than three million copies were sold in the first four years after its publication.

Soon it became clear that organizational culture's importance was being exaggerated. Before long, both the popular press and academic research revealed that many of Peters and Waterman's "excellent" companies quickly had fallen on hard times. Basic themes such as customer service and valuing one's company are quite useful, but these clan control elements often cannot take the place of holding employees accountable for their performance.

Figure 10.18: *Spirited games of kickball can help build an organization's culture, but such events should not substitute for holding employees accountable for delivering results.*

The history of fads allows us to make certain predictions about today's hot ideas, such as empowerment, "good to great," and viral marketing. Executives who distill and act on basic lessons from these fads are likely to enjoy performance improvements. Empowerment, for example, builds on important research findings regarding employees—many workers have important insights to offer to their firms, and these workers become more engaged in their jobs when executives take their insights seriously. Relying too heavily on a fad, however, seldom turns out well.

Just as executives in the 1980s could not treat *In Search of Excellence* as a recipe for success, today's executives should avoid treating James Collins's 2001 best-selling book *Good to Great: Why Some Companies Make the Leap...and Others Don't* as a detailed blueprint for running their companies. Overall, executives should understand that management fads usually contain a core truth that can help organizations improve but that a balance of output, behavioral, and clan control is needed within most organizations. As legendary author Jack Kerouac noted, "Great things are not accomplished by those who yield to trends and fads and popular opinion."

Key Takeaway

- Organizational control systems are a vital aspect of executing strategy because they track performance and identify adjustments that need to be made. Output controls involve measurable results. Behavioral controls involve regulating activities rather than outcomes. Clan control relies on a set of shared values, expectations, traditions, and norms. Over time, a series of fads intended to improve organizational control processes have emerged. Although these fads tend to be seen as cure-alls initially, executives eventually realize that an array of sound business practices is needed to create effective organizational controls.

1. What type of control do you think works most effectively with you and why?
2. What are some common business practices that you predict will be considered fads in the future?
3. How could you integrate each type of control into a college classroom to maximize student learning?

References

Bousquet, S. (2005, September 23). For surly license clerks. a pound of charm. *St Petersburg Times.*

Ketchen, D. J., & Short, J. C. (2011). Separating fads from facts: Lessons from "the good, the fad, and the ugly." *Business Horizons, 54,* 17–22.

Yamanouchi, K. (2011a, February 10). Delta ranks near bottom in on-time performance. *Atlanta-Journal Constitution.*
https://www.ajc.com/business/delta-ranks-near-bottom-time-performance/PbZFT87JuyiSXkNxotBrfN.

Yamanouchi, K. (2011b, July 27). Delta has $198 million profit, says 2,000 took buyouts. *Atlanta-Journal Constitution.*
https://www.ajc.com/business/delta-has-198-million-profit-says-000-took-buyouts/
mqaPWvYuo5nflnAOCcXBUJ.

Image Credits

10.6 Legal Forms of Business

Making a profit is a key goal for the overwhelming majority of firms. How a firm's owners benefit from profits and suffer from losses varies across different legal forms of business. Below we illustrate how profits and losses are treated within different business forms.

Table 10.9 Business Forms

Treatment of Profits and Losses within Different Business Forms
A sole proprietorship is owned by one person. The firm and its owner are treated interchangeably–the owner is the only beneficiary of any profits and is personally responsible for any losses and debts. Most sole proprietorships are small, but entrepreneur James Cash Penney operated JCPenney as one for many years after buying out his two partners.
In a partnership, two or more partners jointly own the firm. A successful partnership requires trust because profits and losses are shared and because each partner is accountable for the actions of others. Partnerships are a common business form for dental practices and law offices.
A corporation such as Southwest Airlines separates ownership and management by issuing ownership shares that are publicly traded in stock markets. Shareholders do not directly receive profits or absorb losses, but profits and losses tend to be reflected in whether the firm's stock price rises or falls. Shareholders can also benefit from profits in the form of dividends. Most large companies are C corporations with multiple stockholders. A disadvantage of this business form is double taxation: taxes are paid on corporate profits and on any dividends that corporate pays to stockholders, at their personal tax rate. An S corporation is limited to 100 stockholders and is more for smaller companies. It does not have double taxation. Taxes are paid on profits distributed to stockholders at their personal tax rate.
A limited liability company (LLC) can be thought of as a hybrid of a corporation and partnership. Like in a corporation, owners are not accountable for the firm's debts. A winner of a legal judgement against an LLC, for example, cannot claim the personal assets of the LLC's owners. LLC's also enjoy the management flexibility of partnerships. For federal tax purposes, an LLC must choose to be treated as a corporation, a partnership, or a sole proprietorship. Many architectural and consulting firms are organized as LLCs.

Choosing a Form of Business

The legal form a firm chooses to operate under is an important decision with implications for how a firm structures its resources and assets. Several legal forms of business are available to executives. Each involves a different approach to dealing with profits and losses (Table 10.9).

There are three primary considerations that firms should take into account when deciding which legal form of business should be chosen. These are:

1. How taxes are handled
2. How liability of the owners is handled
3. How easy to set up and operate the entity

There are five basic forms of business entities:

1. Sole Proprietorship
2. Partnership
3. Corporation
4. S Corporation
5. Limited Liability Company–LLC

A **sole proprietorship** is a firm that is owned by one person. From a legal perspective, the firm and its owner are considered one and the same. On the plus side, this means that all profits are the property of the owner (after taxes are paid, of course). On the minus side, however, the owner is personally responsible for the firm's losses and debts. This presents a tremendous risk. If a sole proprietor is on the losing end of a significant lawsuit, for example, the owner could find his personal assets forfeited. Most sole proprietorships are small and many have no employees. In most towns, for example, there are a number of self-employed repair people, plumbers, and electricians who work alone on home repair jobs. Also, many sole proprietors run their businesses from their homes to avoid expenses associated with operating an office. Along with the disadvantage of personal liability for the owner, sole proprietorships enjoy two advantages. Taxes on profits are assessed at the owner's personal tax rate. Also, this is the easiest form of business to set up and operate.

In a **partnership**, two or more partners share ownership of a firm. A partnership is similar to a sole proprietorship in that the partners are the only beneficiaries of the firm's profits, but they are also responsible for any losses and debts. Partnerships can be especially attractive if each person's expertise complements the others. For example, an accountant who specializes in preparing individual tax returns and another who has mastered business taxes might choose to join forces to offer customers a more complete set of tax services than either could offer alone.

From a practical standpoint, a partnership allows a person to take time off without closing down the business temporarily. Sander & Lawrence is a partnership of two home builders in Tallahassee, Florida. When Lawrence suffered a serious injury a few years ago, Sander was able to take over supervising his projects and see them through to completion. Had Lawrence been a sole proprietor, his customers would have suffered greatly. However, a person who chooses to be part of a partnership rather than operating alone as a sole proprietor also takes on some risk; your partner could make bad decisions that end up costing you a lot of money. Thus developing trust and confidence in one's partner is very important. As with the sole proprietorship, the owners and the partnership are considered as one. Being personally liable for the debts and actions of the partnership and the partner(s) is certainly a downside, however setting up a partnership is relatively easy. Taxes are also paid at the partners individual rate, a tax advantage generally.

Most large firms, such as Southwest Airlines, are organized as **corporations**. A key difference between a corporation and a sole proprietorship or partnership is that corporations involve the separation of ownership and management. Corporations sell shares of ownership that are publicly traded in stock markets, and they are managed by professional executives. These executives may own a significant portion of the corporation's stock, but this is not a legal requirement.

Another unique feature of corporations is how they deal with profits and losses. Unlike in sole proprietorships and partnerships, a corporation's owners (i.e., shareholders) do not directly receive profits or absorb losses. Instead, profits and losses indirectly affect shareholders in two ways. First, profits and losses tend to be reflected in whether the firm's stock price rises or falls. When a shareholder sells her stock, the firm's performance while she has owned the stock will influence whether she makes a profit relative to her stock purchase. Shareholders can also benefit from profits if a firm's executives decide to pay cash dividends to shareholders. Unfortunately, for shareholders, corporate profits and any dividends that these profits support are both taxed. This double taxation is a big disadvantage of corporations. Corporations (also called C corporations) are also the most difficult form of business to set up and have a number of regulations to comply with.

A specialized type of corporation called an **S corporation** is designed for smaller companies.. Much like in a partnership, the firm's profits and losses are reported on owners' personal tax returns in proportion with each owner's share of the firm, so double taxation is avoided. Although this is an attractive feature, an S corporation would be impractical for most large firms because the number of shareholders in an S corporation is capped, usually at one hundred. In contrast, Southwest Airlines has more than ten thousand shareholders. For smaller firms, such as many real-estate agencies, the S corporation is an attractive form of business. S corporations also provide liability protection for their stockholders as C corporations do, and are easier to set up and operate than C corporations.

A final form of business is very popular, yet it is not actually recognized by the federal government as a form of business. Instead, the ability to create a **limited liability company (LLC)** is granted in state laws. LLCs mix attractive features of corporations and partnerships. The owners of an LLC are not personally liable for debts that the LLC accumulates (like in a corporation) and the LLC can be run in a flexible manner (like in a partnership). When paying federal taxes, however, an LLC must choose to be treated as a corporation, a partnership, or a sole proprietorship. Many home builders (including Sander & Lawrence), architectural businesses, and consulting firms are LLCs. The ease of setting up and operating an LLC is similar to a sole proprietorship or partnership.

Table 10.10 Key Factors for Different Forms of Business

	Taxes	Liability	Ease of Operation
Sole Proprietor	Personal tax return	Unlimited liability	Easiest
Partnership	Personal tax return	Unlimited liability	Easy
C Corporation	Double taxation	Limited liability	Hardest
S Corporation	Personal tax return	Limited liability	Hard
Limited Liability Company	Personal tax return	Limited liability	Moderate

Section Video

Finding the Right Business Structure [03:58]

The video for this lesson further explains the various forms of business ownership.

You can view this video here: https://youtu.be/A-Up-JUkaj0.

Key Takeaway

- The five major forms of business in the United States are sole proprietorships, partnerships, LLCs, and C and S corporations. Each form has implications for how individuals are taxed, the personal liability of the owners, and how resources are managed and deployed in the set up and operations.

Exercises

1. Why are so many small firms sole proprietorships?
2. Find an example of a firm that operates as an LLC. Why do you think the owners of this firm chose this form of business over others?
3. Why might different forms of business be more likely to rely on a different organizational structure?

Video Credits

John Deere. (2016, May 26). *Finding the right business structure* [Video]. YouTube. https://youtu.be/A-Up-JUkaj0.

10.7 Conclusion

This chapter explains elements of organizational design that are vital for executing strategy. Leaders of firms, ranging from the smallest sole proprietorship to the largest global corporation, must make decisions about the delegation of authority and responsibility when organizing activities within their firms. Deciding how to best divide labor to increase efficiency and effectiveness is often the starting point for more complex decisions that lead to the creation of formal organizational charts. While small businesses rarely create organization charts, firms that embrace functional, multidivisional, matrix, and boundaryless structures often have reporting relationships with considerable complexity. To execute strategy effectively, managers also depend on the skillful use of organizational control systems that involve output, behavioral, and clan controls. Although introducing more efficient business practices to improve organizational functioning is desirable, executives need to avoid letting their firms become "out of control" by being skeptical of management fads. Finally, the legal form a business takes is an important decision with implications for a firm's organizational structure.

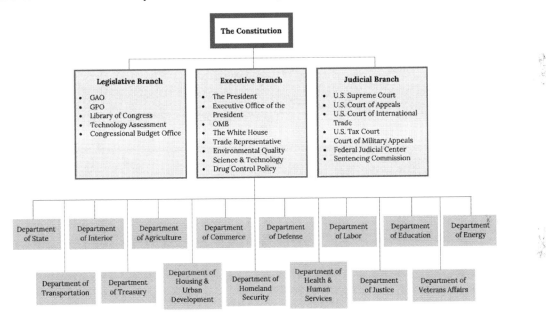

Figure 10.19: Three Government Branches

1. The preceding chart is an organizational chart for the US federal government. What type of the four structures mentioned in this chapter best fits what you see in this chart?
2. How does this structure explain why the government seems to move at an incredibly slow pace?
3. What changes could be made to speed up the government? Would they be beneficial?

Image Credits

Figure 10.19: Kindred Grey (2020). "Three Government Branches." CC BY NC SA 3.0 Adaptation of Figure 9.6 from Mastering Strategic Management (2015) (CC BY NC SA 3.0). Retrieved from https://open.lib.umn.edu/app/uploads/sites/11/2015/04/ea8dfc0653c92ca873e0d4602037591a.jpg.

Chapter 11: Leading an Ethical Organization: Corporate Governance, Corporate Ethics, and Social Responsibility

Learning Objectives

After reading this chapter, you should be able to understand and articulate answers to the following questions:

1. What is the role of the firm's board of directors as it relates to ethical behavior of the firm?
2. What is corporate social responsibility and its strategic role for a firm?
3. What are the implications of the contemporary ethical questions and issues facing companies?

11.1 Introduction

Today, more than ever, stakeholders are placing a variety of ethical and socially responsible demands on firms across industries. Subsequently, strategic management will be unsuccessful if it is performed in an ethical vacuum. Strategy development and implementation must reflect the firm's mission, vision, and values. Ethical assessments of the external and internal environments must be performed using accurate information and transparent processes even in competitive environments. When firms attempt to gain a competitive advantage, many companies engage in legitimate and accepted competitive tactics, but sometimes firms cross the line and enter unethical, and perhaps illegal, space in their quest. The potential costs of unethical corporate business practice is born by the perpetrator—if they are "caught." However, in many cases, like environmental dumping or exploitative labor practices, society and its members may pay the costs years before the firm does. Minimally, business level, corporate level, and international strategy development should always occur within acceptable practices in the industry and in light of the firm's own code of ethics and compliance. As firms move from "doing right" to "doing good," and endorse corporate social responsibility philosophies and activities, employees, managers, customers, and other stakeholders take pride and satisfaction in the impact their company has on improving the society. Further, as contemporary societal expectations have shifted, firms have witnessed new opportunities to turn corporate values and ethical decision-making into a competitive advantage within their marketplace.

TOMS Shoes: Doing Business with Soul

Figure 11.1: Under the business model used by TOMS Shoes, a pair of their signature alpargata footwear is donated for every pair sold.

In 2002 Blake Mycoskie competed with his sister Paige on *The Amazing Race*—a reality show where groups of two people with existing relationships engage in a global race to win valuable prizes, with the winner receiving a coveted grand prize. Although Blake's team finished third in the second season of the show, the experience afforded him the opportunity to visit Argentina, where he returned in 2006 and developed the idea to build a company around the alpargata—a popular style of shoe in that region.

The premise of the company Blake started was a unique one. For every shoe sold, a pair will be given to someone in need. This simple business model was the basis for TOMS Shoes, which has now given away more than one million pairs of shoes to those in need in more than 20 countries worldwide (Oloffson, 2010). The rise of TOMS Shoes has inspired other companies that have adopted the "buy-one-give-one" philosophy. For example, the Good Little Company donates a meal for every package purchased (Nicolas, 2011). This business model has also been successfully applied to selling (and donating) other items such as glasses and books.

The social initiatives that drive TOMS Shoes stand in stark contrast to the criticisms that plagued Nike Corporation, where claims of human rights violations, ranging from the use of sweatshops and child labor to lack of compliance with minimum wage laws, were rampant in the 1990s (McCall, 1998). While Nike struggled to win back confidence in buyers that were concerned with their business practices, TOMS social initiatives are a source of excellent publicity in pride in those who purchase their products. As further testament to their popularity, TOMS has engaged in partnerships with Nordstrom, Disney, and Element Skateboards.

Although the idea of social entrepreneurship and the birth of firms such as TOMS Shoes are relatively new, a push toward social initiatives has been the source of debate for executives for decades. Issues that have sparked particularly fierce debate include CEO pay and the role of today's modern corporation. More than a quarter of a century ago, famed economist Milton Friedman argued, "The social responsibility of business is to increase its profits." This notion is now being challenged by firms such as TOMS and their entrepreneurial CEO, who argue that serving other stakeholders beyond the owners and shareholders can be a powerful, inspiring, and successful motivation for growing business.

This chapter discusses some of the key issues and decisions relevant to understanding corporate and business ethics. These issues include how to govern large corporations in an effective and ethical manner, what behaviors are considered best practices in regard to corporate social performance, and how different generational perspectives and biases may hold a powerful influence on important decisions. Understanding these issues may provide knowledge that can encourage effective organizational leadership like that of TOMS Shoes and discourage the criticisms of many firms associated with the corporate scandals of the late 1990s and early 2000s.

References

McCall, W. (1998). Nike battles backlash from overseas sweatshops. *Marketing News, 9*, 14.

Nicolas, S. (2011, February). The great giveaway. *Director, 64*, 37–39.

Oloffson, K. (2010, September 29). In Toms' shoes: Start-up copy "one-for-one" model. *Wall Street Journal*. https://www.wsj.com/articles/SB10001424052748704116004575522251507063936.

Image Credits

Figure 11.1: Ladd, Parke. "Quinn's new Toms." CC BY 2.0. Retrieved from https://flic.kr/p/9dh984.

11.2 Doing Well by Doing Good

Corporate Scandals and Sarbanes-Oxley Act

Celebrity scandals often create "buzz" and actually make celebrities richer. But scandals in the business world often lead to the forfeiture of millions of dollars as well as prison sentences. We illustrate some notable corporate scandals below.

Table 11.1 Corporate Scandals

Notable Corporate Scandals		
Ponzi schemes are named after Charles Ponzi, who in the 1920s paid returns to investors using money from new investors rather than firm profits. Inevitably this kind of scheme falls apart because it becomes impossible to attract enough new investors to pay existing ones.	Enron executives used accounting loopholes to create shell companies to hide billions in debt from failed deals and projects. Although these smug executives thought they were always "the smartest guys in the room," the loss of $11 billion in stock value and the prison time served by many of them proves otherwise.	Corruption was a family affair at Adelphia Communications Corporation, which was named after the Greek word for brothers. Adelphia was the fifth largest cable company in the United States until father and son team John and Timothy Rigas were found guilty on securities violations tied to their theft of $100 million. Another Rigas son, Michael, pled guilty to falsifying financial reports.
After two crashes that took hundreds of lives, Boeing grounded their 737 Super Max airliner. Their $20 million fine was small compared to the financial losses related to loss of confidence and loss of future sales, as it was discovered that Boeing had failed in several ways with FAA rules, inspections, and training pilots on its software changes.	Although Chiquita Brands sells healthy snacks, their corporate actions upset many stomachs in 2007 when they were fined $25 million by the US Justice Department for having ties to a Colombia paramilitary group on the department's list of foreign terrorists organizations.	The Madoff investment scandal that broke in 2008 provided a modern twist on the classic Ponzi scheme. NASDAQ chairman Bernard Madoff pled guilty to eleven federal crimes that constituted the largest investor fraud ever committed by an individual. Madoff was sentenced to 150 years in prison.

In the 1990s and early 2000s, several corporate scandals were revealed in the United States that showed a lack of board vigilance. Perhaps the most famous involves Enron, whose executive antics were documented in the film *The Smartest Guys in the Room*. Enron used accounting loopholes to hide billions of dollars in failed deals. When their scandal was discovered, top management cashed out millions in stock options while preventing lower-level employees from selling their stock. The collective acts of Enron led many employees to lose all their retirement holdings and their jobs, stockholders lost $74 billion, and many Enron execs were sentenced to prison. This scandal also caused the dissolution of Enron's outside accounting firm, Arthur Anderson, one of the five largest accounting firms in the world at the time.

Around the same time as Enron, other corporate scandals created colossal damage. WorldCom, a telecommunications firm, inflated its assets. When discovered, shareholders lost $180 billion and 30,000 employees lost their jobs. Another famous one is Tyco, where the CEO and CFO stole $150 million and inflated the company revenues by $500 million. Before being discovered, the CEO threw a birthday party for his wife on a Mediterranean island that cost $2 million, paid with company funds. The CEO and CFO both went to prison.

In response to notable corporate scandals at Enron, WorldCom, Tyco, and other firms, Congress passed sweeping new legislation with the hopes of restoring investor confidence while preventing future scandals (Table 11.1). Signed into law by President George W. Bush in 2002, **the Sarbanes-Oxley Act** contained 11 aspects that represented some of the most far-reaching reforms since the presidency of Franklin Roosevelt. These reforms create improved standards that affect all publicly traded firms in the United States. The key elements of each aspect of the act are summarized as follows:

1. Because accounting firms were implicated in corporate scandals, an oversight board was created to oversee auditing activities.
2. Standards now exist to ensure auditors are truly independent and not subject to conflicts of interest in regard to the companies they represent.
3. Enron executives claimed that they had no idea what was going on in their company, but the Sarbanes-Oxley Act requires senior executives to take personal responsibility for the accuracy of financial statements.
4. Enhanced reporting is now required to create more transparency in regard to a firm's financial condition.
5. Securities analysts must disclose potential conflicts of interest.
6. To prevent CEOs from claiming tax fraud is present at their firms, CEOs must personally sign the firm's tax return.
7. The Securities and Exchange Commission (SEC) now has expanded authority to censor or bar securities analysts from acting as brokers, advisers, or dealers.
8. Reports from the comptroller general are required to monitor any consolidations among public accounting firms, the role of credit agencies in securities market operations, securities violations, and enforcement actions.
9. Criminal penalties now exist for altering or destroying financial records.
10. Significant criminal penalties now exist for white-collar crimes.
11. The SEC can freeze unusually large transactions if fraud is suspected.

The changes that encouraged the creation of the Sarbanes-Oxley Act were so sweeping that comedian Jon Stewart quipped, "Did Wall Street have any rules before this? Can you just shoot a guy for looking at you wrong?" Despite the considerable merits of the Sarbanes-Oxley Act, no legislation can provide a cure-all for corporate scandal (Table 11.2). As evidence, the scandal by Bernard Madoff that broke in 2008 represented the largest investor fraud ever committed by an individual. But in contrast to some previous scandals that resulted in relatively minor punishments for their perpetrators, Madoff was sentenced to 150 years in prison.

In the early 2000s, highly publicized fraud at Enron, WorldCom, Tyco, and other firms revealed significant issues including conflicts of interest by auditors and securities analysts, boardroom failures, and inadequate funding of the Securities and Exchange Commission. In response, Senator Paul Sarbanes and Representative Michael Oxley sponsored legislation that contained what former President George. W. Bush called "the most far-reaching reforms of American business practices since the time of Franklin D. Roosevelt." We outline the 11 key aspects of the law below.

Table 11.2 Sarbanes-Oxley Act of 2002 (SOX)

11 Key Aspects of the Sarbanes-Oxley Act of 2002	
Accounting firms were complicit in some fraudulent events. In response, SOX created a board to oversee auditing activities within these firms.	To restore investor confidence in securities analysts, SOX expands the SEC's authority to censure or bar them from acting as a broker, advisor, or dealer.
Concerns about conflicts of interests arising from accounting firms acting as consultants and auditors for the same firm led SOX to establish standards to ensure that auditors would be truly independent.	The comptroller general and the SEC are now required to carefully monitor any consolidation among public accounting firms, the role of credit agencies in securities market operations, securities violations, and enforcement actions.
Senior executives must take individual responsibility for the accuracy of their firms' financial reports and they must forfeit the benefits arising from any non-compliance.	To preserve potentially incriminating documents, SOX creates criminal penalties for altering or destroying financial records.
To create more transparency, SOX enhances reporting standards for off-balance-sheet transactions and requires timely reporting of material changes in a firm's financial condition.	In the past, white-collar crimes often received a proverbial slap on the wrist. SOX significantly increased the penalties associated with white-collar crimes and conspiracies.
Securities analysts must disclose any conflicts of interest involving a firm.	In response to past fraud and records tampering, the SEC can temporarily freeze transactions deemed unusually large.
The CEO is required to sign his/her firm's tax return. This may prevent CEOs from claiming that they did not know tax fraud was occurring within their firms.	

Did the Sarbanes-Oxley Act help reduce corporate scandals? Maybe, but unfortunately they have continued. Some more notable ones are HealthSouth (2003), Freddie Mac (2004), American Insurance Group AIG (2005), Lehman Brothers (2008), Bernie Madoff (2008). Accounting and financial misdeeds are not the only type or corporate scandals that still plague the corporate environment. Sadly, more recent scandals involved Volkswagen (emissions fraud), Uber (sexual harassment), Apple (deliberately slowing devices), Facebook (data harvesting without consent), Boeing (skirting FAA rules), and various pharmaceutical companies that unethically pushed sales of opiate medications, increasing the opioid epidemic. As noted, not all corporate scandals are financial in nature, but typically are driven by greed and provide a financial benefit for individuals or companies.

Section Video

The ethics of business. Where and why it can go wrong [10:55]

This video explains the ethics of business, and where and why it can go wrong.

You can view this video here: https://youtu.be/vAtu_iBbknY.

Ethics and CSR as Corporate Strategy

One positive outcome of the corporate scandals has been an increased focus by firms on corporate ethics. Many companies now have an Ethics and Compliance Officer and a detailed Ethics and Compliance Code. For example, Walmart's Global Ethics and Compliance Program is provided online for the public and has numerous pages (Walmart, n.d.). Many firms provide annual training to all its employees on their company's ethics and compliance standards.

Here is the Table of Contents for Facebook's Code of Conduct. Although this is a typical approach to a Code of Conduct, it doesn't mean a company is necessarily perceived as ethical. This is particularly true lately as Facebook contends with pressure to change its commitments to "free speech" with accusations of promoting hate speech.

Table 11.3 Table of Contents for Facebook's Code of Conduct

Table of Contents
1. Introduction
2. Conflicts of Interest
3. Harassment
4. Communications
5. Public Disclosures
6. Financial Integrity and Responsibility
7. Confidential Information
8. Protection of User Data and Personnel Data
9. Protection and Use of Facebook Assets
10. Compliance with Laws
11. Reporting Violations
12. Policy Prohibiting Retaliation
13. Training
14. Amendment and Waivers

Another form of regulation designed to prevent corporate misbehavior are "whistleblower" laws and policies. Many firms intentionally encourage employees to report any suspected misconduct by the firm, its managers, or employees. A "whistleblower" hotline is often provided where suspected violations can be reported anonymously. Anti-retaliation policies encourage employees to come forward to report misconduct without fear of retaliation or losing their job. Although all these measures are helpful, unfortunately, fraud and misconduct still occur.

In response to persistent "rule-breaking" by corporate actors, Corporate Social Responsibility (CSR) emerged in the 1970s to assert that a "social contract" exists between business and society. At its base is the assumption that businesses thrive when the society it relies on thrives, and therefore, firms have a duty to provide more than profit back to its environment. It is a business model that attempts to "give back" to the members of the community or society that help the firm succeed through the purchasing of its products or services. The goal of CSR is to enhance the success of a business by enhancing the society in which the organization operates. It can take the form of philanthropy or donating funds to causes it believes are important to its stakeholders. Some forms of CSR include corporate volunteerism, such as asking company employees to volunteer to build a Habitat for Humanity house on a Saturday. Improving environmental sustainability is one of the most recognized recent forms of CSR.

Many firms adopt the Triple Bottom Line approach to guide their CSR philosophy. In the triple bottom line, the company focuses on the three P's; profit, planet, and people. CSR is discussed in more detail later in this chapter.

Section Videos

What is business ethics? [04:08]

The video for this lesson explains personal business ethics.

You can view this video here: https://youtu.be/IEmUag1ri6U.

What is Ethics? What is Business Ethics? [04:35]

This second video for the lesson focuses on business ethics.

You can view this video here: https://youtu.be/vmVu66Fpd9U.

Key Takeaway

- Firms can have a positive or negative impact on society. Corporate scandals have caused tremendous losses for shareholders, employees, and other stakeholders. The government has passed various regulations such as the Sarbanes-Oxley Act in attempts to thwart unethical and illegal company behavior, yet this behavior continues. Company boards of directors have the ultimate responsibility of ensuring ethical behavior on the part of the organization and its CEO. Senior management may be tempted to act in their own interest instead of the best interests of the firm, which is called the agency problem. On the positive side, many firms have adopted the philosophy and activities of corporate social responsibility or creating shared value. Ethical issues will confront firms and their leadership teams. Adhering to the companies' core values and keeping the best interests of the firm as the priority will help guide leaders to the best decisions.

1. Divide into groups of 4 or 8, and discuss actions boards of directors can take to help ensure ethical behavior is maintained by the company leadership and the employees. Come up with several ideas to share with the class.
2. You work for Deloitte in Tyson's Corner in Northern Virginia. You have been selected to serve on a team to come up with ideas on how your office can implement corporate social responsibility. What specific CSR ideas will you share with the team?

References

Table 11.3 Facebook. (2019, June 10). Adapted from "Code of Conduct" https://s21.q4cdn.com/399680738/files/doc_downloads/governance_documents/2019/Code-of-Conduct-(June-10-2019).pdf.

Walmart. (n.d.) Global Ethics & Compliance. https://corporate.walmart.com/our-story/global-ethics-compliance.

Video Credits

Cranfield School of Management. (2010, July 13). *The ethics of business. Where and why it can go wrong* [Video]. YouTube. https://youtu.be/vAtu_iBbknY.

Global Ethics Solutions. (2019, November 1). *What is business ethics?* [Video]. https://youtu.be/IEmUag1ri6U.

Markkula Center for Applied Ethics. (2010, October 1). *What is ethics? What is business ethics?* [Video]. https://youtu.be/vmVu66Fpd9U.

11.3 Corporate Governance

The Many Roles of Boards of Directors

"You're fired!" is a commonly used phrase most closely associated with Donald Trump as he dismissed candidates on his reality show, *The Apprentice*. But who would have the power to utter these words to today's CEOs, whose paychecks are on par with many of the top celebrities and athletes in the world? This honor belongs to the board of directors—a group of individuals that oversees the activities of an organization or corporation.

Potentially firing or hiring a CEO is one of many roles played by the board of directors in their charge to provide effective corporate governance for the firm. An effective board plays many roles, ranging from the approval of financial objectives, advising on strategic issues, making the firm aware of relevant laws, and representing stakeholders who have an interest in the long-term performance of the firm (Table 11.1 "Board Roles"). Effective boards may help bring prestige and important resources to the organization. For example, General Electric's board often has included the CEOs of other firms as well as former senators and prestigious academics. Blake Mycoskie of TOMS Shoes was touted as an ideal candidate for an "all-star" board of directors because of his ability to fulfill his company's mission "to show how together we can create a better tomorrow by taking compassionate action today" (Bunting, 2011).

One of the key stakeholders of a corporation is generally agreed to be the shareholders of the company's stock. Most large, publicly traded firms in the United States are made up of thousands of shareholders. While 5% ownership in many ventures may seem modest, this amount is considerable in publicly traded companies, where such ownership is generally limited to other companies, and ownership in this amount could result in representation on the board of directors.

The possibility of **conflicts of interest** is considerable in public corporations. A conflict of interest exists when a person could receive personal benefit from decisions they make in their official capacity. For example, if a firm's purchasing agent's husband owns an office supply company that could sell products to the firm, the purchasing agent has a conflict of interest, On the one hand, CEOs favor large salaries and job stability, and these desires are often accompanied by a tendency to make decisions that would benefit the firm (and their salaries) in the short term at the expense of decisions considered over a longer time horizon. In contrast, shareholders prefer decisions that will grow the value of their stock in the long term. This separation of interest creates an **agency problem** wherein the interests of the individuals that manage the company (agents such as the CEO) may not align with the interest of the owners (such as stockholders).

The Ethisphere® Institute presents an annual listing of the #WorldsMostEthicalCompanies at https://www.worldsmostethicalcompanies.com/honorees.

The composition of the board is critical because the dynamics of the board play an important part in resolving the agency problem. However, who exactly should be on the board is an issue that has been subject to fierce debate. CEOs often favor the use of board insiders who often have intimate knowledge of the firm's business affairs. In contrast, many institutional investors such as mutual funds and pension funds that hold large blocks of stock in the firm often prefer significant representation by board outsiders that provide a fresh, unbiased perspective concerning a firm's actions.

One particularly controversial issue in regard to board composition is the potential for CEO duality, a situation in which the CEO is also the chairman of the board of directors. This has also been known to create a bitter divide within a corporation.

For example, during the 1990s, The Walt Disney Company was often listed in BusinessWeek's rankings for having one of the worst board of directors (Lavelle, 2002). In 2005, Disney's board forced the separation of then CEO (and chairman of the board) Michael Eisner's dual roles. Eisner retained the role of CEO but later stepped down from Disney entirely. Disney's story reflects a changing reality that boards are acting with considerably more influence than in previous decades when they were viewed largely as rubber stamps that generally folded to the whims of the CEO.

William Shakespeare once wrote, "All the world's a stage, and the men and women merely players." This analogy applies well to boards of directors. When the performance of board members is impressive, the company is able to put on a dynamic show. But if a board member phones in their role, failure may soon follow. Discussed below are the different roles board members may play.

Table 11.4 Board Roles

Roles of Board Members	
Accountant	Board members may, at times, approve financial objectives.
Lawyer	Ensuring the firm complies with applicable laws is a key role.
Advisor	Providing advice on strategic issues is a critical role that is overlooked by less effective boards.
Activist	Boards must ensure the rights and interests of stakeholders (especially stockholders) are represented.
Human Resource Manager	Boards must monitor the CEO and engage in hiring, firing, and the administration of CEO compensation.
Agent	Because board members may serve in powerful positions at other companies, a well-networked board member may be able to bring new connections to the firm.

Managing CEO Compensation

One of the most visible roles of boards of directors is setting CEO pay. The valuation of the human capital associated with the rare talent possessed by some CEOs can be illustrated in a story of an encounter one tourist had with the legendary artist Pablo Picasso. As the story goes, Picasso was once spotted by a woman sketching. Overwhelmed with excitement at the serendipitous meeting, the tourist offered Picasso fair market value if he would render a quick sketch of her image. After completing his commission, she was shocked when he asked for five thousand francs, responding, "But it only took you a few minutes." Undeterred, Picasso retorted, "No, it took me all my life" (Kay, 1999).

Figure 11.2: Picasso's Garçon á la pipe was one of the most expensive works ever sold at more than $100 million.

This story illustrates the complexity associated with managing CEO compensation. On the one hand, large corporations must pay competitive wages for the scarce talent that is needed to manage billion-dollar corporations. In addition, like celebrities and sport stars, CEO pay is much more than a function of a day's work for a day's pay. CEO compensation is a market driven function of the competitive wages that other corporations would offer for a potential CEO's services.

On the other hand, boards will face considerable scrutiny from investors if CEO pay is out of line with industry norms. From the year 1980 to 2000, the gap between CEO pay and worker pay grew from 42 to 1 to 475 to 1 (Blumenthal, 2000). Although efforts to close this gap have been made, as recently as 2019 reports indicate the ratio continues to be as high as 278 to 1. This is much higher than other countries, for example, Germany's is half the US ratio (Cox, 2019). Meanwhile, shareholders need to be aware that research studies have found that CEO pay is positively correlated with the size of firms—the bigger the firm, the higher the CEO's compensation (Tosi et al., 2000). Consequently, when a CEO tries to grow a company, such as by acquiring a rival firm, shareholders should question whether such growth is in the company's best interest or whether it is simply an effort by the CEO to get a pay raise.

Within American firms, the average CEO is paid over 200 times what the typical worker makes—one of the highest ratios in the world. Many CEOs also receive perks that the average employee could only dream possible. Such perks are trouble to the extent that they reflect the board's lack of vigilance in monitoring CEO spending. We illustrate a few examples below.

Table 11.5 CEO Perks

Perks of Being a CEO
Former Tyco CEO Dennis Koslowski—now a convicted felon—threw a week-long $2 million birthday bash for his wife that included an ice-sculpture of Michelangelo's David that dispensed vokda—top shelf, of course!
A pint-sized matter compared to the lavish perks of many executives, the sweet tooth should be satisfied for former Ben & Jerry's CEO Robert Holland Jr., who will receive free ice cream for life.
Golden parachutes where CEOs receive large cash settlements if fired are common in publicly traded companies. Less common is the "golden coffin" that provides big settlements if an executive passes away in office. Abercrombie & Fitch CEO Michael Jefferies was offered $6 million for his loyalty to the company...dead or alive.
Foreclosure! Countrywide Financial, now owned by Bank of America, paid nearly $1 million for their executives' country club memberships between 2003 through 2006.
Although Don Tyson of Tyson Foods retired in 2001, Tyson employees mowed his yard and cleaned his house to keep things tidy post retirement.

In most publicly traded firms, CEO compensation generally includes guaranteed salary, cash bonus, and stock options. But perks provide another valuable source of CEO compensation (Table 11.4 "CEO Perks"). In addition to the controversy surrounding CEO pay, such perks associated with holding the position of CEO have also come under considerable scrutiny. The term perks, derived from perquisite, refers to special privileges, or rights, as a function of one's position. CEO perks have ranged in magnitude from the sweet benefit of ice cream for life given to former Ben & Jerry's CEO Robert Holland, to much more extreme benefits that raise the ears of investors while outraging employees. One such perk was provided to John Thain who, as former head of NYSE Euronext, received more than $1 million to renovate his office. While such perks may provide powerful incentives to stay with a company, they may result in considerable negative press and serve only to motivate vigilant investors wary of the value of such investments to shop elsewhere.

As noted earlier in this chapter, sometimes CEOs get involved in corporate scandals, seeking their own self interest instead of the best interests of the company. But this problem can be much more subtle than creating a scandal, and not limited to CEOs. An agency problem exists whenever an "agent" of the company, typically senior management, acts in their own self interest at the expense of the best interests of the firm. For example, a CEO may push for the acquisition of another company to enhance his or her salary and legacy when that acquisition is not a wise move. They may decide to expand into Spain instead of the United Kingdom because they prefer to travel to sunny Spain with its great food instead of the rainy United Kingdom, even though the United Kingdom is the better choice. Selfish or self-centered motives can influence decision making in ways that are difficult to detect. At times, the decision maker may feel justified in the decision and not realize their impure motives behind the decision. The board of directors and the decision makers themselves need to recognize that the agency problem exists and guard against it in their organization. The agency problem also exists in politics, and at times politicians are accused of making decisions that benefit themselves over their constituents.

The Market for Corporate Governance

The terms associated with mergers, acquisitions, and the actions used by executives to block these moves often sound like material from the latest war movie. We explain important terms below.

Table 11.6 Takeover Terms

While a pirate raids a competitor's vessel looking to loot valuable treasures, a **corporate raider** invades a firm by purchasing its stock.	**Hostile takeover** refers to an attempt to purchase a company that is strongly resisted by the target firm's CEO and/or board.
Defenses against takeovers are often referred to as **shark repellent**. We illustrate a few below.	
A **golden parachute** is a financial package (often including stock options and bonuses worth millions of dollars) given to executives likely to lose their jobs after a takeover. These parachutes make taking over a firm more costly and thus less attractive.	When executives are desperate to avoid a takeover they may be forced to swallow a **poison pill**. This involves making the firm's stock unattractive to raiders by letting shareholders buy stock at a discount.
A firm that rescues a target firm by offering a friendly takeover as an alternative to a hostile one is known as a **white knight**.	In contrast to blackmail, where information is withheld unless a demand is met, **greenmail** occurs when an unfriendly firm forces a target company to repurchase a large block of stock at a premium to thwart a takeover attempt.

An old investment cliché encourages individuals to buy low and sell high. When a publicly traded firm loses value, often due to lack of vigilance on the part of the CEO and/or board, a company may become a target of a takeover wherein another firm or set of individuals purchases the company. Generally, the top management team is charged with revitalizing the firm and maximizing its assets.

In some cases, the takeover is in the form of a leveraged buyout (LBO) in which a publicly traded company is purchased with sizable debt and then taken off the stock market. One of the most famous LBOs was of RJR Nabisco, which inspired the book (and later film) *Barbarians at the Gate*. LBOs are historically associated with reduction in workforces to streamline processes and decrease costs. The managers who instigate buyouts generally bring a more entrepreneurial mind-set to the firm with the hopes of creating a turnaround from the same fate that made the company an attractive takeover target (recent poor performance) (Wright et al., 2001).

Many takeover attempts increase shareholder value. However, because most takeovers are associated with the dismissal of previous management, the terminology associated with change of ownership has a decidedly negative slant against the acquiring firm's management team. For example, individuals or firms that hope to conduct a takeover are often referred to as corporate raiders. An unsolicited takeover attempt is often dubbed a hostile takeover, with shark repellent as one of the potential defenses against such attempts. Although the poor management of a targeted firm is often the reason such businesses are potential takeover targets, when another firm that may be more favorable to existing management enters the picture as an alternative buyer, a white knight is said to have entered the picture (Table 11.3 "Takeover Terms").

The negative tone of takeover terminology also extends to the potential target firm. CEOs as well as board members are likely to lose their positions after a successful takeover occurs, and a number of anti-takeover tactics have been used by boards to deter a corporate raid. For example, many firms are said to pay greenmail by repurchasing large blocks of stock at a premium to avoid a potential takeover. Firms may threaten to take a poison pill where additional stock is sold to existing shareholders, increasing the shares needed for a viable takeover. Even if the takeover is successful and the previous CEO is dismissed, a golden parachute that includes a lucrative financial settlement is likely to provide a soft landing for the ousted executive.

Section Video

Role of the Board in Creating an Ethical Corporate Culture [06:48]

The video for this lesson describes the role of the board in creating an ethical corporate culture.

You can view this video here: https://youtu.be/kOm8SC8qI4w.

Exercises

1. Divide the class into teams and see who can find the most egregious CEO perk in the last year.
2. Find a listing of members of a board of directors for a Fortune 500 firm. Does the board seem to be composed of individuals who are likely to fulfill all the board roles effectively?
3. Research a hostile takeover in the past five years and examine the long-term impact on the firm's stock market performance. Was the takeover beneficial or harmful for shareholders?
4. Examine the AFL-CIO Executive Paywatch website https://aflcio.org/paywatch and select a company of interest to see how many years you would need to work to earn a year's pay enjoyed by the firm's CEO.

References

Blumenthal, R. G. (2000, September 4). The pay gap between workers and chiefs looks like a chasm. *Barron's*, 10.

Bunting, C. (2011, February 23). Board of dreams: Fantasy board of directors. *Business News Daily*. http://www.businessnewsdaily.com/681-board-of-directors-fantasy-picks-small-business.html.

Cox, J. (2019, August 16). CEOs see pay grow 1,000% in the last 40 years, now make 278 times the average worker. CNBC. https://www.cnbc.com/2019/08/16/ceos-see-pay-grow-1000percent-and-now-make-278-times-the-average-worker.html.

Kenton, W. (2020). *Sarbanes-Oxley (SOX) Act of 2002*. Investopedia. https://www.investopedia.com/terms/s/sarbanesoxleyact.asp.

Kay, I. (1999). Don't devalue human capital. *Wall Street Journal–Eastern Edition*, 233, A18.

Lavelle, L. (2002, October 7). The best and worst boards: How corporate scandals are sparking a revolution in governance. *BusinessWeek*, 104.

Tosi, H. L., Werner, S., Katz., J. P., & Gomez-Mejia, L. R. (2000). How much does performance matter? A meta-analysis of CEO pay studies. *Journal of Management*, 26, 301–339.

Wright, M., Hoskisson, R. E., & Busenitz, L. W. (2001). Firm rebirth: Buyouts as facilitators of strategic growth and entrepreneurship. *Academy of Management Executive*, 15, 111–125.

Image Credits

Figure 11.2: Picasso, Pablo. "Garçon à la Pipe." Public Domain. Retrieved from https://en.wikipedia.org/wiki/File:Garçon_à_la_pipe.jpg.

Video Credits

Markkula Center for Applied Ethics. 2013, November 26. Role of the Board in Creating an Ethical Corporate Culture. Retrieved from https://youtu.be/kOm8SC8qI4w.

11.4 Corporate Ethics and Social Responsibility

What Is Corporate Social Responsibility?

As introduced early in this chapter, **Corporate Social Responsibility** (CSR) "is a self-regulating business model that helps a company be socially accountable–to itself, its stakeholders, and the public. By practicing corporate social responsibility, also referred to simply as social responsibility, companies can be conscious of the kind of impact they are having on all aspects of society, including economic, social, and environmental" (Chen, 2020). Philanthropy is the simplest form of CSR, where a firm donates funds to a nonprofit organization such as the local volunteer rescue squad or the American Cancer Society. However, CSR can take many forms, with the end result that society benefits in some way. Environmental efforts in CSR might include reducing the company's pollution or helping to clean up the plastic that washes up on beaches. Supporting the local literacy volunteers by encouraging employees to participate to help adults learn to read and write provides a social benefit.

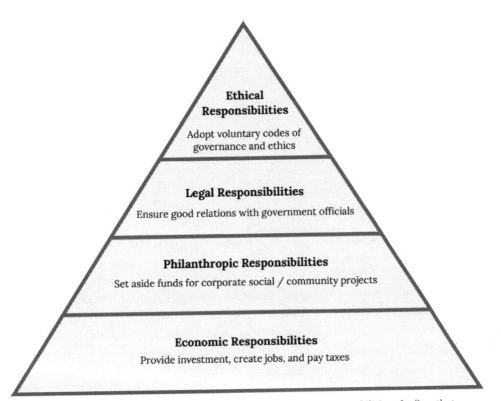

Figure 11.3: The CSR Pyramid shown illustrates the ever-increasing responsibilities of a firm that engages in a CSR philosophy and the associated activities.

The CSR approach is not without controversy. When CSR was introduced, the famous economist Milton Friedman opposed CSR on philosophical grounds. He believed, as some others did, that no profits should be diverted for CSR activities. The logic was that company investors and stockholders took a risk when they invested in the company, and therefore the company's first obligation is to them. On the other hand, many who practice CSR believe that CSR activities ultimately do benefit the company investors and stockholders. The belief is that having a CSR strategy provides good public relations for the firm and enhances their brand image, creating loyalty and more sales long term. For example, some consumers may specifically shop for TOMS shoes because of the firm's Buy One, Give One model, where the consumer feels their purchase is providing a positive social impact.

Some examples of CSR efforts are:

- Reducing their carbon footprint—Coca Cola
- Ensuring contract manufacturers pay a living wage—Patagonia
- Improving sustainable manufacturing—BMW
- Matches employees' donations to nonprofits—Microsoft and Google
- Reducing carbon emissions—United Airlines
- Promoting literacy among children—Twitter

- Eliminating foam cups–Dunkin'
- Donating employees' hours to children's tutoring–Salesforce

One criticism of CSR is that it is seen as an "add on" endeavor for firms. Often, CSR is not an ingrained component of the firm's philosophy and operations. In response to this criticism, a rather new movement emerged in an attempt to remedy this deficiency. Michael Porter and Mark Kramer suggest that instead of CSR, wise corporations are shifting to a **Creating Shared Value (CSV)** model that argues that firms should address social issues by creating shared value, which is fundamentally focused on expanding the total pool of social and economic resources (Porter & Kramer, 2006; Porter & Kramer, 2011). Porter and Kramer re-frame the business proposition by trying to recognize that "societal needs, not just conventional economic needs, define markets, and social harms can create internal costs for firms" (Porter & Kramer, 2011).

Creating shared value (CSV) is a business strategy that creates a direct link between the success of the firm and the improvement of society. Generally, CSV can be considered to be a particular strategic approach within the more general CSR landscape. A key differentiating detail is the explicit focus of CSV in generating positive economic outcomes through its strategic investments. As a company prospers economically, so do those it impacts. However, CSV and CSR both take a longer-term, rather than a short-term, approach to measuring impact. For example, Whole Foods was one of the most high profile companies to adopt CSV as a guiding strategy. This strategy translated into investing in local schools to ensure a well prepared work force and supporting local agricultural communities so it could reliably source produce from local vendors. While one traditional view of "business as usual" is that when a company prospers, it is at the expense of the consumer and society. CSV and CSR flip this view.

Section Videos

Business Ethics: Corporate Social Responsibility [02:56]

The video for this lesson further explains corporate social responsibility.

You can view this video here: https://youtu.be/xoE8XlcDUI8.

Insight: Ideas for Change–Michael Porter–Creating Shared Value [14:09]

The video for this lesson focuses on the differences between CSR and CSV.

You can view this video here: https://youtu.be/xuG-1wYHOjY.

Measuring Corporate Social Performance

TOMS Shoes' commitment to donating a pair of shoes for every pair sold illustrates the concept of social entrepreneurship, in which a business is created with a goal of improving both business and society (Schectman, 2010). Using a CSR model, firms such as TOMS exemplify a desire to improve **corporate social performance** (CSP) in which a commitment to individuals, communities, and the natural environment is valued alongside the goal of creating economic value. Although determining the level of a firm's social responsibility is subjective, this challenge has been addressed by other organizations that rate firms on a number of stakeholder-related issues with the goal of measuring CSP. They conduct ongoing research on social, governance, and environmental performance metrics of publicly traded firms and reports such statistics to institutional investors. For example, the KLD database provides ratings on numerous "strengths" and "concerns" for each firm along a number of dimensions associated with corporate social performance (Table 11.6 "Measuring Corporate Social Performance"). The results of their assessment are used to develop the Domini social investments fund, which has performed at levels roughly equivalent to the S&P 500. Some rating firms use an ESG framework for evaluating a firm. ESG stands for Environmental, Social, and Governance, and measures within each of these three dimensions are used to score a company.

Corporate social performance is defined as the degree to which a firm's actions honor ethical values that respect individuals, communities, and the natural environment. Determining whether a firm is socially responsible is somewhat subjective, but one popular approach has been developed by KLD Research & Analytics. Their work tracks "strengths" and "concerns" for hundreds of firms over time. KLD's findings are used by investors to screen socially responsible firms and by scholars who are interested in explaining corporate social performance. We illustrate the six key dimensions tracked by KLD below.

Table 11.7 Measuring Corporate Social Performance

Corporate Social Performance		
Community strengths include engagement in charitable giving, while involvement in tax controversies exemplifies a community concern.	Product quality/safety strengths include actions such as the establishment of a well-developed quality program, while concerns arise if a firm receives fines related to product quality and/or safety.	Diversity strengths include progressive programs for the employment of people with disabilities, whereas fines or civil penalties that result from an affirmative action constitute a concern.
A no-layoff policy is a strength in regard to employee relations, while poor union relations are a concern.	Environmental strengths include engaging in recycling, while concerns arise when penalties for air or water violations are documented.	Corporate governance strengths include equitable levels of compensation for top management and board members, while concerns are raised if controversies related to accounting, transparency, or political accountability are discovered.

Assessing the community dimension of CSP is accomplished by assessing community strengths, such as charitable or innovative giving that supports housing, education, or relations with indigenous peoples, as well as charitable efforts worldwide, such as volunteer efforts or in-kind giving. A firm's CSP rating is lowered when a firm is involved in tax controversies or other negative actions that affect the community, such as plant closings that can negatively affect property values.

CSP diversity strengths are scored positively when the company is known for promoting women and minorities, especially for board membership and the CEO position. Employment of people with disabilities and the presence of family benefits such as child or elder care would also result in a positive score by KLD. Diversity concerns include fines or civil penalties in conjunction with an affirmative action or other diversity-related controversy. Lack of representation by women on top management positions—suggesting that a glass ceiling is present at a company—would also negatively impact scoring on this dimension.

Figure 11.4: *Chick-fil-A encourages education through their program that has provided more than $92 million in financial aid to more than sixty thousand employees since 1970. [Photo used under Fair Use]*

The employee relations dimension of CSP gauges potential strengths such as notable union relations, profit sharing and employee stock-option plans, favorable retirement benefits, and positive health and safety programs noted by the US Occupational Health and Safety Administration. Employee relations concerns would be evident in poor union relations, as well as fines paid due to violations of health and safety standards. Substantial workforce reductions as well as concerns about adequate funding of pension plans also warrant concern for this dimension.

The environmental dimension records strengths by examining engagement in recycling, preventing pollution, or using alternative energies. KLD would also score a firm positively if profits derived from environmental products or services were a part of the company's business. Environmental concerns such as penalties for hazardous waste, air, water, or other violations or actions such as the production of goods or services that could negatively impact the environment would reduce a firm's CSP score.

Product quality/safety strengths exist when a firm has an established and/or recognized quality program; product quality safety concerns are evident when fines related to product quality and/or safety have been discovered or when a firm has been engaged in questionable marketing practices or paid fines related to antitrust practices or price fixing.

Corporate governance strengths are evident when lower levels of compensation for top management and board members exist, or when the firm owns considerable interest in another company rated favorably by KLD; corporate governance concerns arise when executive compensation is high or when controversies related to accounting, transparency, or political accountability exist.

> **Exercises**
>
> 1. How would your college or university fare if rated on the dimensions of CSR? Of CSV?
> 2. Do you believe that executives behave more ethically as a result of legislation such as the Sarbanes-Oxley Act? Why or why not?

References

Chen, J. (2020, February 22). *Corporate Social Responsibility (CSR)*. Investopedia. https://www.investopedia.com/terms/c/corp-social-responsibility.asp.

Porter, M. E., & Kramer, M. R. (2006). Strategy and society: The Link Between Competitive Advantage and Corporate Social Responsibility. *Harvard Business Review*, 84(12), 78-92.

Porter, M. E., & Kramer, M. R. (2011). Creating Shared Value. *Harvard Business Review*.

Schectman, J. (2010). Good Business. *Newsweek*, 156, 50.

Image Credits

https://thechickenwire.chick-fil-a.com/news/chick-fil-a-to-award-17-million-in-team-member-scholarships-in-2020.

Video Credits

Study.com. (2013, December 31). Business Ethics: Corporate Social Responsibility. Retrieved from https://youtu.be/xoE8XlcDUI8.

World Economic Forum. (2012, September 6). Insight: Ideas for Change-Michael Porter-Creating Shared Value. Retrieved from https://youtu.be/xuG-1wYHOjY.

11.5 Contemporary Questions of Corporate Ethics

The subject of corporate ethics is an ever-evolving theme. Sometimes companies and the individuals in those companies cross the line and commit acts that are unethical, immoral, or illegal. Society has attempted to erect barriers to prevent these activities from happening by passing laws and regulations, expecting a strict code of ethics and conduct, and providing measures of a firm's social contribution. Depending on which party is in power in Washington, laws and regulations are relaxed because they are "bad for business," or they are strengthened to "protect the people." Unfortunately, whatever the legal climate, violations of society's standards and expectations continue to occur, and it is critical to recognize that laws represent the minimum ethical standard tolerated by a society.

Firms committed to ethical business practices must start by recognizing that just because an action is legal, it does not mean it is ethical. Strategists understand the importance of this distinction because it will be the organization's stakeholders, and not the legal system, that will decide if the firm is satisfactorily ethical. For example, the 2020 boycott by advertisers of Facebook was a reaction to Facebook's failure to take a more active position on hate speech, but Facebook's decisions did not break any laws. (Fung, 2020).

This leads to questions about contemporary corporate ethics. In a global economy, where US companies are competing against cell phones from South Korean companies and Belgian chocolates, ethical questions arise as to the best path for a company to follow. Will companies stick to their core values statements when ethical decision making gets tough? Some of these questions are explored below.

Stakeholder Considerations

Bottom of the Pyramid Mini Case

In 2017, 8.6% of the world population controlled 86.3% of global wealth. This disparity continues to increase. This left about 3.5 billion people at the "bottom of the pyramid" (BOP) making $10,000 or less annually. This group has largely been ignored by business, assuming they did not have the means to purchase goods other than subsistence items (Prahalad, 2019).

Some companies are recognizing that this market of nearly half the world's population may be a viable market and in doing so, provide the world's poor with access to low-cost products that would improve the quality of their daily lives. There are three factors causing the increased interest in this market:

- The rise in income of this group in the last several decades.
- The widespread use of cell phone technology among the world's poor, lowering the cost of communication and learning. Banking is even done by cell phone in some poor countries.
- The rise of corporate social responsibility and creating shared value philosophies among companies in richer nations (Prahalad, 2019).

Companies entering this market have used the strategy of "low price, low margins, high volumes" in attempts to gain profitability, but this strategy required appropriately 30% market penetration to be successful. Proctor and Gamble launched its PUR$^{(R)}$ water purification powder on a large scale with this strategy but failed, not achieving sufficient penetration and volumes. Dupont attempted the same strategy selling protein powder packets to fortify foods, but failed for the same reason (Simanis, 2012).

There are criticisms of BOP strategies that extend beyond their failure to achieve market penetration. These BOP critics argue that the targeted marketing of the world's poorest people is exploitative and will systematically keep the poor in poverty by pushing out local suppliers and failing to provide sustainable structures for local employment in their place. Pointedly, they suggest that this approach perpetuates the conditions it is trying to improve.

What can firms like P&G and Dupont do to be successful in the market? How do they need to change their strategy? How can this be a win-win for the company and those at the bottom of the pyramid, or can it? Should firms be engaging in this strategy at all?

Offshoring

As US wages increased, and with improvements in communications and transportation, many US companies offshored their activities. Often, manufacturing operations were closed down in the United States and performed in a country where the labor costs were much cheaper. The result has been the loss of thousands of jobs in the US, with plants closed down and communities left devastated. Another aspect of offshoring has been in the service sector, with US firms setting up their call centers abroad, along with IT services and even accounting services. Importantly, offshoring impacts the working conditions of people around the world, generally in the poorest economies with the least labor protections. Workers in agricultural and garment industries are particularly vulnerable to labor exploitation in the global supply chain (British Standards Institution, 2019), and global concerns about child labor are well documented (Moulds, n.d.).

The ethical question is, "Is offshoring ethical?" Justifications can be made on both sides of the issue. US companies compete in a global marketplace, and the dominant argument has been that if they had to pay US wages, they could not compete internationally. Also, in 2019 before the COVID-19 pandemic, the United States had record low unemployment, so the need to return jobs to the United States was questionable. Conversely, the loss of good jobs and the resulting blight of closed facilities in communities across the country are just not worth the advantage of offshoring, in the opinion of some. As of 2018, efforts are being made by the federal government to encourage manufacturers to return to the United States, which include imposing additional tariffs on some goods made abroad. One outcome of the COVID-19 pandemic was the realization that the United States depends on foreign countries for many essential products, such as pharmaceuticals and face masks. This dependency, especially on China, a political adversary, gave more merit to the argument of reducing offshoring.

Of course, other countries besides the United States pursue cheap labor costs. Sometimes, this can lead to increased labor exploitation abroad, as foreign manufacturers compete against each other on price. This can even lead to labor exploitation at home, with the threat of offshoring to reduce wages and benefits. Conversely, ethical companies have produced the opposite effect abroad, making their suppliers pay fair wages if they want their business. Child labor has been reduced in developing countries because US firms required their suppliers to not use child labor. In an interesting twist, some industries are turning to the American South for cheap manufacturing labor. (Roberts, 2018)

Offshoring is a complicated strategic question, and without considering the full context of the questions facing the firm within its external environment, a strategist could easily make a short-sighted decision.

Environment/Climate Change/Sustainability

Another debate involving multiple world-wide stakeholders relates to environmental sustainability and global warming. As in offshoring, there are opposing forces that tip the scale one way or the other. On one side is the health of the economy and business environment. The opposing side is the health of the planet and its inhabitants; people, animals, and plant life. As environmental forces gain traction and laws and regulations are implemented by governments, some believe this hurts the economy, businesses, and employment. On the flip side, as regulations are loosened, others believe it contributes to increased pollution, poorer human health, and global warming with all its implications for drought, rising sea levels, and loss of animal and plant species.

These arguments have been going on since the early 1970's with the passage of the Clean Air Act and Clean Water Act by Congress. Some take the position that the dichotomy of opposing forces does not have to exist, that movements toward clean renewable energy sources or reducing pollution are overall good for the business environment, stimulating innovation, efficiency, and job creation. Even though it may cost a manufacturer millions of dollars to retrofit their plant to reduce pollution, these costs can be made up and the overall impact is positive. The pendulum swings back and forth on this issue, often depending on who is in power in Washington. European countries have taken the lead in sustainability, with significant conversion to wind power for electricity generation. Others, including China, India, and emerging economies lag behind.

Global Economic Inequality

In 1990, approximately 36% of the world's population lived in extreme poverty. The World Bank defines extreme poverty as living on less than $1.90 per day. Fortunately, this rate has been consistently declining about one percentage point annually, and in 2015 the percentage of people world wide living in extreme poverty was 10%. Approximately 68 million people are no longer considered in extreme poverty (The World Bank, 2018). China is a prime example of poor people moving to cities to take manufacturing jobs, with the result of millions elevating into the middle class.

What created such a drop in those living in extreme poverty? These people have benefited from the increase in global business and foreign direct investment that have impacted developing countries in Asia, Latin America, and Africa. Offshoring to low wage countries, although controversial, has helped millions move from an agrarian lifestyle of poverty to a steady job with steady income. The increase in global trade, particularly in commodities produced by poorer countries, helped in this effort. Likewise, the corporate social responsibility efforts of companies manufacturing in poorer countries insisted on their partners and supply chains to pay a living wage, pay men and women equally, and eliminate child labor, which meant more children received an education.

It is important to understand that even though there has been significant improvements in the number of people world wide living in extreme poverty (less than $1.90 per day), nearly half of the world's population still lives in poverty. Approximately 46% (as of 2015) live on less than $5.50 per day, and 25% live on less than $3.20 per day. Progress has been made but there is still a long way to go. (Walton, 2019).

Since 2015, the rate of decrease in extreme poverty has slowed. The world goal of reaching 3% living in extreme poverty by 2030 is doubtful (The World Bank, 2020). Several more recent factors slow the decline even more. In 2018–2019 the United States implemented tariffs on many products being imported into the country. This had the effect of slowing international trade, lowering manufacturing volumes abroad, and impacting the job growth seen earlier in poorer countries. The trend of reversing offshoring by US companies, called onshoring, will slow the rate as jobs transition to the United States. Lower commodity prices also influenced the decline. The COVID-19 pandemic had a tremendous negative impact on the world economy with a long term effect of increasing the poverty rate. COVID-19 caused economic activity to decline world wide, and employment in poorer countries dropped off considerably.

COVID-19 Mini Case

The world wide pandemic created by the COVID-19 virus had tremendous impact on businesses domestically and globally. For some, sales increased dramatically, such as in the grocery and medical ventilator industries. For most, however, volumes shrunk as countries mandated stay at home orders and social distancing. Local and national economies across the world were devastated, creating vast numbers of unemployed. Governments were tempted to open the economy back up as soon as possible, and sometimes even when the incidence of infections and hospitalization were still on the rise. This conflicted decision was also deliberated by executives and owners of businesses large and small.

The pandemic created an ethical challenge for both political leaders and citizens: Open up to get the economy going and people back to work and school, but risk raising infection rates, or, continue to lock down to control and diminish the impact of the virus but keep people unemployed, or some balance in between.

(1) Suppose you are the governor of a state. Should lock down continue, at the cost of more unemployment over a longer time frame, or open the economy up at the expense of more coronavirus cases, hospitalizations, and even deaths? What do you do?

(2) Suppose you are the CEO of a 200 person company that makes specialized parts for airplanes. You outsource the manufacturing to another company in Mexico. With the coronavirus outbreak, you initially followed the governor's guidance, closed the office and had people work from home. Productivity is suffering, and you have a lab where 30 people work in two shifts who cannot work from home. You have paid them for the first 4 weeks anyway, but now you are running in the red with sales down. What do you do? Bring everyone back to the office, and risk them getting infected? Bring only the lab staff back, with the same risk? Lay off the lab staff? Furlough everyone to stop the bleeding until this passes? Continue paying everyone and risk bankrupting the company? Some combination of these options? Or is there another option you haven't thought of yet? What's your decision, CEO?

(3) In the midst of this chaos, there are strategic opportunities for those firms positioned to take advantage of the new environment. What might some of those opportunities be?

(4) Suppose you own Sharkey's in Blacksburg. Students are gone and your business has collapsed. Now you're closed per the governor's order, and all staff are furloughed. You tried to stay open for take-out only but it didn't work. The governor has announced that Phase 2 will start next week, and you can open with 25% capacity. It's July, there are a few students around, with many more expected in August. You have enough cash in the bank to stay closed and pay the bills until the semester starts. You'll lose even more money if you open now at 25% capacity and have to pay staff. They need their jobs, however, coming back also increases their risk of infection. What do you do? What's the best decision? You first decide that you hate these ethical dilemmas. Then what?

Section Video

What are the ethical issues facing business today? [02:25]

The video for this lesson explores the ethical issues that businesses face today.

You can view this video here: https://youtu.be/_pLh6bOKbQE.

Key Takeaway

- Living in the United States isolates and insulates its citizens from most of the extreme problems of the world; war, dire poverty, starvation, poor housing, lack of water for drinking, bathing, and cleaning, as well as toxic environments. Global business and economic activities over the last few decades have had a positive impact on the conditions of approximately half of the world's population that struggle financially. Foreign direct investment and offshoring by wealthy countries, as well as buying commodities from poorer countries have contributed to the rise in incomes in poorer nations. Ethical questions remain on how business can impact positively not only on the world's poor, but also on citizens at home, and on the health of the planet.

References

British Standards Institution. (2019). *Risk Factors for Labor Exploitation in Global Supply Chains*. https://www.bsigroup.com/en-US/blog/supply-chain-blog/risk-management/risk-factors-for-labor-exploitation-in-global-supply-chains/.

Fung, B. (2020). *Hundreds of brands are pulling advertisements from Facebook. Its largest advertisers aren't among them*. CNN Business. https://www.cnn.com/2020/07/01/tech/facebook-top-advertisers/index.html.

Moulds, J. (n.d.). *Child labour in the fashion supply chain*. The Guardian. https://labs.theguardian.com/unicef-child-labour.

Prahalad, D. (2019, January 2). *The new fortune at the bottom of the pyramid*. Strategy + Business. https://www.strategy-business.com/article/The-New-Fortune-at-the-Bottom-of-the-Pyramid?gko=c5f11.

Roberts, K. (2018, January 22). *Insult to injury: Foreign manufacturers now making more case in the U.S. than U.S. companies*. Forbes. https://www.forbes.com/sites/kenroberts/2018/01/22/insult-to-injury-foreign-manufacturers-now-making-more-cars-in-u-s-than-u-s-companies.

Simanis, E. (2012, January). *Reality Check at the Bottom of the Pyramid*. Harvard Business Review. https://hbr.org/2012/06/reality-check-at-the-bottom-of-the-pyramid.

Walton, D. (2019). *Poverty trends: global, regional, and national*. Development Initiatives. https://devinit.org/resources/poverty-trends-global-regional-and-national.

The World Bank. (2018). Decline of global extreme poverty continues but has slowed: World Bank. https://www.worldbank.org/en/news/press-release/2018/09/19/decline-of-global-extreme-poverty-continues-but-has-slowed-world-bank.

The World Bank. (2020). Poverty overview. https://www.worldbank.org/en/topic/poverty/overview.

Video Credits

Institute of Business Ethics. (2016, February 1). What are the ethical issues facing business today? Retrieved from https://youtu.be/_pLh6bOKbQE.

11.6 Conclusion

This chapter explains the role of boards of directors in the corporate governance of organizations such as large, publicly traded corporations. Wise boards work to manage the agency problem that creates a conflict of interest between top managers such as the CEO and other groups with a stake in the firm. When boards fail to do their duties, numerous scandals may ensue. Corporate scandals became so widespread that new legislation such as the Sarbanes-Oxley Act of 2002 has been developed with the hope of impeding future actions by executives associated with unethical or illegal behavior. Companies have adopted practices such as ethics and compliance codes and corporate social responsibility activities to improve their accountability to the communities and society they serve. Globally, business activities have lowered poverty rates, but ethical issues remain regarding balancing competing interests on many issues such as offshoring, pollution, sustainability, and economic inequality.

Exercises

1. Divide your class into four or eight groups, depending on the size of the class. Each group should select a different industry. Find positive and negative examples of corporate social performance based on the dimensions used by KLD.

2. This chapter discussed Blake Mycoskie and TOMS Shoes. What other opportunities exist to create new organizations that serve both social and financial goals?

About the Author

Some original material for this book was published in 2010 under a Creative Commons NonCommercial-ShareAlike 3.0 license by a publisher who requested that they and the original authors be unnamed. We express gratitude for their contributions.

This version has been adapted and significantly updated by: Reed Kennedy, with Eli Jamison, Joe Simpson, Pankaj Kumar, Ayenda Kemp, Kiran Awate, and Kathleen (Katie) Manning. Editorial oversight and project management was provided by Anita Walz with Kindred Grey and Kathleen (Katie) Manning. Production was manged by Robert Browder with Grace Baggett and Loren Holt.

Primary Contributor and Content Expert Coordinator

Reed B. Kennedy, Associate Professor of Practice

Pamplin College of Business, Virginia Tech

Reed B. Kennedy is an Associate Professor of Management Practice in the Management Department, where he teaches management courses. He began his career as a naval officer before entering his primary career in healthcare administration, where he served in senior executive roles in various hospitals for over 20 years. He then worked as a business consultant for the Small Business Development Center for the New River Valley at Radford University. His education includes a Bachelor of Science in Aerospace Engineering from the U.S. Naval Academy, a Masters of Healthcare Administration from Medical College of Virginia / Virginia Commonwealth University, a Masters in Public Health and a Graduate Certificate in Global Planning and International Development from Virginia Tech. Reed served as the chief textbook reviser on this project. He worked with the contributor and editorial teams from project start to completion.

Reviewers and Contributors

Eli Jamison, Assistant Professor of Practice

Pamplin College of Business, Virginia Tech

Eli completed her Ph.D. in Virginia Tech's ASPECT program (Alliance for Social, Political, Ethical, and Cultural Thought) in 2015 with concentrations in social and political thought and earned the Women and Gender Studies (WGS) Graduate Certificate. Previously, she earned her M.B.A. at Vanderbilt University with dual concentrations in Human Resource Management and Organizational Behavior. Eli has over twenty years of experience across public, private, and nonprofit sector organizations in the fields of leadership and organizational development working in internal and external consulting roles. Currently, she is a member of the Roanoke City (VA) School Board. Her research focus has centered on questions at the intersection of corporate social responsibility, power networks, and their potential for impacting social justice outcomes for marginalized communities. Eli made significant edits and revisions to the text and contributed extensive original text.

Joseph Simpson, Collegiate Assistant Professor

Department of Management, Pamplin College of Business, Virginia Tech

Joseph Simpson is a Collegiate Assistant Professor of Management and Director of the Integrated Security Education and Research Center (ISERC). An Army veteran, his experience includes ten years of military special operations and nuclear weapons security. For the last six years, he has served on a few boards of directors and owned multiple businesses including two outpatient treatment facilities and a real estate holding company. His research focuses on security and its effect on attitudes, decision-making and firm outcomes. He received his Ph.D from the University of Texas. He teaches Strategic Management and other security related courses. Joe reviewed and made edits in all the chapters and contributed some original text.

Pankaj Kumar, Assistant Professor

Department of Management, Pamplin College of Business, Virginia Tech

Pankaj Kumar is an assistant professor in the Department of Management at the Virginia Tech Pamplin College of Business, where he teaches Strategic Management. He received his Ph.D. in business administration from the Carlson School of Management, University of Minnesota. His research interests lie at the intersection of strategy and organization theory, with a focus on innovation, interfirm relationships (networks), strategic alliances, and geography. He has published in the Academy of Management Journal. Pankaj worked as a CFO at Universidad Veritas in Costa Rica and was a member of board of directors of CPI Panama. He also worked as a consultant for the Bain and Co. affiliate Mesoamerica in Costa Rica and as an assistant manager for Larsen and Toubro in India. Pankaj was the primary developer of the revised outline of the textbook, deciding what content to add and what to delete, and reviewed the textbook upon completion.

Ayenda Kemp, Assistant Professor

Department of Management, Pamplin College of Business, Virginia Tech

Ayenda Kemp is an assistant professor in the Department of Management at the Virginia Tech Pamplin College of Business. He received his Ph.D. in international management from the Jindal School of Management, University of Texas at Dallas. His research interests lie at the intersection of strategy and organization theory, with a focus on understanding how firms may structure intrafirm and interfirm relationships (networks) to best enhance organizational learning, innovation, and performance outcomes. His work appears in the Academy of Management Best Paper Proceedings. Prior to joining academia Ayenda worked as a forecasting analyst in the energy industry. As a teacher of Strategic Management, he helped with the development of the textbook outline and reviewed the book when completed.

Kiran Awate, Assistant Professor

Pamplin College of Business, Virginia Tech

Kiran's research interests lie at the intersection of organizational learning and innovation. His dissertation examines how firms learn from failures during the drug discovery process in the pharmaceutical industry. His work highlights that failures help firms reconsider their existing beliefs and seek out better and more refined theoretical explanations. He won the best research presentation award twice at the Hayes Research Forum and his work was nominated for the best paper award at the Academy of International Business annual conference. He taught undergraduate course in international business at the Ohio State University. Before PhD, Kiran worked in the software technology industry for about nine years where he got an opportunity to experience diverse cultures from countries such as the United Kingdom, Saudi Arabia, and South Korea. Kiran teaches Strategic Management and helped develop the outline and reviewed the textbook.

Kathleen (Katie) Manning, Research and Editorial Assistant

Pamplin College of Business and University Libraries, Virginia Tech

Kathleen Manning is a recent graduate of the Pamplin College of Business at Virginia Tech where she majored in Accounting and Information Systems. She started her professional career at Deloitte in Fall 2020 in their Risk and Financial Advisory practice. Having recently completed Virginia Tech's capstone course in Strategic Management, Katie served as a student reviewer of the text, and became an indispensable part of both content development and editorial processes. She identified significant areas for improvement in content and provided context to greatly improve relevancy of the text for today's students. In addition to identifying numerous short videos, case studies, and examples of recognizable brands and companies, she also completed the painstaking process of transferring newly drafted text from a collaborative writing environment into the Pressbooks publishing software, and followed through with the detailed work of formatting, editing, collaborating on image selection, and proofreading. Kathleen's contributions have made the text much more usable and relatable for today's students.

Editorial and Production Teams

Editorial Team

Kindred Grey, Design Specialist

University Libraries, Virginia Tech

Kindred Grey is a Senior undergraduate student at Virginia Tech graduating in late 2020 with a B.S. in Statistics and Psychology. Apart from her studies, she enjoys graphic design and color theory. Kindred's creative abilities are demonstrated in the visual elements of the book: cover art, interior color palette selection, and creation of new and adapted figures. She designed with color contract (and accessibility) in mind and also wrote the alternative-text for each figure used in the book. She was instrumental in maintaining methods for tracking and updating the over two hundred and fifty figures and tables which were reviewed, revised, or replaced through the course of the project. Kindred's contributions have resulted in a text that is accessible to a wider range of readers, uses visual content to illustrate and more clearly convey conceptual information, and which is more lucid, visually cohesive – and beautiful.

Kathleen (Katie) Manning, Research and Editorial Assistant

Pamplin College of Business and University Libraries, Virginia Tech

Kathleen Manning is a recent graduate of the Pamplin College of Business at Virginia Tech where she majored in Accounting and Information Systems. She started her professional career at Deloitte in Fall 2020 in their Risk and Financial Advisory practice. Having recently completed Virginia Tech's capstone course in Strategic Management, Katie served as a student reviewer of the text, and became an indispensable part of both content development and editorial processes. She identified significant areas for improvement in content and provided context to greatly improve relevancy of the text for today's students. In addition to identifying numerous short videos, case studies, and examples of recognizable brands and companies, she also completed the painstaking process of transferring newly drafted text from a collaborative writing environment into the Pressbooks publishing software, and followed through with the detailed work of formatting, editing, collaborating on image selection, and proofreading. Kathleen's contributions have made the text much more usable and relatable for today's students.

Anita Walz, Managing Editor

University Libraries, Virginia Tech

Anita Walz is associate professor, and assistant director of open education and scholarly communication librarian in the University Libraries at Virginia Tech. She received her M.S. in Library and Information Science from the University of Illinois at Urbana-Champaign and has worked in university, government, school, and international libraries for eighteen years. She is the founder of the Open Education Initiative at Virginia Tech and the managing editor of several open textbooks adapted or created at Virginia Tech, including *Fundamentals of Business*, Virginia Tech's first open textbook and first open textbook partnership with the Pamplin College of Business. Her work appears in *Open: The Philosophy and Practices that are Revolutionizing Education and Science*, *OER: A Field Guide for Academic Librarians*, *The Evolution of Affordable Content Efforts in the Higher*

Education Environment, and other scholarly books, journals, and reports. She enjoys design and management of collaborative, productive, project-based experiential learning opportunities involving instructors and students. Ms. Walz worked closely with the Chief Contributor, editorial and production teams. She provided overall and day-by-day project coordination, planning, guidance, and oversight.

Version Notes

Version Notes

The book you are reading is deeply adapted from an openly licensed textbook titled *Mastering Strategic Management* published in 2015 under a Creative Commons Attribution NonCommercial ShareAlike 3.0 licence by the University of Minnesota Libraries Publishing Service. Below is a record of changes made to the book.

All Chapters

- Deleted all all section Learning Objectives; added Learning Objectives at the chapter level only
- Revised section headings and subheadings format
- Added Introduction to each chapter
- Updated many illustrations and vignettes to make more current
- Added video links for each major section
- Updated reference lists

Chapter 1

- Deleted the 5 P's
- Added a sub-section called Contemporary Critique of Strategic Management at the end of the History of Strategic Management section
- Deleted 2 paragraphs in the sub-section called Lessons Offered by Military Strategy
- Moved sections 2 and 3 under section 1
- Deleted the heading Modeling the Strategy Process

Chapter 2

- Added a section called Corporate Values
- Deleted the section on CEO as Celebrity
- Added a section on Competitive Advantage

- Moved section on Entrepreneurial Orientation to Chapter 7, Innovation

Chapter 3

- Deleted vignette on Subway, replaced with Panera Bread
- Added a section on Interpreting the Five Forces
- Added section called Understanding Groups
- Added section called Designing a Strategic Group Map

Chapter 4

- Updated the Southwest Airlines example
- Organized Resources and Capabilities section ahead of VRIO: Four Characteristics of Strategic Resources
- Changed N = Nonsubstituable to O= Organized to Capture Value
- Deleted The Marketing Mix
- Deleted Is Resource-Based Theory Old News
- Added section on isolating mechanisms
- Deleted section on From the Value Chain to Best Value Supply Chains
- Deleted section on Beyond Resource-Based Theory: Other Views on Company Performance
- Moved Section on SWOT Analysis to new Chapter 5

Chapter 5

(Additional Chapter Added)

- Added SWOT Analysis from Chapter 4\
- Composed new section on Strategic Issue Identification
- Added conclusion

Chapter 6

(formerly Chapter 5 Selecting Business-Level Strategies)

- Updated the Target example and picture
- Replaced Yugo example with K-Mart

Chapter 7

(formerly Chapter 6 Supporting the Business Level Strategy: Competitive and Cooperative Moves)

- Changed the title to Innovation Strategies
- Added the Entrepreneurial Orientation section from Chapter 2 as the first section
- Changed original first section to Why Innovate
- Added section on Innovate to Capture Markets
- Moved the Get Moving illustration to earlier in the chapter
- Moved Blue Ocean to earlier in the chapter
- Deleted Autonomy and Competitive Aggressiveness in the Entrepreneurial Orientation section
- Deleted the section on Merck
- Replaced section Responding to Competitors Moves to Types of Innovation
- Added Incremental, Architectural, and Radical to Disruptive Innovation
- Changed Making Cooperative Moves section to Implementing Innovation
- Deleted Co-opetition and Co-location, added Internal Development and Acquisitions
- Added Product Life Cycle and Crossing the Chasm
- Replaced section Making Cooperative Moves to Responding to Innovation in the Market, included Co-opetition and co-location here

Chapter 8

- Updated Disney illustration at the beginning
- Added section defining corporate strategy and synergy
- Deleted section on Concentration Strategies
- Added section on the 3 types of diversification
- Moved Diversification Strategies section to before section on Vertical Integration Strategies
- Updated many of the illustrations and examples
- Added section on Geographic Diversification
- Added major section on Implementing Corporate Strategies
- Added section on Diversification Discount
- Added 2 graphics on the BCG Matrix and section on how to plot, interpret, and make decisions using the BCG Matrix.

Chapter 9

- Added section defining international strategy and providing context
- Made various edits and updates to figures and text

- Added a major section on the CAGE framework
- Added a section on a fourth international strategy – International, and a graphic showing all four
- Rearranged the options for competing in international markets and added graphics to range from exporting to greenfield to show continuum of least risk, control, and profit potential to most.

Chapter 10

- Added section on Why Organizational Design?
- Deleted section on simple organizational structure
- Added section on boundary less organizational structure
- Added more text and illustration to matrix section
- Multiple edits to update text and illustrations
- Added more content to the Forms of Business section

Chapter 11

- Added a large section, 11.1 Doing Well By Doing Good, that included corporate scandals, resulting in Sarbanes-Oxley Act and firm emphasis on code of ethics and compliance. Introduced corporate ethics and CSR
- Deleted the section on Stages of Moral Development
- Deleted section on Understanding Thought Patterns
- Added section on Corporate Ethics and Social Responsibility
- Added major section on Contemporary Questions of Corporate Ethics
- Added section on offshoring
- Added section on Environmental/Climate Change/Sustainability
- Added section on Global Economic Inequality
- Added a mini case on the ethical decisions for selling to the "bottom of the pyramid"
- Added a mini case on the ethical dilemma presented by the Covid-19 pandemic
- Various edits, smaller additions and deletions

Glossary

acquisitions

When one firm, usually the larger one, buys another firm

agency problem

When the interests of the individuals that manage the company (agents such as the CEO) may not align with the interest of the owners (such as stockholders)

backward vertical integration

Moving back along the value chain and entering a supplier's business

behavioral control

Focuses on controlling the actions of individuals through rules and procedures

best-cost

A strategy where the firm attempts to offer a hybrid of both lower cost and differentiated products or services, combining the two basic strategies

blue ocean strategy

Creating a new, untapped market rather than competing with rivals in an existing market

broad cost leadership

A strategy that offers the lowest price in the market for that product or service

broad differentiation

A strategy that offers something unique that differentiates their product or service from others

Causal Ambiguity

The reason for achieving a competitive advantage is not apparent, and therefore difficult to imitate

clan control

Relies on shared traditions, expectations, values, and norms to lead people to work toward the good of their organization

competitive advantage

When the economic value creation of a firm is greater than its competitors.

conflicts of interest

When a person could receive personal benefit from decisions they make in their official capacity

Copyrights

Provide exclusive rights to the creators of original artistic works such as books, movies, songs, and screenplays

core competency

A skill set that is difficult for competitors to imitate

core values

The important guiding principles of an organization, that every employee should embrace

corporate social performance

Measuring the impact of a firm's activities in corporate social responsibility

Corporate social responsibility

Efforts by a firm to be socially accountable by contributing to community and/or societal goals through philanthropic, activist, or charitable activities

Corporate Strategy

Specifies actions taken by the firm to gain a competitive advantage by selecting and managing a group of different businesses in several industries and/or product markets

corporations

A legal business entity that separates the owners from the liabilities of the business. Owners are issued stock, and profits are taxed twice, at the corporate and individual owner levels

Creating Shared Value (CSV)

A business model whereby society's needs and challenges are addressed as a firm prospers achieving its mission

Cultural risk

The potential for a company's operations in a country to struggle because of differences in language, customs, norms, and customer preferences

diversification discount

When the value of a conglomerate is less than the value of the sum of its business units

Economic risk

The potential for a country's economic conditions and policies, property rights protections, and currency exchange rates to harm a firm's operations within a country

Economies of scale

Created when the unit cost of goods and services decreases as a firm is able to produce and sell more items

Emergent strategy

An unplanned strategy that arises in response to unexpected opportunities and challenges

Entrepreneurial orientation

The processes, practices, and decision-making styles of organizations that act entrepreneurially

fighting brand

A lower-end brand that a firm introduces to try to protect the firm's market share without damaging the firm's existing brands

focused cost leadership

A strategy that attempts to provide the lowest cost to a narrow, niche target market

focused differentiation

A strategy that provides unique or differentiated products or services to a narrow, niche target market

foothold

A small position that a firm intentionally establishes within a market in which it does not yet compete

forward vertical integration

Moving further down the value chain to enter a buyer's business

Geographic Diversification

Expanding geographically into different markets

hierarchy of authority

The chain of command that shows who reports to whom

horizontal integration

Pursuing a diversification strategy by acquiring or merging with a rival company

Innovativeness

The tendency to pursue creativity and experimentation aimed at developing new products, services, and processes

intangible resources

Resources that are not physical, like a firm's reputation, a patent, or employee knowledge

Intellectual property

Creations of the mind, such as inventions, artistic products, and symbols.

intended strategy

The strategy that an organization hopes to execute

internal development

Adding new capabilities or products and services using a firm's resources or hiring those resources

International strategy

How a firm conducts its business outside the borders of its home country

isolating mechanisms

Methods that prevent a competitor from imitating the resource or capability that provides a competitive advantage

joint venture

A cooperative arrangement that involves two or more organizations each contributing to the creation of a jointly owned, new company

limited liability company (LLC)

A limited liability company with some of the ease of operation of a sole proprietorship or partnership but owners are separated from the liabilities of the business

merger

Two firms, usually similar in size, combine into one entity, often gaining strength in the market

mission

An organization's purpose, why it exists, beyond making a profit

multinational corporation (MNC)

A firm that has operations in more than one country

Offshoring

Relocating a business activity to another country, such as manufacturing or a call center

organizational performance indicators

Quantitative measures that indicate how an organization performs in comparison to historical trends and/or competitors.

Output control

Focuses on measurable results within an organization

partnership

A business that is not incorporated with two or more owners/partners, personally responsible for the liabilities of the business

Patents

Legal decrees that protect inventions from direct imitation for a limited period of time

path dependence

The historical path a firm takes over time, including the decisions, accumulated learning, and experience gained along the historical path are not easily duplicated.

performance benchmarks

Reference points that a firm can use to compare its performance against others.

performance measures

Quantitative measures that indicate how an organization performs in comparison to historical trends and/or competitors.

PESTEL analysis

Evaluation of six forces in an industry's macro-environment: political, economic, socio-cultural, technological, environmental, and legal.

Political risk

The potential for government upheaval or interference with business to harm an operation within a country

Proactiveness

The tendency to anticipate and act on future needs rather than reacting to events after they unfold

realized strategy

The strategy that an organization actually follows

Related Diversification

When a firm moves into a new industry that has important similarities with the firm's existing industry or industries

reshoring

Returning offshored jobs and activities back to the home country

S corporation

A special form of a corporation for smaller companies, with a limited number of owners/stock holders who are separated from the liabilities of the business. Profits are only taxed at the individual owners level.

Sarbanes-Oxley

Federal legislation in 2002 that reformed financial regulations, in the wake of multiple corporate scandals

SMART

Goals that are specific, measurable, attainable, realistic, and time-bound

social complexity

The interrelationships within a firm, along with relationships within or across a business process, that are difficult for competitors to imitate.

sole proprietorship

The simplest form of business, with only one owner who is personally responsible for the liabilities of the business, whereby the owner and the business are considered one and the same

strategic alliance

A cooperative arrangement governed by contract between two or more organizations for their mutual benefit.

strategic issue

The primary matter faced by an organization that must be addressed for the organization to survive, excel, or achieve a major strategic initiative

strategic management

An ongoing process used by firms to set an organizational vision, analyze the external, competitive, and internal environments, and develop strategies for success

strategic resources

Resources that provide an organization with an opportunity to develop competitive advantages over its rivals

strategy

A broad goal that an organization needs to achieve to be successful in the marketplace

stuck in the middle

Firms that attempt a hybrid, best cost strategy of low cost and differentiation, but are not able to achieve either effectively

Synergy

In the business context means the cooperation or interaction of two or more busi - ness units so that they perform more effectively together than they would if independent

Tangible resources

Resources that can be readily seen, touched, and quantified, such as cash or equipment

three P's

Measuring a firm's overall success based on People, Planet, and Profit, instead of the traditional view of only profit.

Trade secrets

Refer to formulas, practices, and designs that are central to a firm's business and that remain unknown to competitors

Trademarks

Phrases, pictures, names, or symbols used to identify a particular organization

unrealized strategy

A strategy that was developed but not accomplished

Unrelated Diversification

When a firm enters an industry that lacks any important similarities with the firm's existing industry or industries

value chain

The path and steps by which products and services are created and eventually sold to customers, including supporting activities

value statements

The principles that are important to an organization, that all employees should adopt and live by

vertical integration

Diversifying by entering an industry in the firm's value chain, such as a supplier upstream or a buyer downstream

vision

What the organization hopes to become, its aspirational goal for the future

VRIO framework

A tool used to assess if a firm's resource or capability is Valuable, Rare, Difficult to Imitate, and Organized to create value, and therefore what type of competitive advantage it provides.

Made in the USA
Middletown, DE
28 August 2023

37487565R00197